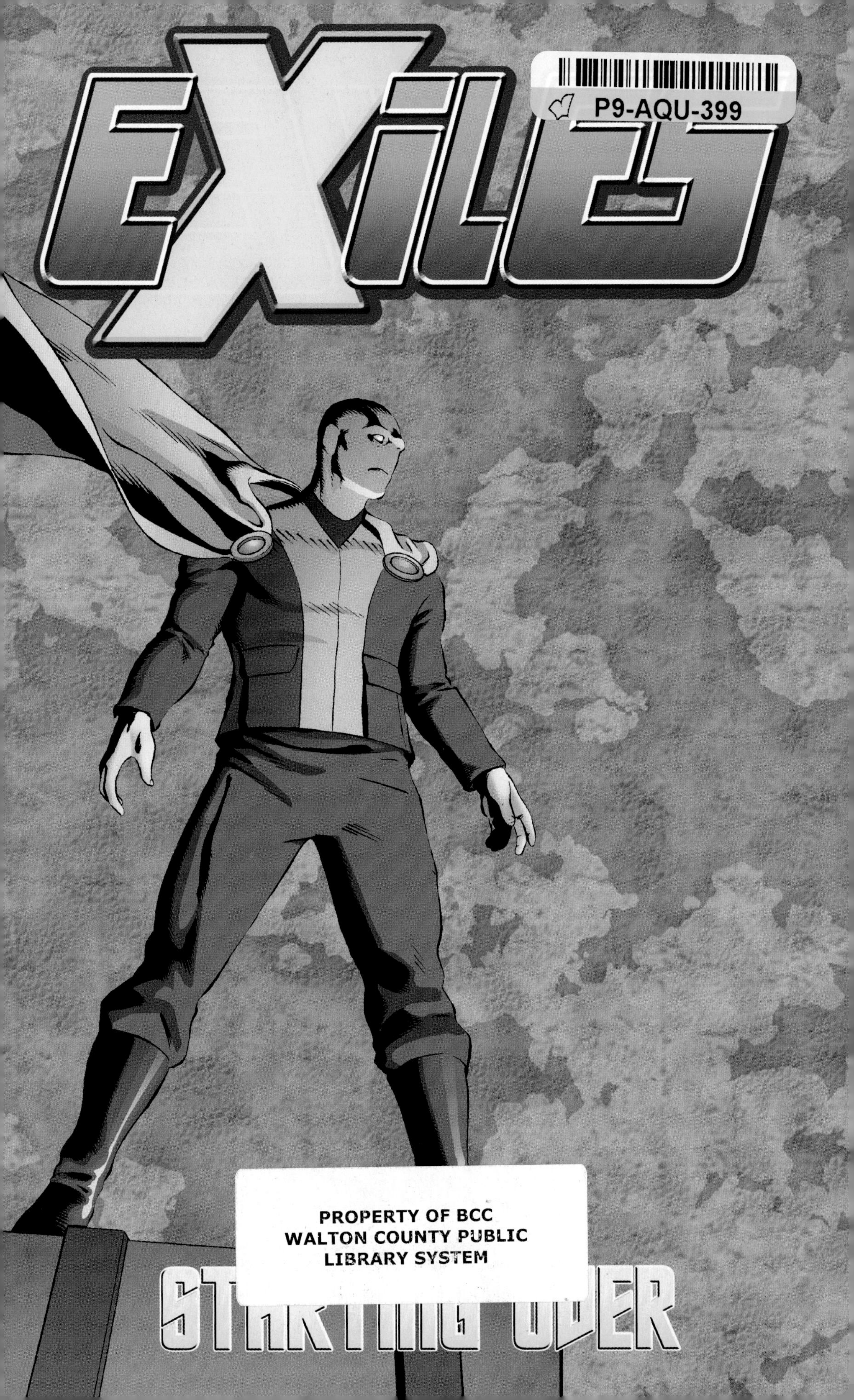
EXILES
STARTING OVER

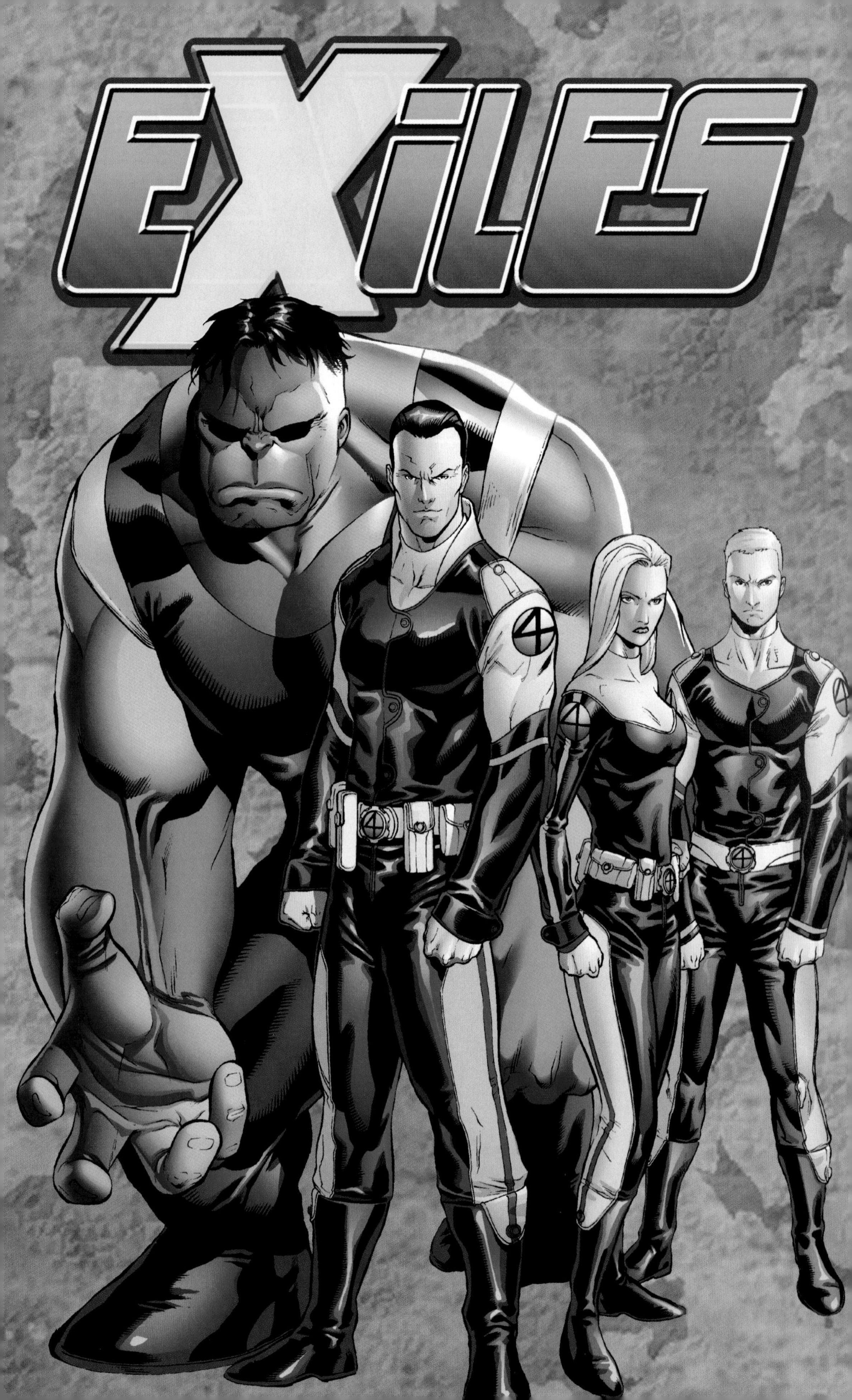
EXILES

STARTING OVER

Writer: Chris Claremont
Pencilers: Clayton Henry, Steve Scott,
Ronan Cliquet & Tom Grummett
Inkers: Norman Lee, Amilton Santos
& Scott Hanna
Colorist: Wil Quintana
Letterer: Simon Bowland
Cover Artists: Tomm Coker & Tom Grummett, Terry Pallot
& Wil Quintana
Assistant Editors: Nathan Cosby & Jordan D. White
Editor: Mark Paniccia

DAYS OF THEN AND NOW
Writer: Mike Raicht
Chapter 1: A World Without Heroes
Pencils: Carlos Ferreira
Inks: Terry Pallot
Colors: Wes Dzioba
Chapter 2: A Quentin in Time
Pencils & Inks: Zach Howard
Colors: Beth Sotelo
Chapter 3: Legacy
Pencils & Inks: Paul Azaceta
Colors: Lee Loughridge
Chapter 4: World Tour
Pencils: Mario Gully
Inks: Sandu Florea
Colors: Michelle Madsen
Chapter 5: The Lost Son
Pencils: Arnold Pander
Inks: Vicente Cifuentes
Colors: June Chung
Chapter 6: Meet the Exiles
Pencils: Wayne Nichols
Inks: Scott Koblish
Colors: Sotocolor's A. Street
Chapter 7: Home
Pencils: Carlos Ferreira
Inks: Terry Pallot
Colors: Wes Dzioba
Chapter 8: Moving On
Pencils: Wayne Nichols
Inks: Scott Koblish
Colors: Sotocolor's A. Street
Cover art: Francis Tsai

Collection Editor: Jennifer Grünwald
Assistant Editors: Cory Levine & John Denning
Editor, Special Projects: Mark D. Beazley
Senior Editor, Special Projects: Jeff Youngquist
Senior Vice President of Sales: David Gabriel
Production: Jerron Quality Color & Jerry Kalinowski
Vice President of Creative: Tom Marvelli

Editor in Chief: Joe Quesada
Publisher: Dan Buckley

THERE ARE REALITIES OUTSIDE OUR OWN; SOME SIMILAR, OTHERS ABNORMAL. SOMETIMES THESE REALITIES ARE DAMAGED, AND NEED SOME HELP.
THAT'S WHERE WE COME IN...

Stolen from countless different realities, the Exiles' roster is constantly shifting, depending on the specific mission.

CURRENT ROSTER:

SABRETOOTH
AGE OF APOCALYPSE

MORPH
EARTH-58163

PSYLOCKE
EARTH-616

BLINK
AGE OF APOCALYPSE

LONGSHOT
MOJOVERSE

TEAM COORDINATOR

SPIDER-MAN 2099
EARTH-6375

HEATHER HUDSON
EARTH-3470

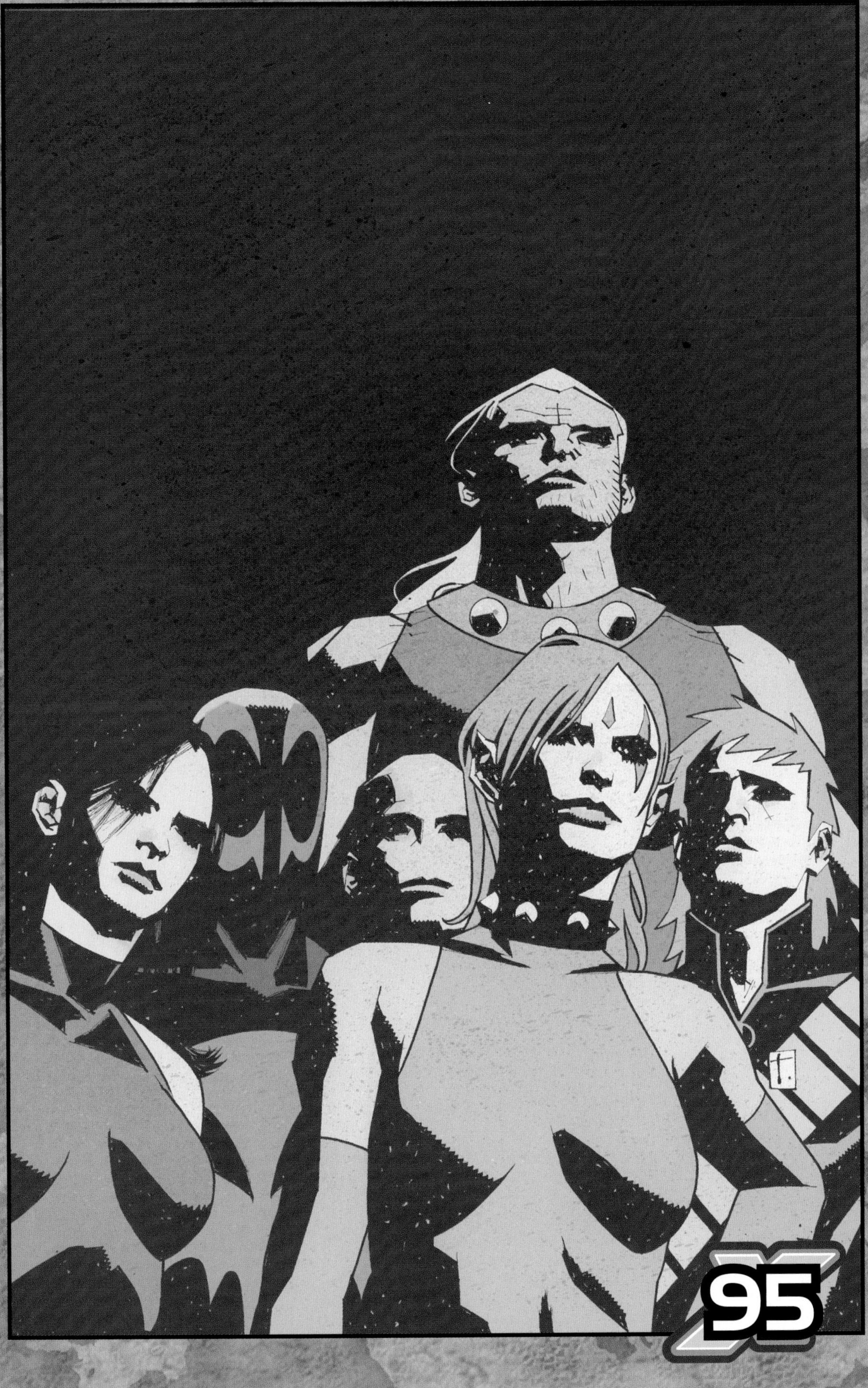
95

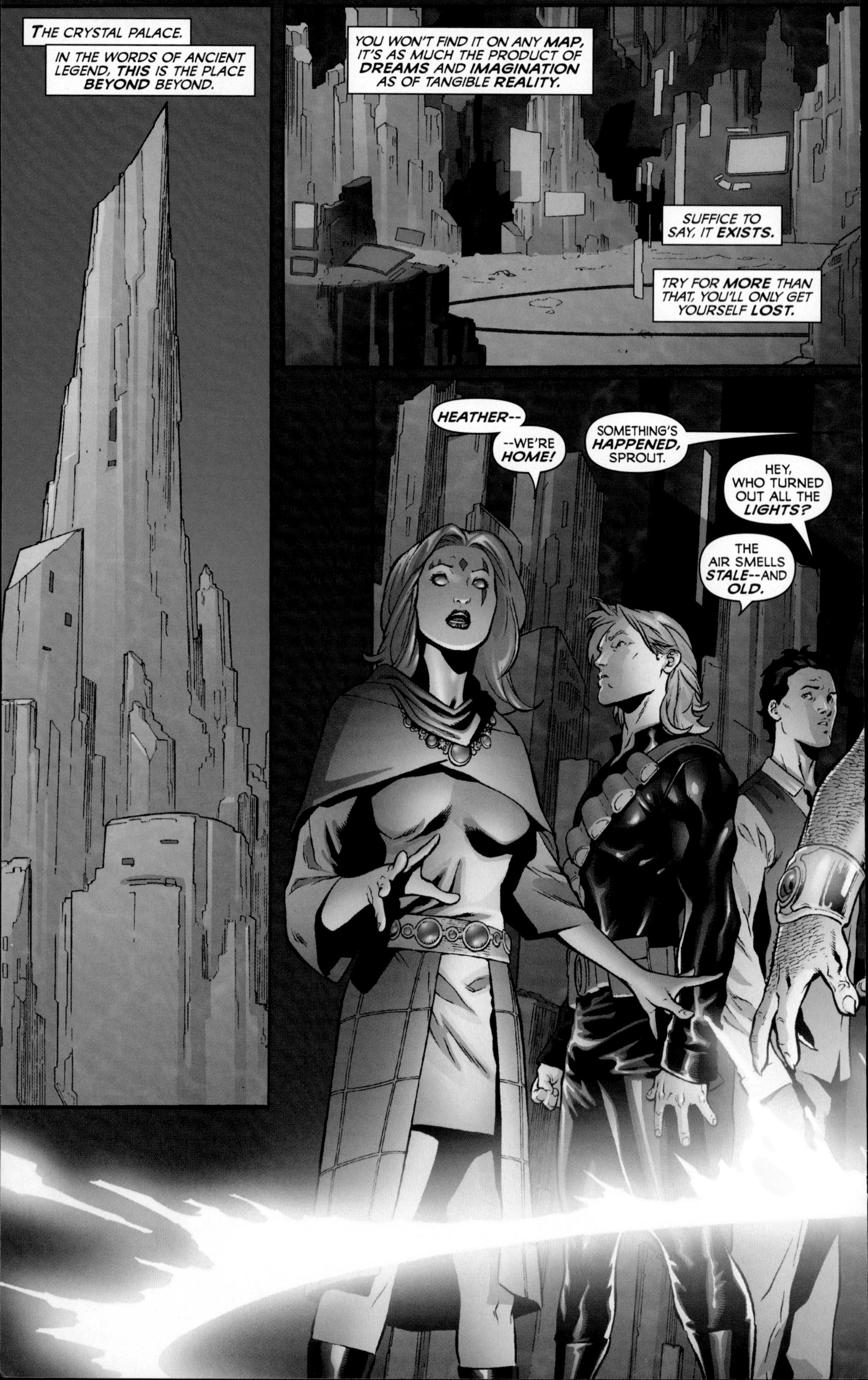

THE CRYSTAL PALACE.
IN THE WORDS OF ANCIENT LEGEND, **THIS** IS THE PLACE **BEYOND** BEYOND.
YOU WON'T FIND IT ON ANY **MAP**, IT'S AS MUCH THE PRODUCT OF **DREAMS** AND **IMAGINATION** AS OF TANGIBLE **REALITY**.
SUFFICE TO SAY, IT **EXISTS**.
TRY FOR **MORE** THAN THAT, YOU'LL ONLY GET YOURSELF **LOST**.
HEATHER--
--WE'RE HOME!
SOMETHING'S **HAPPENED**, SPROUT.
HEY, WHO TURNED OUT ALL THE **LIGHTS?**
THE AIR SMELLS **STALE**--AND **OLD**.

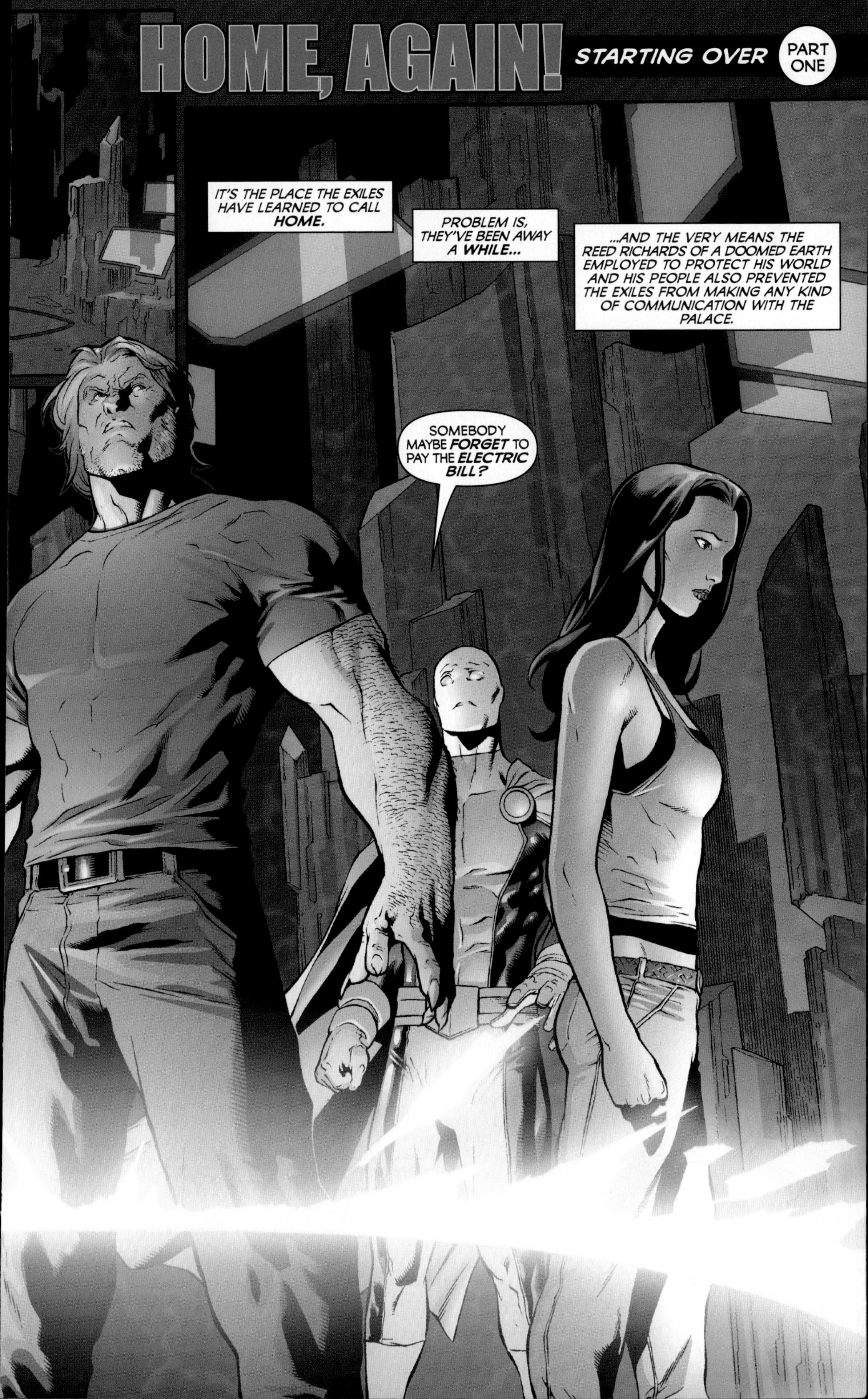

HOME, AGAIN!
STARTING OVER
PART ONE
IT'S THE PLACE THE EXILES HAVE LEARNED TO CALL HOME.
PROBLEM IS, THEY'VE BEEN AWAY A WHILE...
...AND THE VERY MEANS THE REED RICHARDS OF A DOOMED EARTH EMPLOYED TO PROTECT HIS WORLD AND HIS PEOPLE ALSO PREVENTED THE EXILES FROM MAKING ANY KIND OF COMMUNICATION WITH THE PALACE.
SOMEBODY MAYBE FORGET TO PAY THE ELECTRIC BILL?

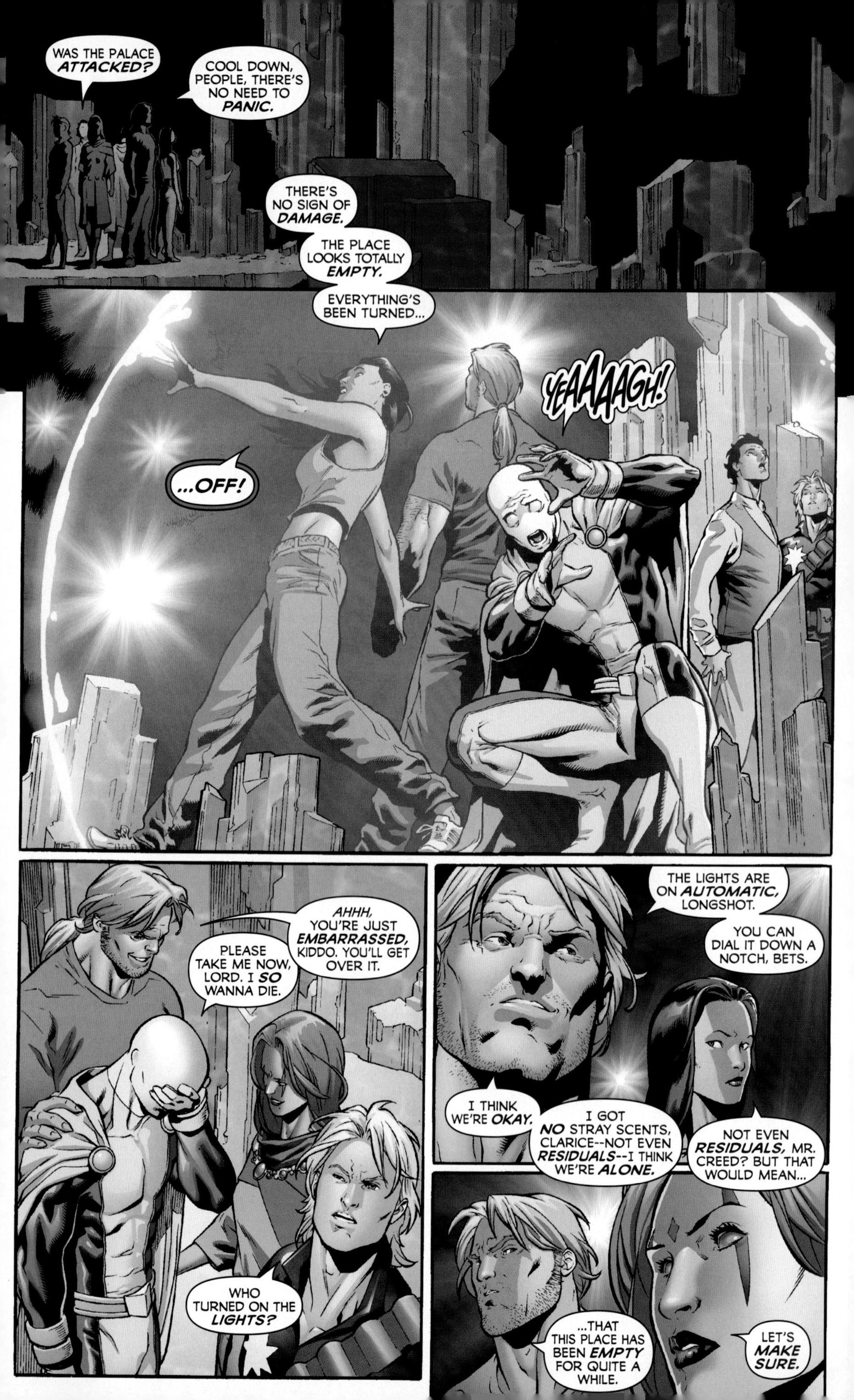
WAS THE PALACE *ATTACKED?*
COOL DOWN, PEOPLE, THERE'S NO NEED TO *PANIC.*
THERE'S NO SIGN OF *DAMAGE.*
THE PLACE LOOKS TOTALLY *EMPTY.*
EVERYTHING'S BEEN TURNED...
YEAAAAAGH!
...OFF!
AHHH, YOU'RE JUST *EMBARRASSED,* KIDDO. YOU'LL GET OVER IT.
PLEASE TAKE ME NOW, LORD. I *SO* WANNA DIE.
WHO TURNED ON THE *LIGHTS?*
THE LIGHTS ARE ON *AUTOMATIC,* LONGSHOT.
YOU CAN DIAL IT DOWN A NOTCH, BETS.
I THINK WE'RE *OKAY.*
I GOT *NO* STRAY SCENTS, CLARICE--NOT EVEN *RESIDUALS*--I THINK WE'RE *ALONE.*
NOT EVEN *RESIDUALS,* MR. CREED? BUT THAT WOULD MEAN...
...THAT THIS PLACE HAS BEEN *EMPTY* FOR QUITE A WHILE.
LET'S *MAKE SURE.*

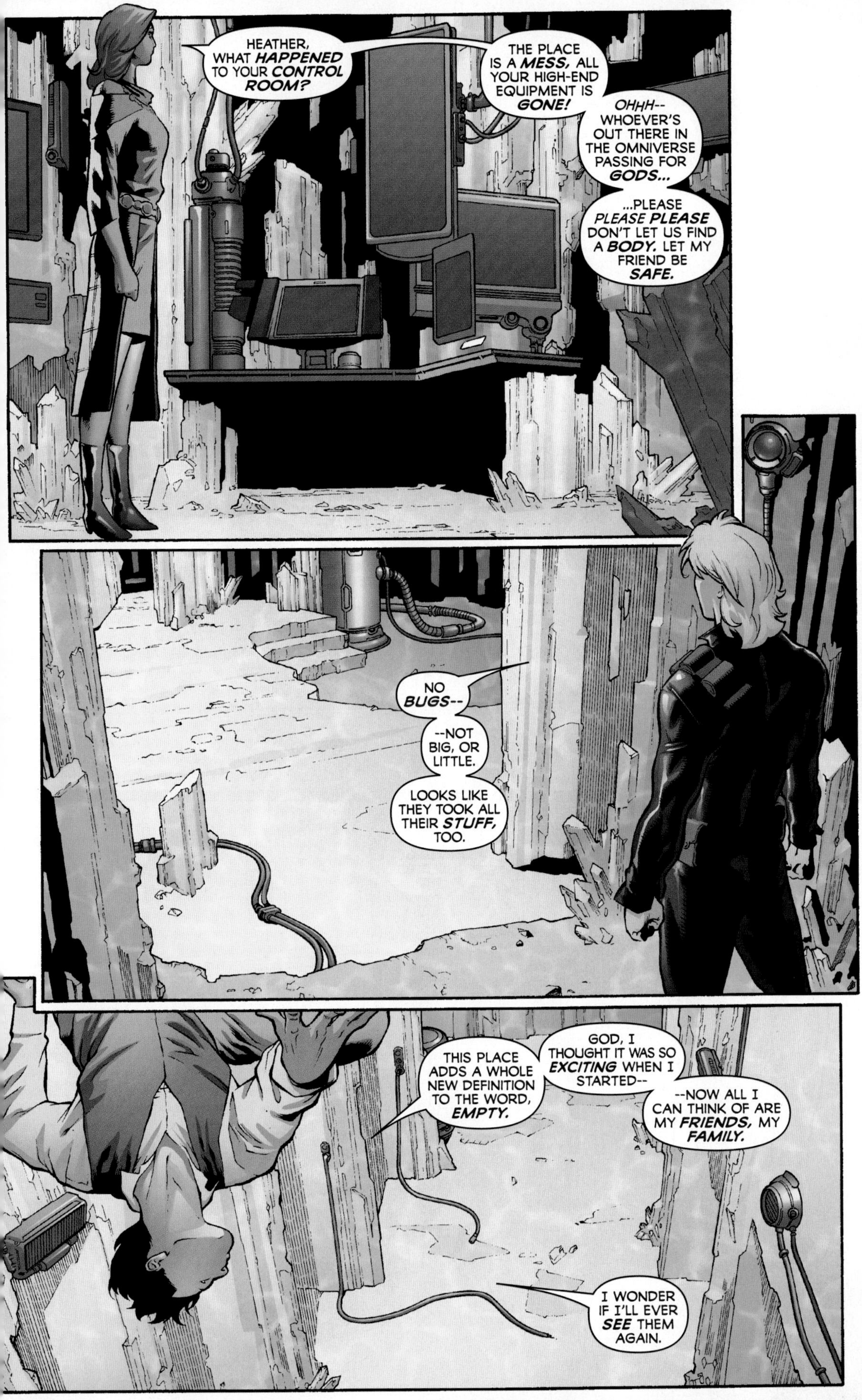
HEATHER, WHAT HAPPENED TO YOUR CONTROL ROOM?
THE PLACE IS A MESS, ALL YOUR HIGH-END EQUIPMENT IS GONE!
OHHH-- WHOEVER'S OUT THERE IN THE OMNIVERSE PASSING FOR GODS...
...PLEASE PLEASE PLEASE DON'T LET US FIND A BODY. LET MY FRIEND BE SAFE.
NO BUGS--
--NOT BIG, OR LITTLE.
LOOKS LIKE THEY TOOK ALL THEIR STUFF, TOO.
THIS PLACE ADDS A WHOLE NEW DEFINITION TO THE WORD, EMPTY.
GOD, I THOUGHT IT WAS SO EXCITING WHEN I STARTED--
--NOW ALL I CAN THINK OF ARE MY FRIENDS, MY FAMILY.
I WONDER IF I'LL EVER SEE THEM AGAIN.

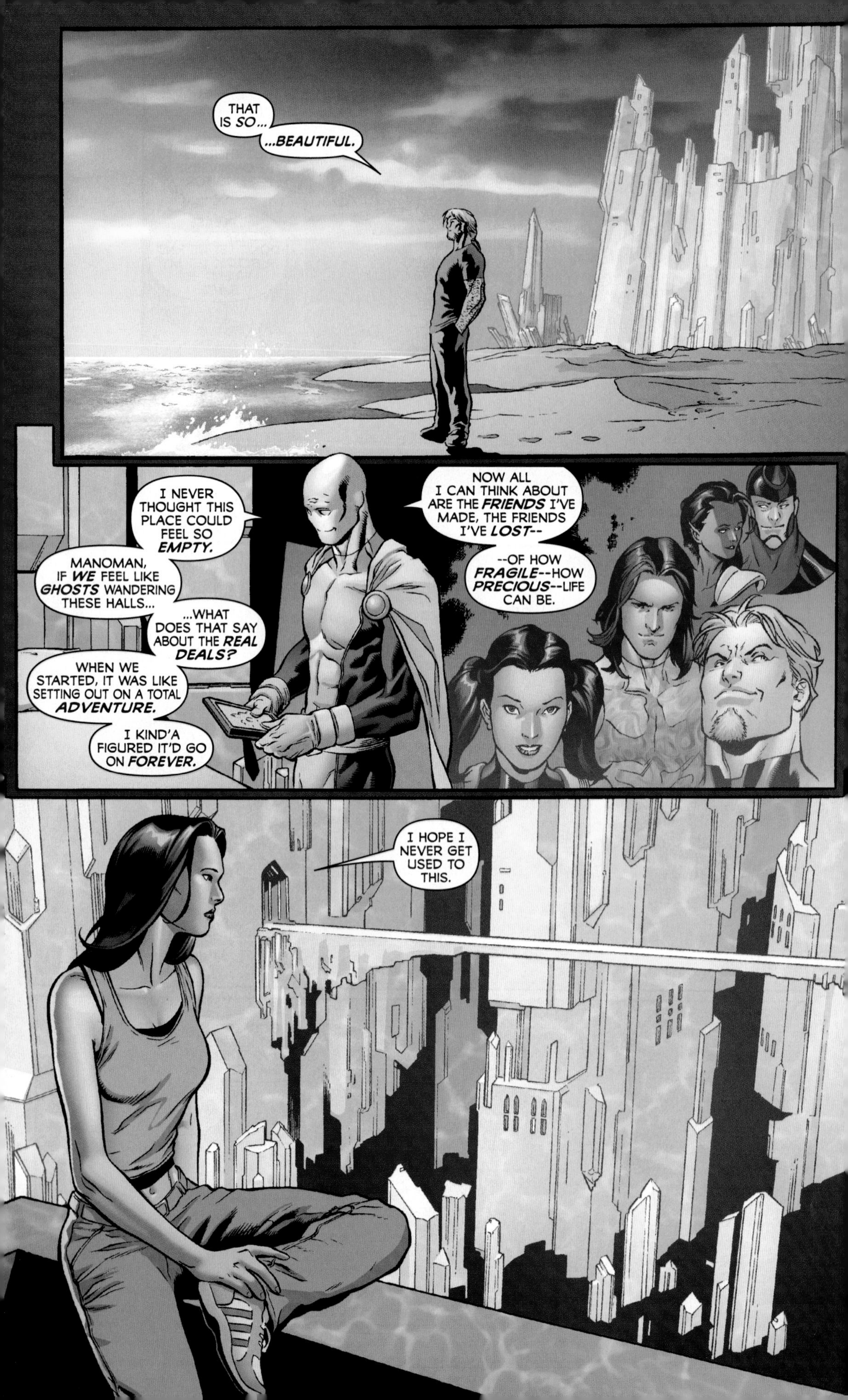
THAT IS SO... ...BEAUTIFUL.
I NEVER THOUGHT THIS PLACE COULD FEEL SO EMPTY.
MANOMAN, IF WE FEEL LIKE GHOSTS WANDERING THESE HALLS...
...WHAT DOES THAT SAY ABOUT THE REAL DEALS?
WHEN WE STARTED, IT WAS LIKE SETTING OUT ON A TOTAL ADVENTURE.
I KIND'A FIGURED IT'D GO ON FOREVER.
NOW ALL I CAN THINK ABOUT ARE THE FRIENDS I'VE MADE, THE FRIENDS I'VE LOST--
--OF HOW FRAGILE--HOW PRECIOUS--LIFE CAN BE.
I HOPE I NEVER GET USED TO THIS.

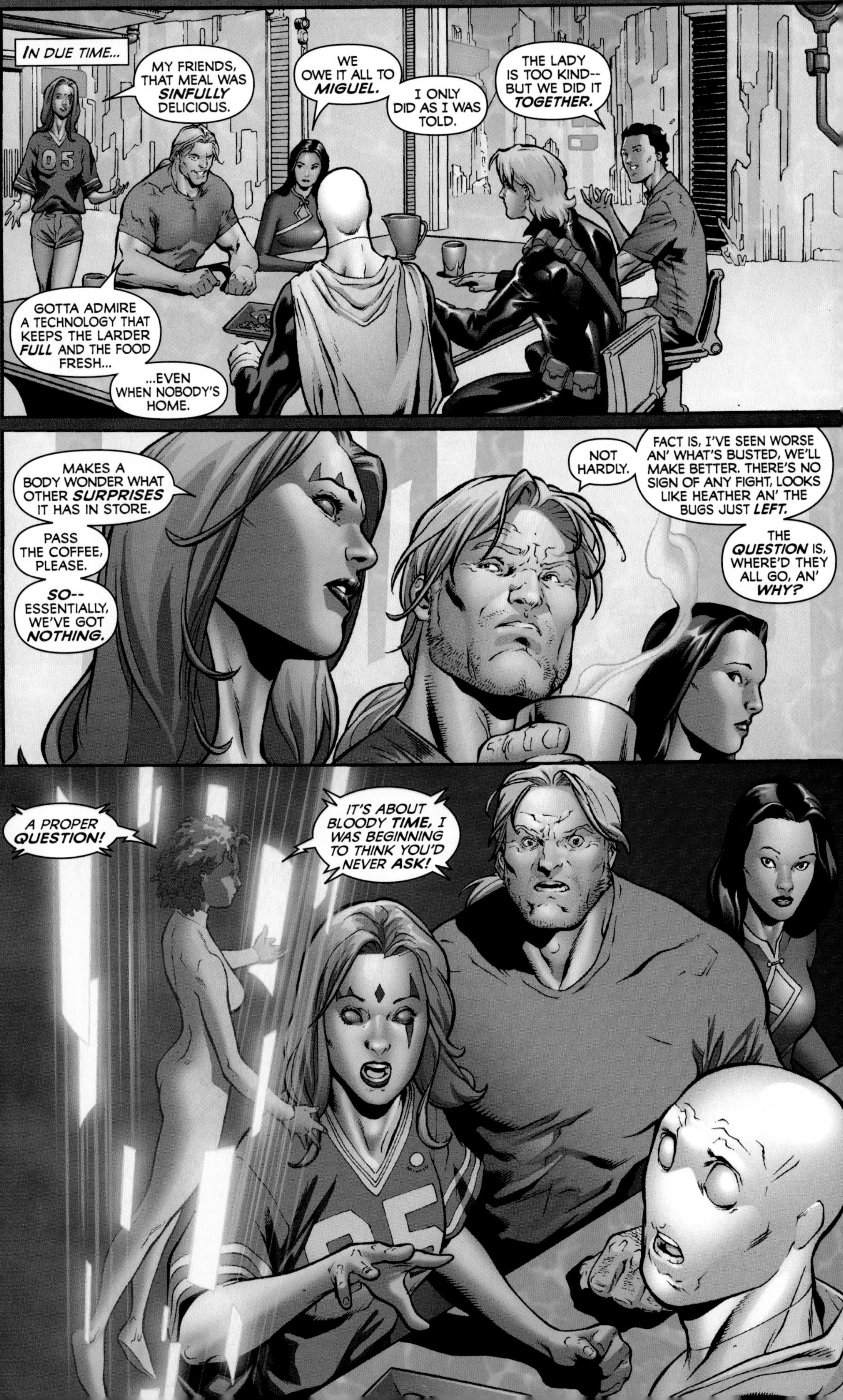
IN DUE TIME...
MY FRIENDS, THAT MEAL WAS SINFULLY DELICIOUS.
WE OWE IT ALL TO MIGUEL.
I ONLY DID AS I WAS TOLD.
THE LADY IS TOO KIND-- BUT WE DID IT TOGETHER.
GOTTA ADMIRE A TECHNOLOGY THAT KEEPS THE LARDER FULL AND THE FOOD FRESH...
...EVEN WHEN NOBODY'S HOME.
MAKES A BODY WONDER WHAT OTHER SURPRISES IT HAS IN STORE.
PASS THE COFFEE, PLEASE.
SO-- ESSENTIALLY, WE'VE GOT NOTHING.
NOT HARDLY.
FACT IS, I'VE SEEN WORSE AN' WHAT'S BUSTED, WE'LL MAKE BETTER. THERE'S NO SIGN OF ANY FIGHT, LOOKS LIKE HEATHER AN' THE BUGS JUST LEFT.
THE QUESTION IS, WHERE'D THEY ALL GO, AN' WHY?
A PROPER QUESTION!
IT'S ABOUT BLOODY TIME, I WAS BEGINNING TO THINK YOU'D NEVER ASK!

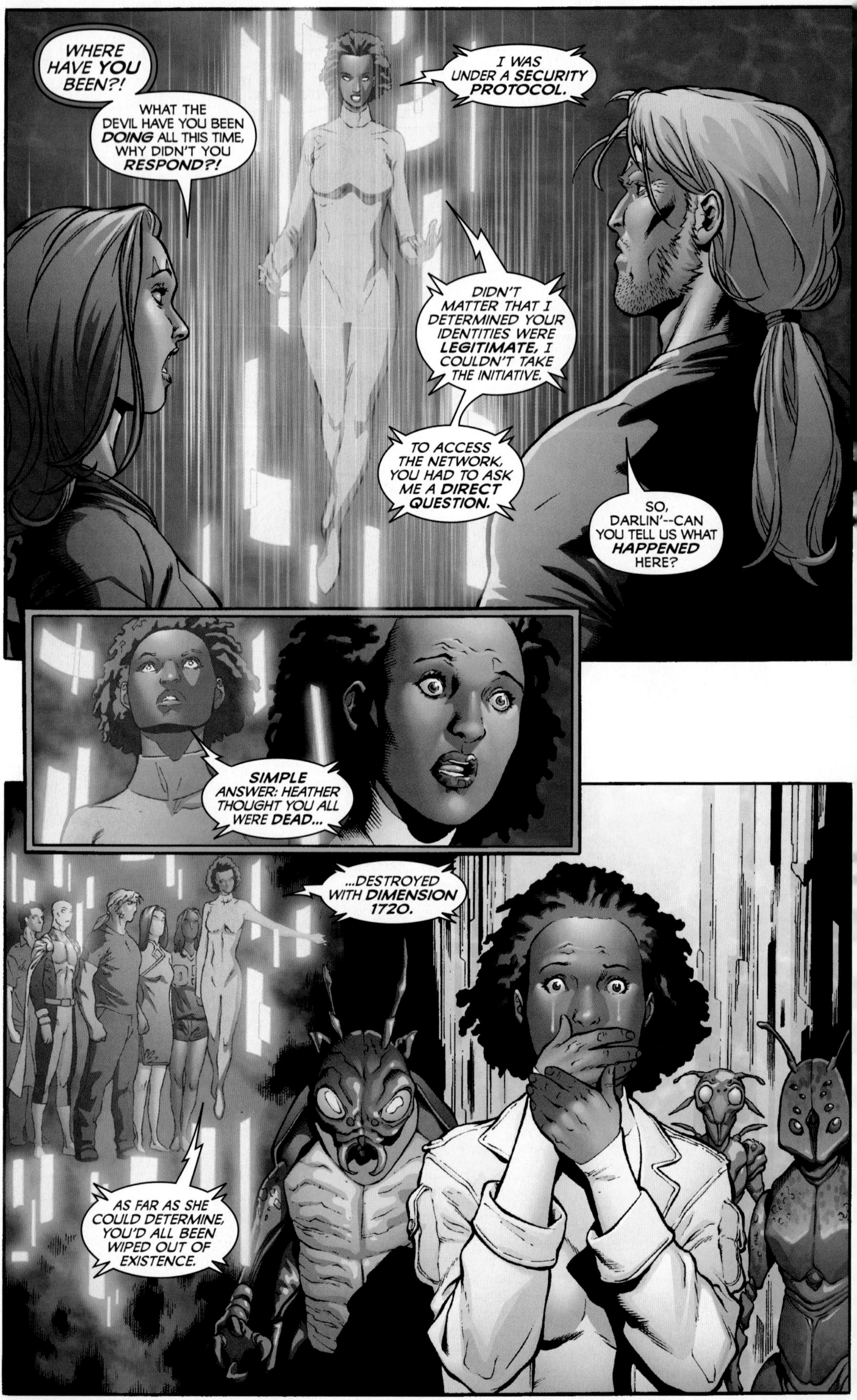
WHERE HAVE YOU BEEN?!
WHAT THE DEVIL HAVE YOU BEEN DOING ALL THIS TIME, WHY DIDN'T YOU RESPOND?!
I WAS UNDER A SECURITY PROTOCOL.
DIDN'T MATTER THAT I DETERMINED YOUR IDENTITIES WERE LEGITIMATE, I COULDN'T TAKE THE INITIATIVE.
TO ACCESS THE NETWORK, YOU HAD TO ASK ME A DIRECT QUESTION.
SO, DARLIN'--CAN YOU TELL US WHAT HAPPENED HERE?
SIMPLE ANSWER: HEATHER THOUGHT YOU ALL WERE DEAD...
...DESTROYED WITH DIMENSION 1720.
AS FAR AS SHE COULD DETERMINE, YOU'D ALL BEEN WIPED OUT OF EXISTENCE.

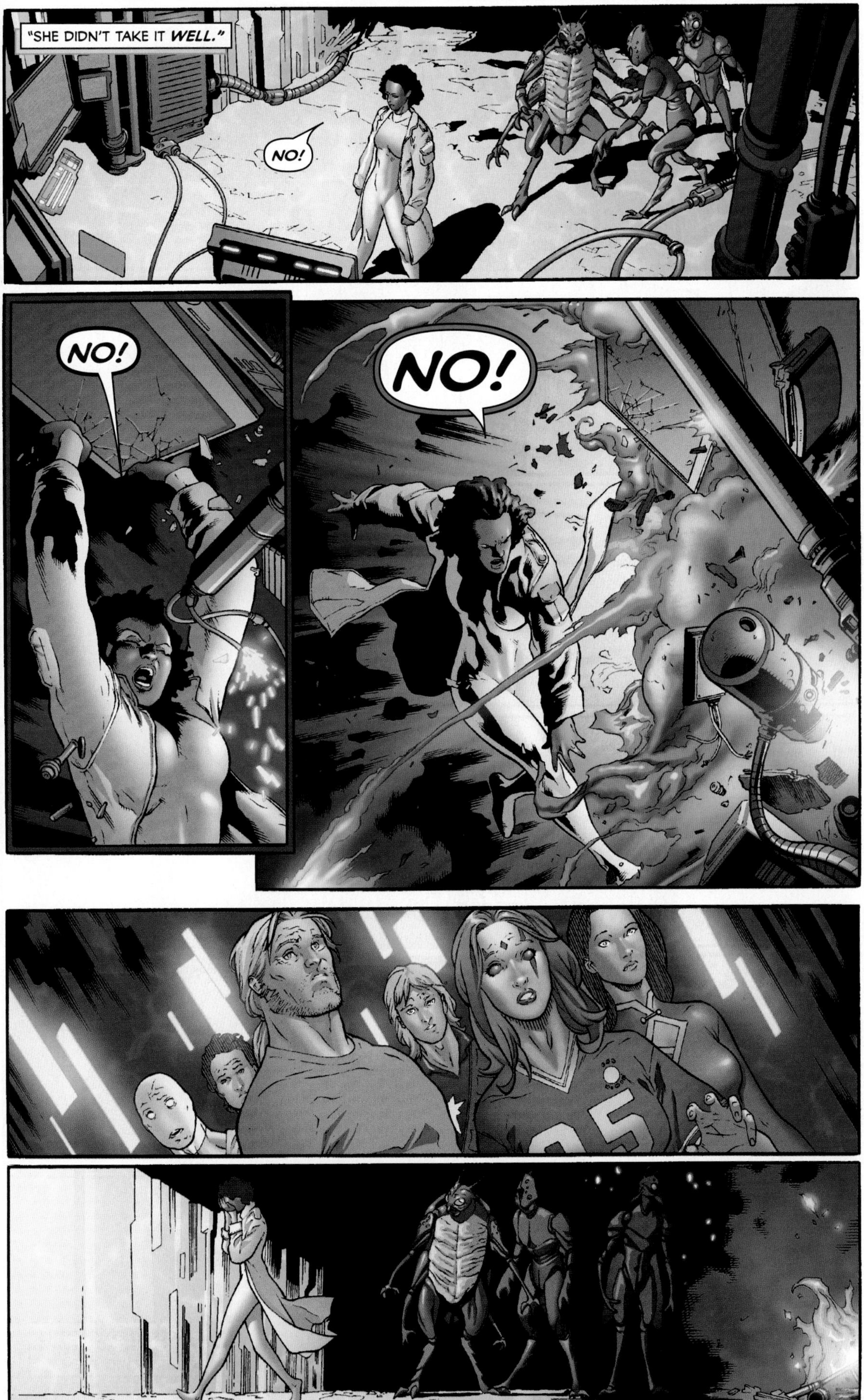
"SHE DIDN'T TAKE IT WELL."
NO!
NO!
NO!

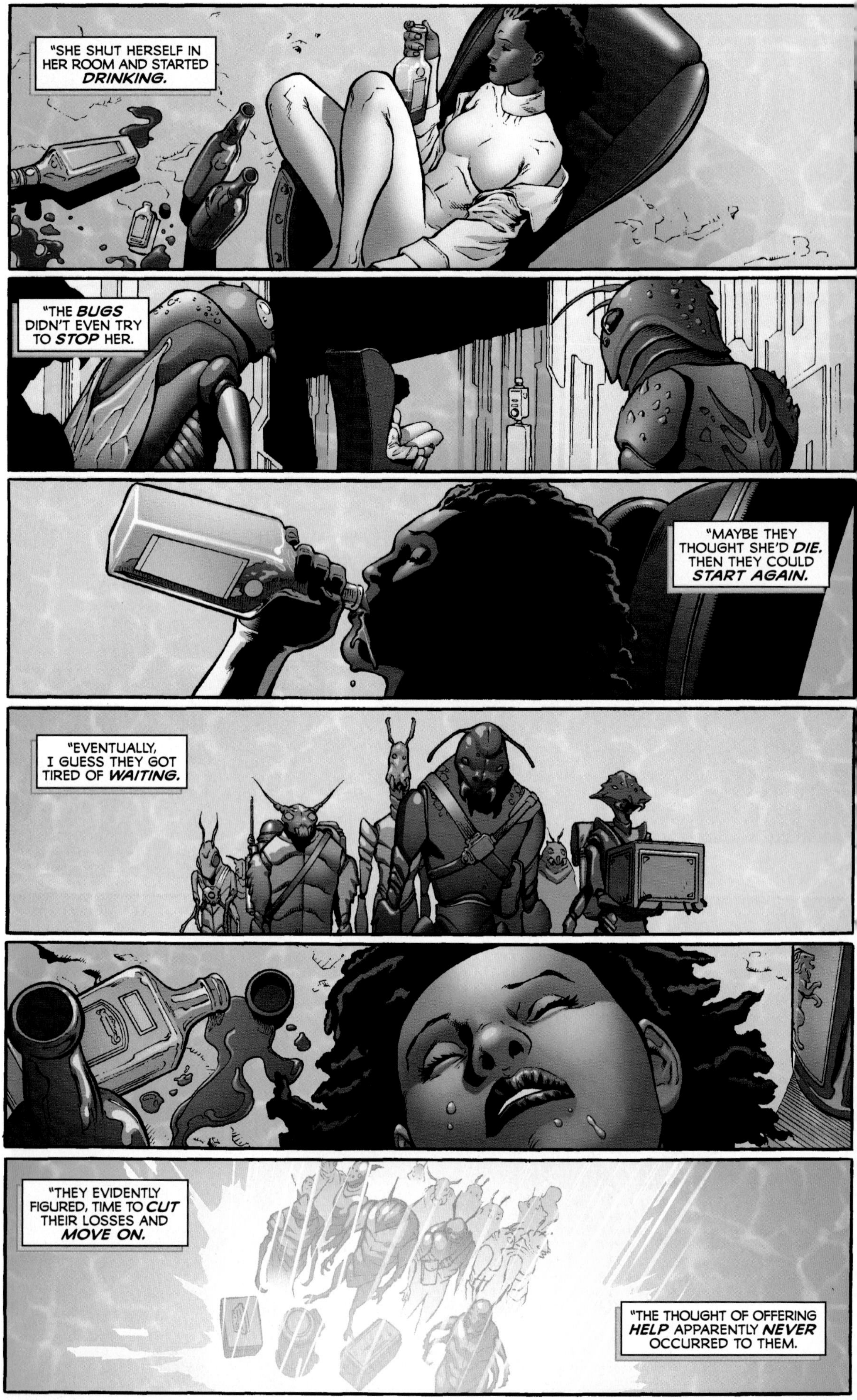
"SHE SHUT HERSELF IN HER ROOM AND STARTED *DRINKING.*
"THE *BUGS* DIDN'T EVEN TRY TO *STOP* HER.
"MAYBE THEY THOUGHT SHE'D *DIE.* THEN THEY COULD *START AGAIN.*
"EVENTUALLY, I GUESS THEY GOT TIRED OF *WAITING.*
"THEY EVIDENTLY FIGURED, TIME TO *CUT* THEIR LOSSES AND *MOVE ON.*
"THE THOUGHT OF OFFERING *HELP* APPARENTLY *NEVER* OCCURRED TO THEM.

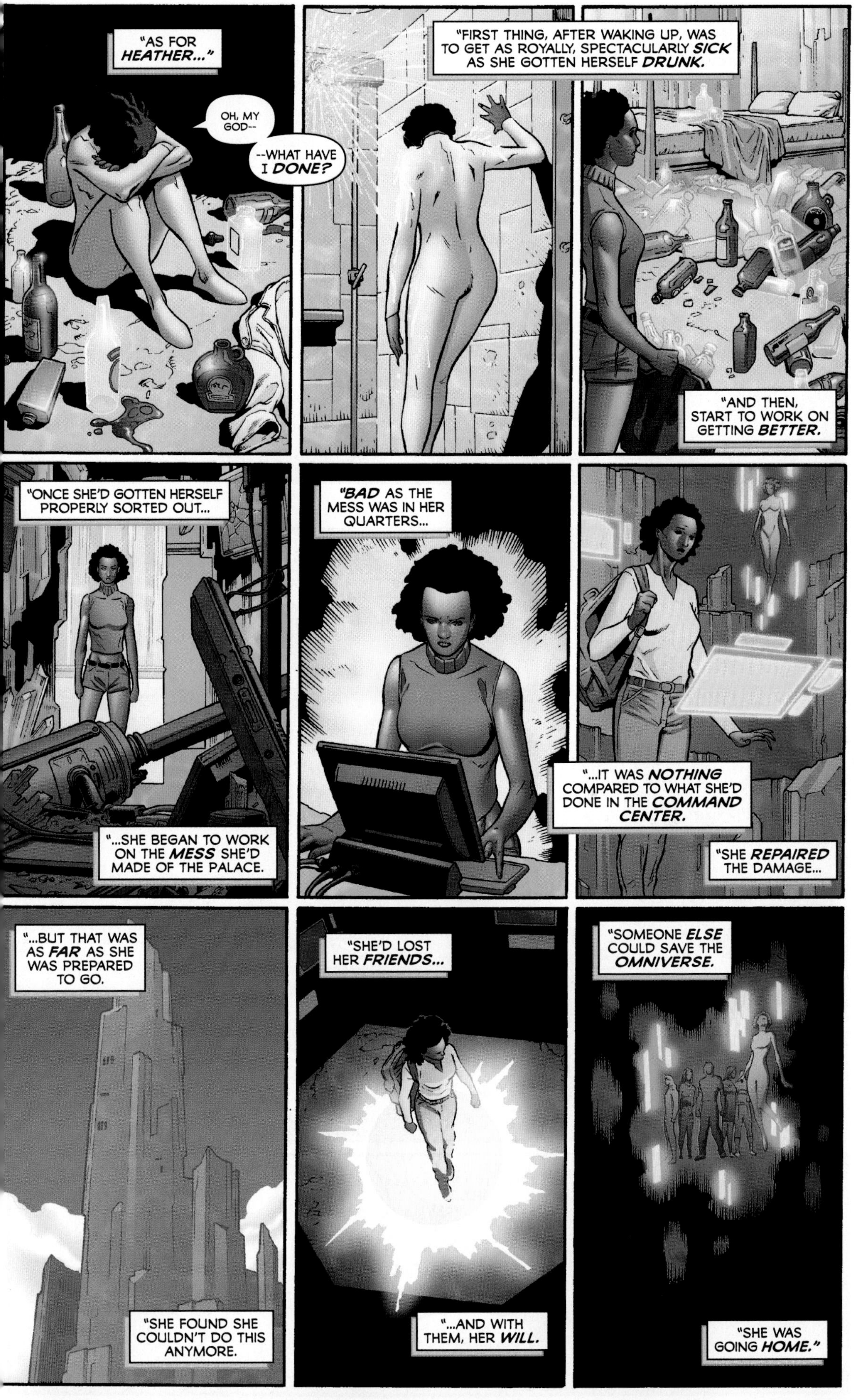
"AS FOR *HEATHER...*"
OH, MY GOD--
--WHAT HAVE I *DONE?*
"FIRST THING, AFTER WAKING UP, WAS TO GET AS ROYALLY, SPECTACULARLY *SICK* AS SHE GOTTEN HERSELF *DRUNK.*
"AND THEN, START TO WORK ON GETTING *BETTER.*
"ONCE SHE'D GOTTEN HERSELF PROPERLY SORTED OUT...
"...SHE BEGAN TO WORK ON THE *MESS* SHE'D MADE OF THE PALACE.
"*BAD* AS THE MESS WAS IN HER QUARTERS...
"...IT WAS *NOTHING* COMPARED TO WHAT SHE'D DONE IN THE *COMMAND CENTER.*
"SHE *REPAIRED* THE DAMAGE...
"...BUT THAT WAS AS *FAR* AS SHE WAS PREPARED TO GO.
"SHE FOUND SHE COULDN'T DO THIS ANYMORE.
"SHE'D LOST HER *FRIENDS...*
"...AND WITH THEM, HER *WILL.*
"SOMEONE *ELSE* COULD SAVE THE *OMNIVERSE.*
"SHE WAS GOING *HOME.*"

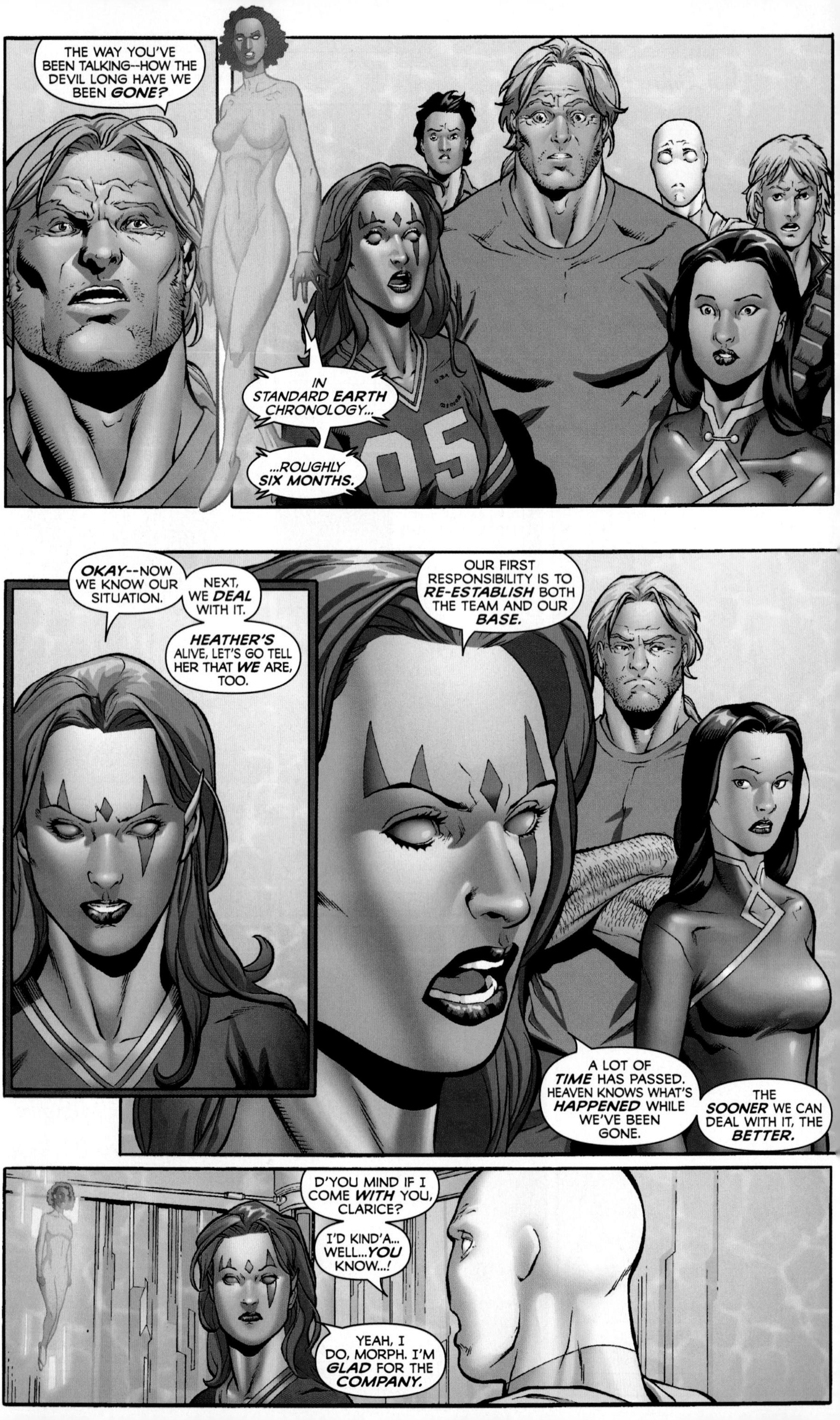

THE WAY YOU'VE BEEN TALKING--HOW THE DEVIL LONG HAVE WE BEEN GONE?
IN STANDARD EARTH CHRONOLOGY...
...ROUGHLY SIX MONTHS.
05
OKAY--NOW WE KNOW OUR SITUATION.
NEXT, WE DEAL WITH IT.
HEATHER'S ALIVE, LET'S GO TELL HER THAT WE ARE, TOO.
OUR FIRST RESPONSIBILITY IS TO RE-ESTABLISH BOTH THE TEAM AND OUR BASE.
A LOT OF TIME HAS PASSED. HEAVEN KNOWS WHAT'S HAPPENED WHILE WE'VE BEEN GONE.
THE SOONER WE CAN DEAL WITH IT, THE BETTER.
D'YOU MIND IF I COME WITH YOU, CLARICE?
I'D KIND'A... WELL...YOU KNOW...!
YEAH, I DO, MORPH. I'M GLAD FOR THE COMPANY.

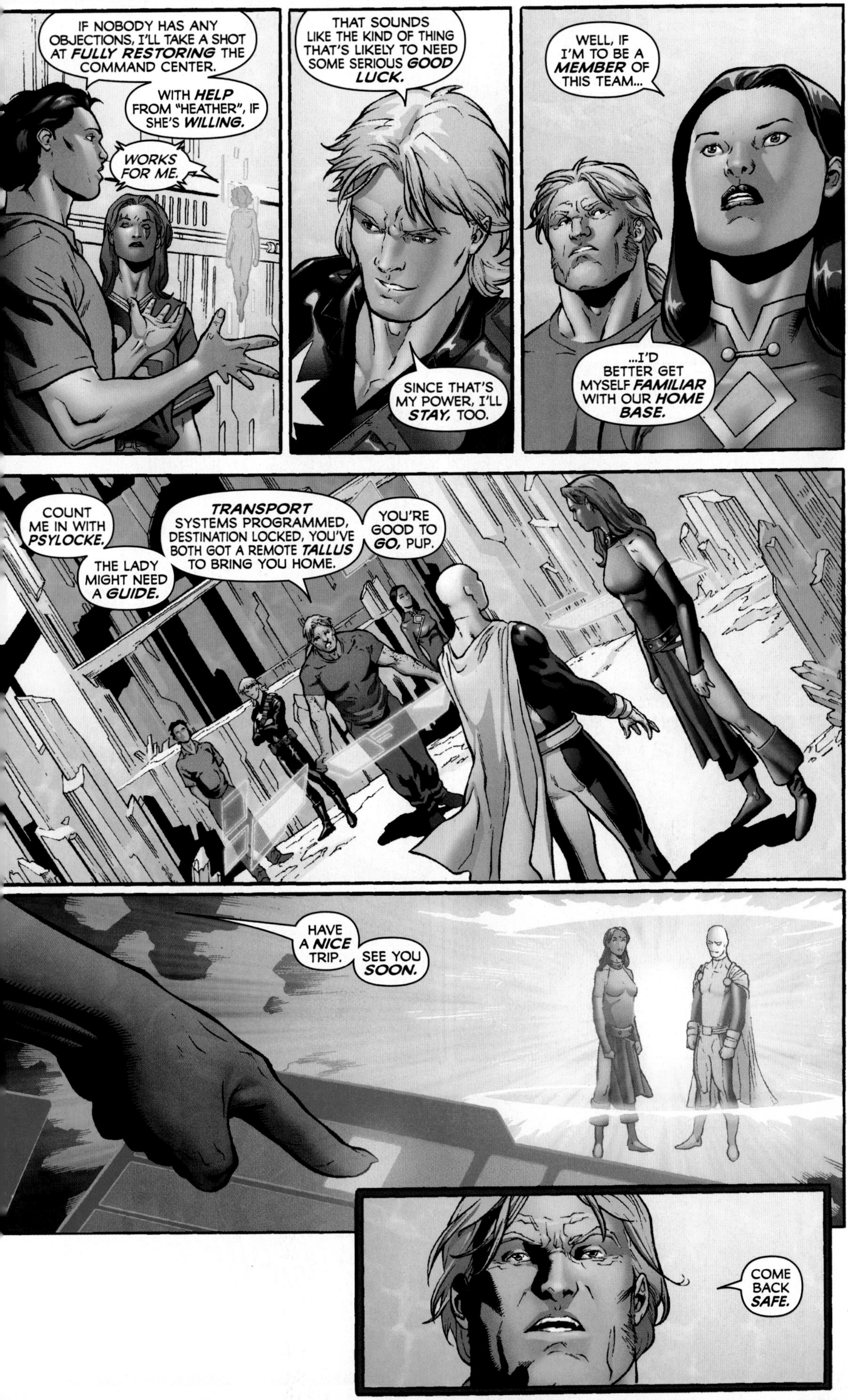
IF NOBODY HAS ANY OBJECTIONS, I'LL TAKE A SHOT AT *FULLY RESTORING* THE COMMAND CENTER.
WITH *HELP* FROM "HEATHER", IF SHE'S *WILLING.*
WORKS FOR ME.
THAT SOUNDS LIKE THE KIND OF THING THAT'S LIKELY TO NEED SOME SERIOUS *GOOD LUCK.*
SINCE THAT'S MY POWER, I'LL *STAY,* TOO.
WELL, IF I'M TO BE A *MEMBER* OF THIS TEAM...
...I'D BETTER GET MYSELF *FAMILIAR* WITH OUR *HOME BASE.*
COUNT ME IN WITH *PSYLOCKE.*
THE LADY MIGHT NEED A *GUIDE.*
TRANSPORT SYSTEMS PROGRAMMED, DESTINATION LOCKED, YOU'VE BOTH GOT A REMOTE *TALLUS* TO BRING YOU HOME.
YOU'RE GOOD TO *GO,* PUP.
HAVE A *NICE* TRIP.
SEE YOU *SOON.*
COME BACK *SAFE.*

EARTH 3470.

YOU *SURE* THIS IS THE RIGHT ADDRESS? IS IT THE *RIGHT* EARTH?

MORPH-- JUST RING THE *DOORBELL!*

DINK-DONG
DING-DONG

HEY, *HEATHER*-- GUESS WHO'S *NOT DEAD!*

MORPH?

HEATHER?!?

?

!

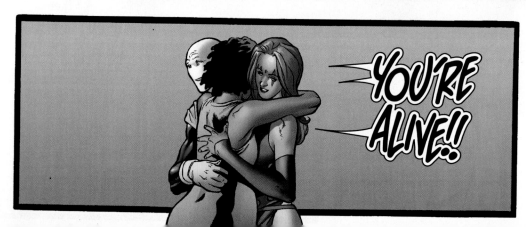

YOU'RE ALIVE!!

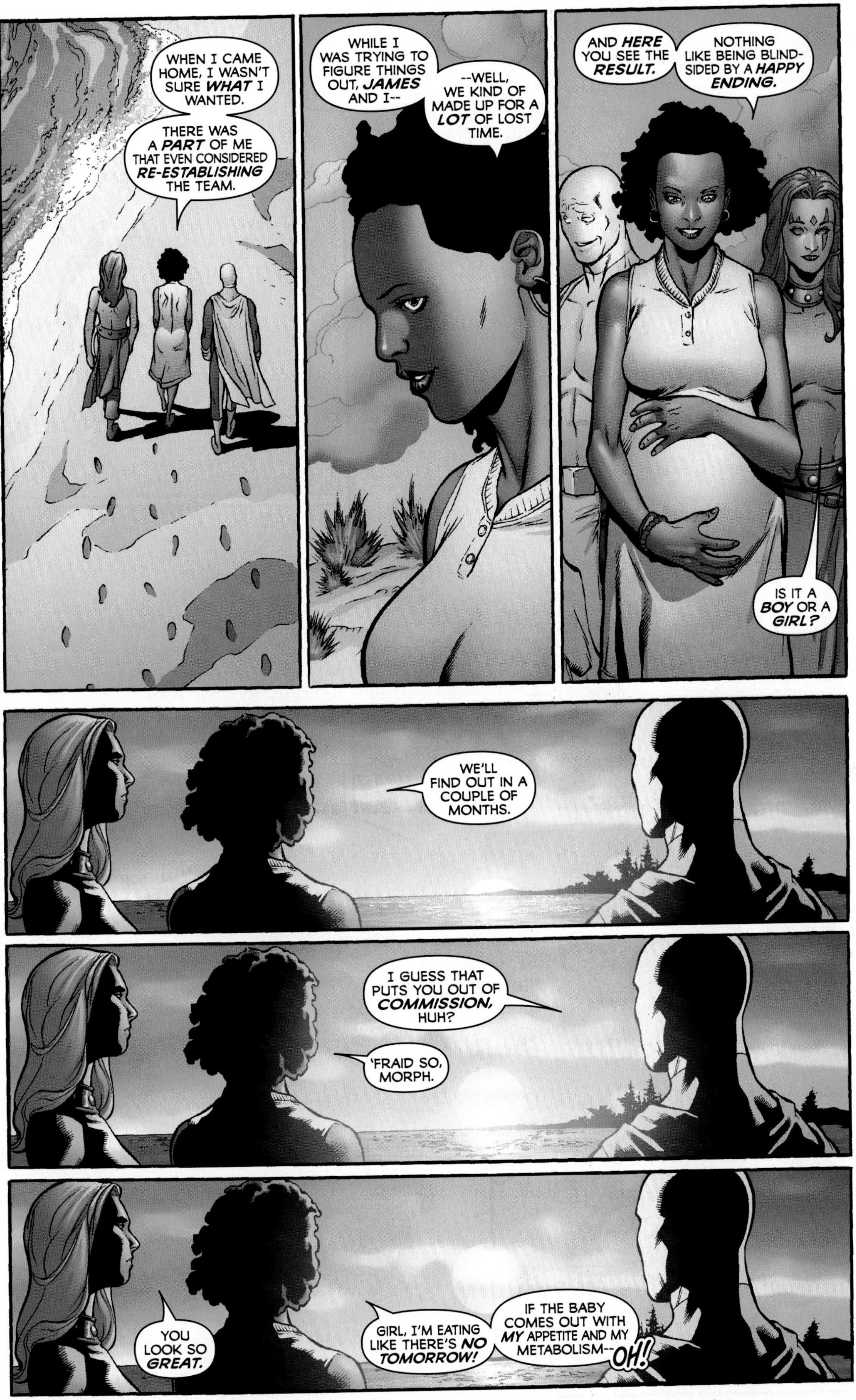
WHEN I CAME HOME, I WASN'T SURE *WHAT* I WANTED.
THERE WAS A *PART* OF ME THAT EVEN CONSIDERED *RE-ESTABLISHING* THE TEAM.
WHILE I WAS TRYING TO FIGURE THINGS OUT, *JAMES* AND I--
--WELL, WE KIND OF MADE UP FOR A *LOT* OF LOST TIME.
AND *HERE* YOU SEE THE *RESULT.*
NOTHING LIKE BEING BLIND-SIDED BY A *HAPPY ENDING.*
IS IT A *BOY* OR A *GIRL?*
WE'LL FIND OUT IN A COUPLE OF MONTHS.
I GUESS THAT PUTS YOU OUT OF *COMMISSION,* HUH?
'FRAID SO, MORPH.
YOU LOOK SO *GREAT.*
GIRL, I'M EATING LIKE THERE'S *NO TOMORROW!*
IF THE BABY COMES OUT WITH *MY* APPETITE AND MY METABOLISM--
OH!

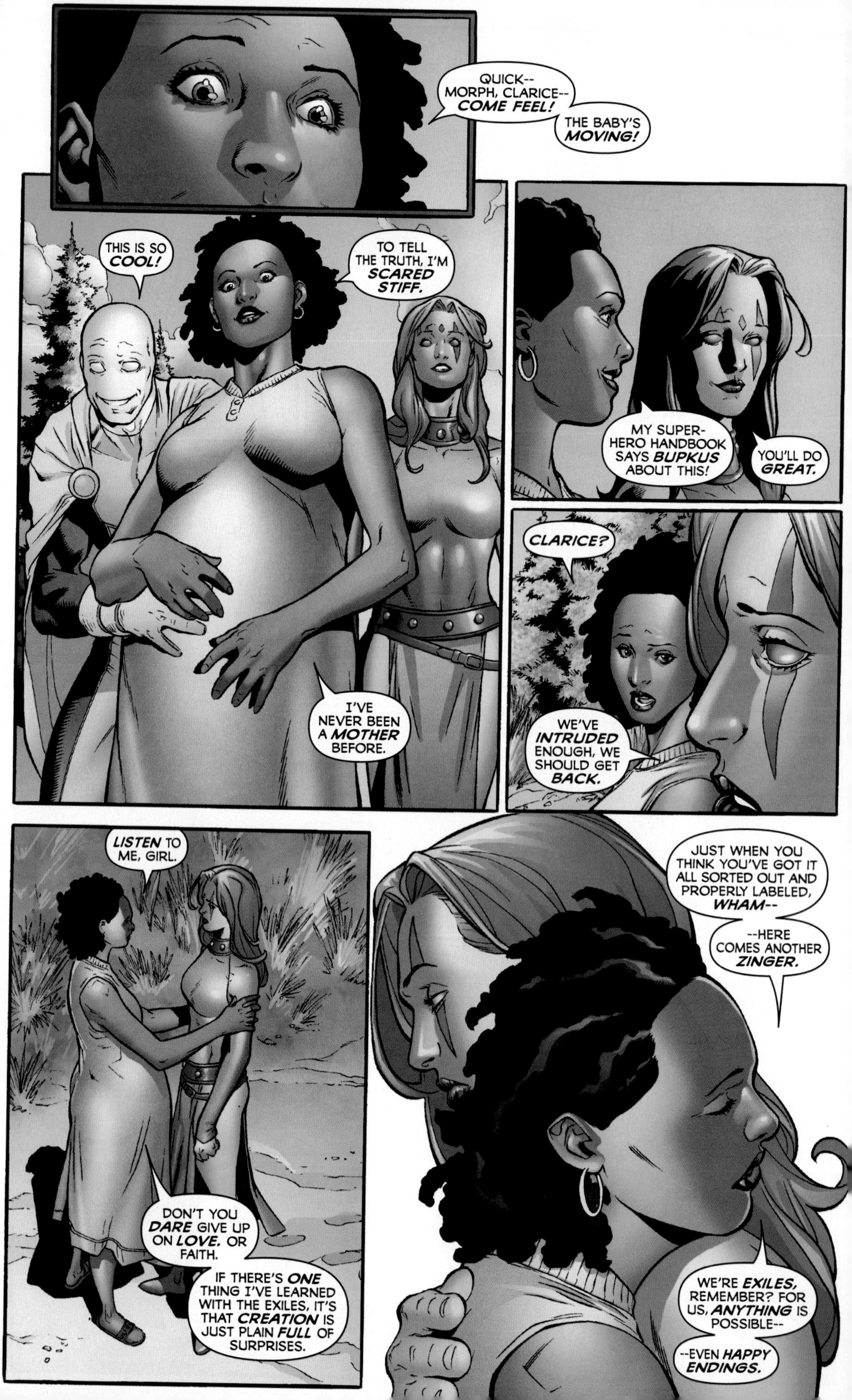
QUICK-- MORPH, CLARICE-- COME FEEL!
THE BABY'S MOVING!
THIS IS SO COOL!
TO TELL THE TRUTH, I'M SCARED STIFF.
I'VE NEVER BEEN A MOTHER BEFORE.
MY SUPER-HERO HANDBOOK SAYS BUPKUS ABOUT THIS!
YOU'LL DO GREAT.
CLARICE?
WE'VE INTRUDED ENOUGH, WE SHOULD GET BACK.
LISTEN TO ME, GIRL.
DON'T YOU DARE GIVE UP ON LOVE. OR FAITH.
IF THERE'S ONE THING I'VE LEARNED WITH THE EXILES, IT'S THAT CREATION IS JUST PLAIN FULL OF SURPRISES.
JUST WHEN YOU THINK YOU'VE GOT IT ALL SORTED OUT AND PROPERLY LABELED, WHAM--
--HERE COMES ANOTHER ZINGER.
WE'RE EXILES, REMEMBER? FOR US, ANYTHING IS POSSIBLE--
--EVEN HAPPY ENDINGS.

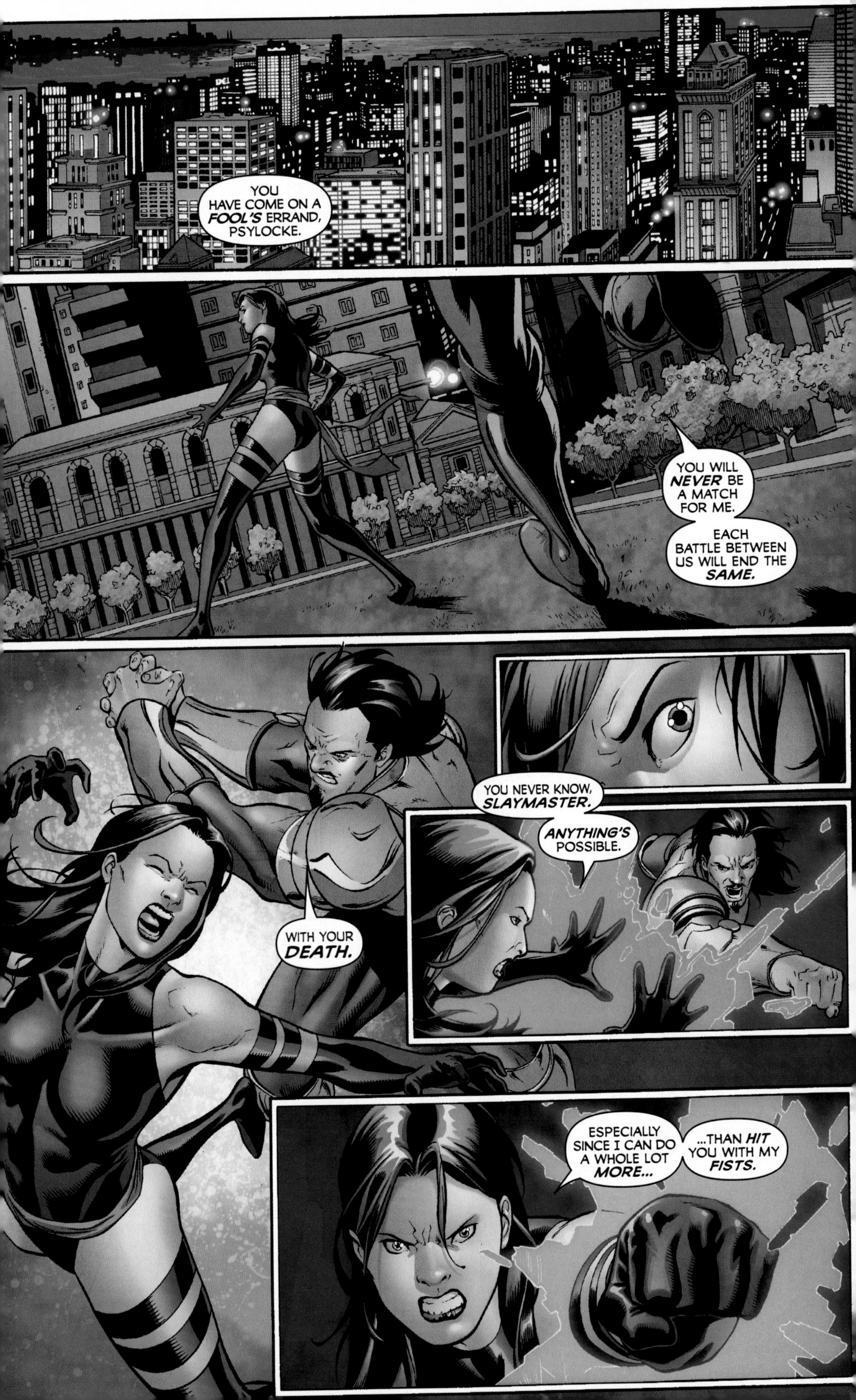
YOU HAVE COME ON A FOOL'S ERRAND, PSYLOCKE.
YOU WILL NEVER BE A MATCH FOR ME.
EACH BATTLE BETWEEN US WILL END THE SAME.
WITH YOUR DEATH.
YOU NEVER KNOW, SLAYMASTER.
ANYTHING'S POSSIBLE.
ESPECIALLY SINCE I CAN DO A WHOLE LOT MORE...
...THAN HIT YOU WITH MY FISTS.

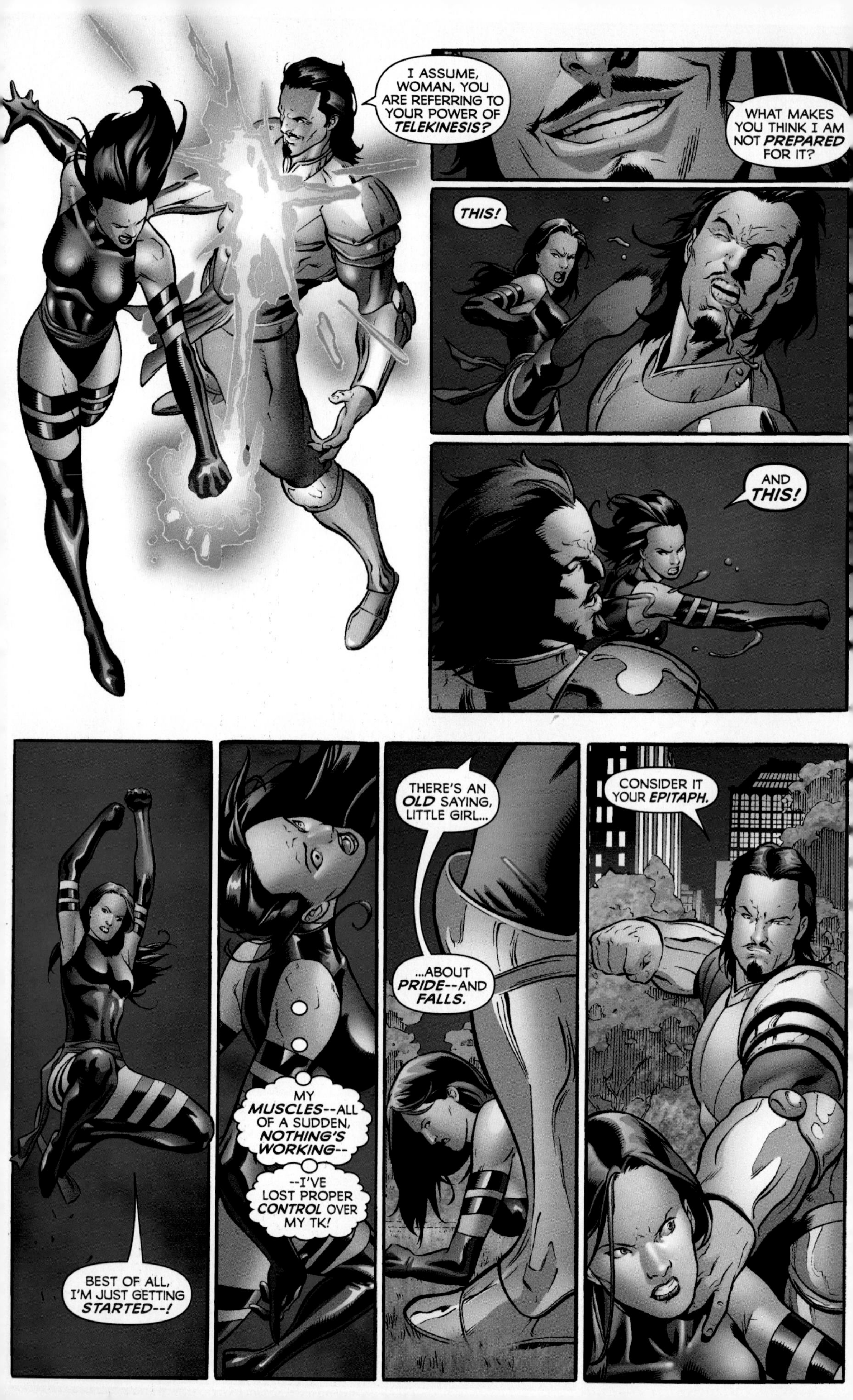
I ASSUME, WOMAN, YOU ARE REFERRING TO YOUR POWER OF TELEKINESIS?
WHAT MAKES YOU THINK I AM NOT PREPARED FOR IT?
THIS!
AND THIS!
BEST OF ALL, I'M JUST GETTING STARTED--!
MY MUSCLES--ALL OF A SUDDEN, NOTHING'S WORKING--
--I'VE LOST PROPER CONTROL OVER MY TK!
THERE'S AN OLD SAYING, LITTLE GIRL...
...ABOUT PRIDE--AND FALLS.
CONSIDER IT YOUR EPITAPH.

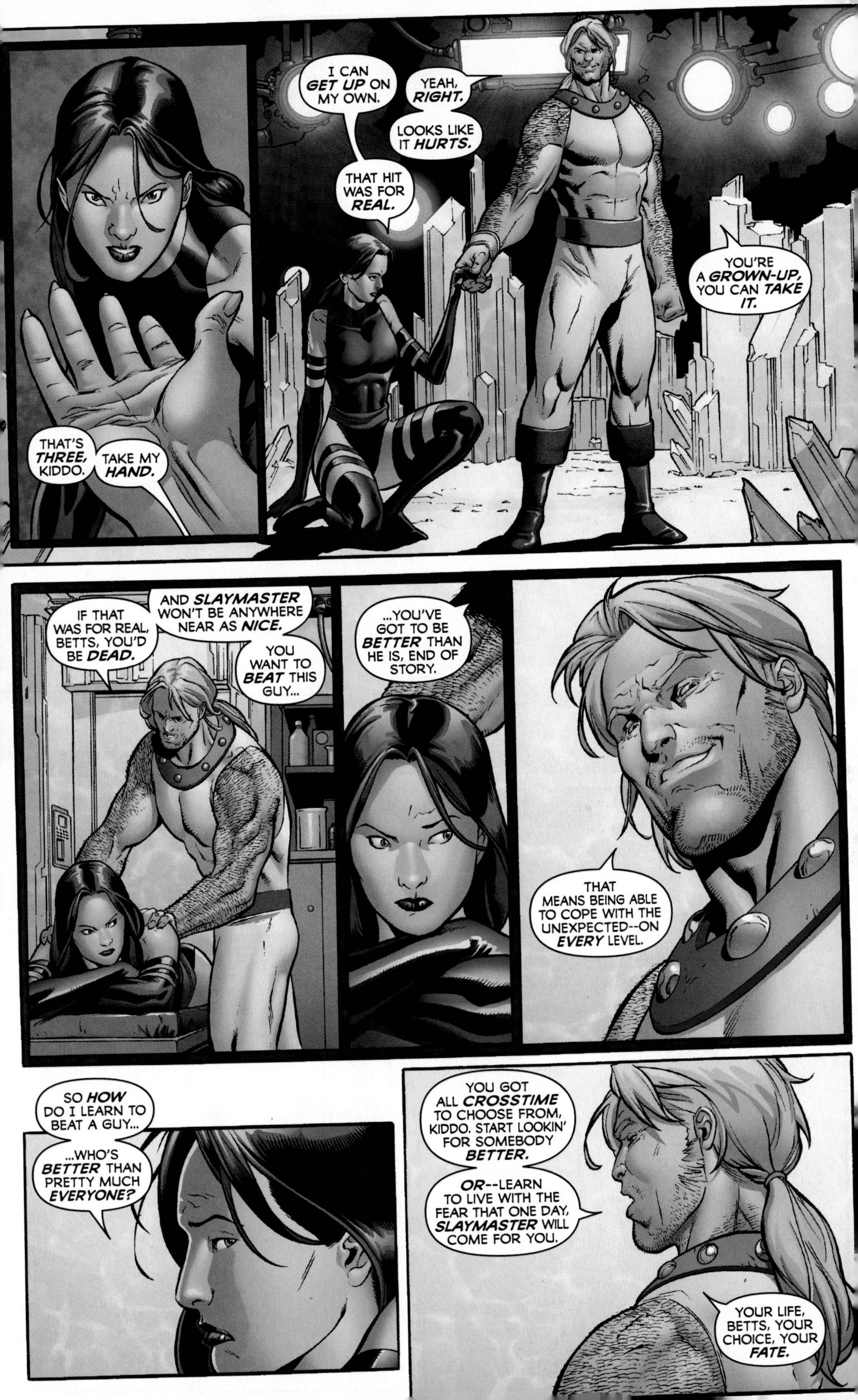
THAT'S THREE, KIDDO.
TAKE MY HAND.
I CAN GET UP ON MY OWN.
YEAH, RIGHT.
LOOKS LIKE IT HURTS.
THAT HIT WAS FOR REAL.
YOU'RE A GROWN-UP, YOU CAN TAKE IT.
IF THAT WAS FOR REAL, BETTS, YOU'D BE DEAD.
AND SLAYMASTER WON'T BE ANYWHERE NEAR AS NICE.
YOU WANT TO BEAT THIS GUY...
...YOU'VE GOT TO BE BETTER THAN HE IS, END OF STORY.
THAT MEANS BEING ABLE TO COPE WITH THE UNEXPECTED--ON EVERY LEVEL.
SO HOW DO I LEARN TO BEAT A GUY...
...WHO'S BETTER THAN PRETTY MUCH EVERYONE?
YOU GOT ALL CROSSTIME TO CHOOSE FROM, KIDDO. START LOOKIN' FOR SOMEBODY BETTER.
OR--LEARN TO LIVE WITH THE FEAR THAT ONE DAY, SLAYMASTER WILL COME FOR YOU.
YOUR LIFE, BETTS, YOUR CHOICE, YOUR FATE.

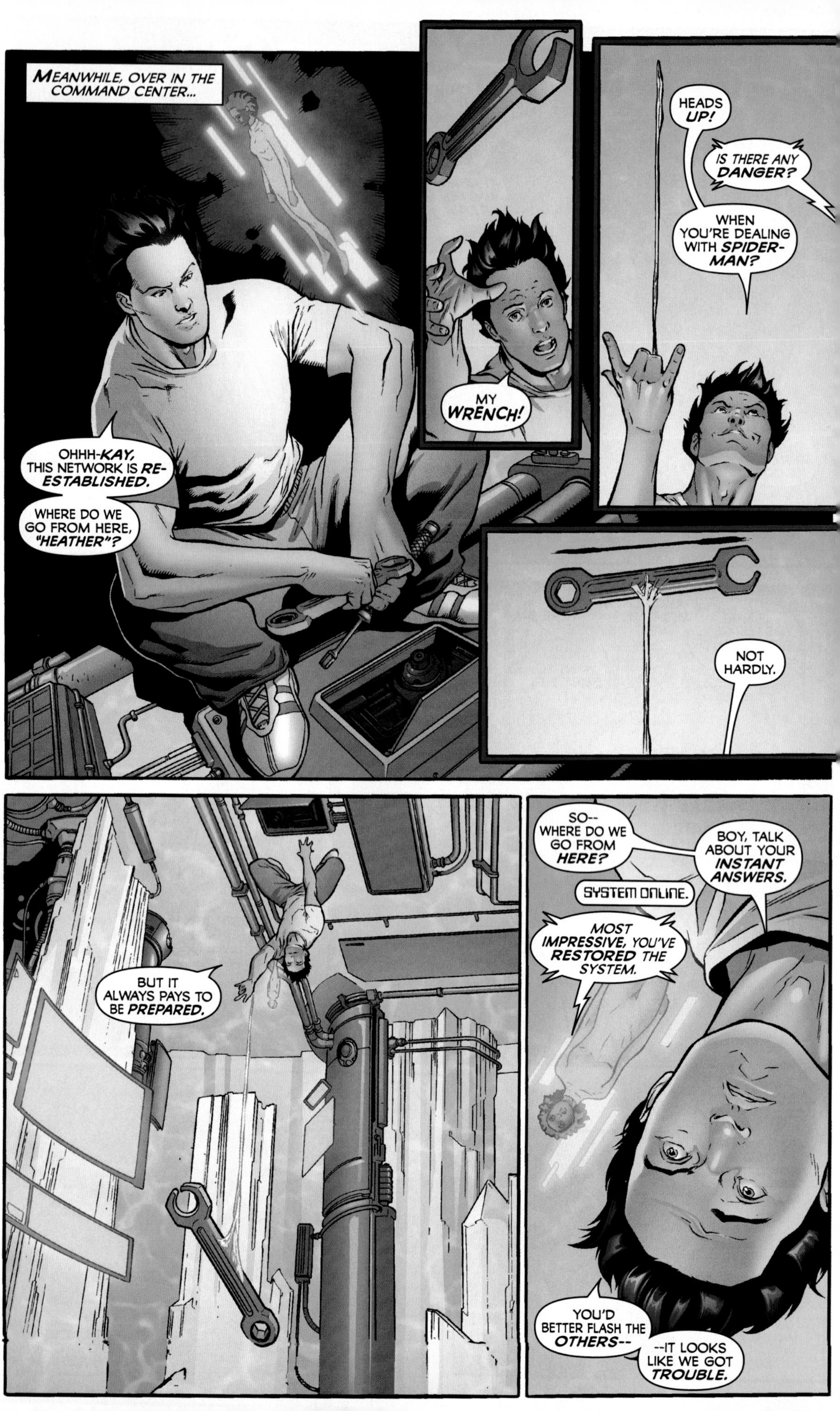
MEANWHILE, OVER IN THE COMMAND CENTER...
OHHH-KAY, THIS NETWORK IS RE-ESTABLISHED.
WHERE DO WE GO FROM HERE, "HEATHER"?
MY WRENCH!
HEADS UP!
IS THERE ANY DANGER?
WHEN YOU'RE DEALING WITH SPIDER-MAN?
NOT HARDLY.
BUT IT ALWAYS PAYS TO BE PREPARED.
SO-- WHERE DO WE GO FROM HERE?
BOY, TALK ABOUT YOUR INSTANT ANSWERS.
SYSTEM ONLINE.
MOST IMPRESSIVE, YOU'VE RESTORED THE SYSTEM.
YOU'D BETTER FLASH THE OTHERS--
--IT LOOKS LIKE WE GOT TROUBLE.

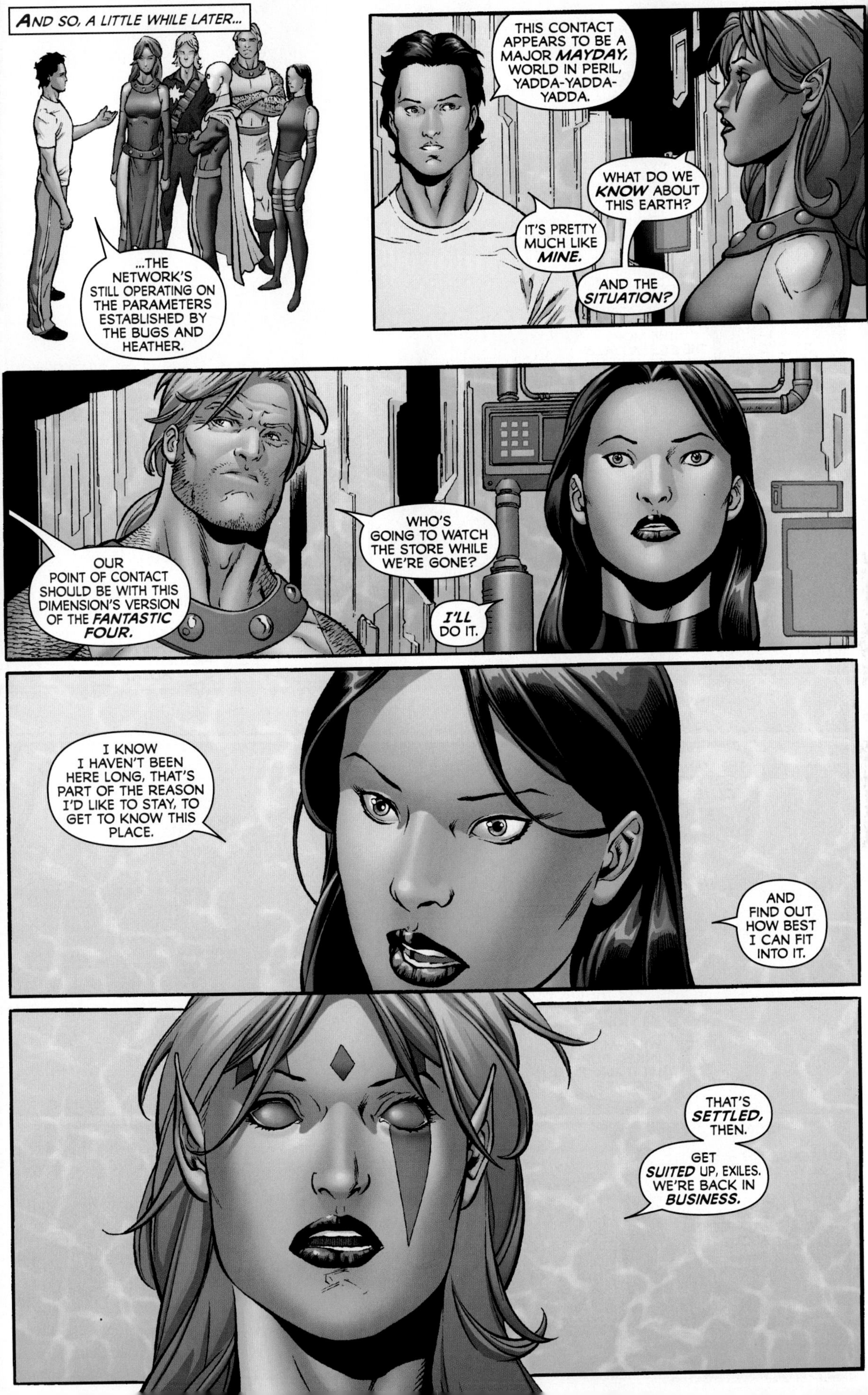
AND SO, A LITTLE WHILE LATER...
...THE NETWORK'S STILL OPERATING ON THE PARAMETERS ESTABLISHED BY THE BUGS AND HEATHER.
THIS CONTACT APPEARS TO BE A MAJOR MAYDAY, WORLD IN PERIL, YADDA-YADDA-YADDA.
WHAT DO WE KNOW ABOUT THIS EARTH?
IT'S PRETTY MUCH LIKE MINE.
AND THE SITUATION?
OUR POINT OF CONTACT SHOULD BE WITH THIS DIMENSION'S VERSION OF THE FANTASTIC FOUR.
WHO'S GOING TO WATCH THE STORE WHILE WE'RE GONE?
I'LL DO IT.
I KNOW I HAVEN'T BEEN HERE LONG, THAT'S PART OF THE REASON I'D LIKE TO STAY, TO GET TO KNOW THIS PLACE.
AND FIND OUT HOW BEST I CAN FIT INTO IT.
THAT'S SETTLED, THEN.
GET SUITED UP, EXILES. WE'RE BACK IN BUSINESS.

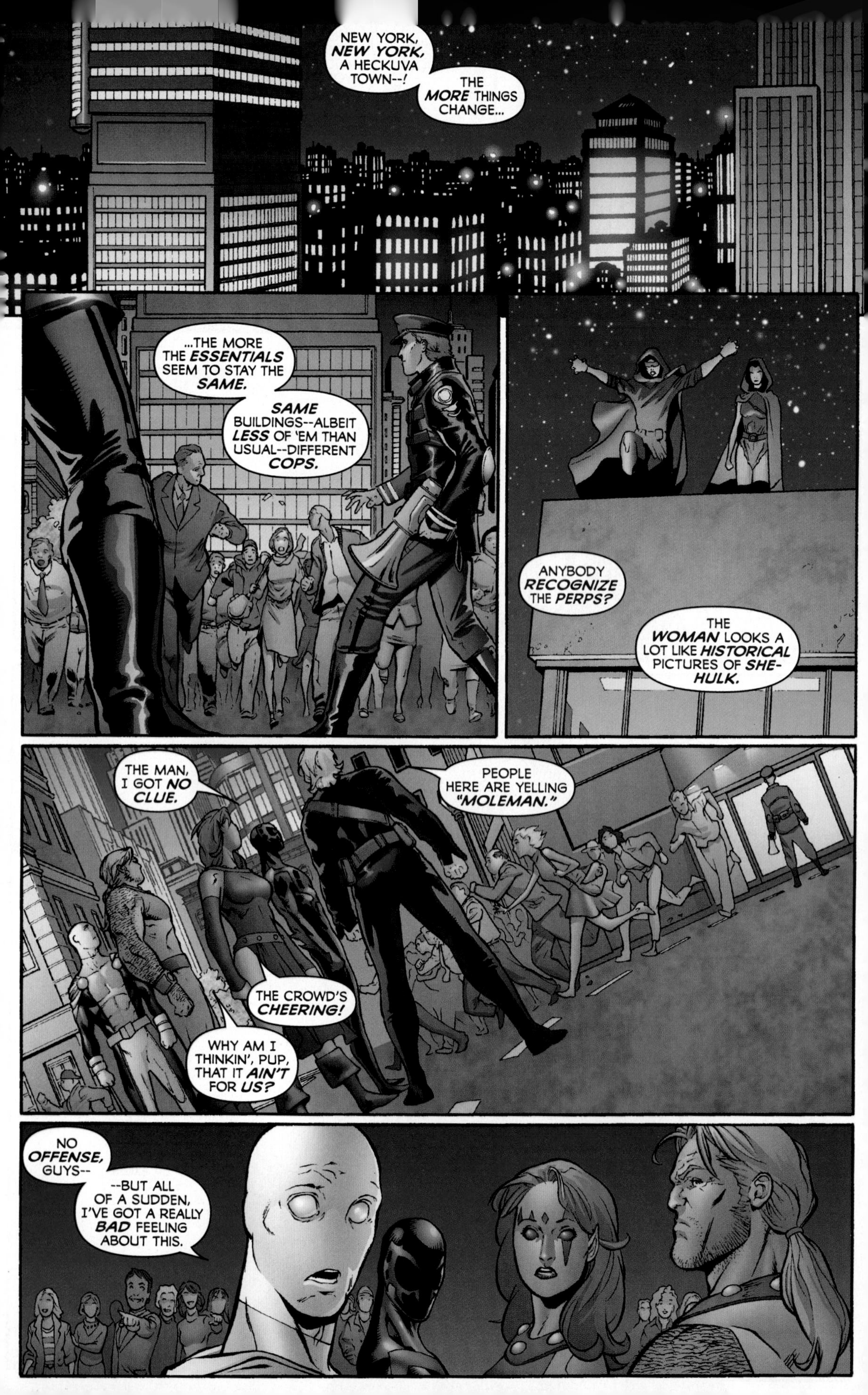
NEW YORK, NEW YORK, A HECKUVA TOWN--!
THE MORE THINGS CHANGE...
...THE MORE THE ESSENTIALS SEEM TO STAY THE SAME.
SAME BUILDINGS--ALBEIT LESS OF 'EM THAN USUAL--DIFFERENT COPS.
ANYBODY RECOGNIZE THE PERPS?
THE WOMAN LOOKS A LOT LIKE HISTORICAL PICTURES OF SHE-HULK.
THE MAN, I GOT NO CLUE.
PEOPLE HERE ARE YELLING "MOLEMAN."
THE CROWD'S CHEERING!
WHY AM I THINKIN', PUP, THAT IT AIN'T FOR US?
NO OFFENSE, GUYS--
--BUT ALL OF A SUDDEN, I'VE GOT A REALLY BAD FEELING ABOUT THIS.

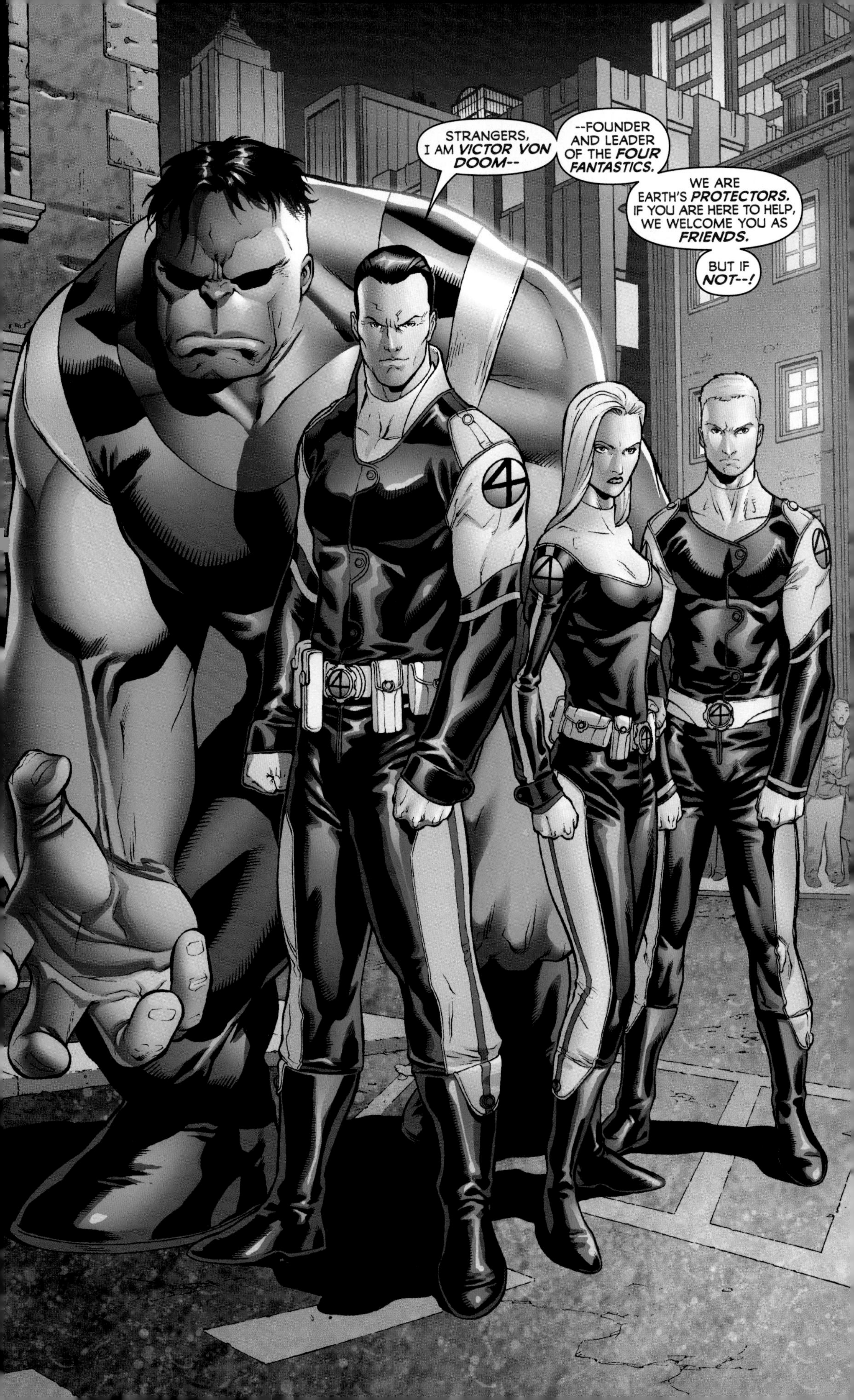
STRANGERS, I AM *VICTOR VON DOOM*--
--FOUNDER AND LEADER OF THE *FOUR FANTASTICS.*
WE ARE EARTH'S *PROTECTORS.* IF YOU ARE HERE TO HELP, WE WELCOME YOU AS *FRIENDS.*
BUT IF *NOT*--!

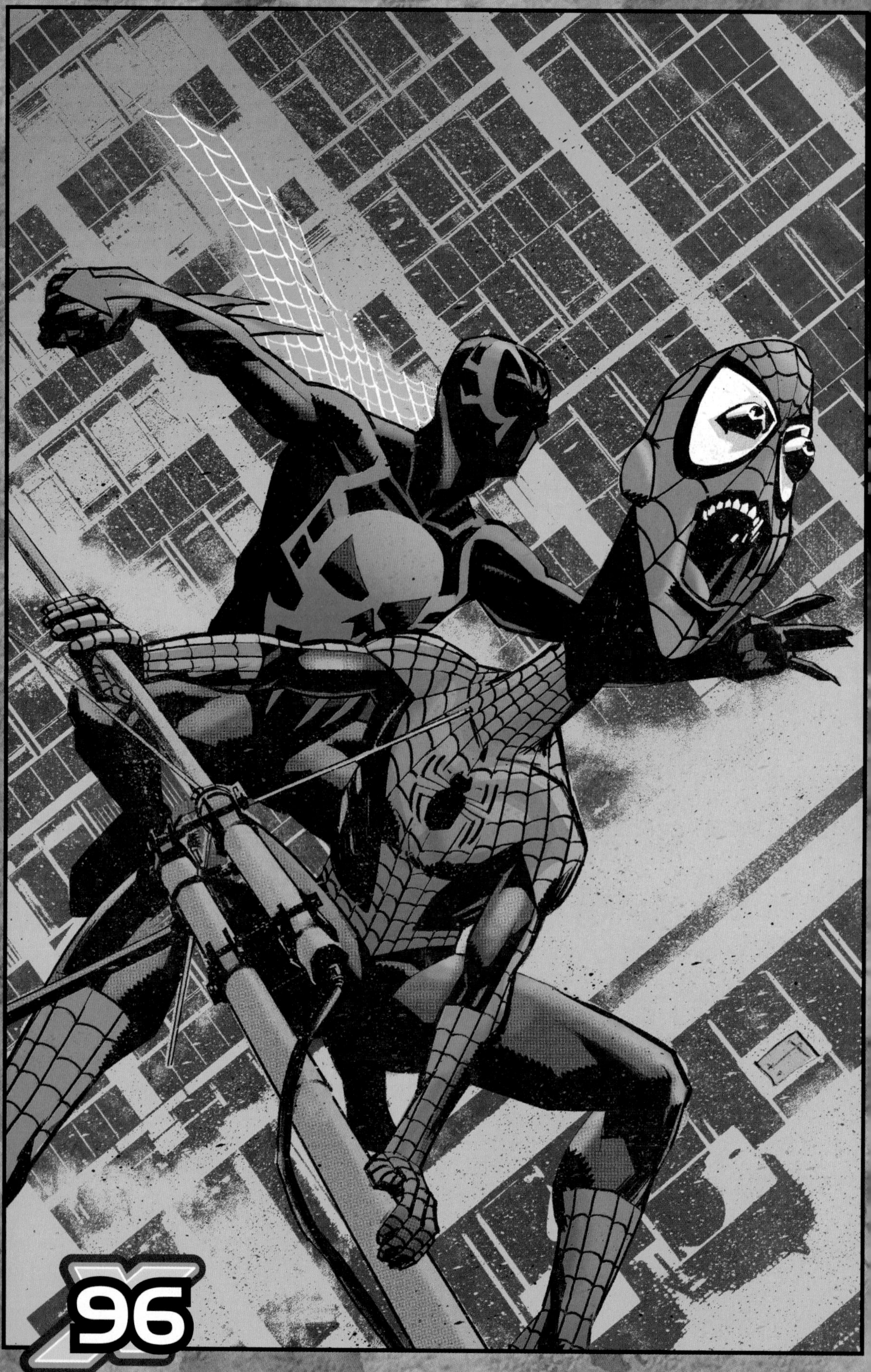
96

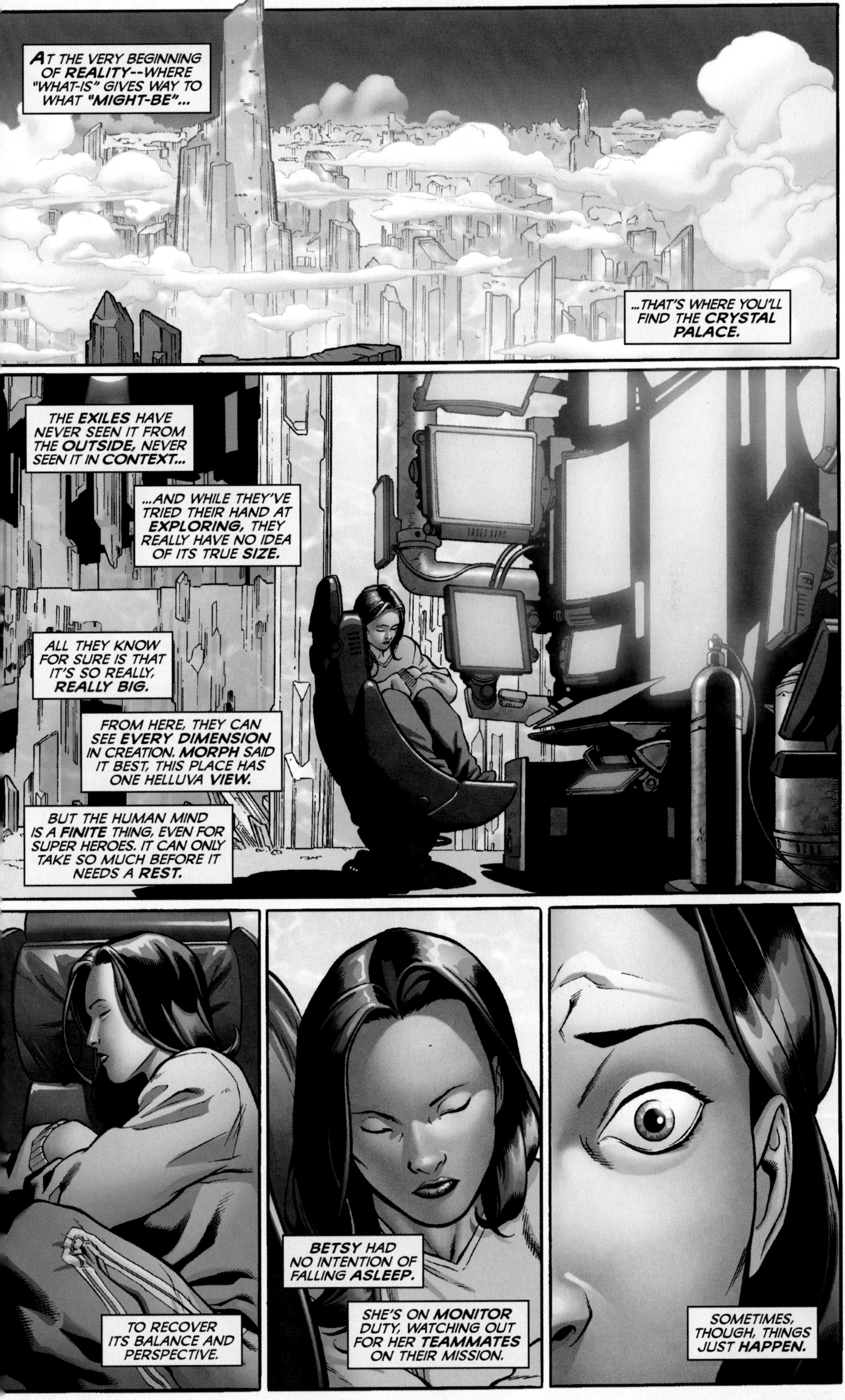

AT THE VERY BEGINNING OF REALITY--WHERE "WHAT-IS" GIVES WAY TO WHAT "MIGHT-BE"...
...THAT'S WHERE YOU'LL FIND THE CRYSTAL PALACE.
THE EXILES HAVE NEVER SEEN IT FROM THE OUTSIDE, NEVER SEEN IT IN CONTEXT...
...AND WHILE THEY'VE TRIED THEIR HAND AT EXPLORING, THEY REALLY HAVE NO IDEA OF ITS TRUE SIZE.
ALL THEY KNOW FOR SURE IS THAT IT'S SO REALLY, REALLY BIG.
FROM HERE, THEY CAN SEE EVERY DIMENSION IN CREATION. MORPH SAID IT BEST, THIS PLACE HAS ONE HELLUVA VIEW.
BUT THE HUMAN MIND IS A FINITE THING, EVEN FOR SUPER HEROES. IT CAN ONLY TAKE SO MUCH BEFORE IT NEEDS A REST.
TO RECOVER ITS BALANCE AND PERSPECTIVE.
BETSY HAD NO INTENTION OF FALLING ASLEEP.
SHE'S ON MONITOR DUTY, WATCHING OUT FOR HER TEAMMATES ON THEIR MISSION.
SOMETIMES, THOUGH, THINGS JUST HAPPEN.

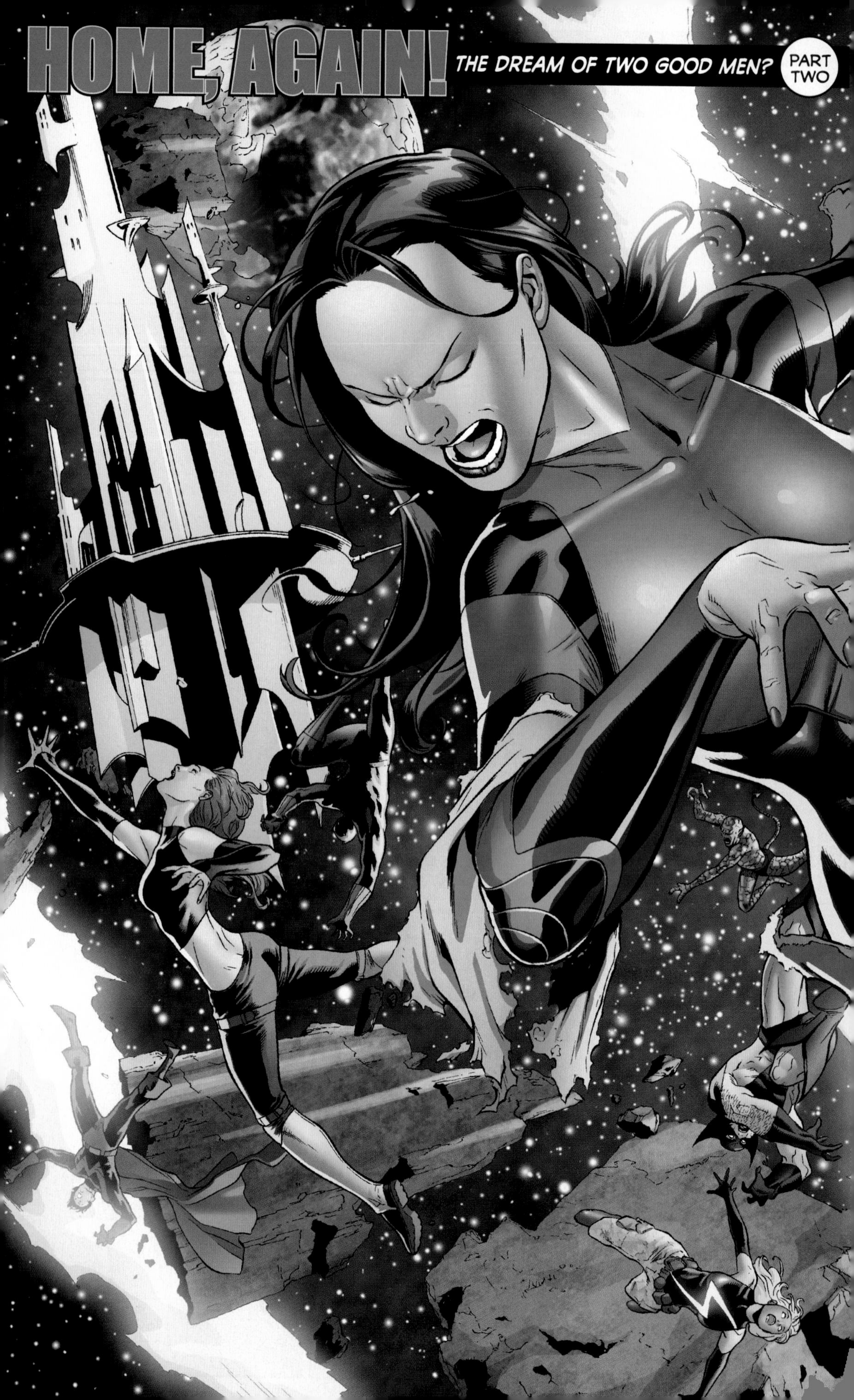
HOME, AGAIN!
THE DREAM OF TWO GOOD MEN?
PART TWO

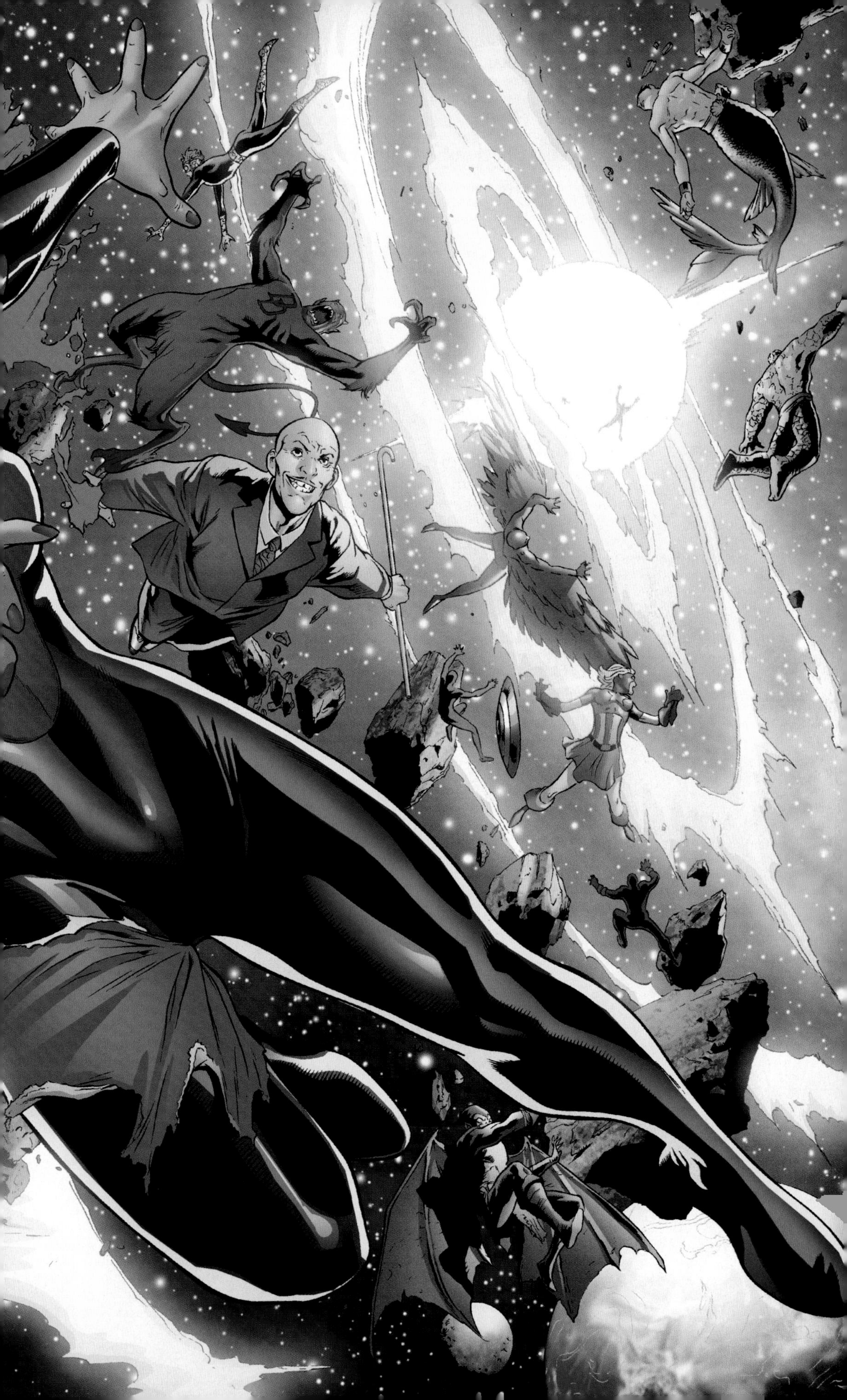

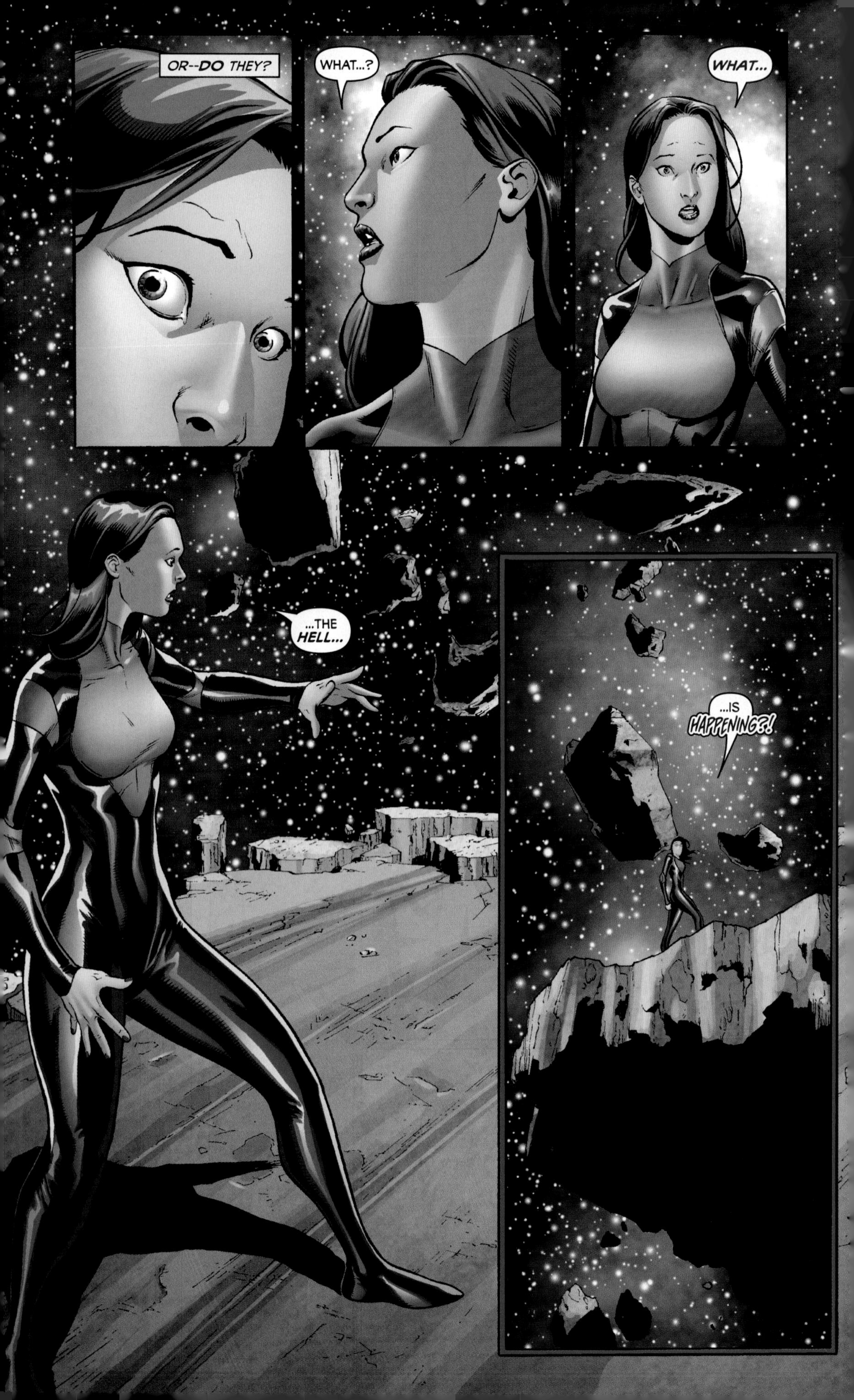
OR--DO THEY?
WHAT...?
WHAT...
...THE HELL...
...IS HAPPENING?!

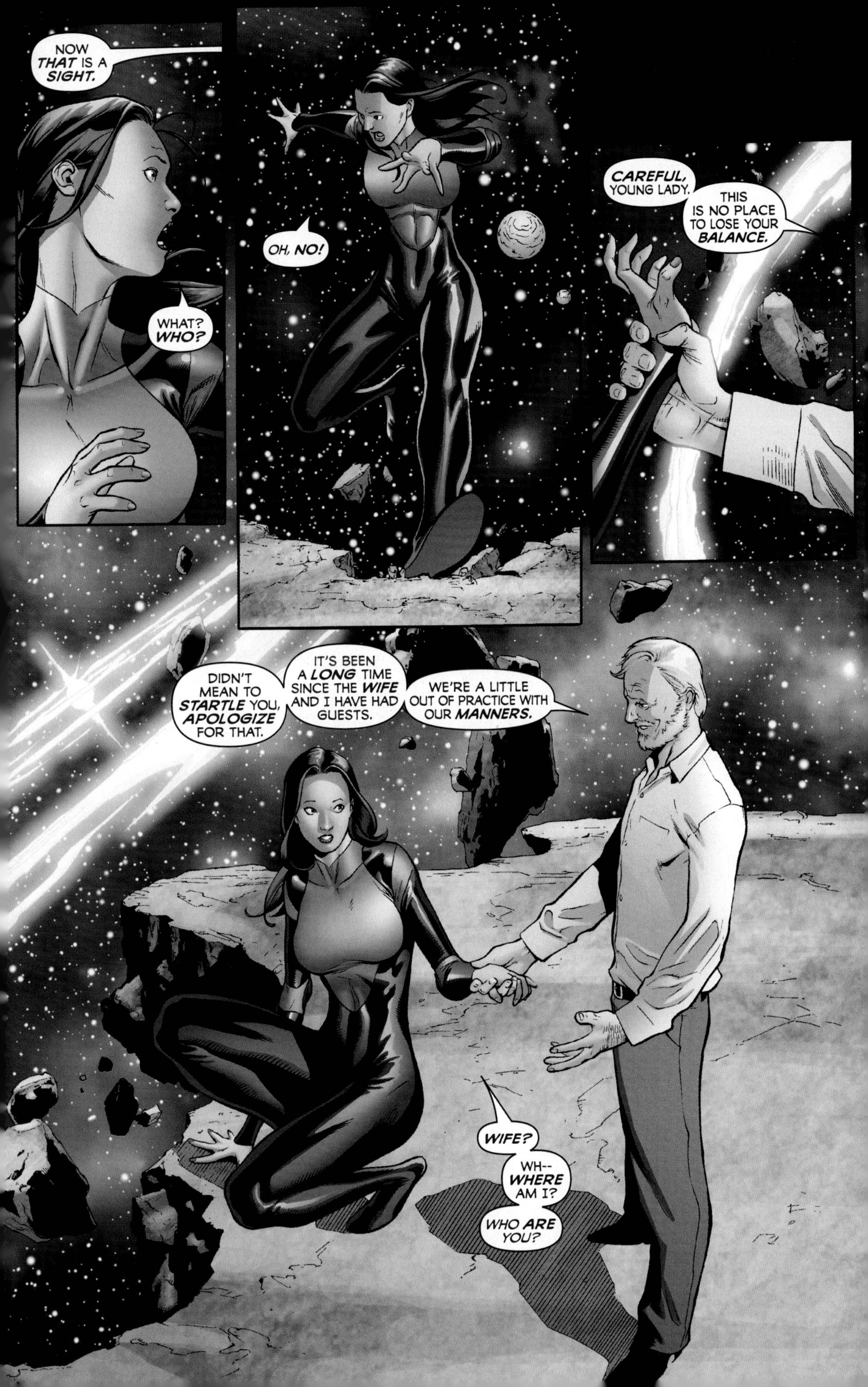
NOW THAT IS A SIGHT.
WHAT? WHO?
OH, NO!
CAREFUL, YOUNG LADY.
THIS IS NO PLACE TO LOSE YOUR BALANCE.
DIDN'T MEAN TO STARTLE YOU, APOLOGIZE FOR THAT.
IT'S BEEN A LONG TIME SINCE THE WIFE AND I HAVE HAD GUESTS.
WE'RE A LITTLE OUT OF PRACTICE WITH OUR MANNERS.
WIFE?
WH-- WHERE AM I?
WHO ARE YOU?

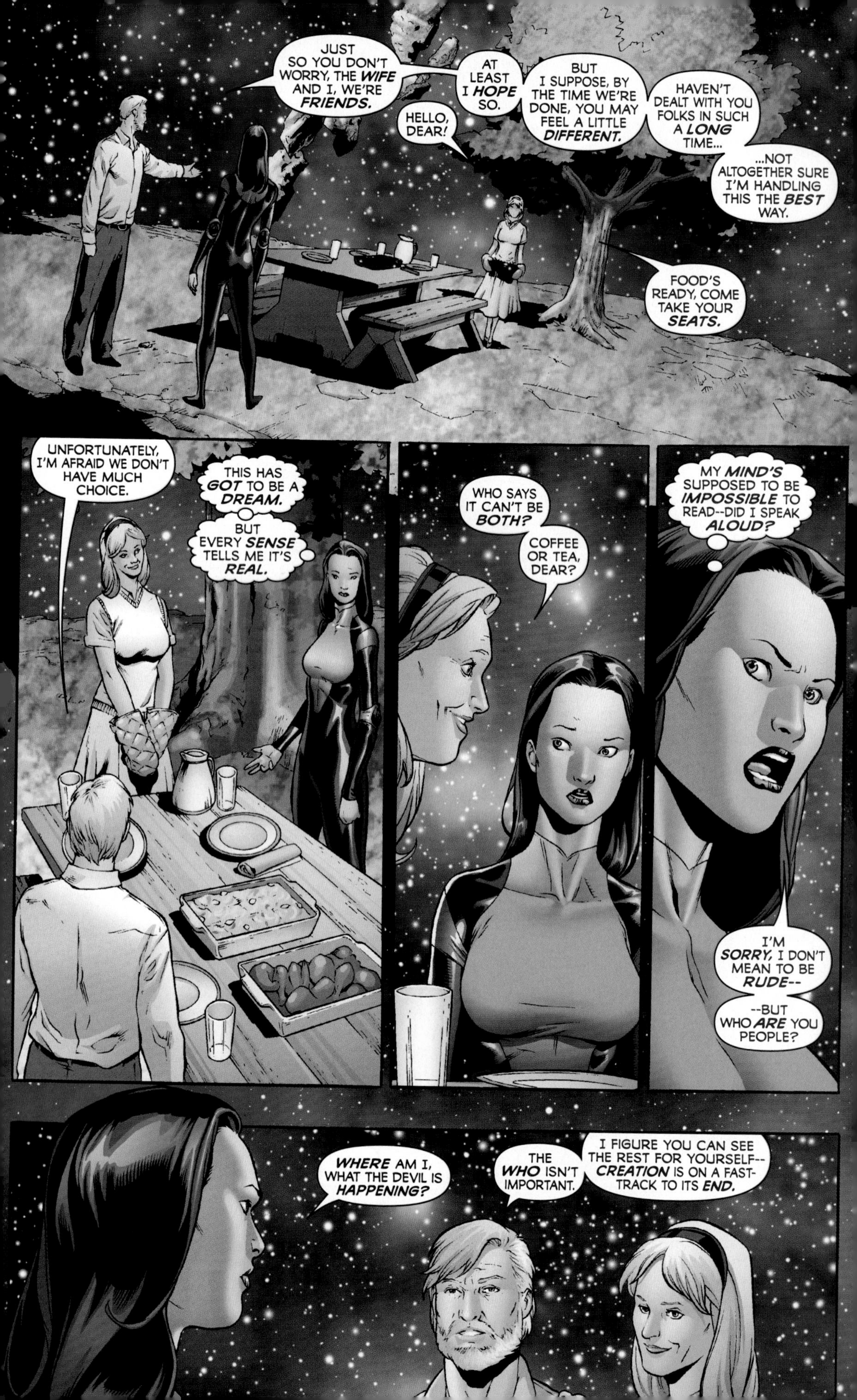

JUST SO YOU DON'T WORRY, THE WIFE AND I, WE'RE FRIENDS.
AT LEAST I HOPE SO.
BUT I SUPPOSE, BY THE TIME WE'RE DONE, YOU MAY FEEL A LITTLE DIFFERENT.
HAVEN'T DEALT WITH YOU FOLKS IN SUCH A LONG TIME...
...NOT ALTOGETHER SURE I'M HANDLING THIS THE BEST WAY.
HELLO, DEAR!
FOOD'S READY, COME TAKE YOUR SEATS.
UNFORTUNATELY, I'M AFRAID WE DON'T HAVE MUCH CHOICE.
THIS HAS GOT TO BE A DREAM.
BUT EVERY SENSE TELLS ME IT'S REAL.
WHO SAYS IT CAN'T BE BOTH?
COFFEE OR TEA, DEAR?
MY MIND'S SUPPOSED TO BE IMPOSSIBLE TO READ--DID I SPEAK ALOUD?
I'M SORRY, I DON'T MEAN TO BE RUDE--
--BUT WHO ARE YOU PEOPLE?
WHERE AM I, WHAT THE DEVIL IS HAPPENING?
THE WHO ISN'T IMPORTANT.
I FIGURE YOU CAN SEE THE REST FOR YOURSELF-- CREATION IS ON A FAST-TRACK TO ITS END.

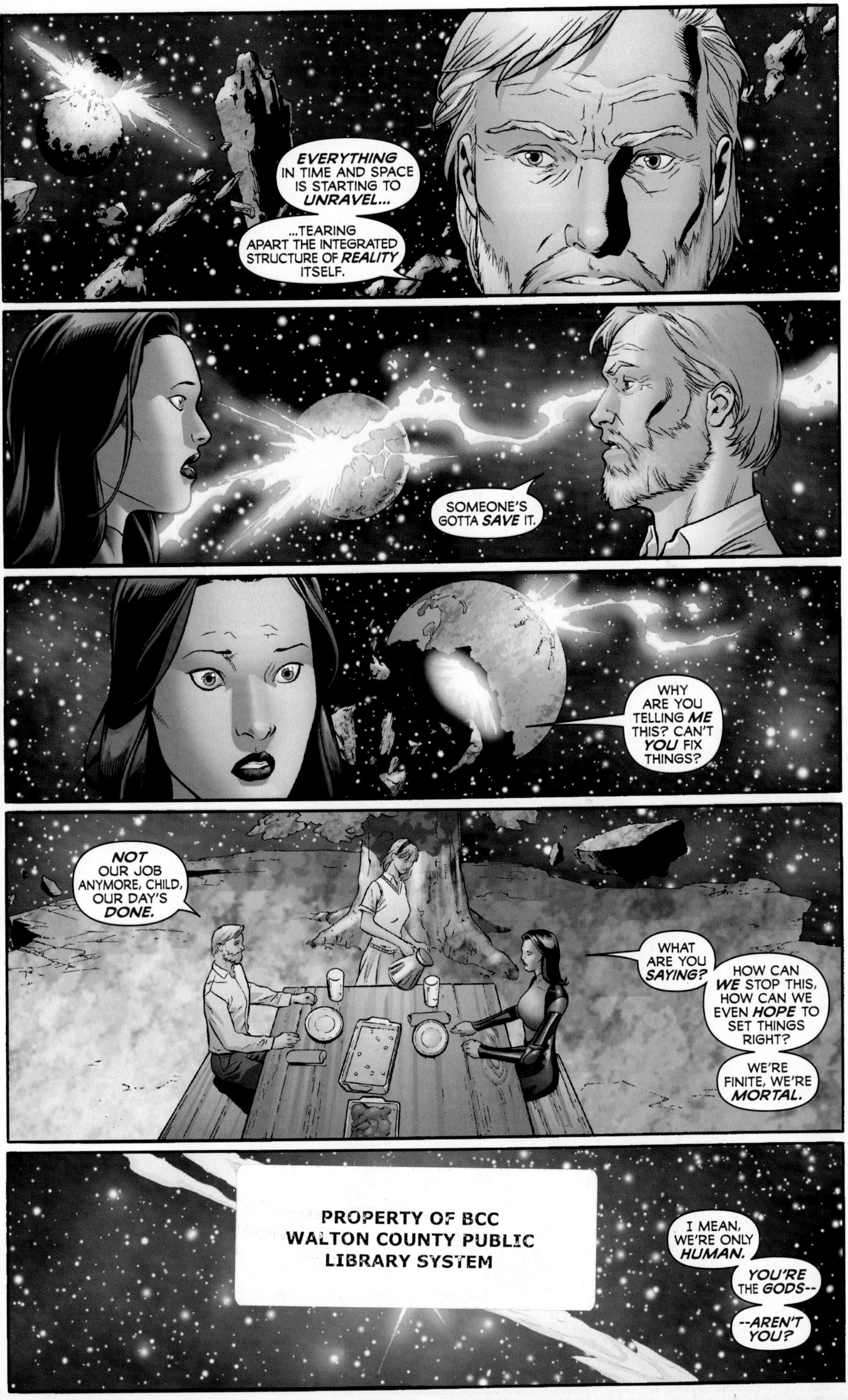
EVERYTHING IN TIME AND SPACE IS STARTING TO UNRAVEL...
...TEARING APART THE INTEGRATED STRUCTURE OF REALITY ITSELF.
SOMEONE'S GOTTA SAVE IT.
WHY ARE YOU TELLING ME THIS? CAN'T YOU FIX THINGS?
NOT OUR JOB ANYMORE, CHILD, OUR DAY'S DONE.
WHAT ARE YOU SAYING?
HOW CAN WE STOP THIS, HOW CAN WE EVEN HOPE TO SET THINGS RIGHT?
WE'RE FINITE, WE'RE MORTAL.
I MEAN, WE'RE ONLY HUMAN.
YOU'RE THE GODS--
--AREN'T YOU?

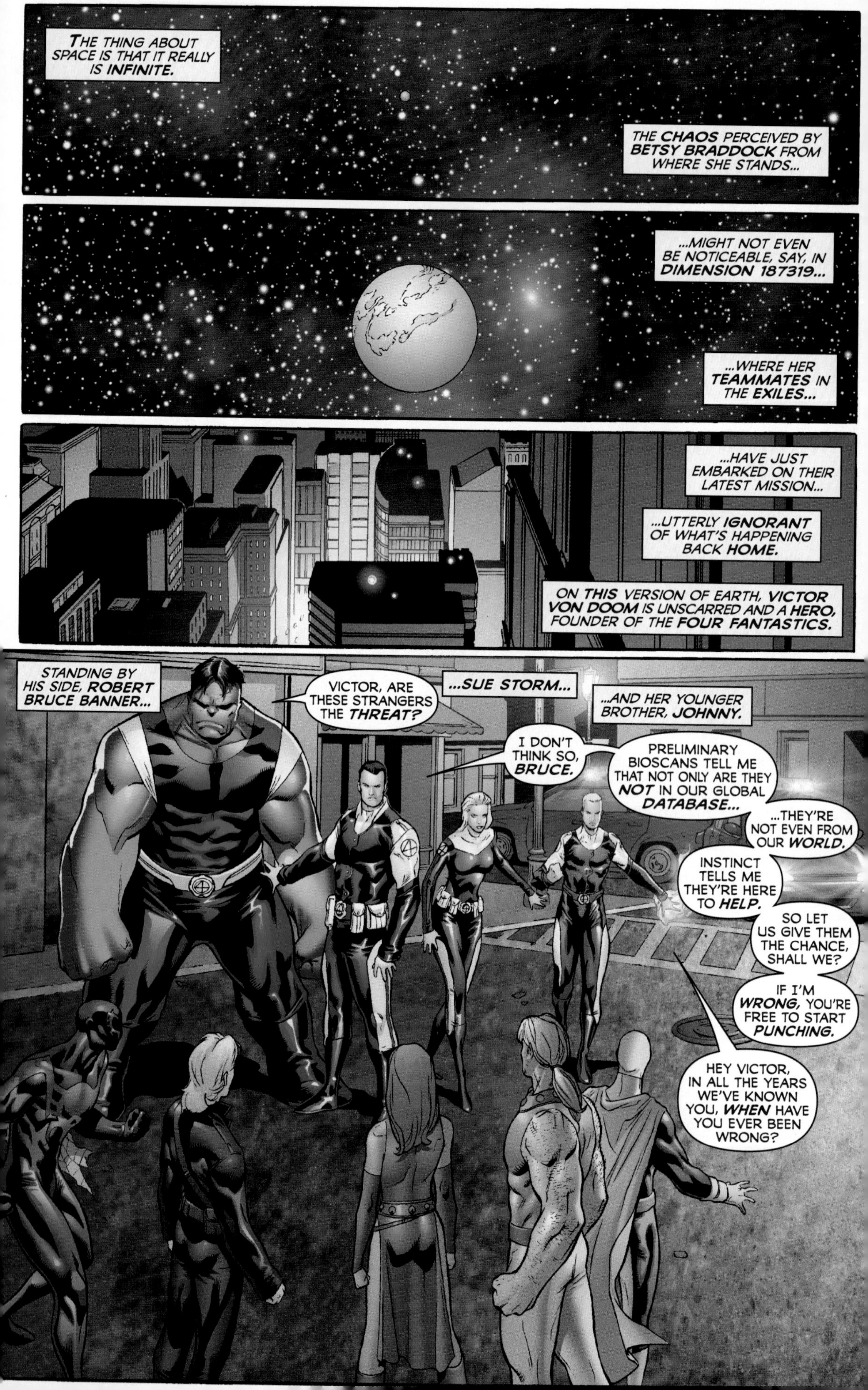
THE THING ABOUT SPACE IS THAT IT REALLY IS INFINITE.
THE CHAOS PERCEIVED BY BETSY BRADDOCK FROM WHERE SHE STANDS...
...MIGHT NOT EVEN BE NOTICEABLE, SAY, IN DIMENSION 187319...
...WHERE HER TEAMMATES IN THE EXILES...
...HAVE JUST EMBARKED ON THEIR LATEST MISSION...
...UTTERLY IGNORANT OF WHAT'S HAPPENING BACK HOME.
ON THIS VERSION OF EARTH, VICTOR VON DOOM IS UNSCARRED AND A HERO, FOUNDER OF THE FOUR FANTASTICS.
STANDING BY HIS SIDE, ROBERT BRUCE BANNER...
VICTOR, ARE THESE STRANGERS THE THREAT?
...SUE STORM...
...AND HER YOUNGER BROTHER, JOHNNY.
I DON'T THINK SO, BRUCE.
PRELIMINARY BIOSCANS TELL ME THAT NOT ONLY ARE THEY NOT IN OUR GLOBAL DATABASE...
...THEY'RE NOT EVEN FROM OUR WORLD.
INSTINCT TELLS ME THEY'RE HERE TO HELP.
SO LET US GIVE THEM THE CHANCE, SHALL WE?
IF I'M WRONG, YOU'RE FREE TO START PUNCHING.
HEY VICTOR, IN ALL THE YEARS WE'VE KNOWN YOU, WHEN HAVE YOU EVER BEEN WRONG?

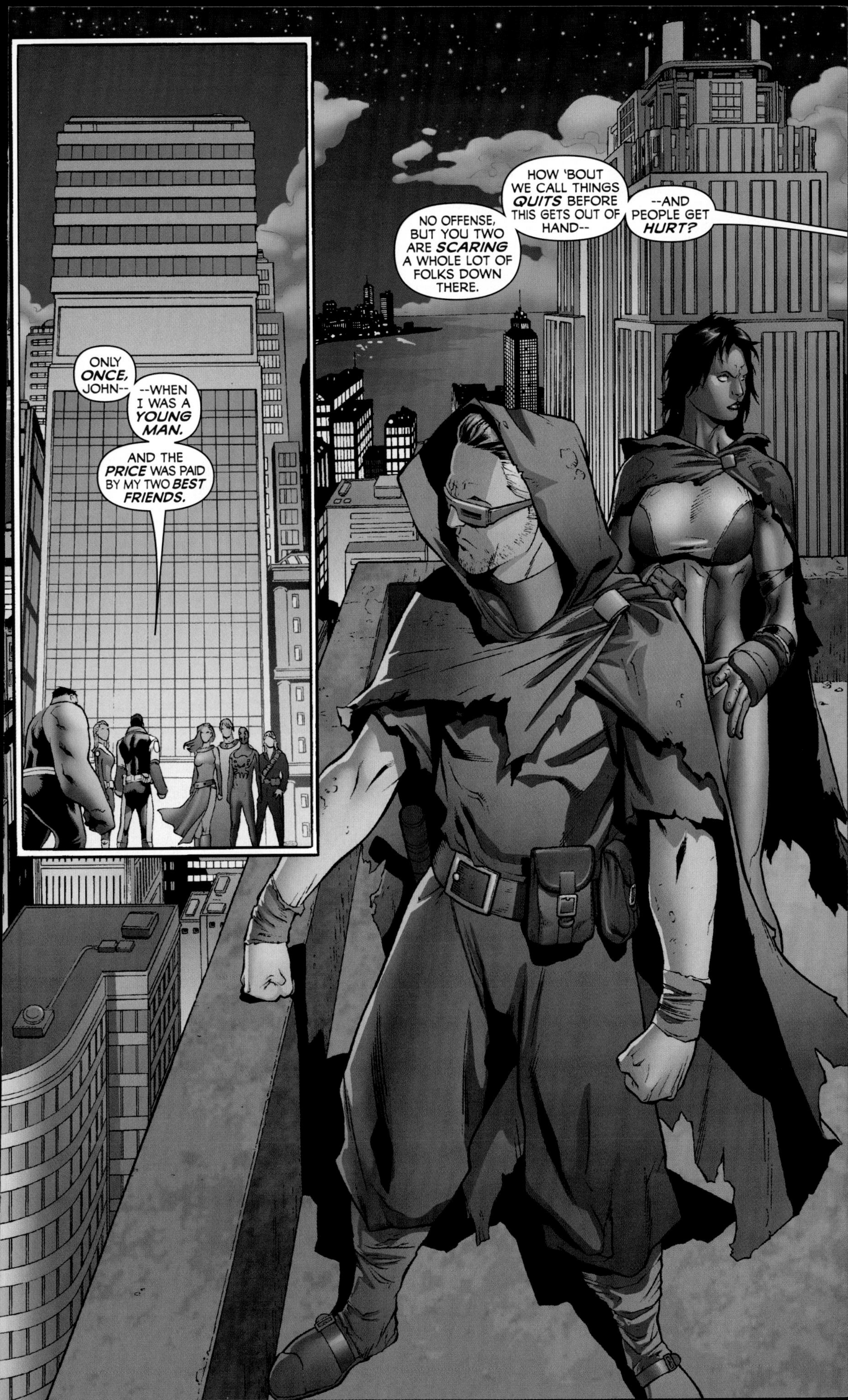
ONLY ONCE, JOHN--
--WHEN I WAS A YOUNG MAN.
AND THE PRICE WAS PAID BY MY TWO BEST FRIENDS.
NO OFFENSE, BUT YOU TWO ARE SCARING A WHOLE LOT OF FOLKS DOWN THERE.
HOW 'BOUT WE CALL THINGS QUITS BEFORE THIS GETS OUT OF HAND--
--AND PEOPLE GET HURT?

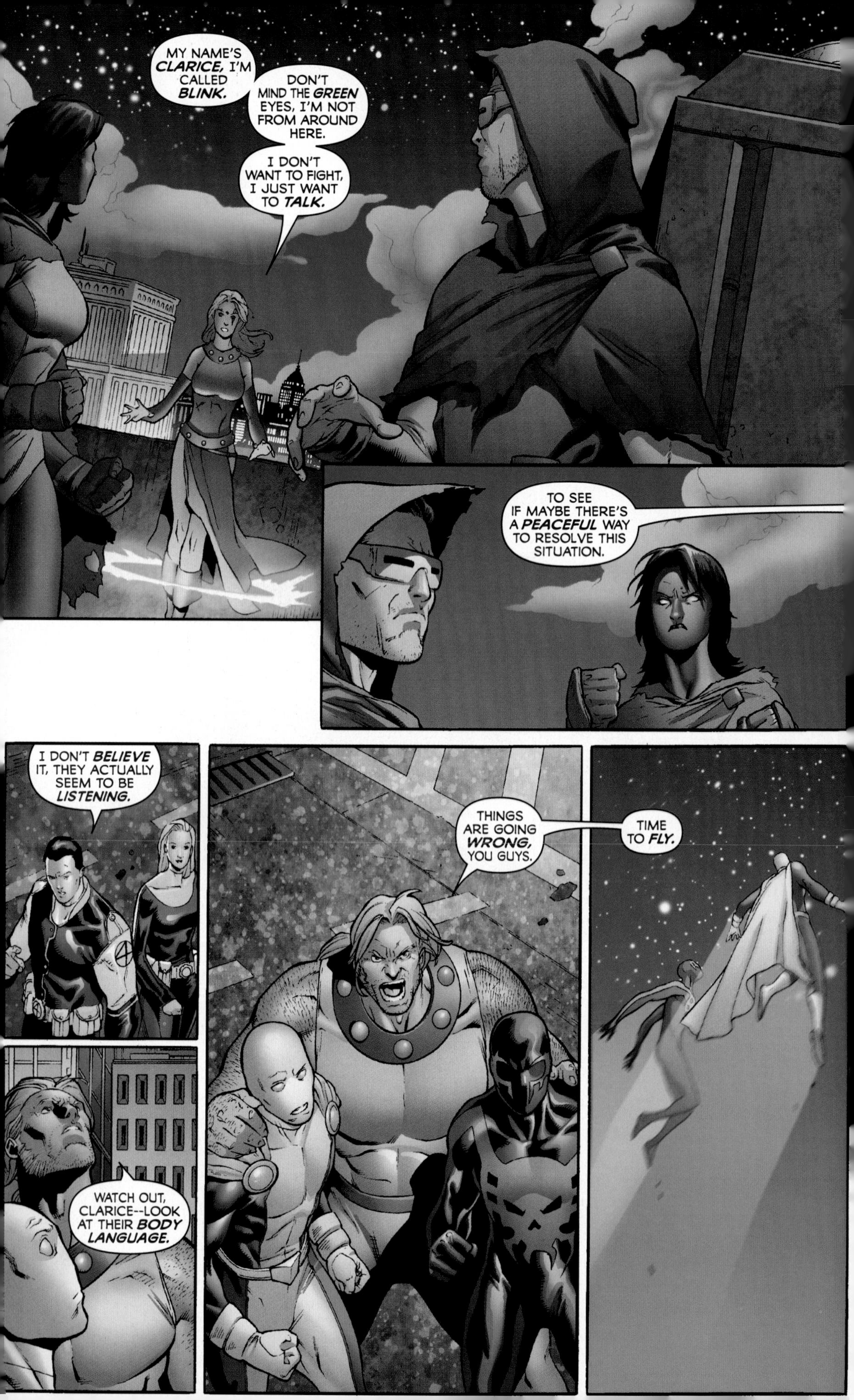
MY NAME'S CLARICE, I'M CALLED BLINK.
DON'T MIND THE GREEN EYES, I'M NOT FROM AROUND HERE.
I DON'T WANT TO FIGHT, I JUST WANT TO TALK.
TO SEE IF MAYBE THERE'S A PEACEFUL WAY TO RESOLVE THIS SITUATION.
I DON'T BELIEVE IT, THEY ACTUALLY SEEM TO BE LISTENING.
WATCH OUT, CLARICE--LOOK AT THEIR BODY LANGUAGE.
THINGS ARE GOING WRONG, YOU GUYS.
TIME TO FLY.

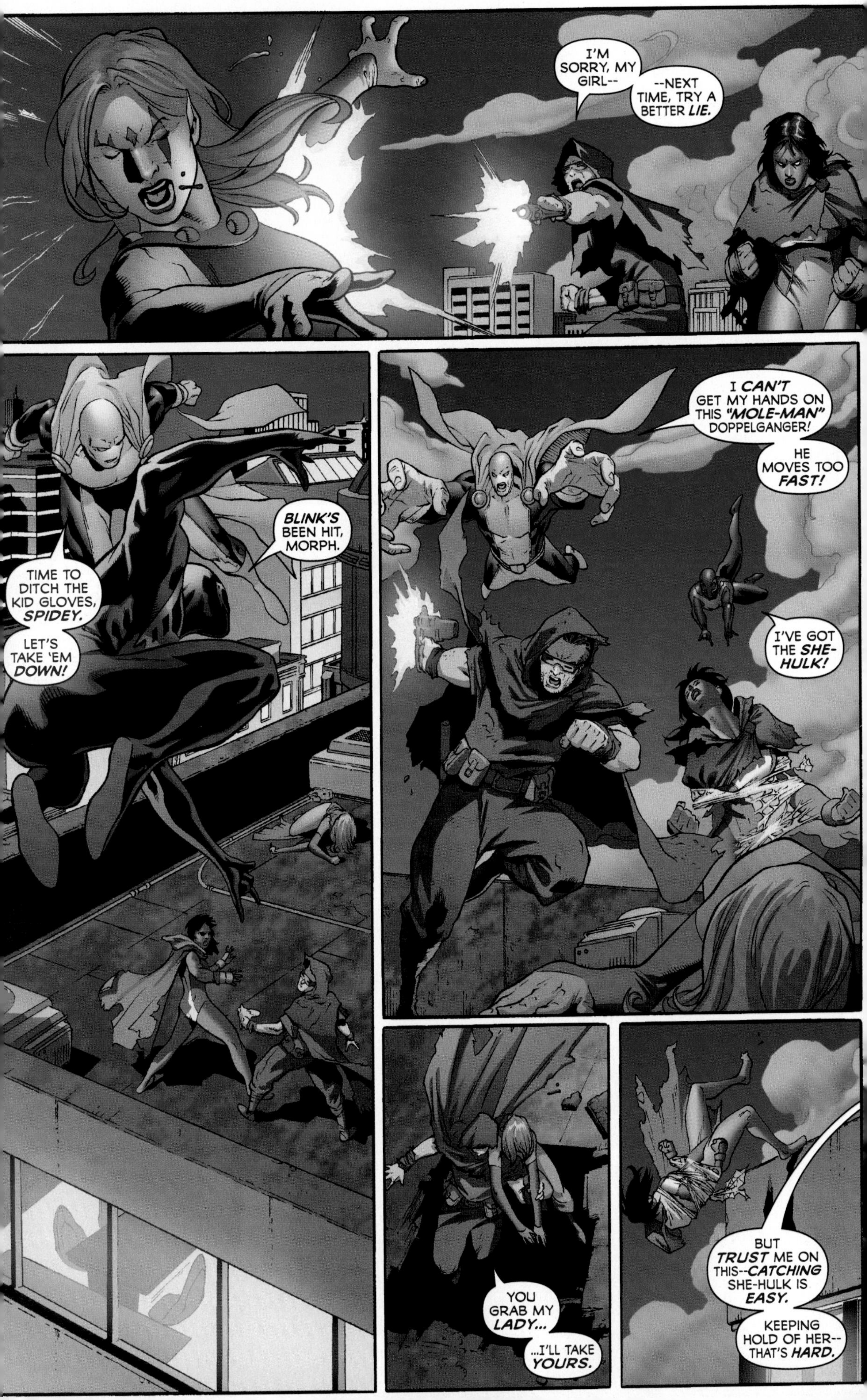
I'M SORRY, MY GIRL--
--NEXT TIME, TRY A BETTER LIE.
BLINK'S BEEN HIT, MORPH.
TIME TO DITCH THE KID GLOVES, SPIDEY.
LET'S TAKE 'EM DOWN!
I CAN'T GET MY HANDS ON THIS "MOLE-MAN" DOPPELGANGER!
HE MOVES TOO FAST!
I'VE GOT THE SHE-HULK!
YOU GRAB MY LADY...
...I'LL TAKE YOURS.
BUT TRUST ME ON THIS--CATCHING SHE-HULK IS EASY.
KEEPING HOLD OF HER--THAT'S HARD.

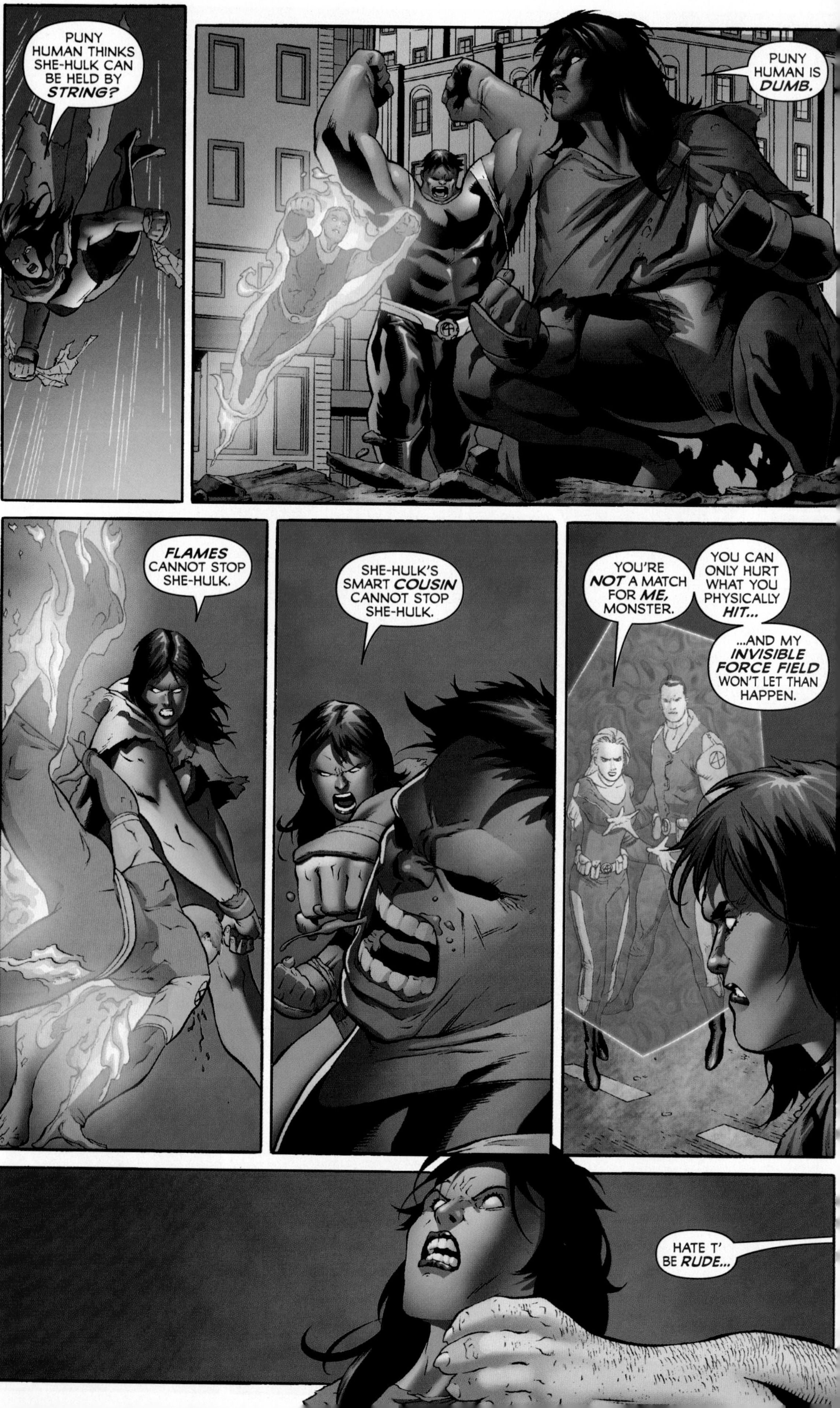
PUNY HUMAN THINKS SHE-HULK CAN BE HELD BY STRING?
PUNY HUMAN IS DUMB.
FLAMES CANNOT STOP SHE-HULK.
SHE-HULK'S SMART COUSIN CANNOT STOP SHE-HULK.
YOU'RE NOT A MATCH FOR ME, MONSTER.
YOU CAN ONLY HURT WHAT YOU PHYSICALLY HIT...
...AND MY INVISIBLE FORCE FIELD WON'T LET THAN HAPPEN.
HATE T' BE RUDE...

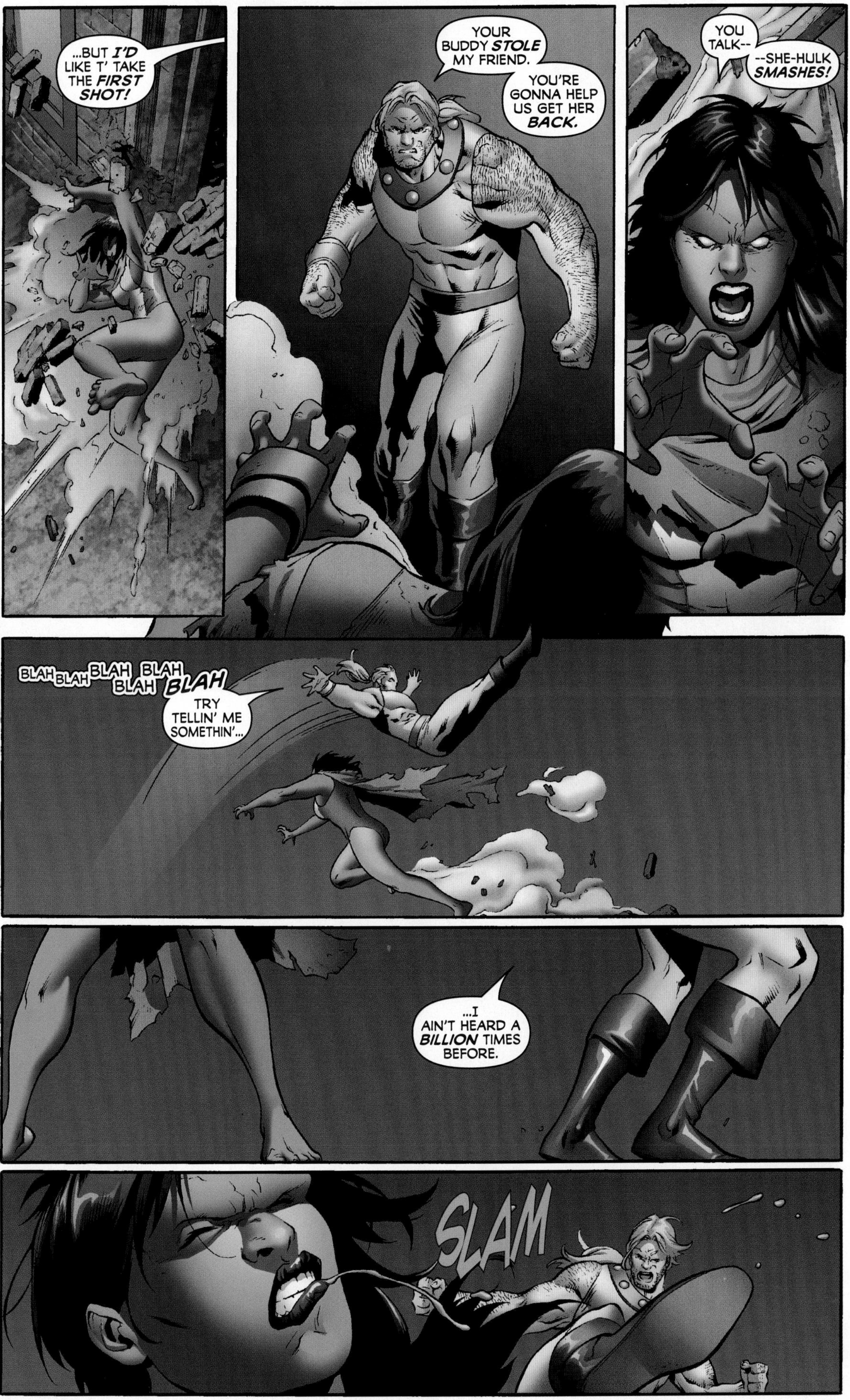
...BUT I'D LIKE T' TAKE THE FIRST SHOT!
YOUR BUDDY STOLE MY FRIEND.
YOU'RE GONNA HELP US GET HER BACK.
YOU TALK--
--SHE-HULK SMASHES!
BLAH BLAH BLAH BLAH BLAH BLAH
TRY TELLIN' ME SOMETHIN'...
...I AIN'T HEARD A BILLION TIMES BEFORE.
SLAM

YOU *LAUGH* AT SHE-HULK!

SHE-HULK WILL MAKE YOU *CRY!*

ONLY IF YOU MAKE *CONTACT.*

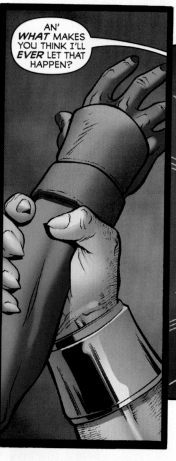

AN' *WHAT* MAKES YOU THINK I'LL *EVER* LET THAT HAPPEN?

RAW *STRENGTH* IS WHERE FOLKS LIKE US *START.*

WHAT COMES NEXT-- WHAT MAKES THE *DIFFERENCE*--IS KNOWIN' HOW TO *USE* IT.

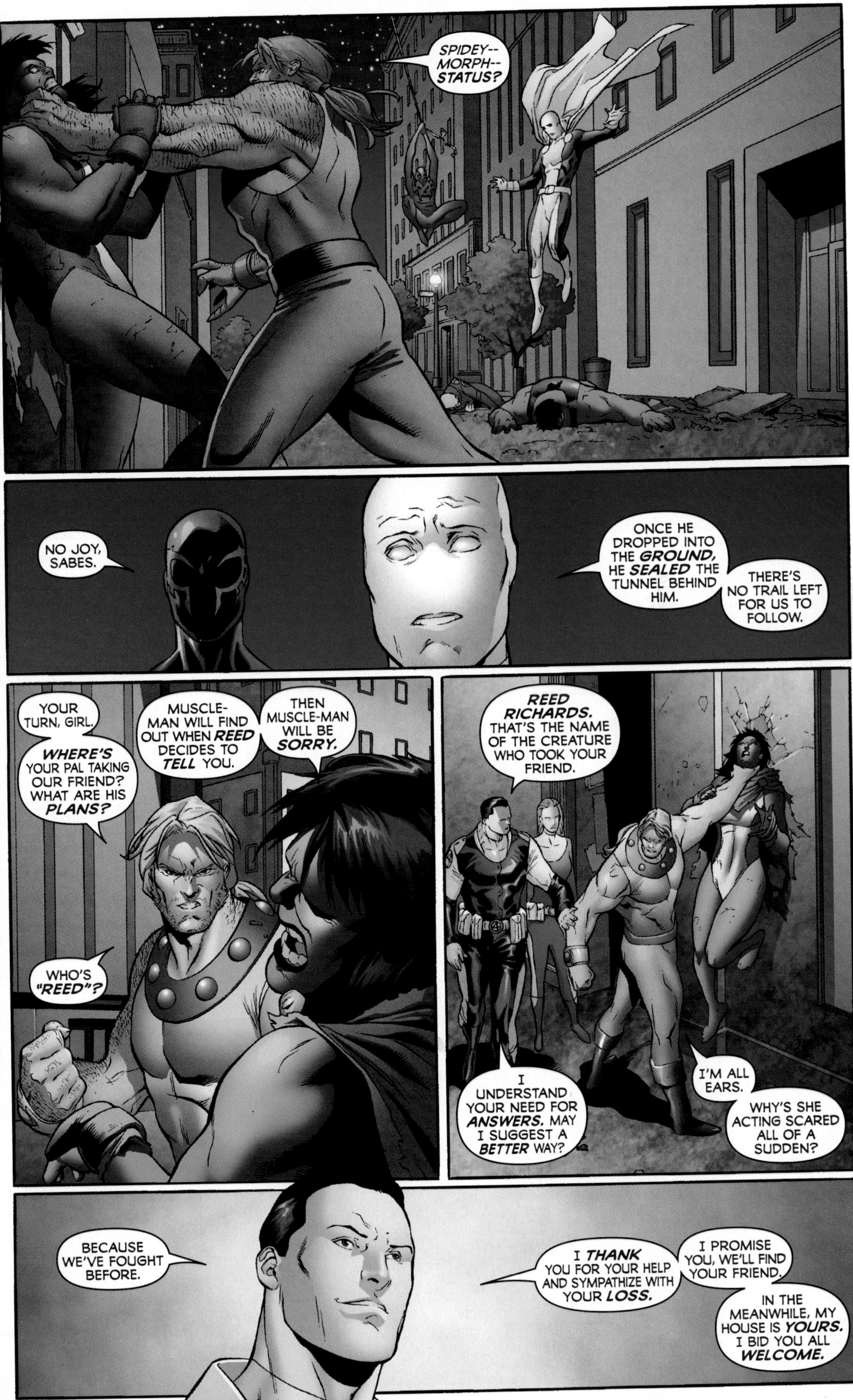
SPIDEY-- MORPH-- STATUS?
NO JOY, SABES.
ONCE HE DROPPED INTO THE GROUND, HE SEALED THE TUNNEL BEHIND HIM.
THERE'S NO TRAIL LEFT FOR US TO FOLLOW.
YOUR TURN, GIRL.
WHERE'S YOUR PAL TAKING OUR FRIEND? WHAT ARE HIS PLANS?
MUSCLE-MAN WILL FIND OUT WHEN REED DECIDES TO TELL YOU.
THEN MUSCLE-MAN WILL BE SORRY.
WHO'S "REED"?
REED RICHARDS. THAT'S THE NAME OF THE CREATURE WHO TOOK YOUR FRIEND.
I UNDERSTAND YOUR NEED FOR ANSWERS. MAY I SUGGEST A BETTER WAY?
I'M ALL EARS.
WHY'S SHE ACTING SCARED ALL OF A SUDDEN?
BECAUSE WE'VE FOUGHT BEFORE.
I THANK YOU FOR YOUR HELP AND SYMPATHIZE WITH YOUR LOSS.
I PROMISE YOU, WE'LL FIND YOUR FRIEND.
IN THE MEANWHILE, MY HOUSE IS YOURS. I BID YOU ALL WELCOME.

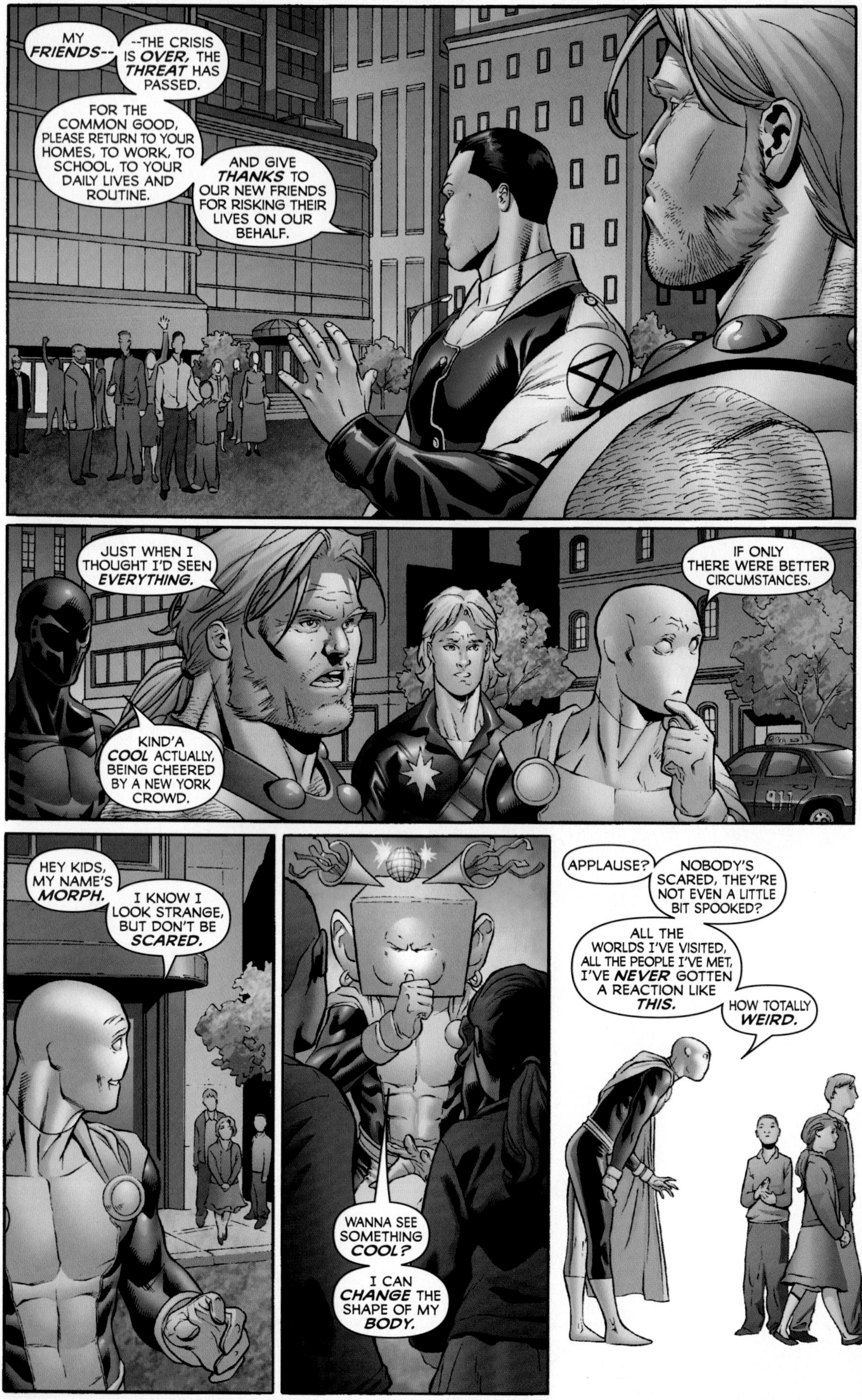
MY FRIENDS--
--THE CRISIS IS OVER, THE THREAT HAS PASSED.
FOR THE COMMON GOOD, PLEASE RETURN TO YOUR HOMES, TO WORK, TO SCHOOL, TO YOUR DAILY LIVES AND ROUTINE.
AND GIVE THANKS TO OUR NEW FRIENDS FOR RISKING THEIR LIVES ON OUR BEHALF.
JUST WHEN I THOUGHT I'D SEEN EVERYTHING.
KIND'A COOL ACTUALLY, BEING CHEERED BY A NEW YORK CROWD.
IF ONLY THERE WERE BETTER CIRCUMSTANCES.
HEY KIDS, MY NAME'S MORPH.
I KNOW I LOOK STRANGE, BUT DON'T BE SCARED.
WANNA SEE SOMETHING COOL?
I CAN CHANGE THE SHAPE OF MY BODY.
APPLAUSE?
NOBODY'S SCARED, THEY'RE NOT EVEN A LITTLE BIT SPOOKED?
ALL THE WORLDS I'VE VISITED, ALL THE PEOPLE I'VE MET, I'VE NEVER GOTTEN A REACTION LIKE THIS.
HOW TOTALLY WEIRD.

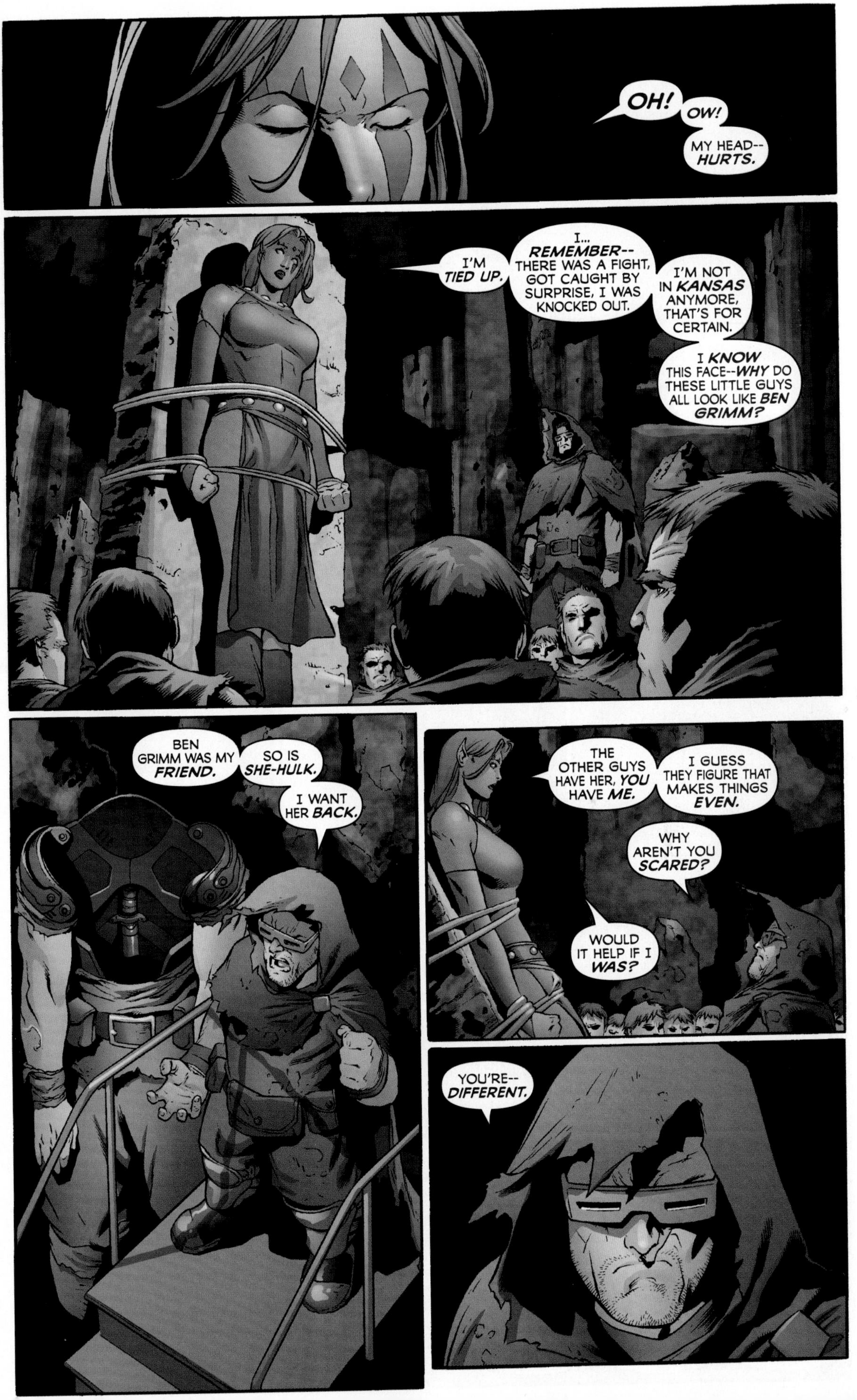
OH!
OW!
MY HEAD-- HURTS.
I'M TIED UP.
I... REMEMBER-- THERE WAS A FIGHT, GOT CAUGHT BY SURPRISE, I WAS KNOCKED OUT.
I'M NOT IN KANSAS ANYMORE, THAT'S FOR CERTAIN.
I KNOW THIS FACE--WHY DO THESE LITTLE GUYS ALL LOOK LIKE BEN GRIMM?
BEN GRIMM WAS MY FRIEND.
SO IS SHE-HULK.
I WANT HER BACK.
THE OTHER GUYS HAVE HER, YOU HAVE ME.
I GUESS THEY FIGURE THAT MAKES THINGS EVEN.
WHY AREN'T YOU SCARED?
WOULD IT HELP IF I WAS?
YOU'RE-- DIFFERENT.

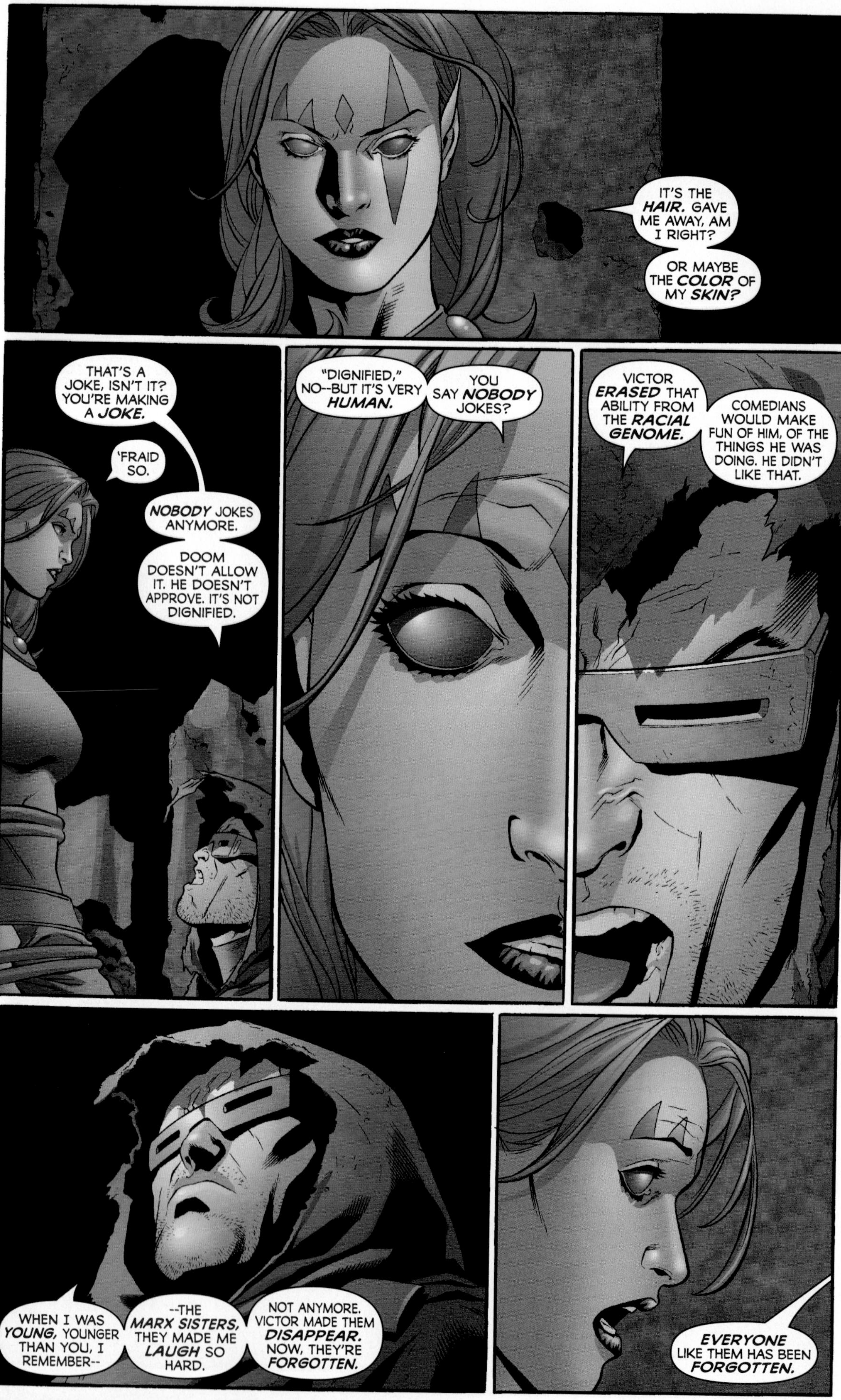
IT'S THE HAIR. GAVE ME AWAY, AM I RIGHT?
OR MAYBE THE COLOR OF MY SKIN?
THAT'S A JOKE, ISN'T IT? YOU'RE MAKING A JOKE.
'FRAID SO.
NOBODY JOKES ANYMORE.
DOOM DOESN'T ALLOW IT. HE DOESN'T APPROVE. IT'S NOT DIGNIFIED.
"DIGNIFIED," NO--BUT IT'S VERY HUMAN.
YOU SAY NOBODY JOKES?
VICTOR ERASED THAT ABILITY FROM THE RACIAL GENOME.
COMEDIANS WOULD MAKE FUN OF HIM, OF THE THINGS HE WAS DOING. HE DIDN'T LIKE THAT.
WHEN I WAS YOUNG, YOUNGER THAN YOU, I REMEMBER--
--THE MARX SISTERS, THEY MADE ME LAUGH SO HARD.
NOT ANYMORE. VICTOR MADE THEM DISAPPEAR. NOW, THEY'RE FORGOTTEN.
EVERYONE LIKE THEM HAS BEEN FORGOTTEN.

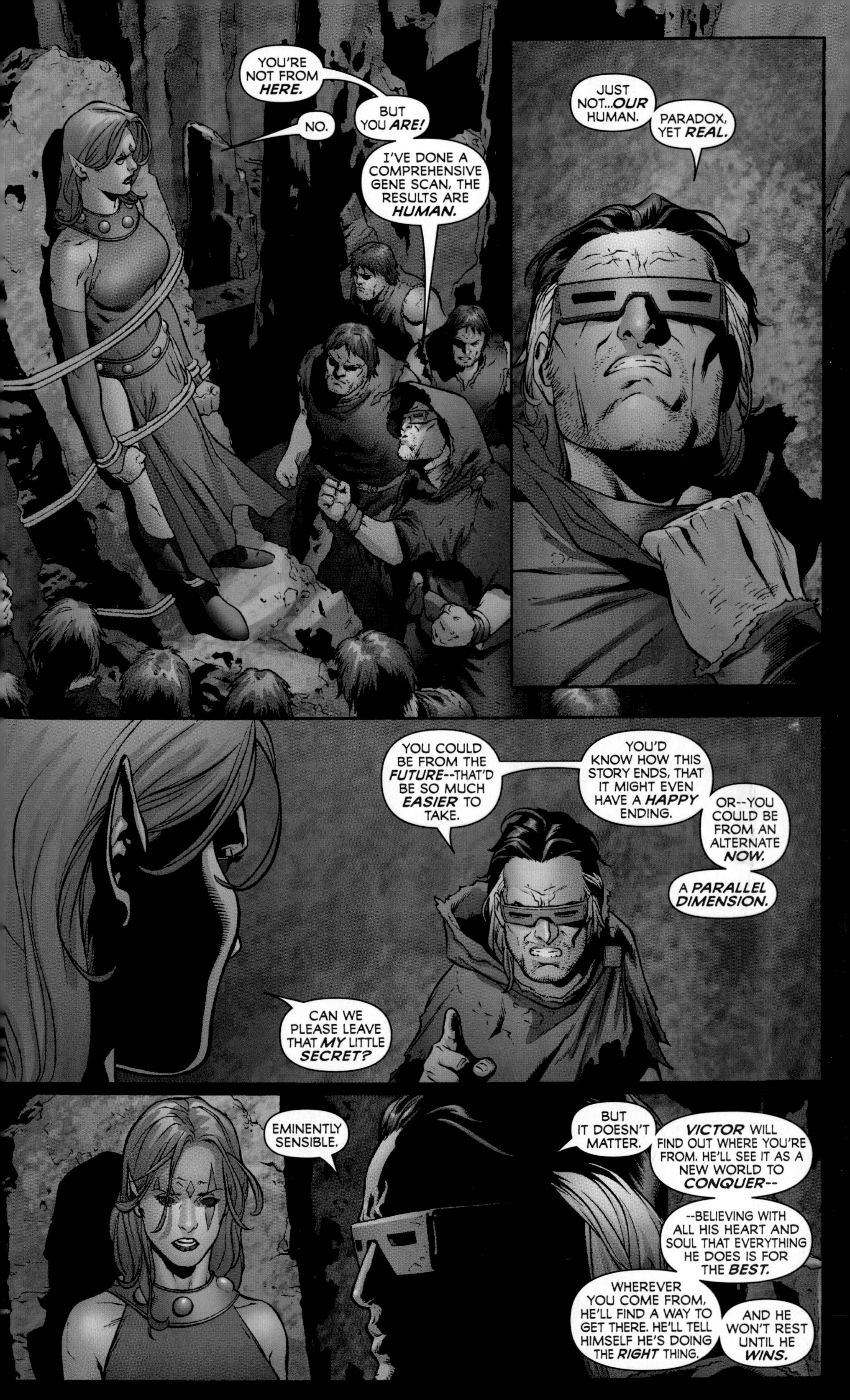

YOU'RE NOT FROM *HERE.*
NO.
BUT YOU *ARE!*
I'VE DONE A COMPREHENSIVE GENE SCAN, THE RESULTS ARE *HUMAN.*
JUST NOT...*OUR* HUMAN.
PARADOX, YET *REAL.*
YOU COULD BE FROM THE *FUTURE*--THAT'D BE SO MUCH *EASIER* TO TAKE.
YOU'D KNOW HOW THIS STORY ENDS, THAT IT MIGHT EVEN HAVE A *HAPPY* ENDING.
OR--YOU COULD BE FROM AN ALTERNATE *NOW.*
A *PARALLEL DIMENSION.*
CAN WE PLEASE LEAVE THAT *MY* LITTLE *SECRET?*
EMINENTLY SENSIBLE.
BUT IT DOESN'T MATTER.
VICTOR WILL FIND OUT WHERE YOU'RE FROM. HE'LL SEE IT AS A NEW WORLD TO *CONQUER*--
--BELIEVING WITH ALL HIS HEART AND SOUL THAT EVERYTHING HE DOES IS FOR THE *BEST.*
WHEREVER YOU COME FROM, HE'LL FIND A WAY TO GET THERE. HE'LL TELL HIMSELF HE'S DOING THE *RIGHT* THING.
AND HE WON'T REST UNTIL HE *WINS.*

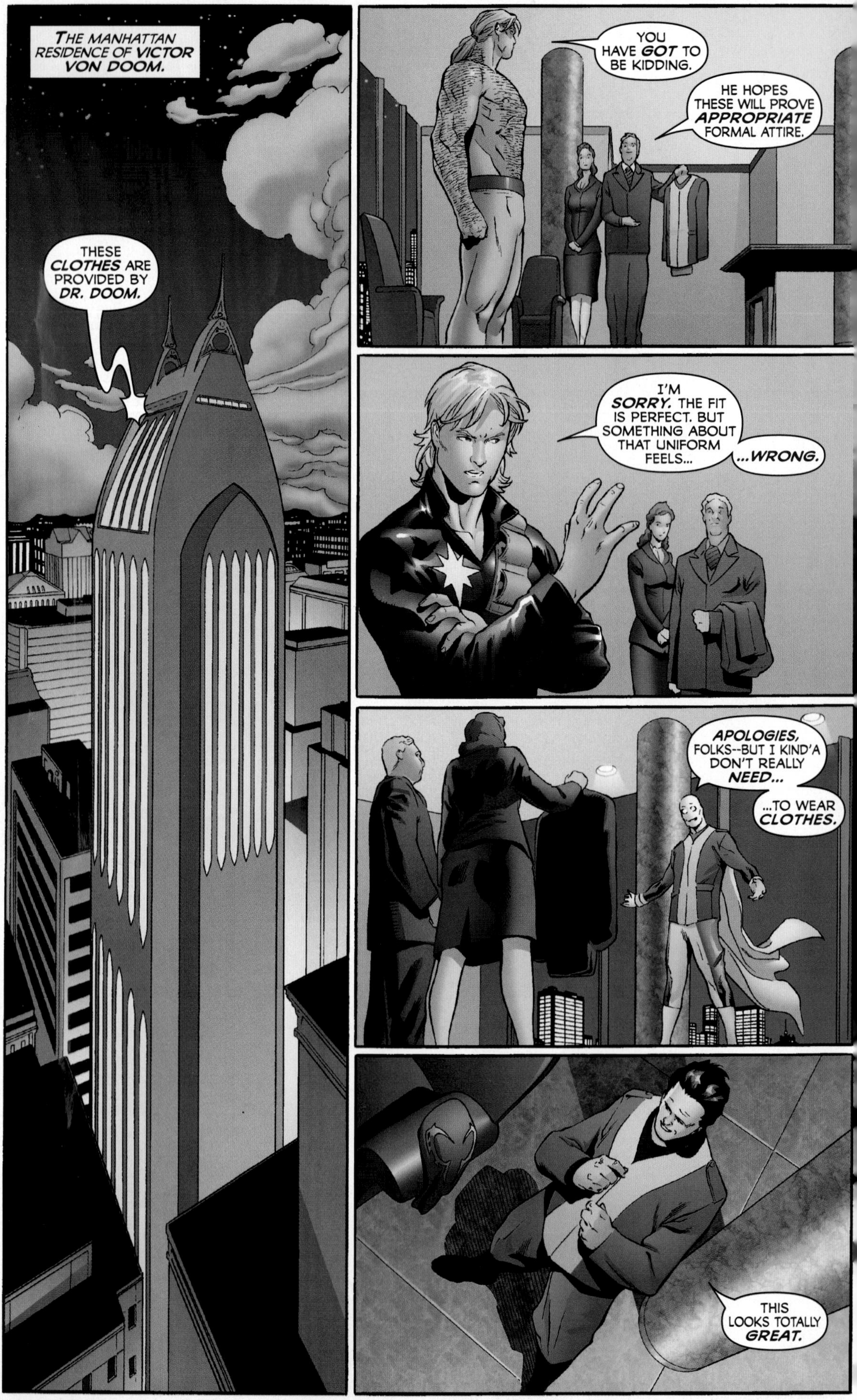
THE MANHATTAN RESIDENCE OF VICTOR VON DOOM.
THESE CLOTHES ARE PROVIDED BY DR. DOOM.
YOU HAVE GOT TO BE KIDDING.
HE HOPES THESE WILL PROVE APPROPRIATE FORMAL ATTIRE.
I'M SORRY. THE FIT IS PERFECT. BUT SOMETHING ABOUT THAT UNIFORM FEELS...
...WRONG.
APOLOGIES, FOLKS--BUT I KIND'A DON'T REALLY NEED...
...TO WEAR CLOTHES.
THIS LOOKS TOTALLY GREAT.

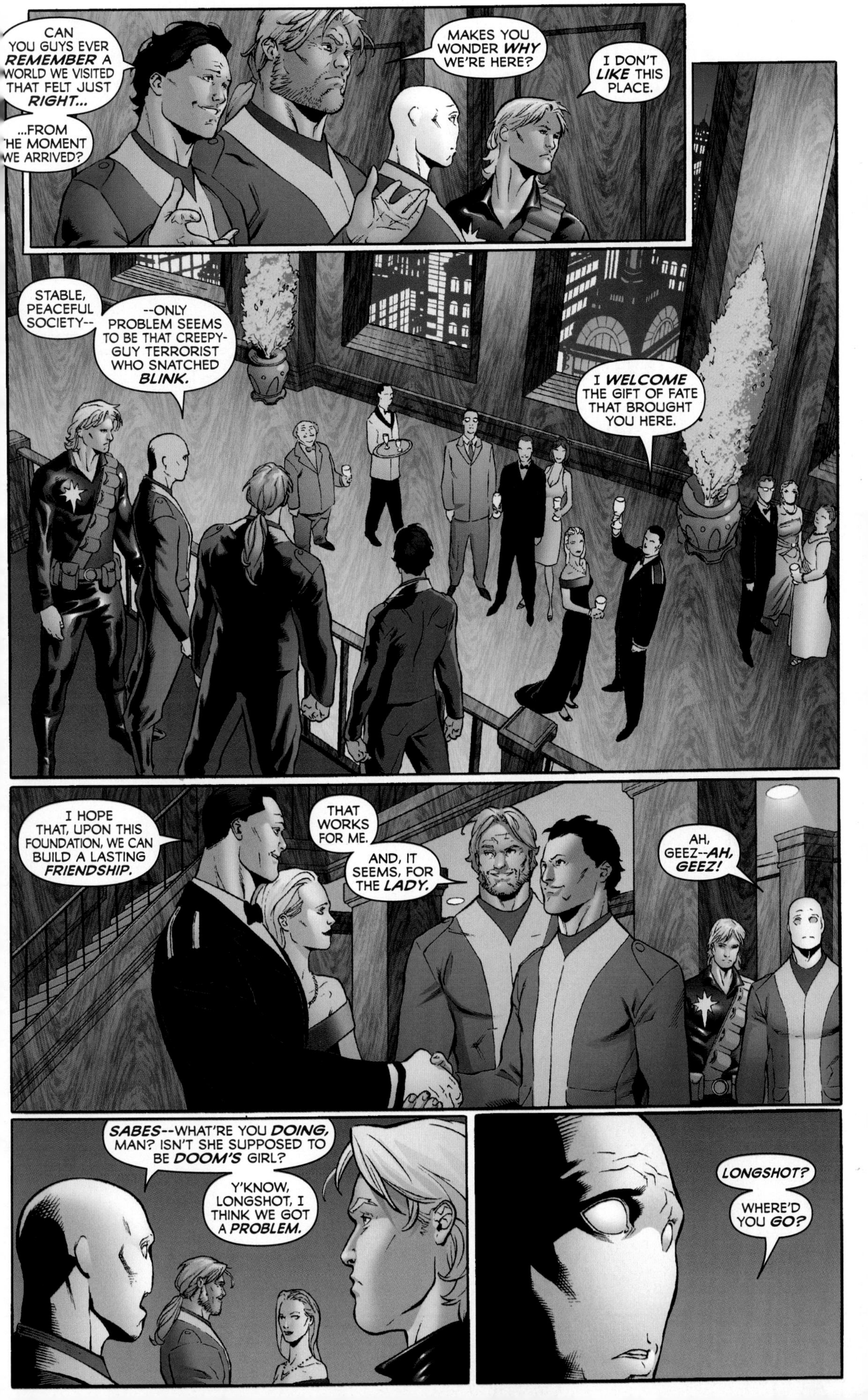
CAN YOU GUYS EVER *REMEMBER* A WORLD WE VISITED THAT FELT JUST *RIGHT...*
...FROM THE MOMENT WE ARRIVED?
MAKES YOU WONDER *WHY* WE'RE HERE?
I DON'T *LIKE* THIS PLACE.
STABLE, PEACEFUL SOCIETY--
--ONLY PROBLEM SEEMS TO BE THAT CREEPY-GUY TERRORIST WHO SNATCHED *BLINK.*
I *WELCOME* THE GIFT OF FATE THAT BROUGHT YOU HERE.
I HOPE THAT, UPON THIS FOUNDATION, WE CAN BUILD A LASTING *FRIENDSHIP.*
THAT WORKS FOR ME.
AND, IT SEEMS, FOR THE *LADY.*
AH, GEEZ--*AH, GEEZ!*
SABES--WHAT'RE YOU *DOING,* MAN? ISN'T SHE SUPPOSED TO BE *DOOM'S* GIRL?
Y'KNOW, LONGSHOT, I THINK WE GOT A *PROBLEM.*
LONGSHOT?
WHERE'D YOU *GO?*

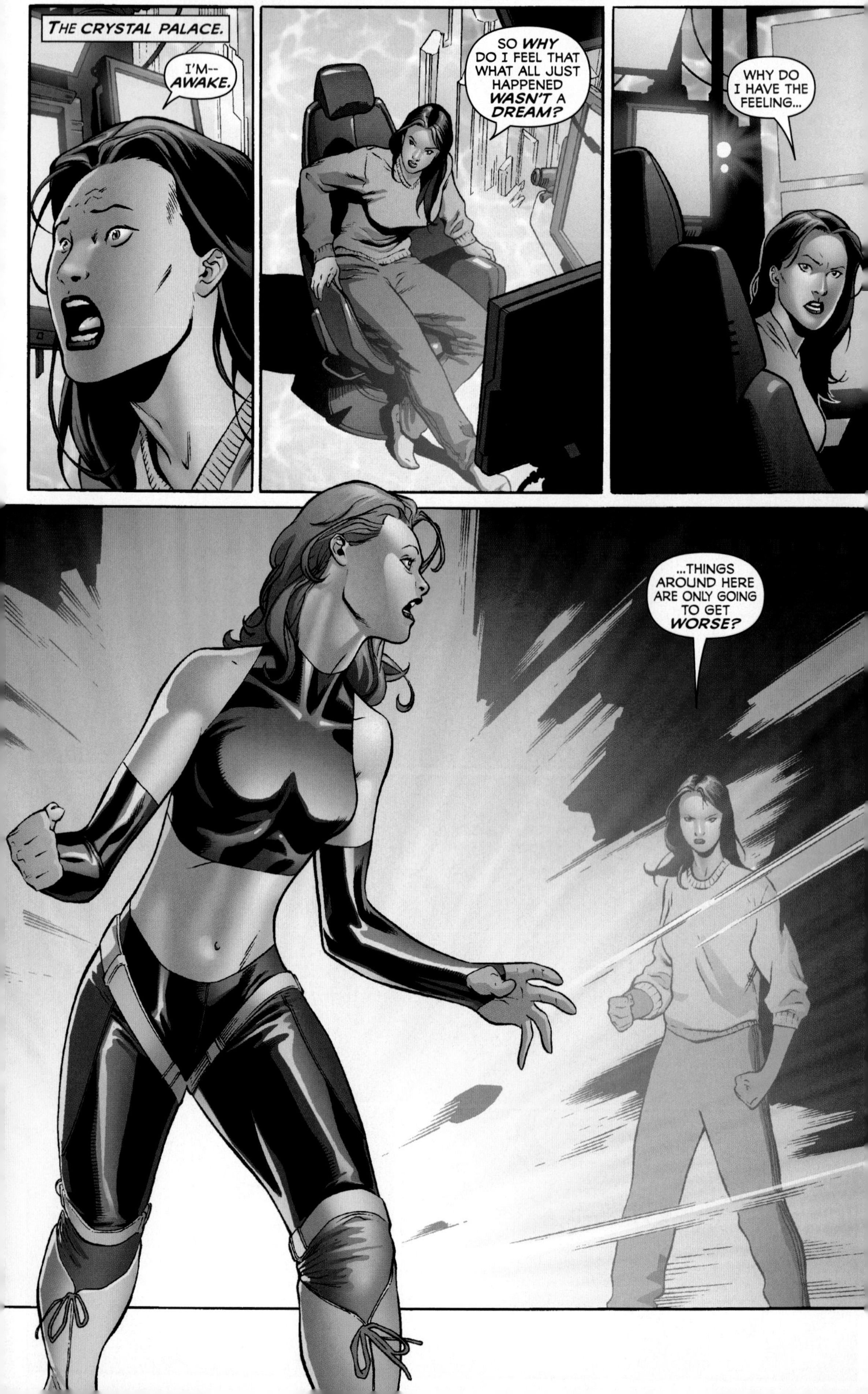
THE CRYSTAL PALACE.
I'M--AWAKE.
SO WHY DO I FEEL THAT WHAT ALL JUST HAPPENED WASN'T A DREAM?
WHY DO I HAVE THE FEELING...
...THINGS AROUND HERE ARE ONLY GOING TO GET WORSE?

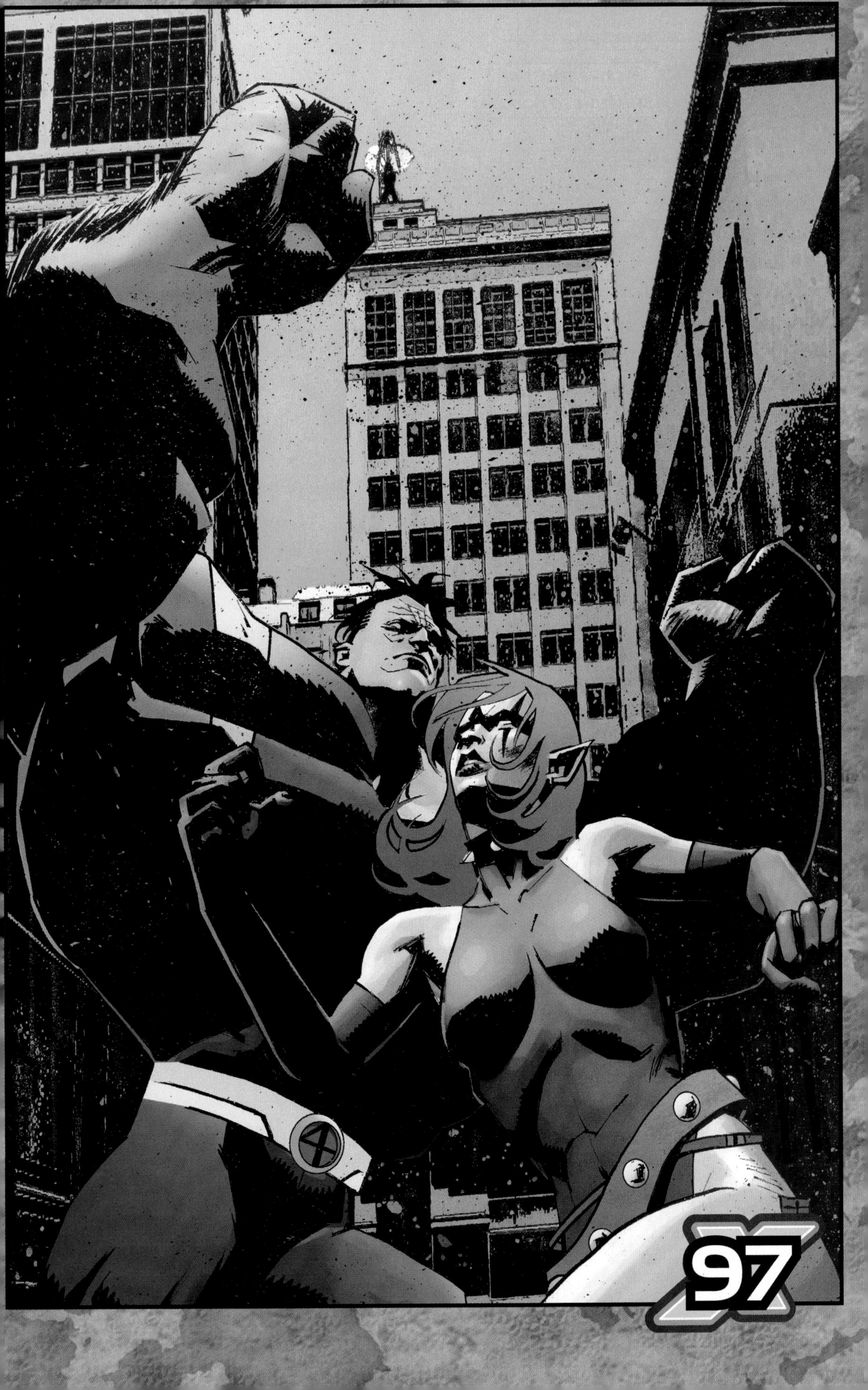

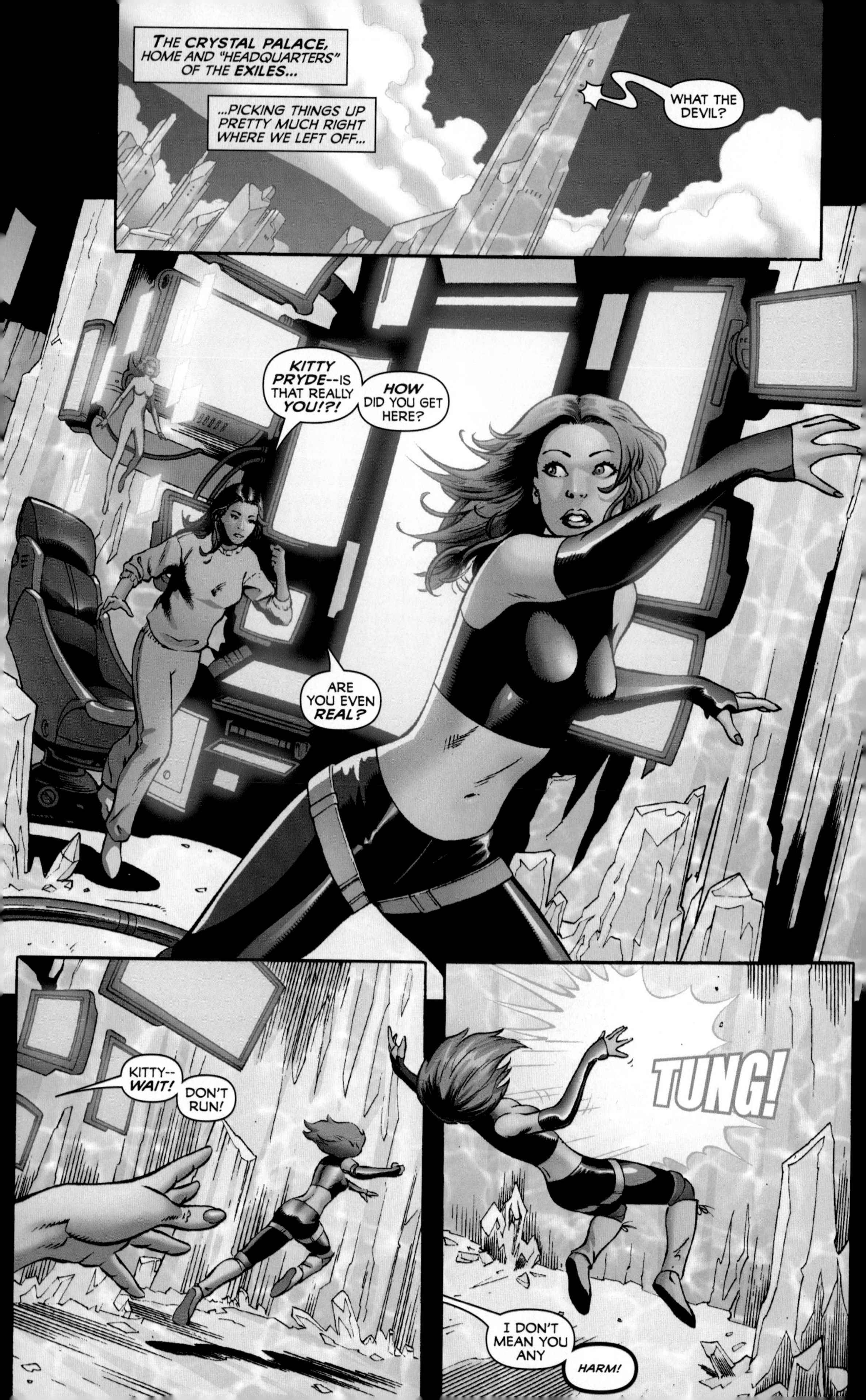
THE CRYSTAL PALACE, HOME AND "HEADQUARTERS" OF THE EXILES...
...PICKING THINGS UP PRETTY MUCH RIGHT WHERE WE LEFT OFF...
WHAT THE DEVIL?
KITTY PRYDE--IS THAT REALLY YOU!?!
HOW DID YOU GET HERE?
ARE YOU EVEN REAL?
KITTY--WAIT!
DON'T RUN!
TUNG!
I DON'T MEAN YOU ANY
HARM!

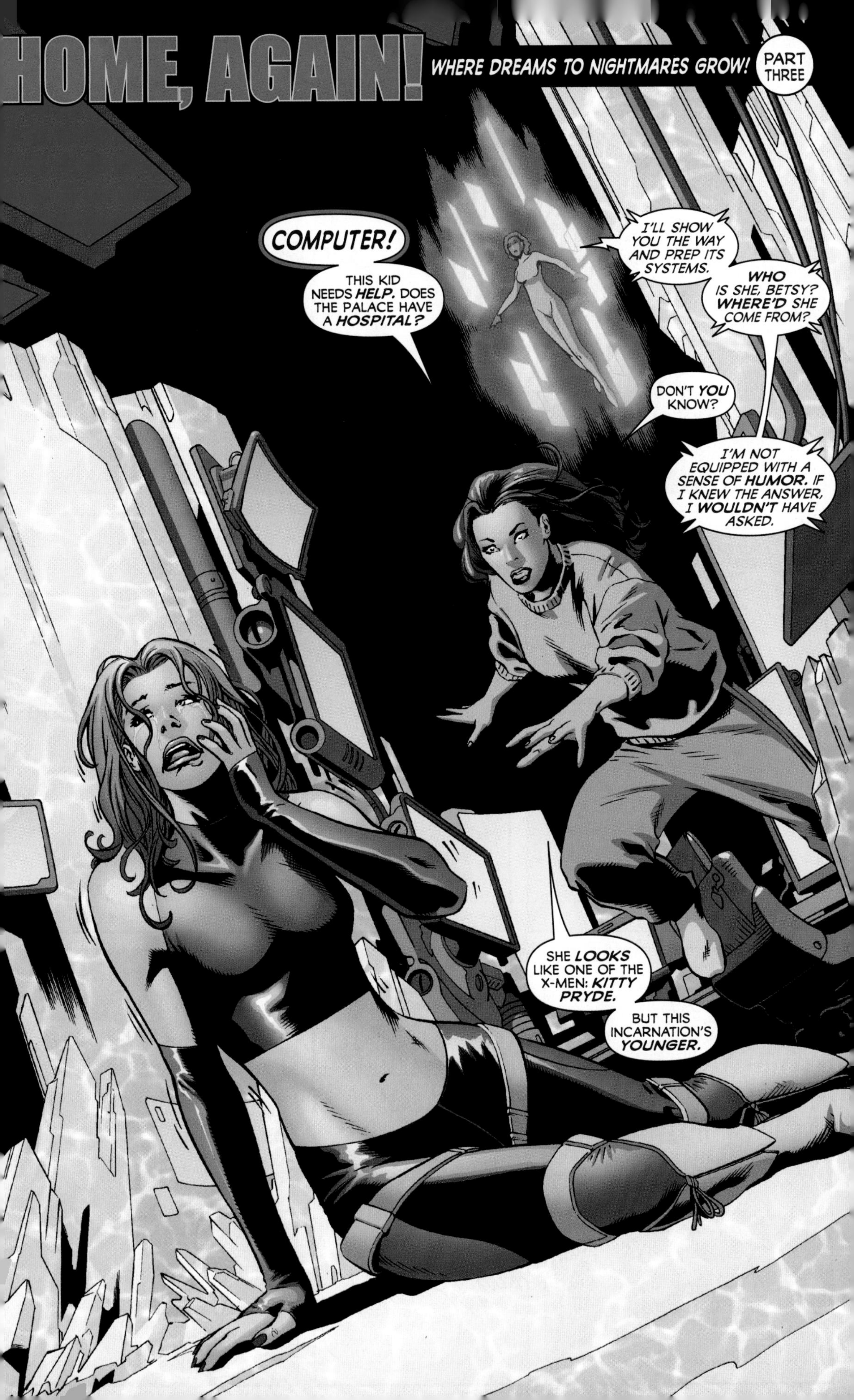
HOME, AGAIN!
WHERE DREAMS TO NIGHTMARES GROW!
PART THREE
COMPUTER!
THIS KID NEEDS HELP. DOES THE PALACE HAVE A HOSPITAL?
I'LL SHOW YOU THE WAY AND PREP ITS SYSTEMS.
WHO IS SHE, BETSY? WHERE'D SHE COME FROM?
DON'T YOU KNOW?
I'M NOT EQUIPPED WITH A SENSE OF HUMOR. IF I KNEW THE ANSWER, I WOULDN'T HAVE ASKED.
SHE LOOKS LIKE ONE OF THE X-MEN: KITTY PRYDE.
BUT THIS INCARNATION'S YOUNGER.

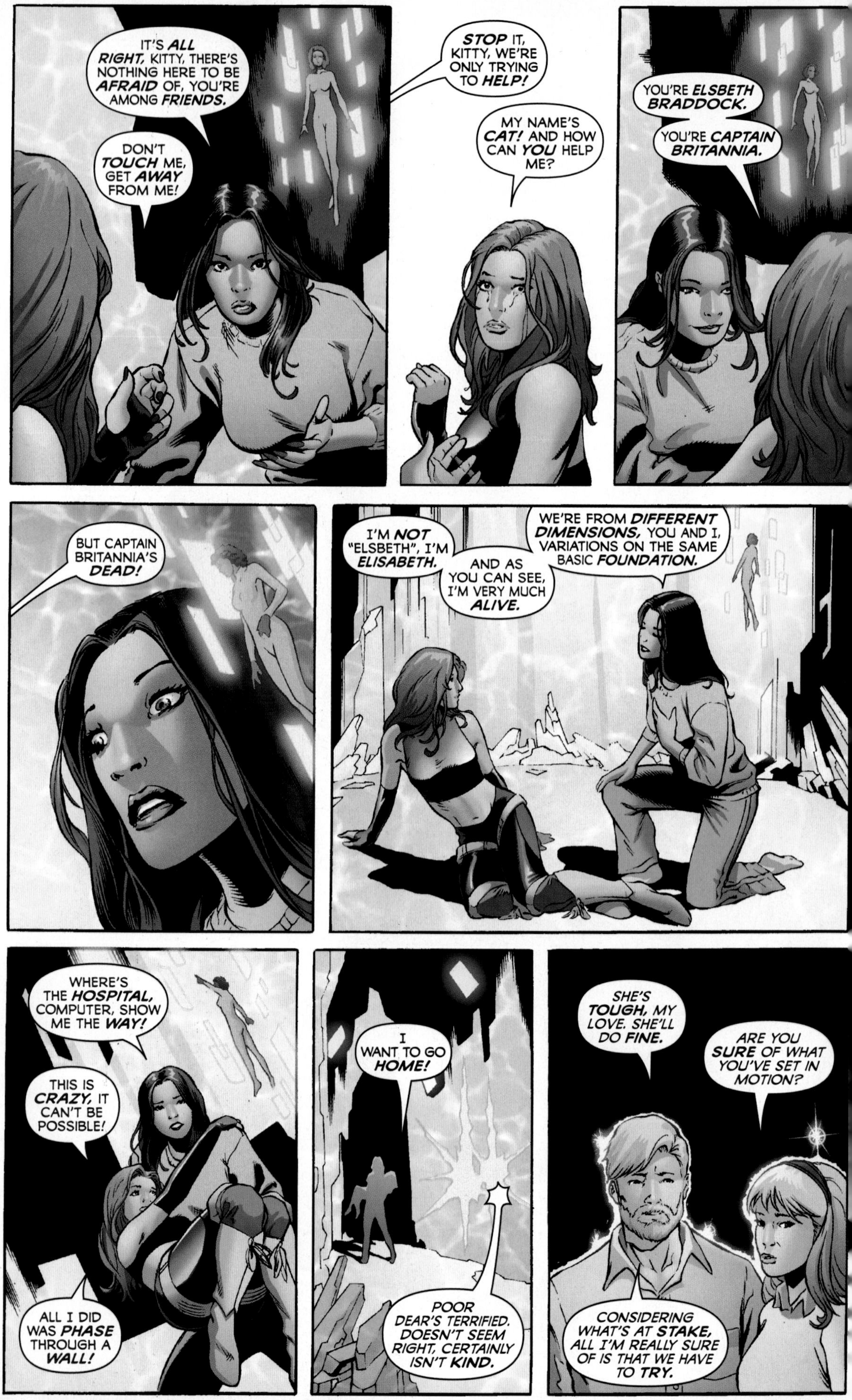
IT'S ALL RIGHT, KITTY, THERE'S NOTHING HERE TO BE AFRAID OF, YOU'RE AMONG FRIENDS.
DON'T TOUCH ME, GET AWAY FROM ME!
STOP IT, KITTY, WE'RE ONLY TRYING TO HELP!
MY NAME'S CAT! AND HOW CAN YOU HELP ME?
YOU'RE ELSBETH BRADDOCK.
YOU'RE CAPTAIN BRITANNIA.
BUT CAPTAIN BRITANNIA'S DEAD!
I'M NOT "ELSBETH", I'M ELISABETH.
WE'RE FROM DIFFERENT DIMENSIONS, YOU AND I, VARIATIONS ON THE SAME BASIC FOUNDATION.
AND AS YOU CAN SEE, I'M VERY MUCH ALIVE.
WHERE'S THE HOSPITAL, COMPUTER, SHOW ME THE WAY!
THIS IS CRAZY, IT CAN'T BE POSSIBLE!
ALL I DID WAS PHASE THROUGH A WALL!
I WANT TO GO HOME!
POOR DEAR'S TERRIFIED. DOESN'T SEEM RIGHT, CERTAINLY ISN'T KIND.
SHE'S TOUGH, MY LOVE. SHE'LL DO FINE.
ARE YOU SURE OF WHAT YOU'VE SET IN MOTION?
CONSIDERING WHAT'S AT STAKE, ALL I'M REALLY SURE OF IS THAT WE HAVE TO TRY.

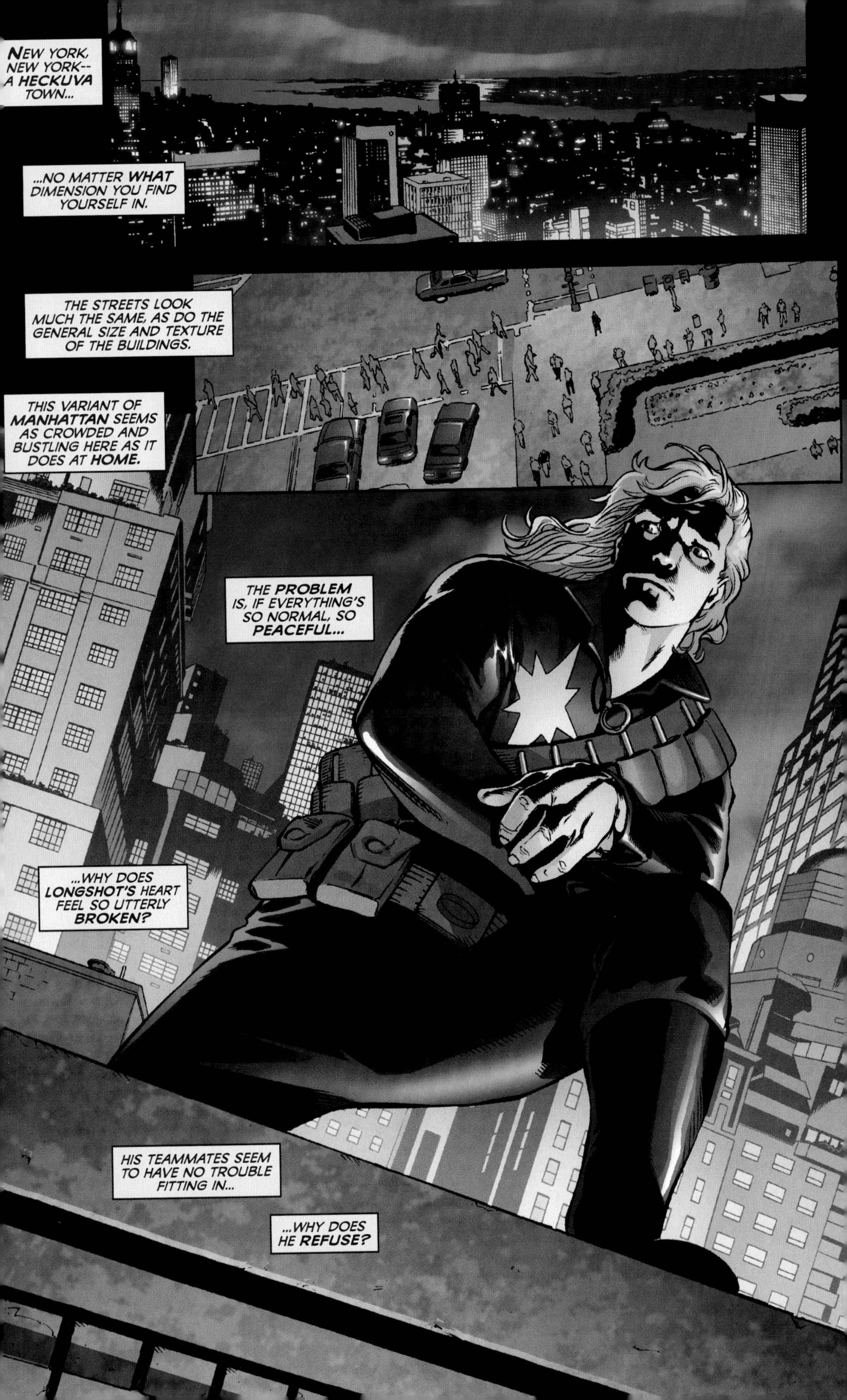
NEW YORK, NEW YORK-- A HECKUVA TOWN...
...NO MATTER WHAT DIMENSION YOU FIND YOURSELF IN.
THE STREETS LOOK MUCH THE SAME, AS DO THE GENERAL SIZE AND TEXTURE OF THE BUILDINGS.
THIS VARIANT OF MANHATTAN SEEMS AS CROWDED AND BUSTLING HERE AS IT DOES AT HOME.
THE PROBLEM IS, IF EVERYTHING'S SO NORMAL, SO PEACEFUL...
...WHY DOES LONGSHOT'S HEART FEEL SO UTTERLY BROKEN?
HIS TEAMMATES SEEM TO HAVE NO TROUBLE FITTING IN...
...WHY DOES HE REFUSE?

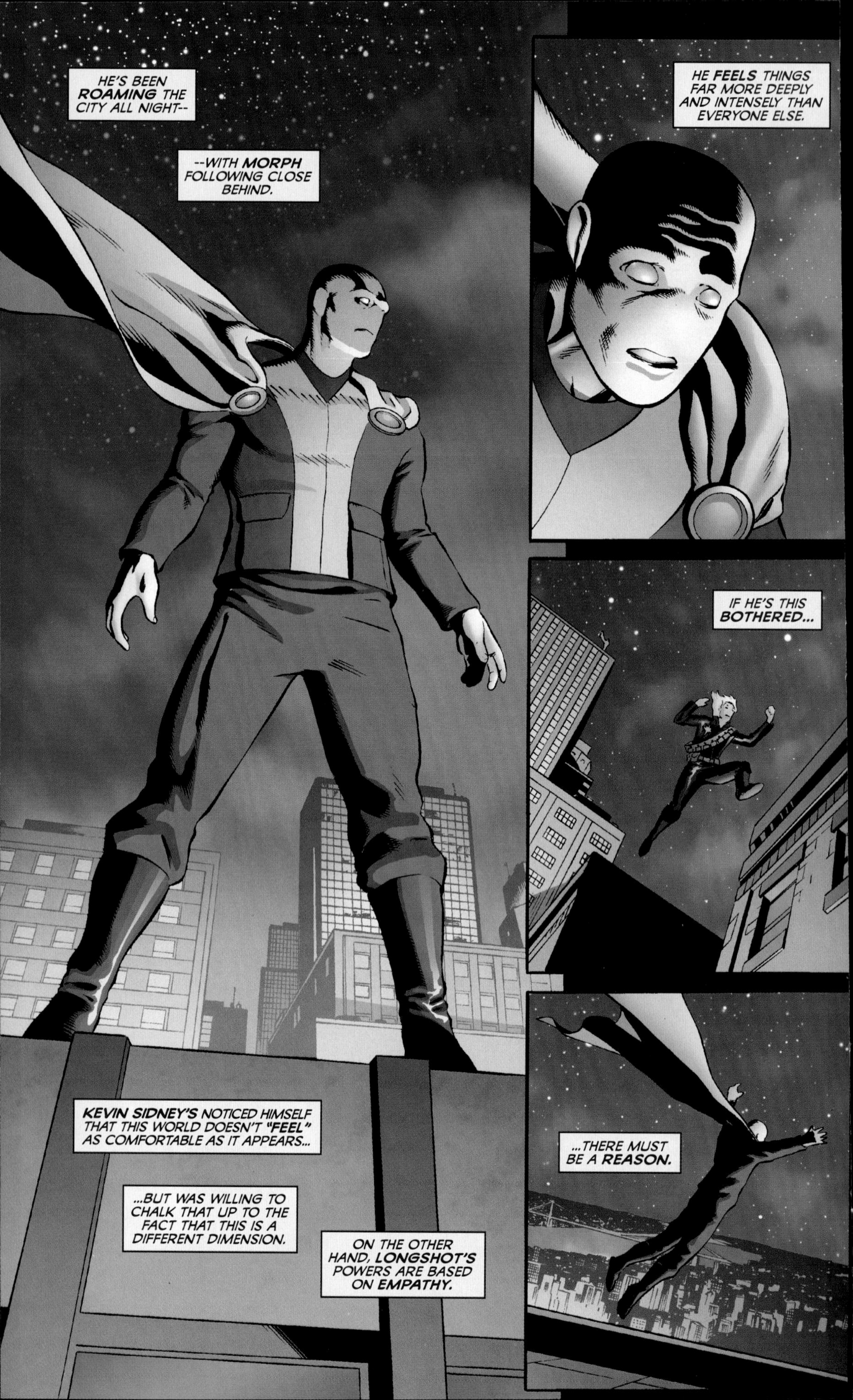
HE'S BEEN ROAMING THE CITY ALL NIGHT--
--WITH MORPH FOLLOWING CLOSE BEHIND.
HE FEELS THINGS FAR MORE DEEPLY AND INTENSELY THAN EVERYONE ELSE.
IF HE'S THIS BOTHERED...
...THERE MUST BE A REASON.
KEVIN SIDNEY'S NOTICED HIMSELF THAT THIS WORLD DOESN'T "FEEL" AS COMFORTABLE AS IT APPEARS...
...BUT WAS WILLING TO CHALK THAT UP TO THE FACT THAT THIS IS A DIFFERENT DIMENSION.
ON THE OTHER HAND, LONGSHOT'S POWERS ARE BASED ON EMPATHY.

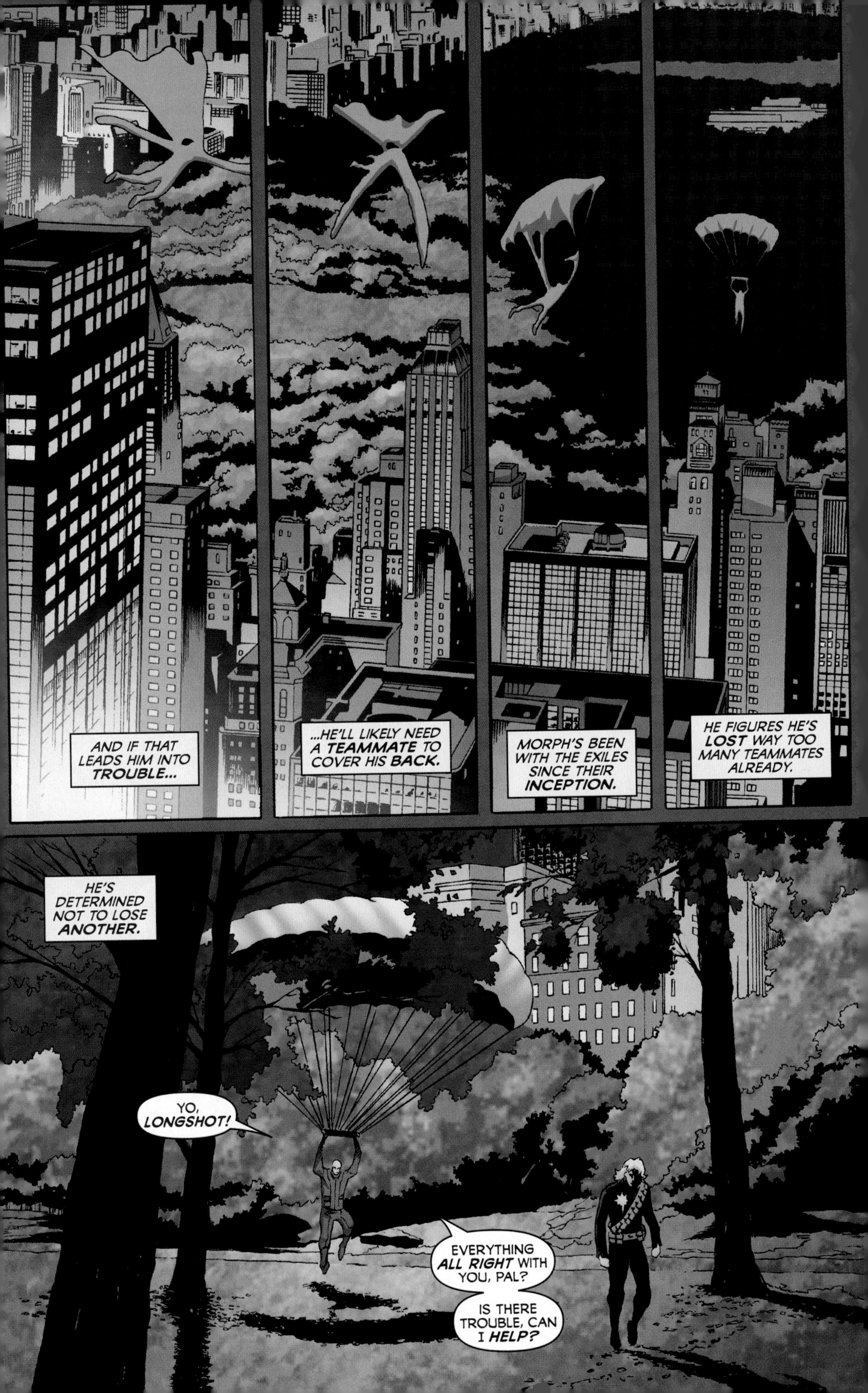
AND IF THAT LEADS HIM INTO TROUBLE...
...HE'LL LIKELY NEED A TEAMMATE TO COVER HIS BACK.
MORPH'S BEEN WITH THE EXILES SINCE THEIR INCEPTION.
HE FIGURES HE'S LOST WAY TOO MANY TEAMMATES ALREADY.
HE'S DETERMINED NOT TO LOSE ANOTHER.
YO, LONGSHOT!
EVERYTHING ALL RIGHT WITH YOU, PAL?
IS THERE TROUBLE, CAN I HELP?

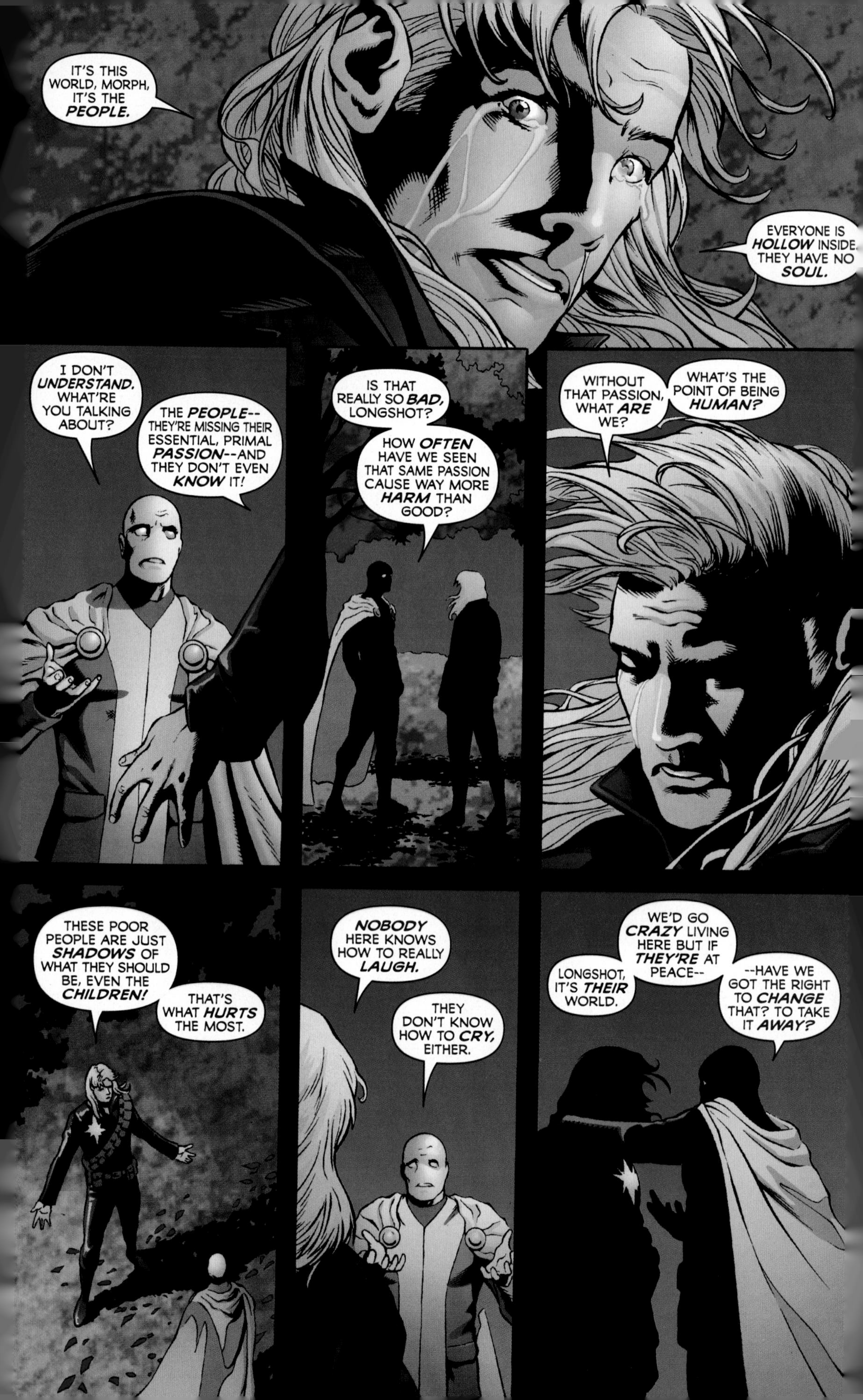
IT'S THIS WORLD, MORPH, IT'S THE PEOPLE.
EVERYONE IS HOLLOW INSIDE. THEY HAVE NO SOUL.
I DON'T UNDERSTAND. WHAT'RE YOU TALKING ABOUT?
THE PEOPLE-- THEY'RE MISSING THEIR ESSENTIAL, PRIMAL PASSION--AND THEY DON'T EVEN KNOW IT!
IS THAT REALLY SO BAD, LONGSHOT?
HOW OFTEN HAVE WE SEEN THAT SAME PASSION CAUSE WAY MORE HARM THAN GOOD?
WITHOUT THAT PASSION, WHAT ARE WE?
WHAT'S THE POINT OF BEING HUMAN?
THESE POOR PEOPLE ARE JUST SHADOWS OF WHAT THEY SHOULD BE, EVEN THE CHILDREN!
THAT'S WHAT HURTS THE MOST.
NOBODY HERE KNOWS HOW TO REALLY LAUGH.
THEY DON'T KNOW HOW TO CRY, EITHER.
LONGSHOT, IT'S THEIR WORLD.
WE'D GO CRAZY LIVING HERE BUT IF THEY'RE AT PEACE--
--HAVE WE GOT THE RIGHT TO CHANGE THAT? TO TAKE IT AWAY?

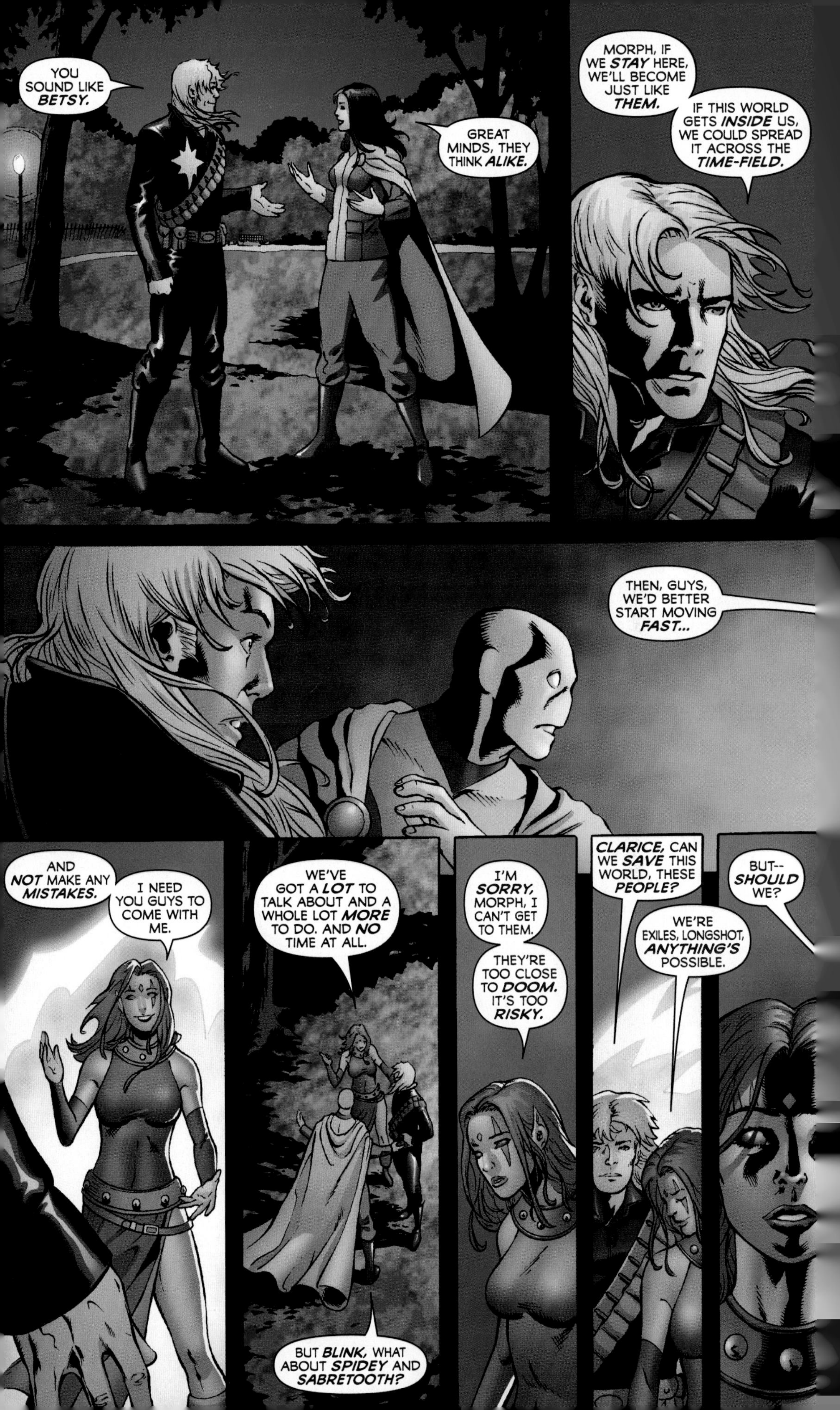

YOU SOUND LIKE BETSY.
GREAT MINDS, THEY THINK ALIKE.
MORPH, IF WE STAY HERE, WE'LL BECOME JUST LIKE THEM.
IF THIS WORLD GETS INSIDE US, WE COULD SPREAD IT ACROSS THE TIME-FIELD.
THEN, GUYS, WE'D BETTER START MOVING FAST...
AND NOT MAKE ANY MISTAKES.
I NEED YOU GUYS TO COME WITH ME.
WE'VE GOT A LOT TO TALK ABOUT AND A WHOLE LOT MORE TO DO. AND NO TIME AT ALL.
BUT BLINK, WHAT ABOUT SPIDEY AND SABRETOOTH?
I'M SORRY, MORPH, I CAN'T GET TO THEM.
THEY'RE TOO CLOSE TO DOOM. IT'S TOO RISKY.
CLARICE, CAN WE SAVE THIS WORLD, THESE PEOPLE?
WE'RE EXILES, LONGSHOT, ANYTHING'S POSSIBLE.
BUT-- SHOULD WE?

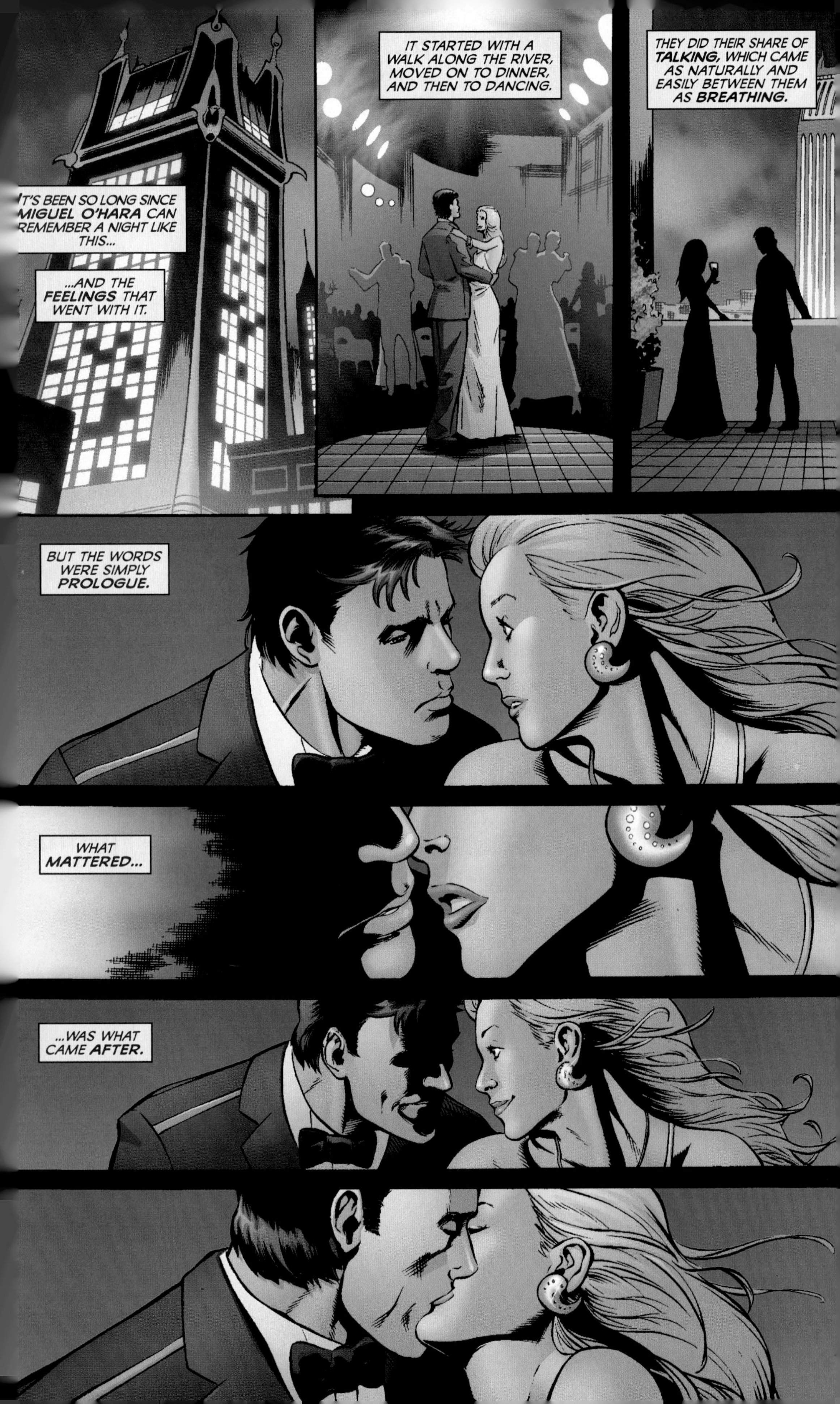

IT'S BEEN SO LONG SINCE MIGUEL O'HARA CAN REMEMBER A NIGHT LIKE THIS...
...AND THE FEELINGS THAT WENT WITH IT.
IT STARTED WITH A WALK ALONG THE RIVER, MOVED ON TO DINNER, AND THEN TO DANCING.
THEY DID THEIR SHARE OF TALKING, WHICH CAME AS NATURALLY AND EASILY BETWEEN THEM AS BREATHING.
BUT THE WORDS WERE SIMPLY PROLOGUE.
WHAT MATTERED...
...WAS WHAT CAME AFTER.

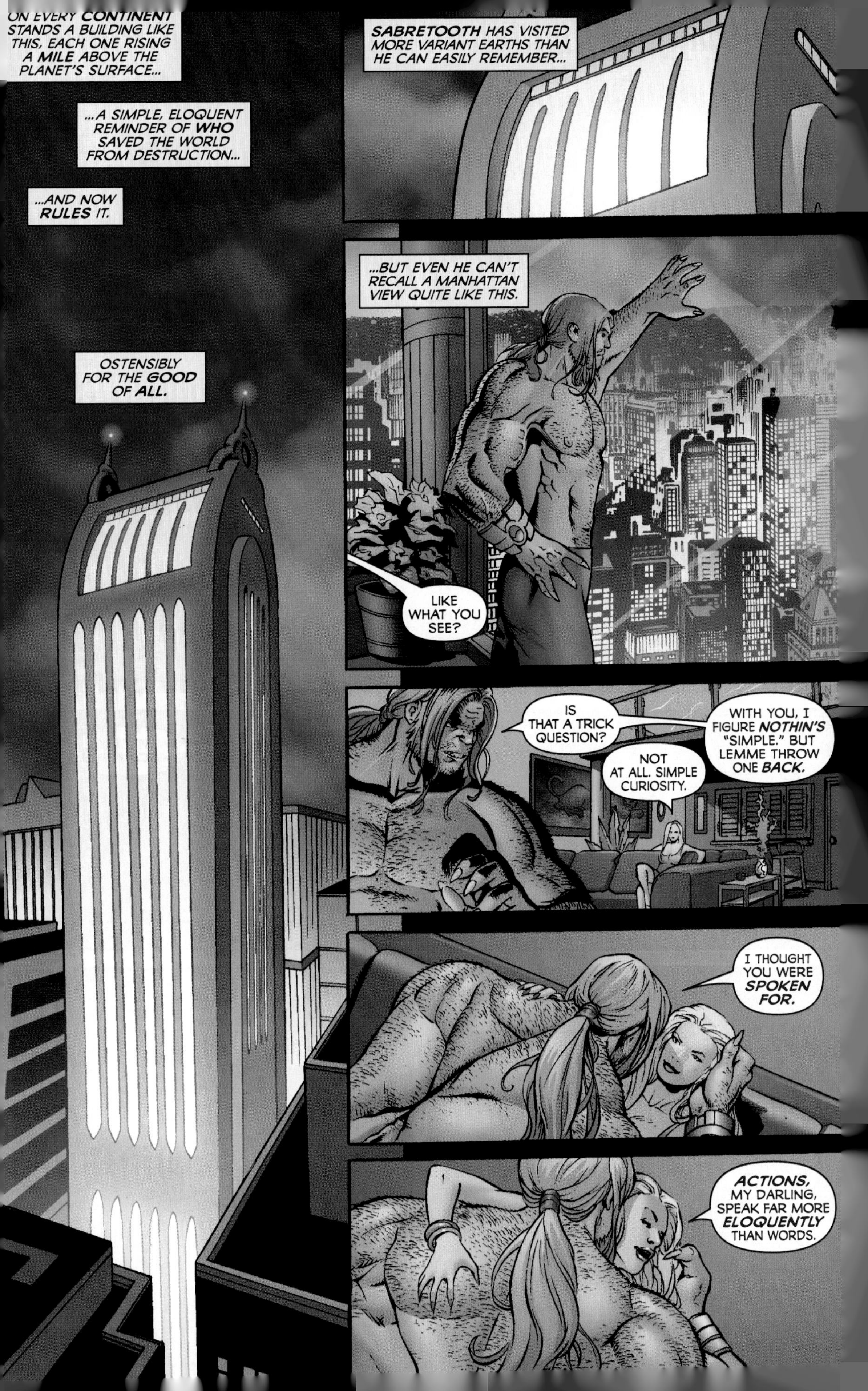
ON EVERY CONTINENT STANDS A BUILDING LIKE THIS, EACH ONE RISING A MILE ABOVE THE PLANET'S SURFACE...
...A SIMPLE, ELOQUENT REMINDER OF WHO SAVED THE WORLD FROM DESTRUCTION...
...AND NOW RULES IT.
OSTENSIBLY FOR THE GOOD OF ALL.
SABRETOOTH HAS VISITED MORE VARIANT EARTHS THAN HE CAN EASILY REMEMBER...
...BUT EVEN HE CAN'T RECALL A MANHATTAN VIEW QUITE LIKE THIS.
LIKE WHAT YOU SEE?
IS THAT A TRICK QUESTION?
NOT AT ALL. SIMPLE CURIOSITY.
WITH YOU, I FIGURE NOTHIN'S "SIMPLE." BUT LEMME THROW ONE BACK.
I THOUGHT YOU WERE SPOKEN FOR.
ACTIONS, MY DARLING, SPEAK FAR MORE ELOQUENTLY THAN WORDS.

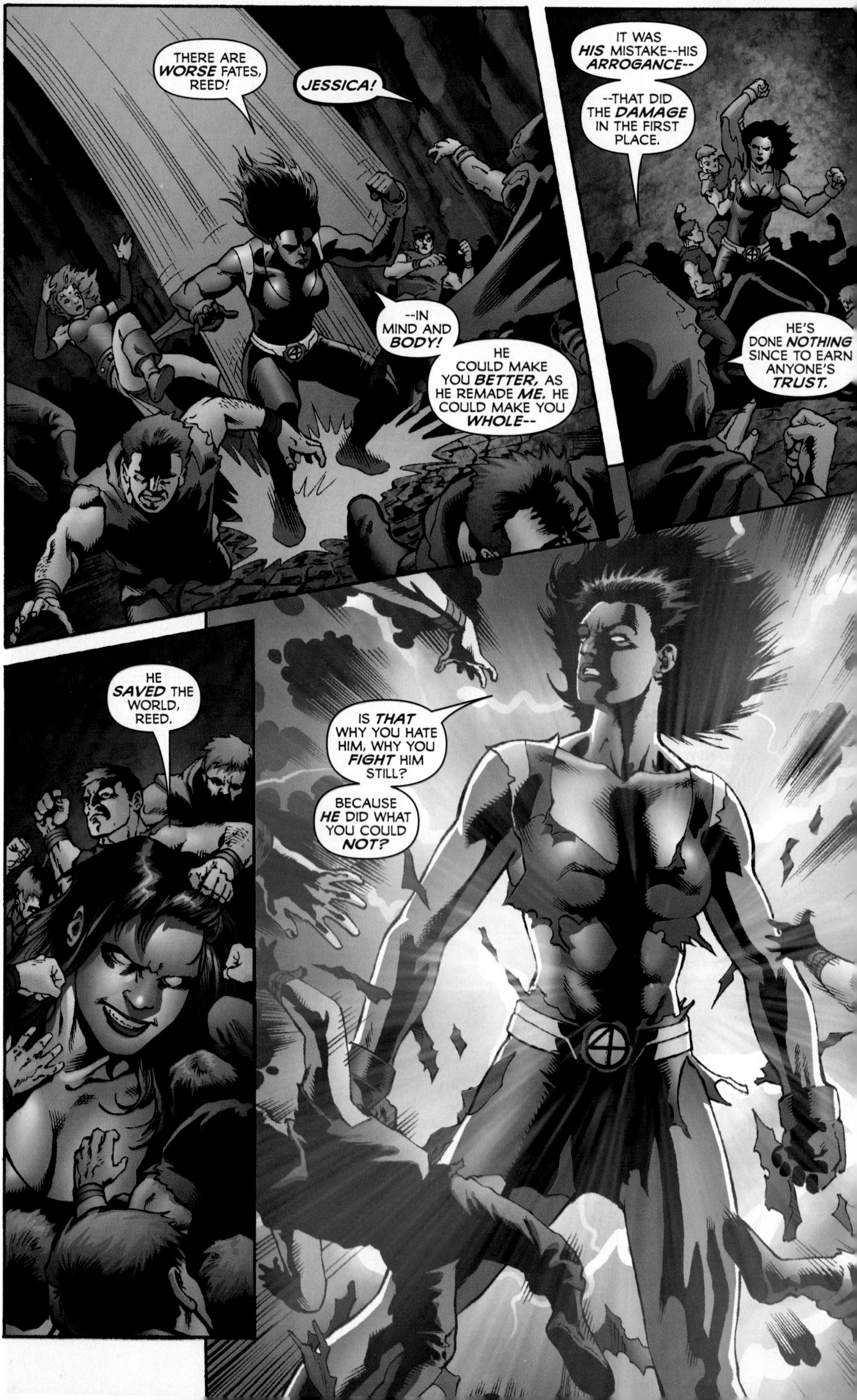

THERE ARE WORSE FATES, REED!
JESSICA!
--IN MIND AND BODY!
HE COULD MAKE YOU BETTER, AS HE REMADE ME. HE COULD MAKE YOU WHOLE--
IT WAS HIS MISTAKE--HIS ARROGANCE--
--THAT DID THE DAMAGE IN THE FIRST PLACE.
HE'S DONE NOTHING SINCE TO EARN ANYONE'S TRUST.
HE SAVED THE WORLD, REED.
IS THAT WHY YOU HATE HIM, WHY YOU FIGHT HIM STILL?
BECAUSE HE DID WHAT YOU COULD NOT?

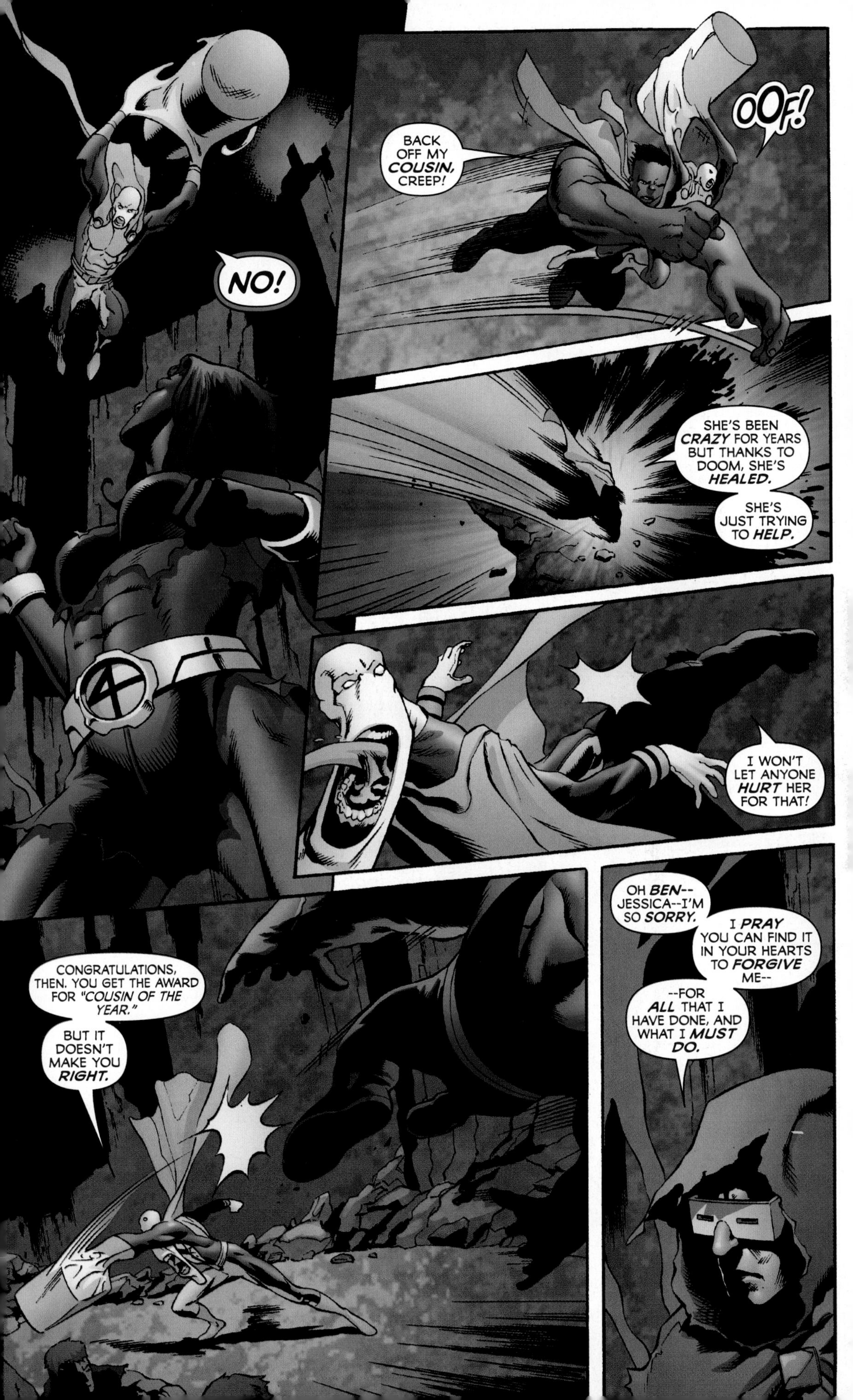

NO!
BACK OFF MY COUSIN, CREEP!
OOF!
SHE'S BEEN CRAZY FOR YEARS BUT THANKS TO DOOM, SHE'S HEALED.
SHE'S JUST TRYING TO HELP.
I WON'T LET ANYONE HURT HER FOR THAT!
CONGRATULATIONS, THEN. YOU GET THE AWARD FOR "COUSIN OF THE YEAR."
BUT IT DOESN'T MAKE YOU RIGHT.
OH BEN-- JESSICA--I'M SO SORRY.
I PRAY YOU CAN FIND IT IN YOUR HEARTS TO FORGIVE ME--
--FOR ALL THAT I HAVE DONE, AND WHAT I MUST DO.

HEY *FREAKS,* WHAT DID'JA THINK--

--THAT WE'D LET THE *NEW GAL* COME AFTER YOU *ALONE?*

TEAM EFFORT, CAN'TCHA TELL?

WE KNOW *SOMETHING* ABOUT THAT, FELLA.

BLINK

MATTER OF FACT, *TEAMWORK* IS THE EXILES' STOCK IN TRADE.

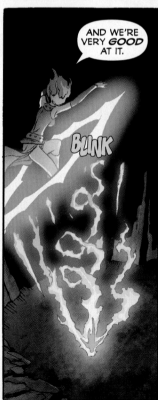

AND WE'RE VERY *GOOD* AT IT.

BLINK

"CAN'TCHA TELL?"

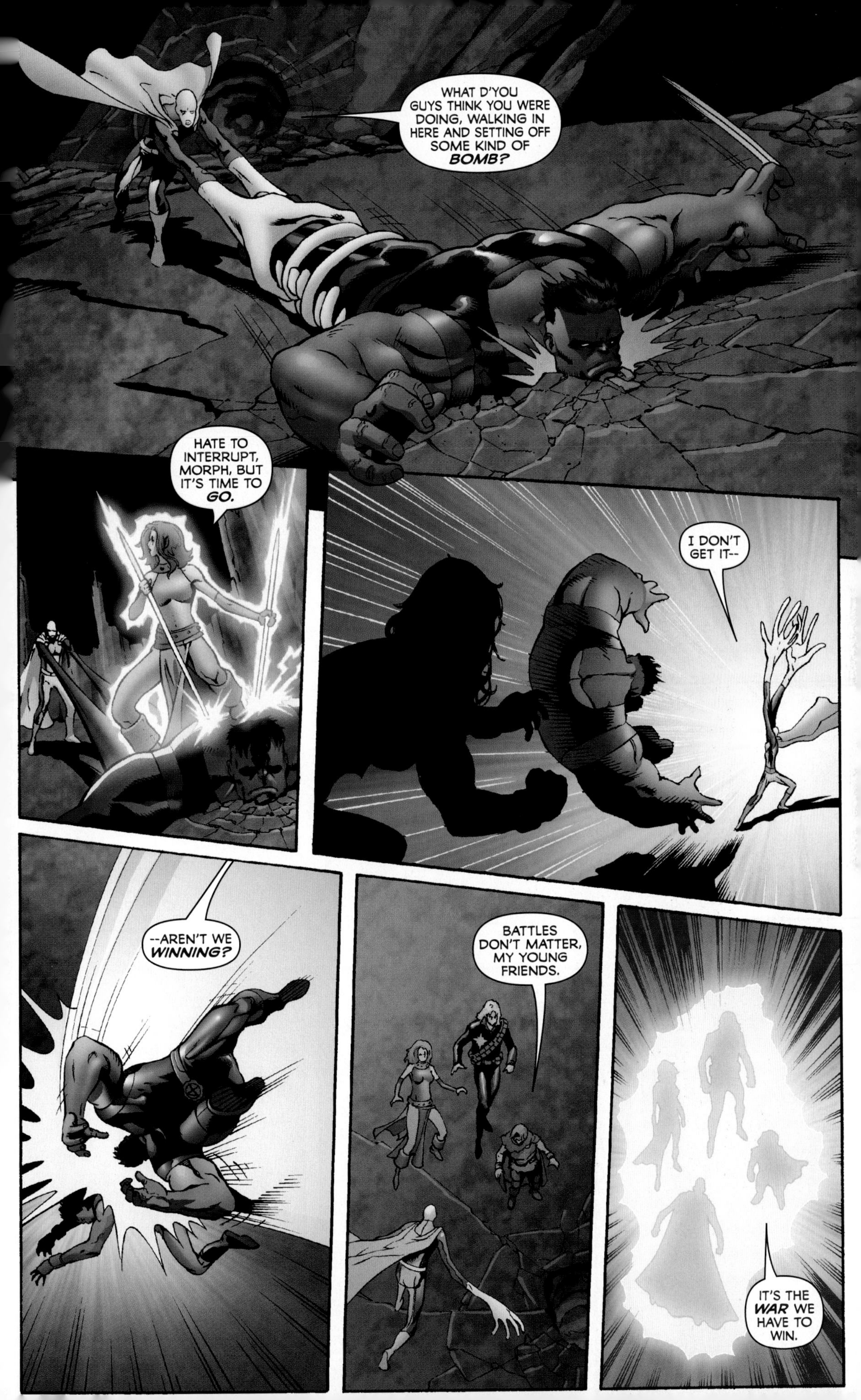

WHAT D'YOU GUYS THINK YOU WERE DOING, WALKING IN HERE AND SETTING OFF SOME KIND OF *BOMB?*
HATE TO INTERRUPT, MORPH, BUT IT'S TIME TO *GO.*
I DON'T GET IT--
--AREN'T WE *WINNING?*
BATTLES DON'T MATTER, MY YOUNG FRIENDS.
IT'S THE *WAR* WE HAVE TO WIN.

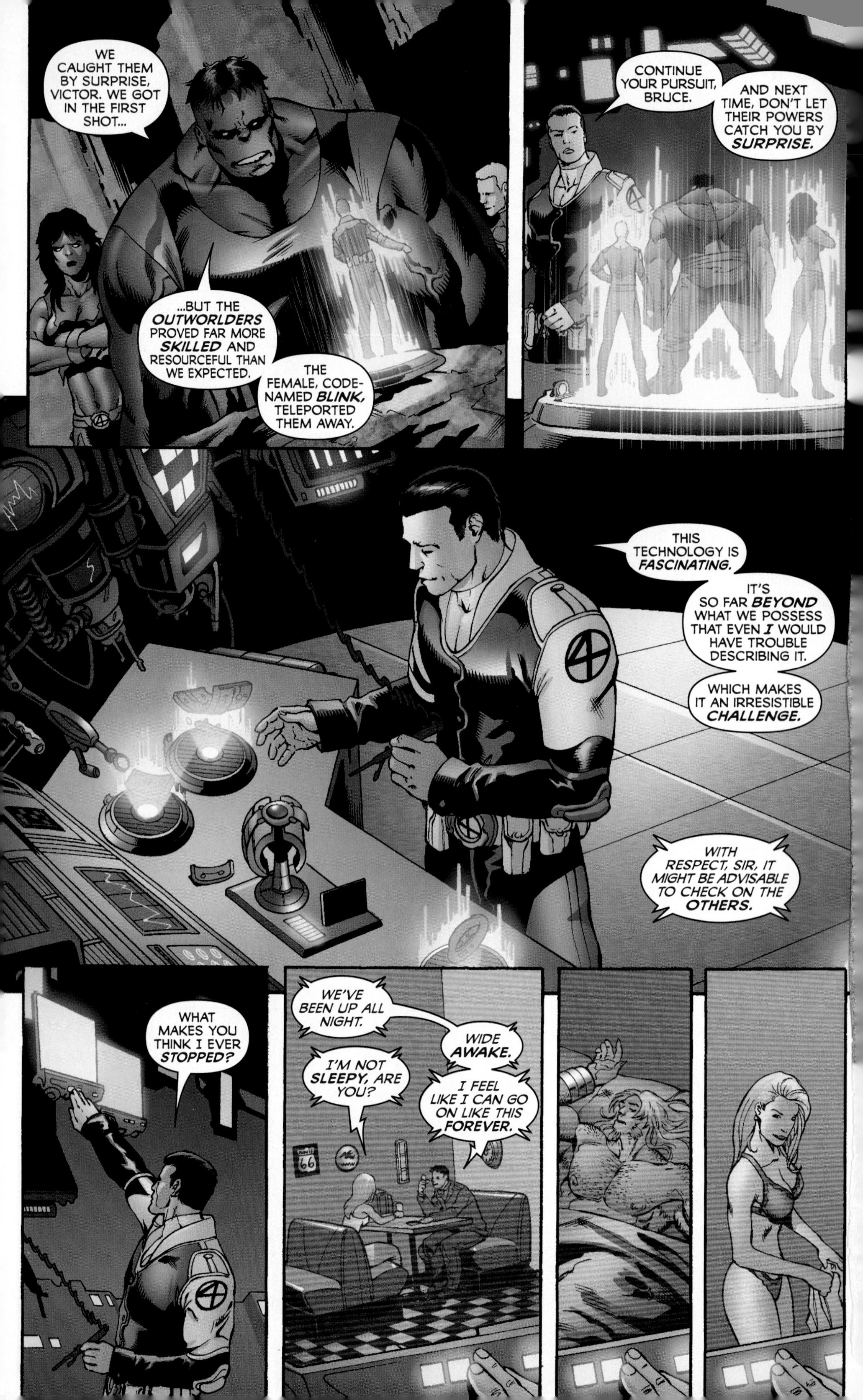
WE CAUGHT THEM BY SURPRISE, VICTOR. WE GOT IN THE FIRST SHOT...
...BUT THE OUTWORLDERS PROVED FAR MORE SKILLED AND RESOURCEFUL THAN WE EXPECTED.
THE FEMALE, CODE-NAMED BLINK, TELEPORTED THEM AWAY.
CONTINUE YOUR PURSUIT, BRUCE.
AND NEXT TIME, DON'T LET THEIR POWERS CATCH YOU BY SURPRISE.
THIS TECHNOLOGY IS FASCINATING.
IT'S SO FAR BEYOND WHAT WE POSSESS THAT EVEN I WOULD HAVE TROUBLE DESCRIBING IT.
WHICH MAKES IT AN IRRESISTIBLE CHALLENGE.
WITH RESPECT, SIR, IT MIGHT BE ADVISABLE TO CHECK ON THE OTHERS.
WHAT MAKES YOU THINK I EVER STOPPED?
WE'VE BEEN UP ALL NIGHT.
WIDE AWAKE.
I'M NOT SLEEPY, ARE YOU?
I FEEL LIKE I CAN GO ON LIKE THIS FOREVER.
66

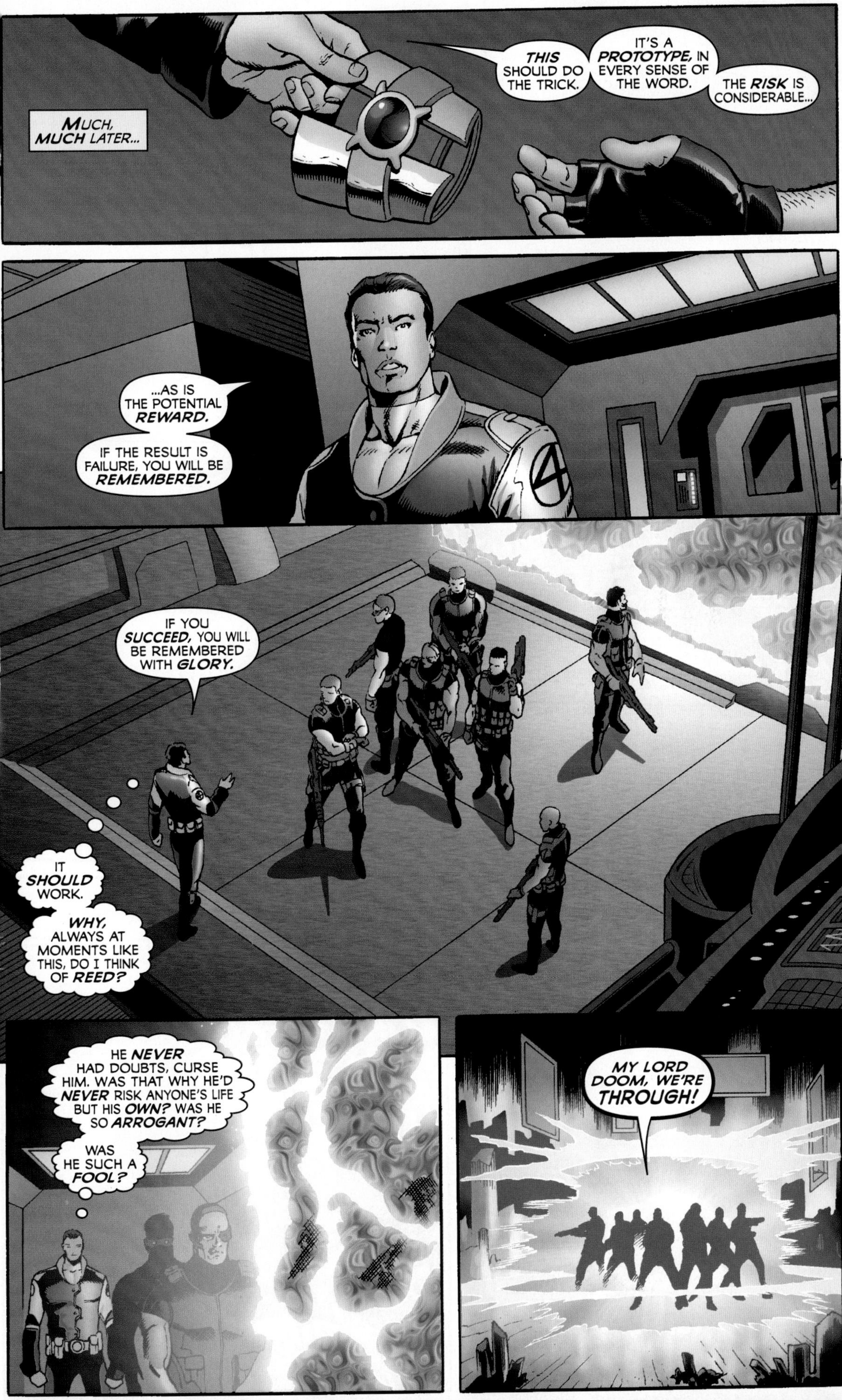
MUCH, MUCH LATER...
THIS SHOULD DO THE TRICK.
IT'S A PROTOTYPE, IN EVERY SENSE OF THE WORD.
THE RISK IS CONSIDERABLE...
...AS IS THE POTENTIAL REWARD.
IF THE RESULT IS FAILURE, YOU WILL BE REMEMBERED.
IF YOU SUCCEED, YOU WILL BE REMEMBERED WITH GLORY.
IT SHOULD WORK.
WHY, ALWAYS AT MOMENTS LIKE THIS, DO I THINK OF REED?
HE NEVER HAD DOUBTS, CURSE HIM. WAS THAT WHY HE'D NEVER RISK ANYONE'S LIFE BUT HIS OWN? WAS HE SO ARROGANT?
WAS HE SUCH A FOOL?
MY LORD DOOM, WE'RE THROUGH!

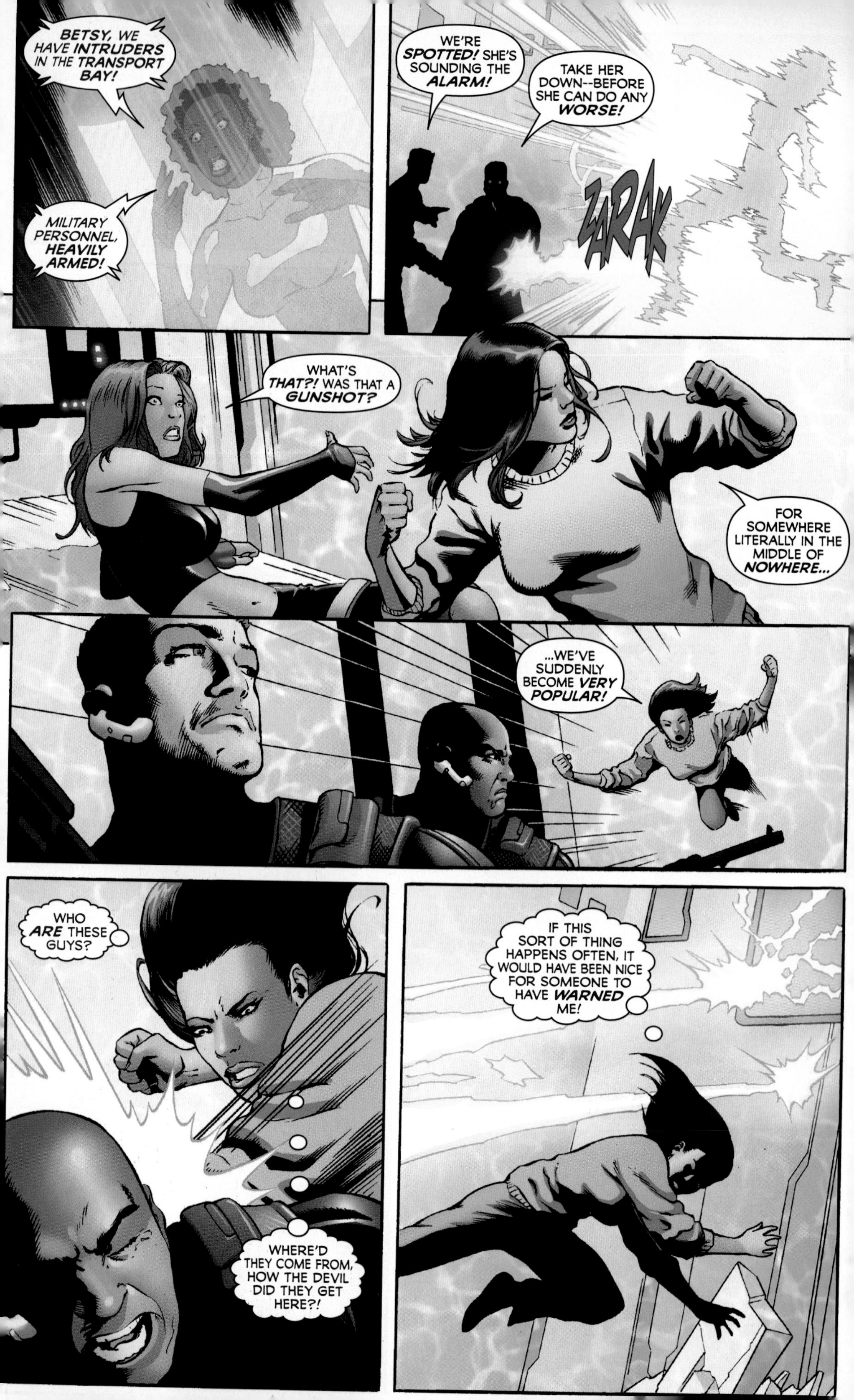
BETSY, WE HAVE INTRUDERS IN THE TRANSPORT BAY!
MILITARY PERSONNEL, HEAVILY ARMED!
WE'RE SPOTTED! SHE'S SOUNDING THE ALARM!
TAKE HER DOWN--BEFORE SHE CAN DO ANY WORSE!
ZARAK
WHAT'S THAT?! WAS THAT A GUNSHOT?
FOR SOMEWHERE LITERALLY IN THE MIDDLE OF NOWHERE...
...WE'VE SUDDENLY BECOME VERY POPULAR!
WHO ARE THESE GUYS?
WHERE'D THEY COME FROM, HOW THE DEVIL DID THEY GET HERE?!
IF THIS SORT OF THING HAPPENS OFTEN, IT WOULD HAVE BEEN NICE FOR SOMEONE TO HAVE WARNED ME!

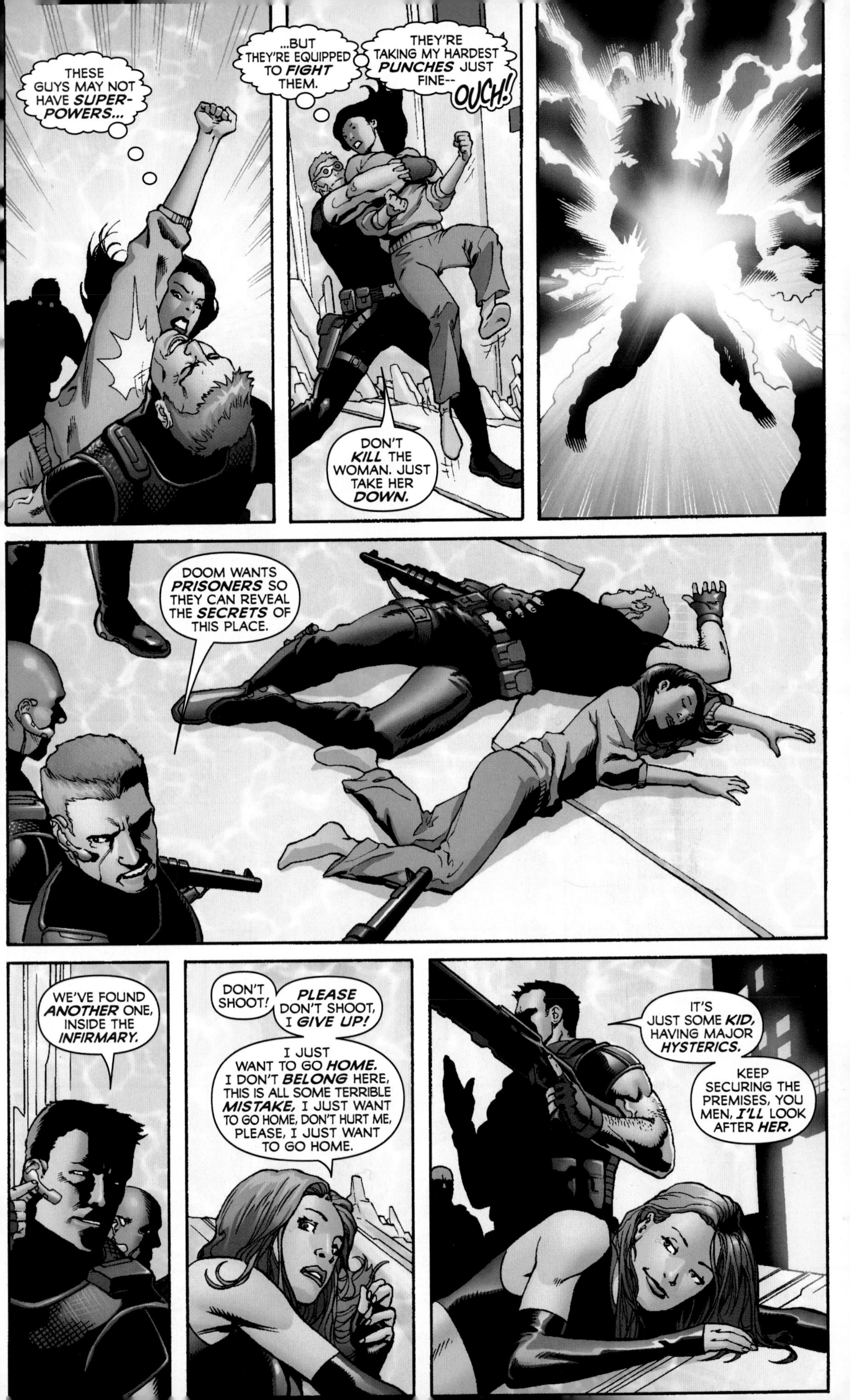
THESE GUYS MAY NOT HAVE SUPER-POWERS...
...BUT THEY'RE EQUIPPED TO FIGHT THEM.
THEY'RE TAKING MY HARDEST PUNCHES JUST FINE--
OUCH!
DON'T KILL THE WOMAN. JUST TAKE HER DOWN.
DOOM WANTS PRISONERS SO THEY CAN REVEAL THE SECRETS OF THIS PLACE.
WE'VE FOUND ANOTHER ONE, INSIDE THE INFIRMARY.
DON'T SHOOT!
PLEASE DON'T SHOOT, I GIVE UP!
I JUST WANT TO GO HOME. I DON'T BELONG HERE, THIS IS ALL SOME TERRIBLE MISTAKE, I JUST WANT TO GO HOME, DON'T HURT ME, PLEASE, I JUST WANT TO GO HOME.
IT'S JUST SOME KID, HAVING MAJOR HYSTERICS.
KEEP SECURING THE PREMISES, YOU MEN, I'LL LOOK AFTER HER.

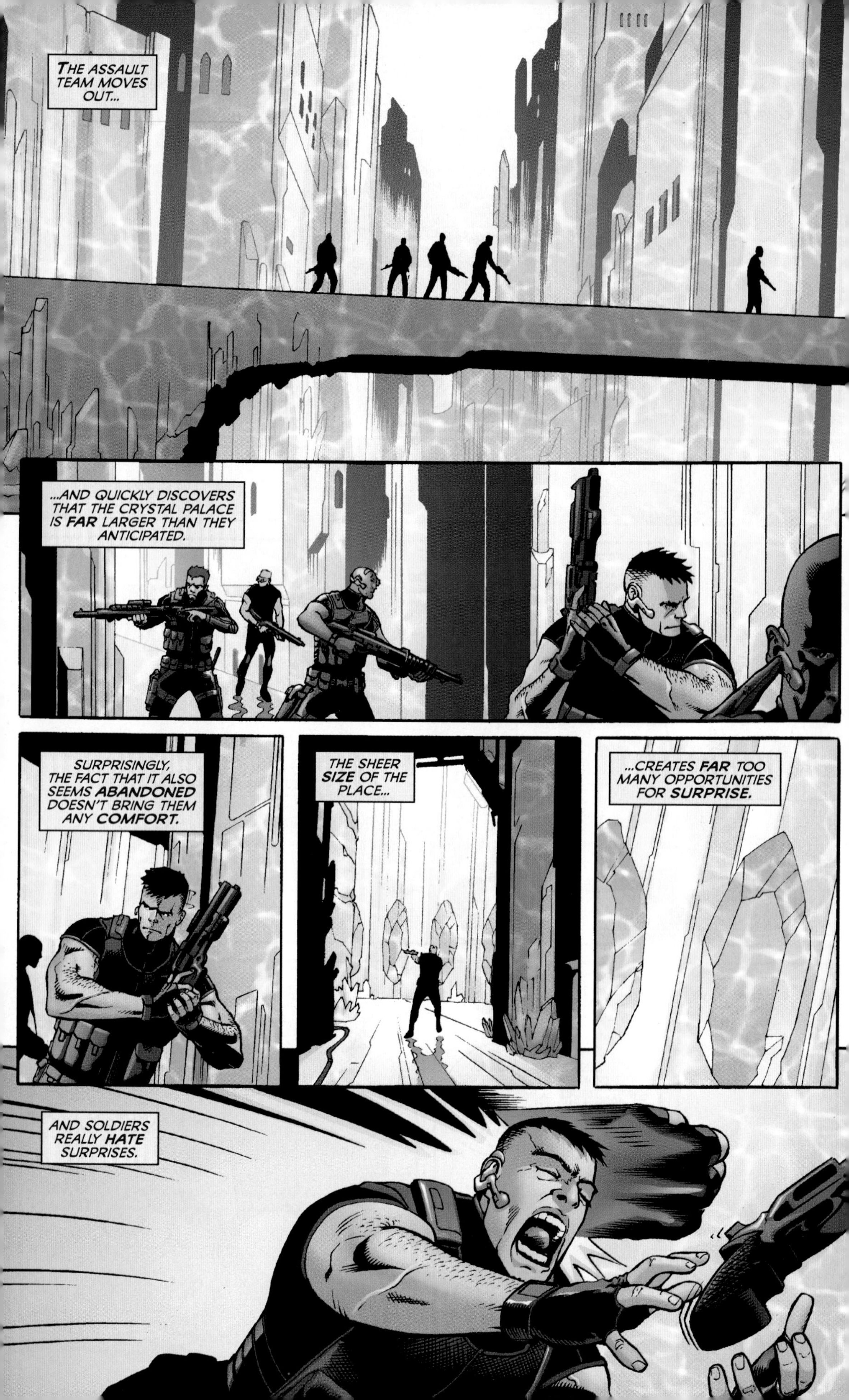

THE ASSAULT TEAM MOVES OUT...
...AND QUICKLY DISCOVERS THAT THE CRYSTAL PALACE IS FAR LARGER THAN THEY ANTICIPATED.
SURPRISINGLY, THE FACT THAT IT ALSO SEEMS ABANDONED DOESN'T BRING THEM ANY COMFORT.
THE SHEER SIZE OF THE PLACE...
...CREATES FAR TOO MANY OPPORTUNITIES FOR SURPRISE.
AND SOLDIERS REALLY HATE SURPRISES.

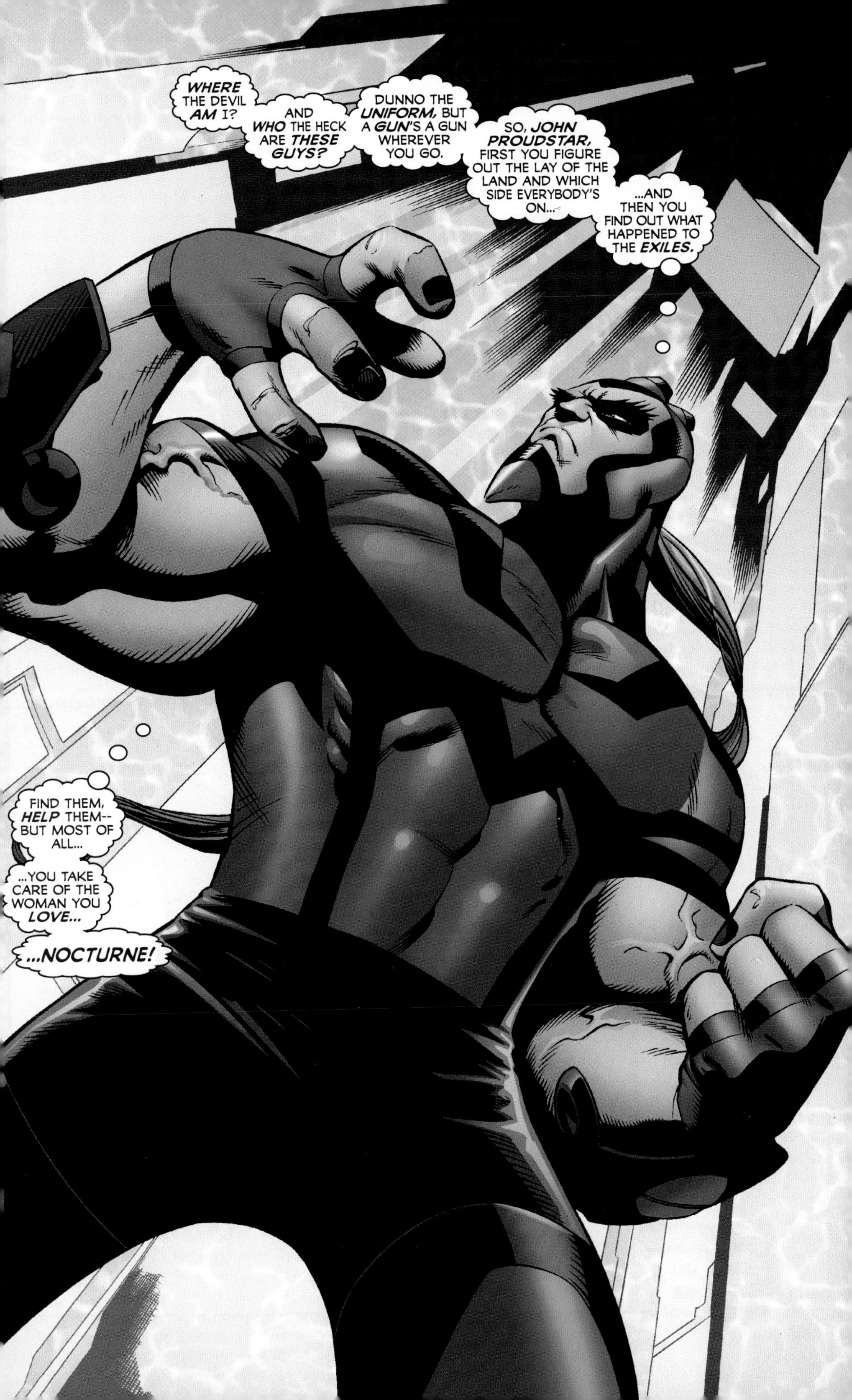
WHERE THE DEVIL AM I?
AND WHO THE HECK ARE THESE GUYS?
DUNNO THE UNIFORM, BUT A GUN'S A GUN WHEREVER YOU GO.
SO, JOHN PROUDSTAR, FIRST YOU FIGURE OUT THE LAY OF THE LAND AND WHICH SIDE EVERYBODY'S ON...
...AND THEN YOU FIND OUT WHAT HAPPENED TO THE EXILES.
FIND THEM, HELP THEM-- BUT MOST OF ALL...
...YOU TAKE CARE OF THE WOMAN YOU LOVE...
...NOCTURNE!

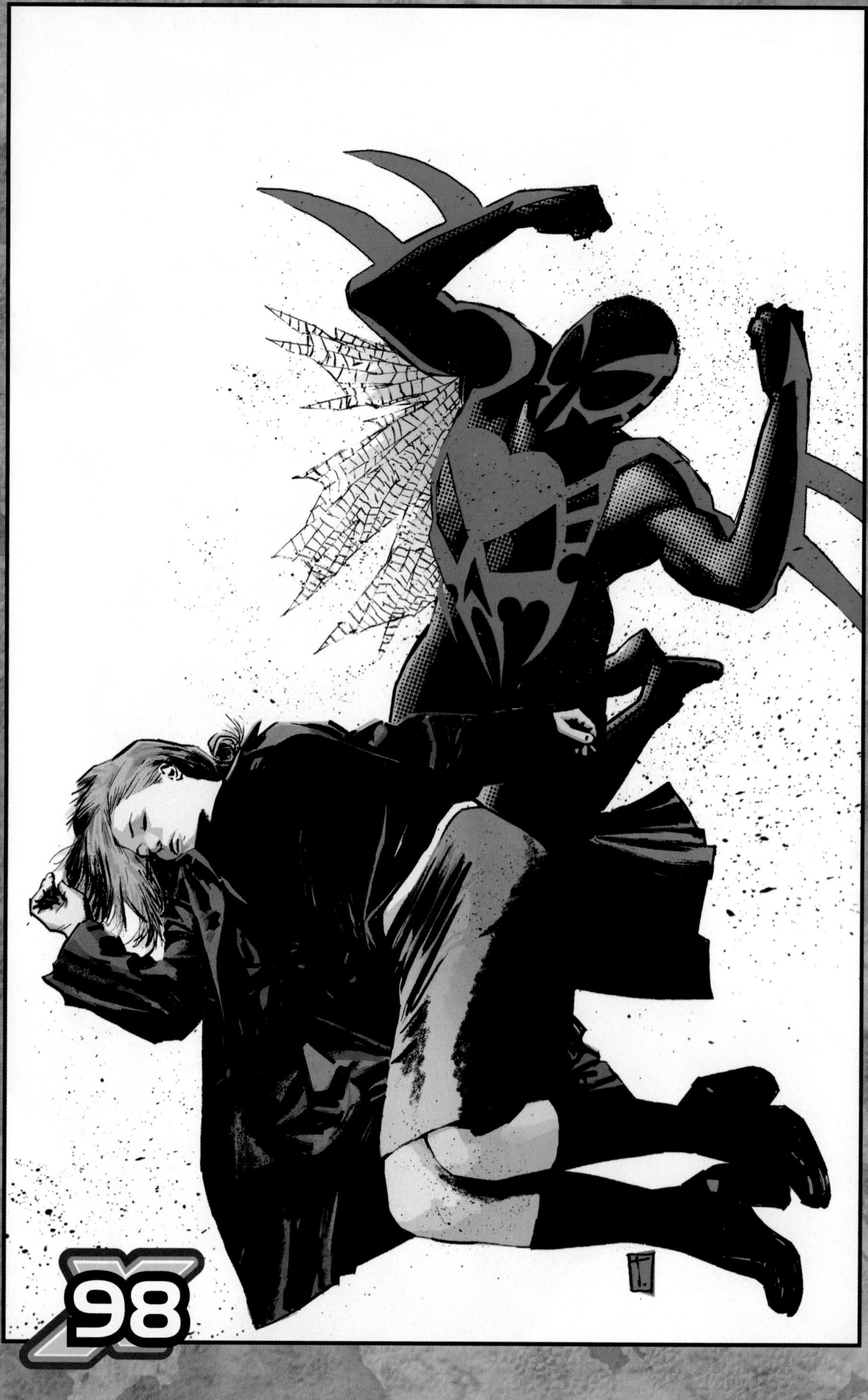
98

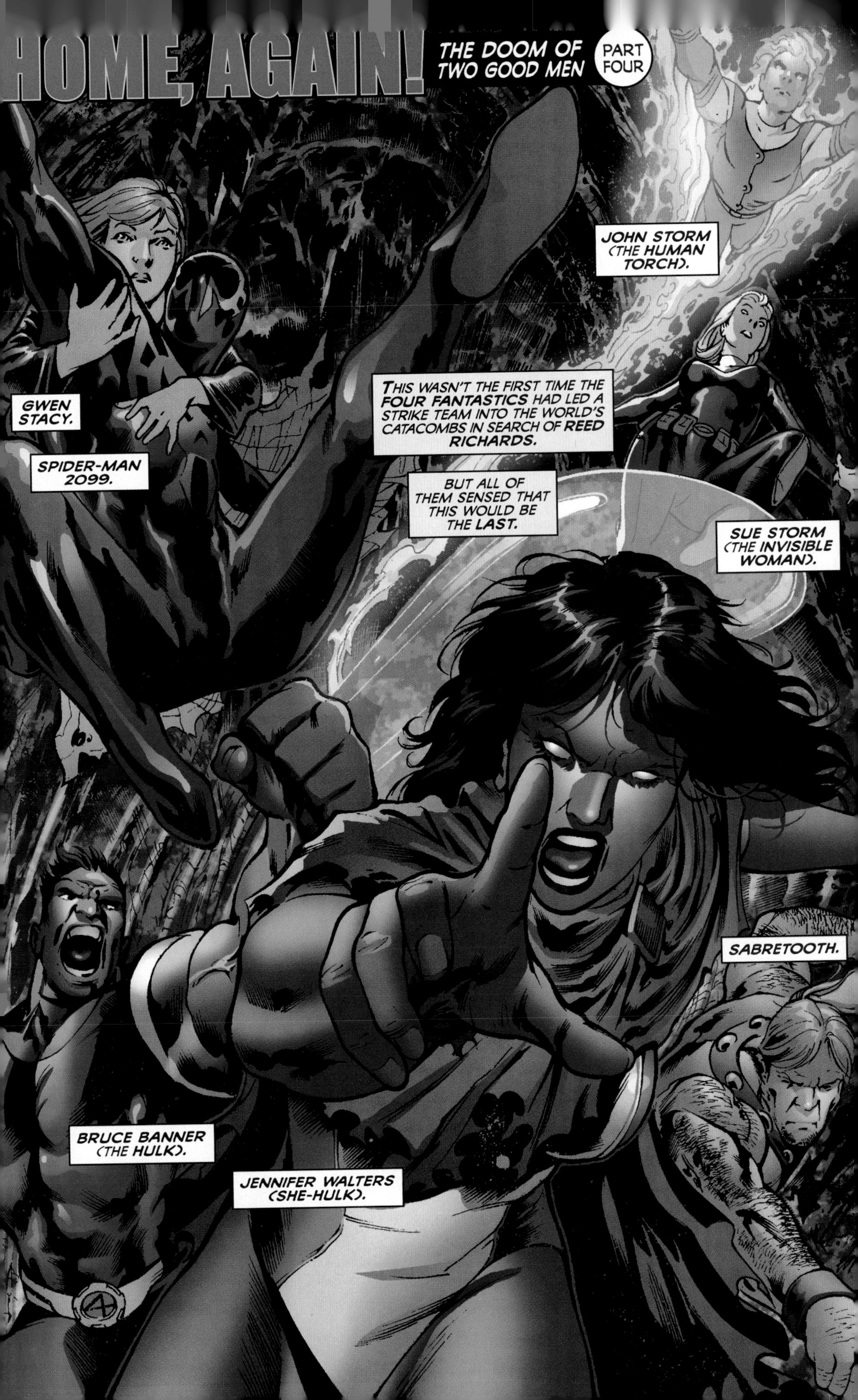
HOME, AGAIN!
THE DOOM OF TWO GOOD MEN
PART FOUR
JOHN STORM (THE HUMAN TORCH).
THIS WASN'T THE FIRST TIME THE FOUR FANTASTICS HAD LED A STRIKE TEAM INTO THE WORLD'S CATACOMBS IN SEARCH OF REED RICHARDS.
GWEN STACY.
SPIDER-MAN 2099.
BUT ALL OF THEM SENSED THAT THIS WOULD BE THE LAST.
SUE STORM (THE INVISIBLE WOMAN).
SABRETOOTH.
BRUCE BANNER (THE HULK).
JENNIFER WALTERS (SHE-HULK).

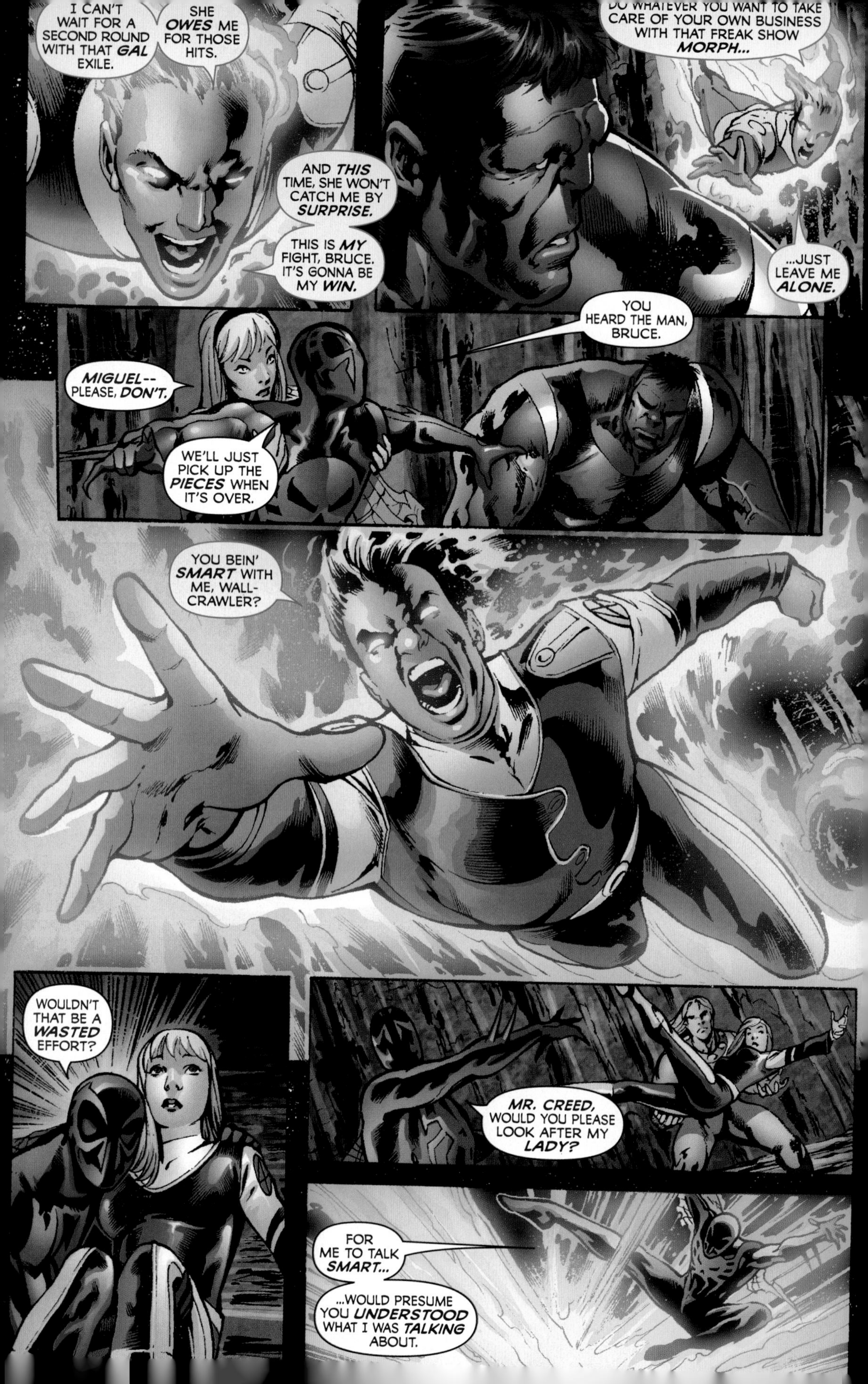
I CAN'T WAIT FOR A SECOND ROUND WITH THAT GAL EXILE.
SHE OWES ME FOR THOSE HITS.
AND THIS TIME, SHE WON'T CATCH ME BY SURPRISE.
THIS IS MY FIGHT, BRUCE. IT'S GONNA BE MY WIN.
DO WHATEVER YOU WANT TO TAKE CARE OF YOUR OWN BUSINESS WITH THAT FREAK SHOW MORPH...
...JUST LEAVE ME ALONE.
YOU HEARD THE MAN, BRUCE.
MIGUEL-- PLEASE, DON'T.
WE'LL JUST PICK UP THE PIECES WHEN IT'S OVER.
YOU BEIN' SMART WITH ME, WALL-CRAWLER?
WOULDN'T THAT BE A WASTED EFFORT?
MR. CREED, WOULD YOU PLEASE LOOK AFTER MY LADY?
FOR ME TO TALK SMART...
...WOULD PRESUME YOU UNDERSTOOD WHAT I WAS TALKING ABOUT.

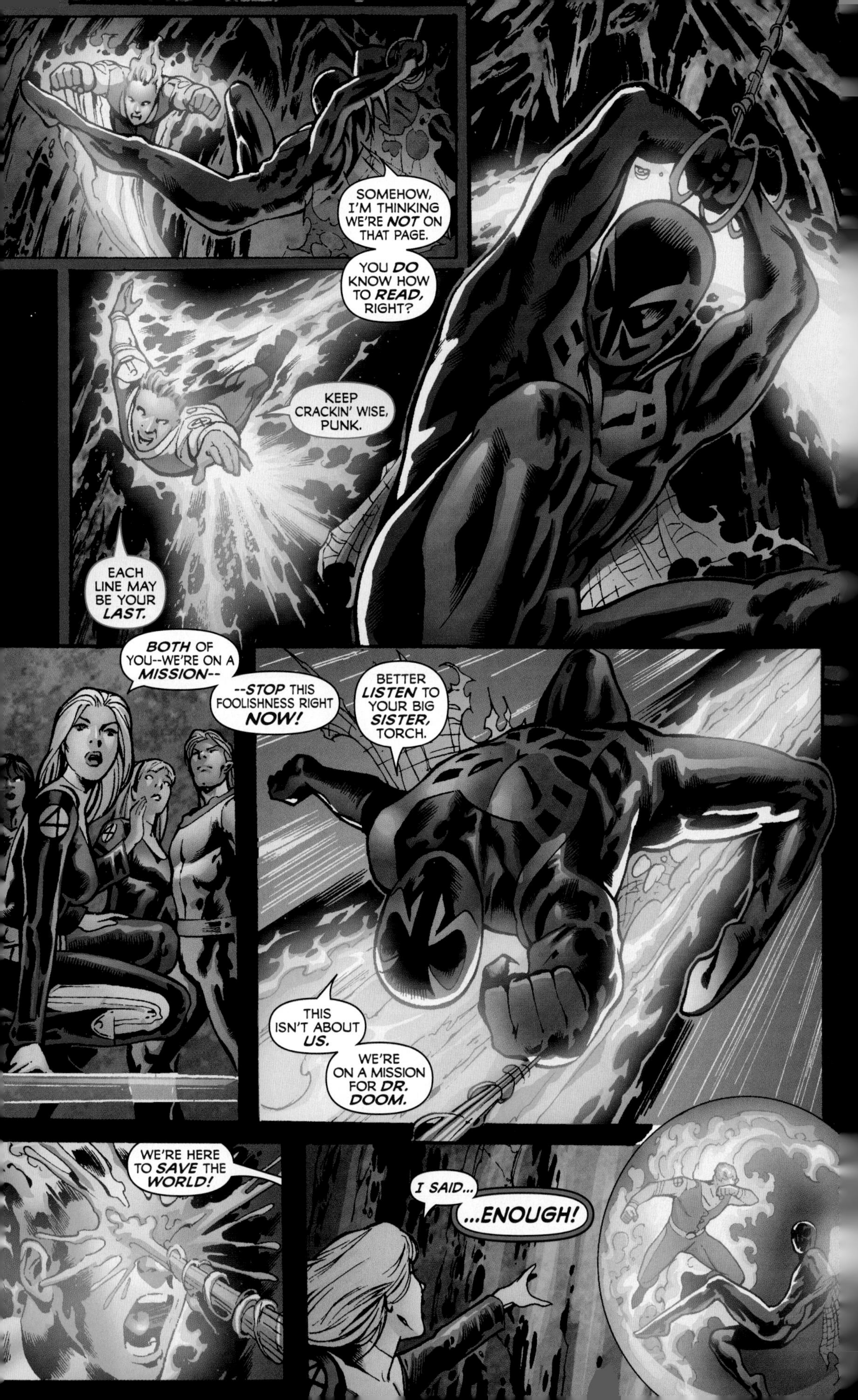
SOMEHOW, I'M THINKING WE'RE NOT ON THAT PAGE.
YOU DO KNOW HOW TO READ, RIGHT?
KEEP CRACKIN' WISE, PUNK.
EACH LINE MAY BE YOUR LAST.
BOTH OF YOU--WE'RE ON A MISSION--
--STOP THIS FOOLISHNESS RIGHT NOW!
BETTER LISTEN TO YOUR BIG SISTER, TORCH.
THIS ISN'T ABOUT US.
WE'RE ON A MISSION FOR DR. DOOM.
WE'RE HERE TO SAVE THE WORLD!
I SAID...
...ENOUGH!

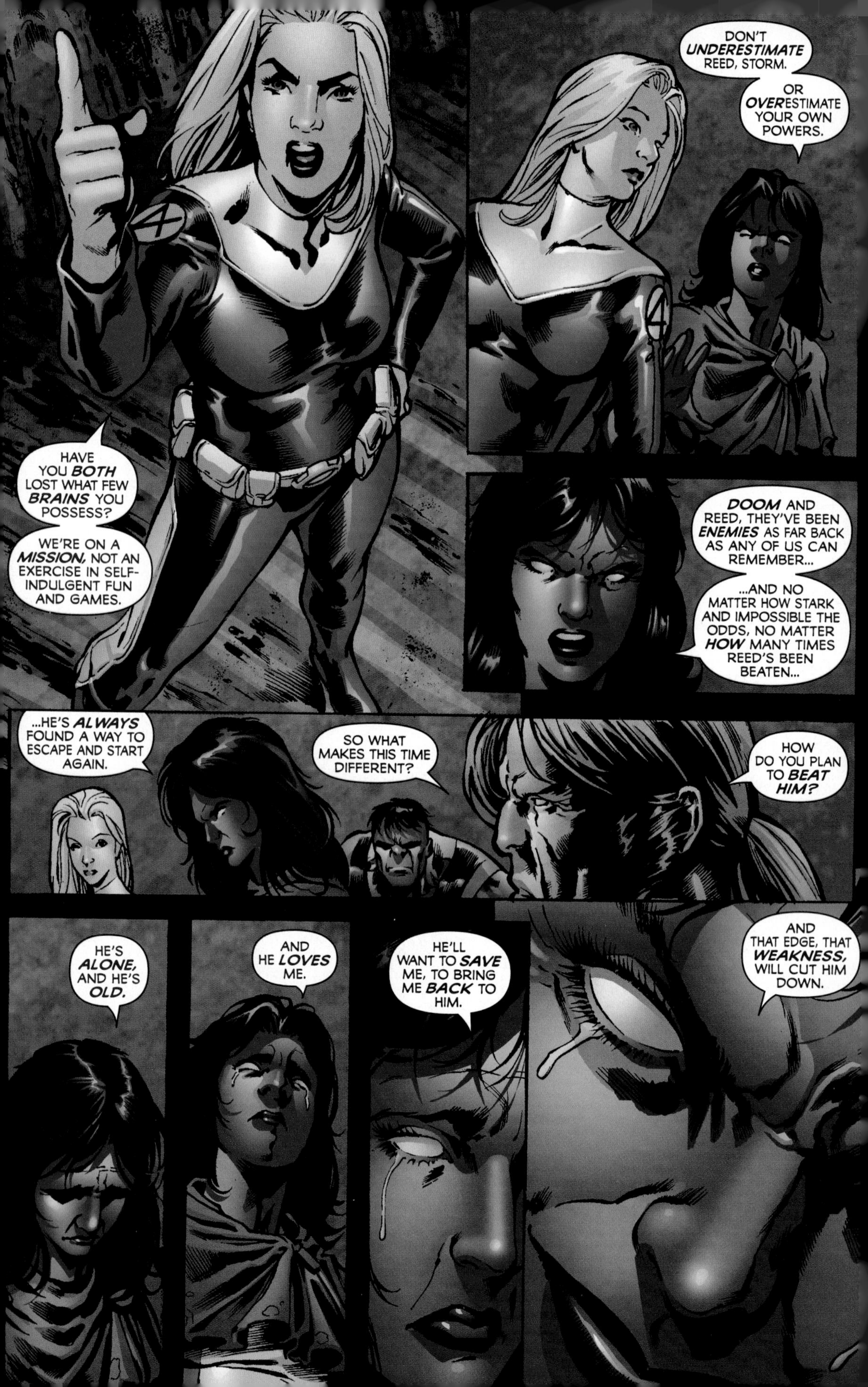

HAVE YOU BOTH LOST WHAT FEW BRAINS YOU POSSESS?
WE'RE ON A MISSION, NOT AN EXERCISE IN SELF-INDULGENT FUN AND GAMES.
DON'T UNDERESTIMATE REED, STORM.
OR OVERESTIMATE YOUR OWN POWERS.
DOOM AND REED, THEY'VE BEEN ENEMIES AS FAR BACK AS ANY OF US CAN REMEMBER...
...AND NO MATTER HOW STARK AND IMPOSSIBLE THE ODDS, NO MATTER HOW MANY TIMES REED'S BEEN BEATEN...
...HE'S ALWAYS FOUND A WAY TO ESCAPE AND START AGAIN.
SO WHAT MAKES THIS TIME DIFFERENT?
HOW DO YOU PLAN TO BEAT HIM?
HE'S ALONE, AND HE'S OLD.
AND HE LOVES ME.
HE'LL WANT TO SAVE ME, TO BRING ME BACK TO HIM.
AND THAT EDGE, THAT WEAKNESS, WILL CUT HIM DOWN.

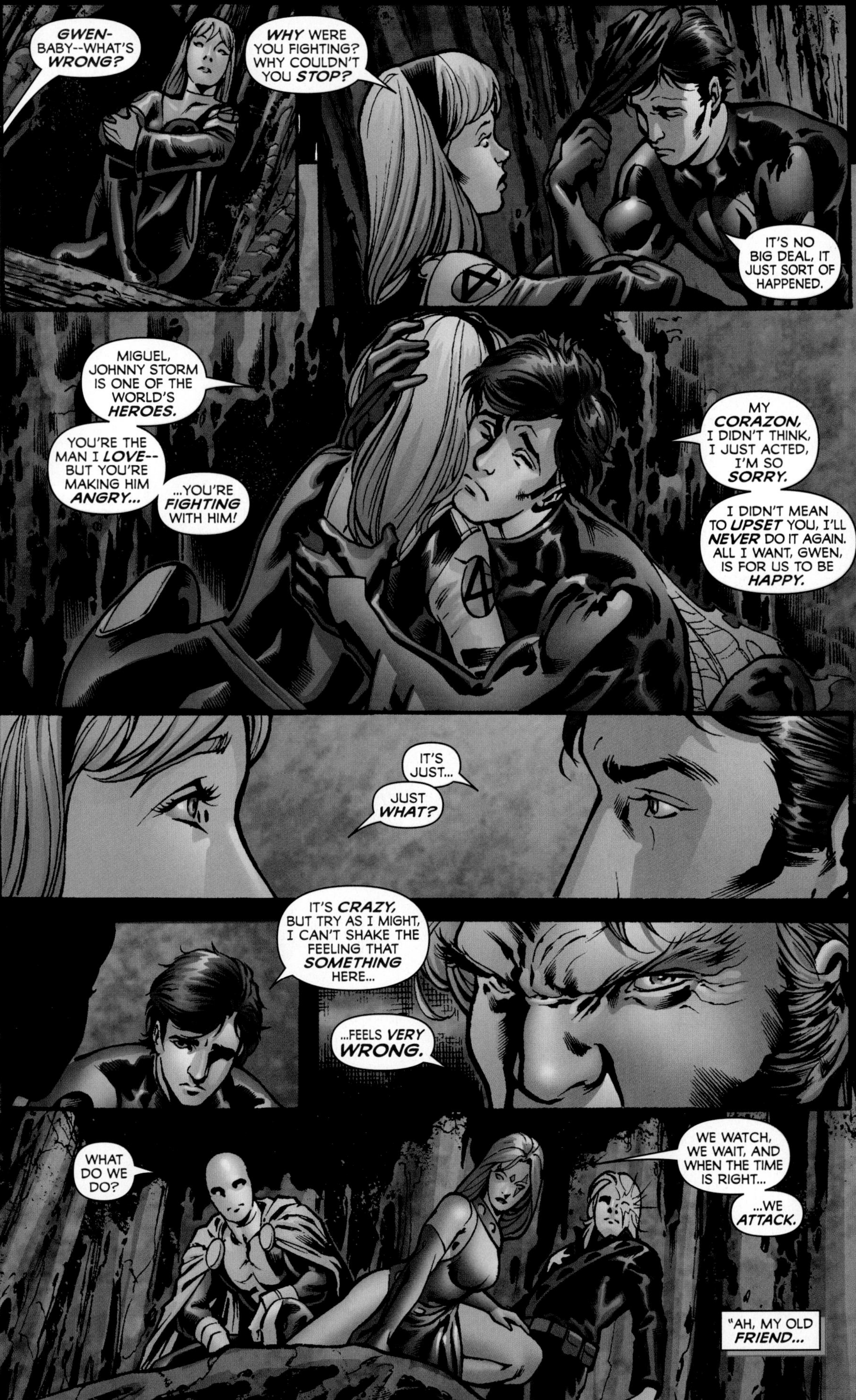
GWEN-BABY--WHAT'S WRONG?
WHY WERE YOU FIGHTING? WHY COULDN'T YOU STOP?
IT'S NO BIG DEAL, IT JUST SORT OF HAPPENED.
MIGUEL, JOHNNY STORM IS ONE OF THE WORLD'S HEROES.
YOU'RE THE MAN I LOVE--BUT YOU'RE MAKING HIM ANGRY...
...YOU'RE FIGHTING WITH HIM!
MY CORAZON, I DIDN'T THINK, I JUST ACTED, I'M SO SORRY.
I DIDN'T MEAN TO UPSET YOU, I'LL NEVER DO IT AGAIN. ALL I WANT, GWEN, IS FOR US TO BE HAPPY.
IT'S JUST...
JUST WHAT?
IT'S CRAZY, BUT TRY AS I MIGHT, I CAN'T SHAKE THE FEELING THAT SOMETHING HERE...
...FEELS VERY WRONG.
WHAT DO WE DO?
WE WATCH, WE WAIT, AND WHEN THE TIME IS RIGHT...
...WE ATTACK.
"AH, MY OLD FRIEND...

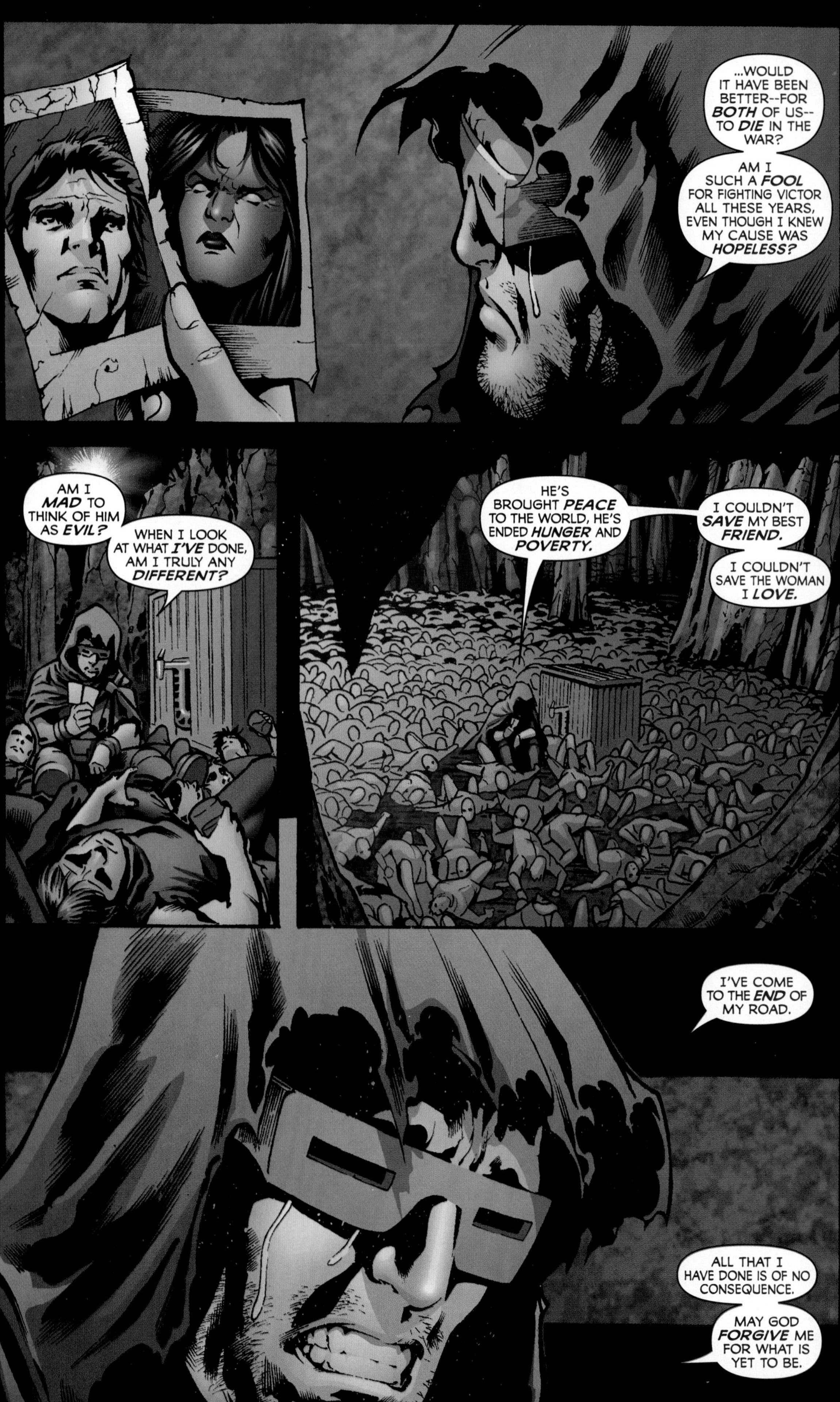
...WOULD IT HAVE BEEN BETTER--FOR BOTH OF US--TO DIE IN THE WAR?
AM I SUCH A FOOL FOR FIGHTING VICTOR ALL THESE YEARS, EVEN THOUGH I KNEW MY CAUSE WAS HOPELESS?
AM I MAD TO THINK OF HIM AS EVIL?
WHEN I LOOK AT WHAT I'VE DONE, AM I TRULY ANY DIFFERENT?
HE'S BROUGHT PEACE TO THE WORLD, HE'S ENDED HUNGER AND POVERTY.
I COULDN'T SAVE MY BEST FRIEND.
I COULDN'T SAVE THE WOMAN I LOVE.
I'VE COME TO THE END OF MY ROAD.
ALL THAT I HAVE DONE IS OF NO CONSEQUENCE.
MAY GOD FORGIVE ME FOR WHAT IS YET TO BE.

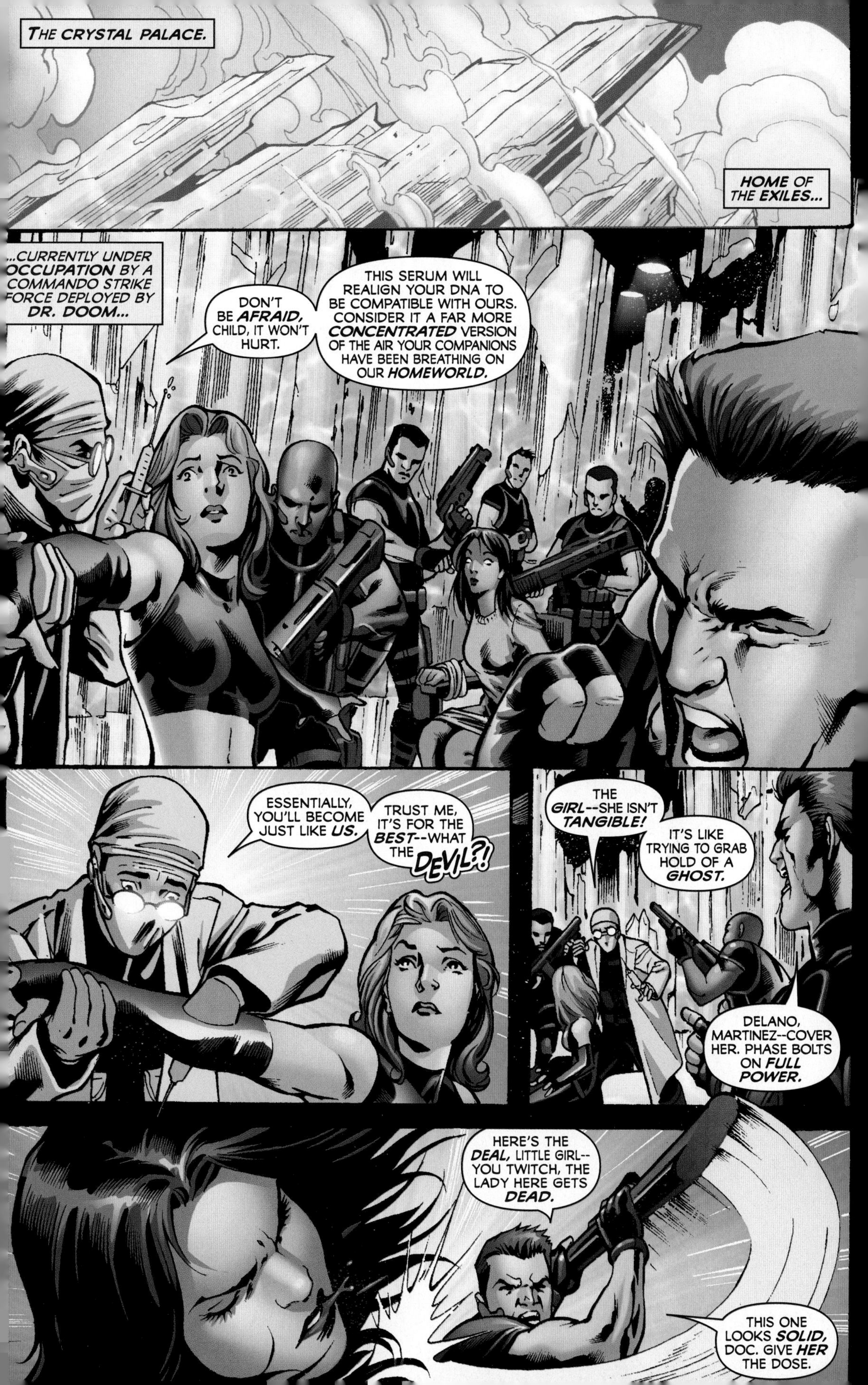
THE CRYSTAL PALACE.
HOME OF THE EXILES...
...CURRENTLY UNDER OCCUPATION BY A COMMANDO STRIKE FORCE DEPLOYED BY DR. DOOM...
DON'T BE AFRAID, CHILD, IT WON'T HURT.
THIS SERUM WILL REALIGN YOUR DNA TO BE COMPATIBLE WITH OURS. CONSIDER IT A FAR MORE CONCENTRATED VERSION OF THE AIR YOUR COMPANIONS HAVE BEEN BREATHING ON OUR HOMEWORLD.
ESSENTIALLY, YOU'LL BECOME JUST LIKE US.
TRUST ME, IT'S FOR THE BEST--WHAT THE DEVIL?!
THE GIRL--SHE ISN'T TANGIBLE!
IT'S LIKE TRYING TO GRAB HOLD OF A GHOST.
DELANO, MARTINEZ--COVER HER. PHASE BOLTS ON FULL POWER.
HERE'S THE DEAL, LITTLE GIRL-- YOU TWITCH, THE LADY HERE GETS DEAD.
THIS ONE LOOKS SOLID, DOC. GIVE HER THE DOSE.

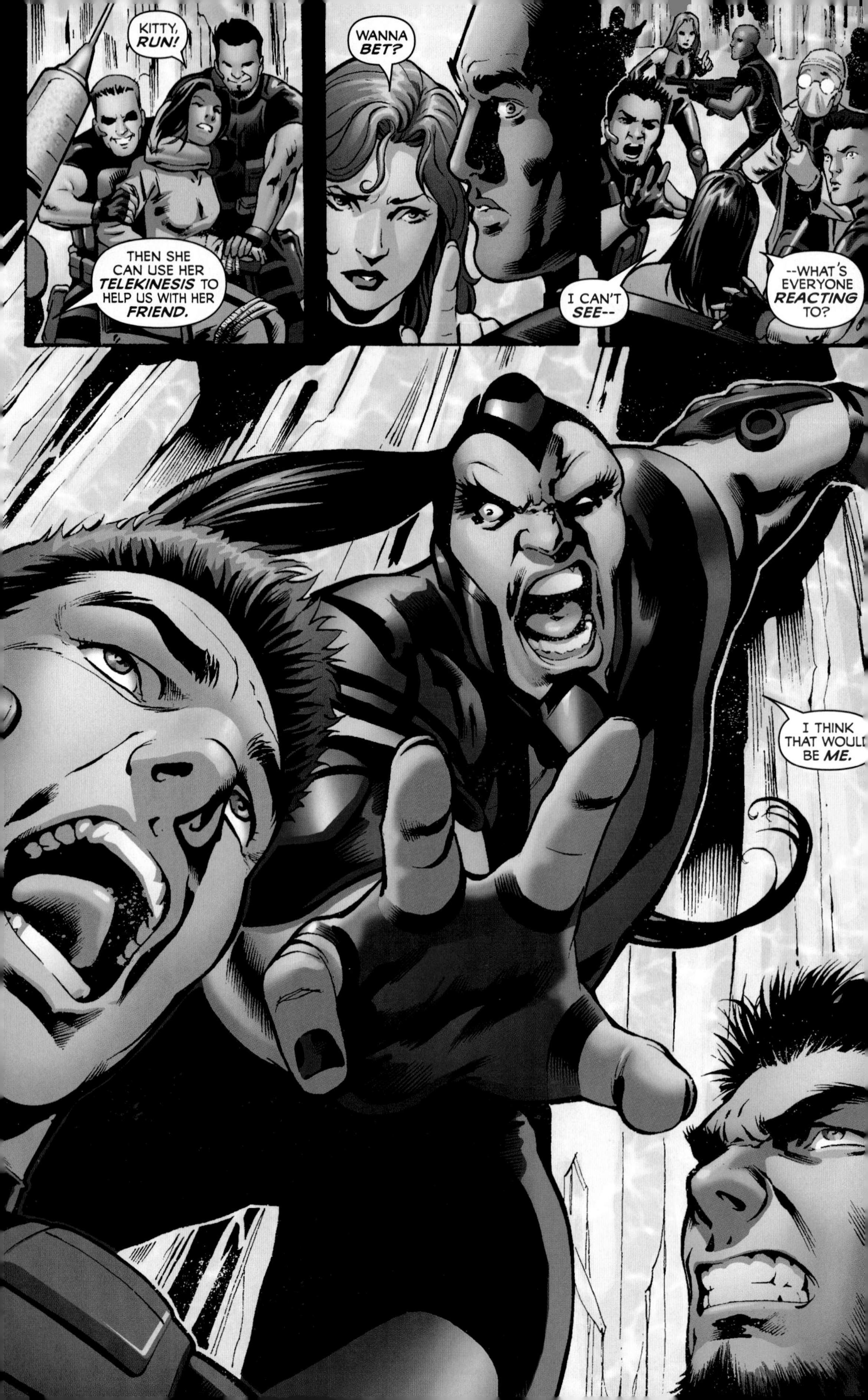
KITTY, RUN!
THEN SHE CAN USE HER TELEKINESIS TO HELP US WITH HER FRIEND.
WANNA BET?
I CAN'T SEE--
--WHAT'S EVERYONE REACTING TO?
I THINK THAT WOULD BE ME.

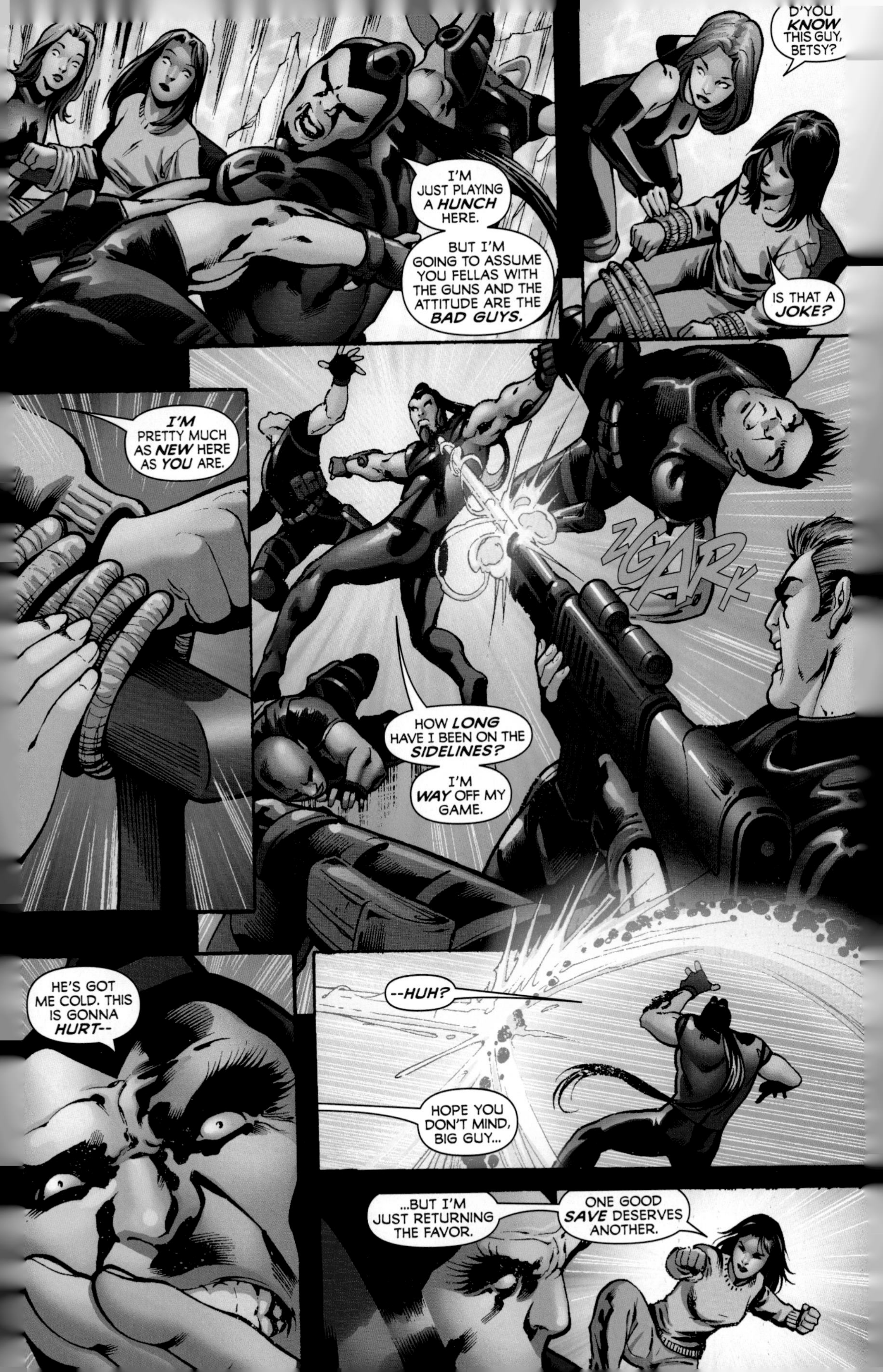
I'M JUST PLAYING A HUNCH HERE.
BUT I'M GOING TO ASSUME YOU FELLAS WITH THE GUNS AND THE ATTITUDE ARE THE BAD GUYS.
D'YOU KNOW THIS GUY, BETSY?
IS THAT A JOKE?
I'M PRETTY MUCH AS NEW HERE AS YOU ARE.
ZGARK
HOW LONG HAVE I BEEN ON THE SIDELINES?
I'M WAY OFF MY GAME.
HE'S GOT ME COLD. THIS IS GONNA HURT--
--HUH?
HOPE YOU DON'T MIND, BIG GUY...
...BUT I'M JUST RETURNING THE FAVOR.
ONE GOOD SAVE DESERVES ANOTHER.

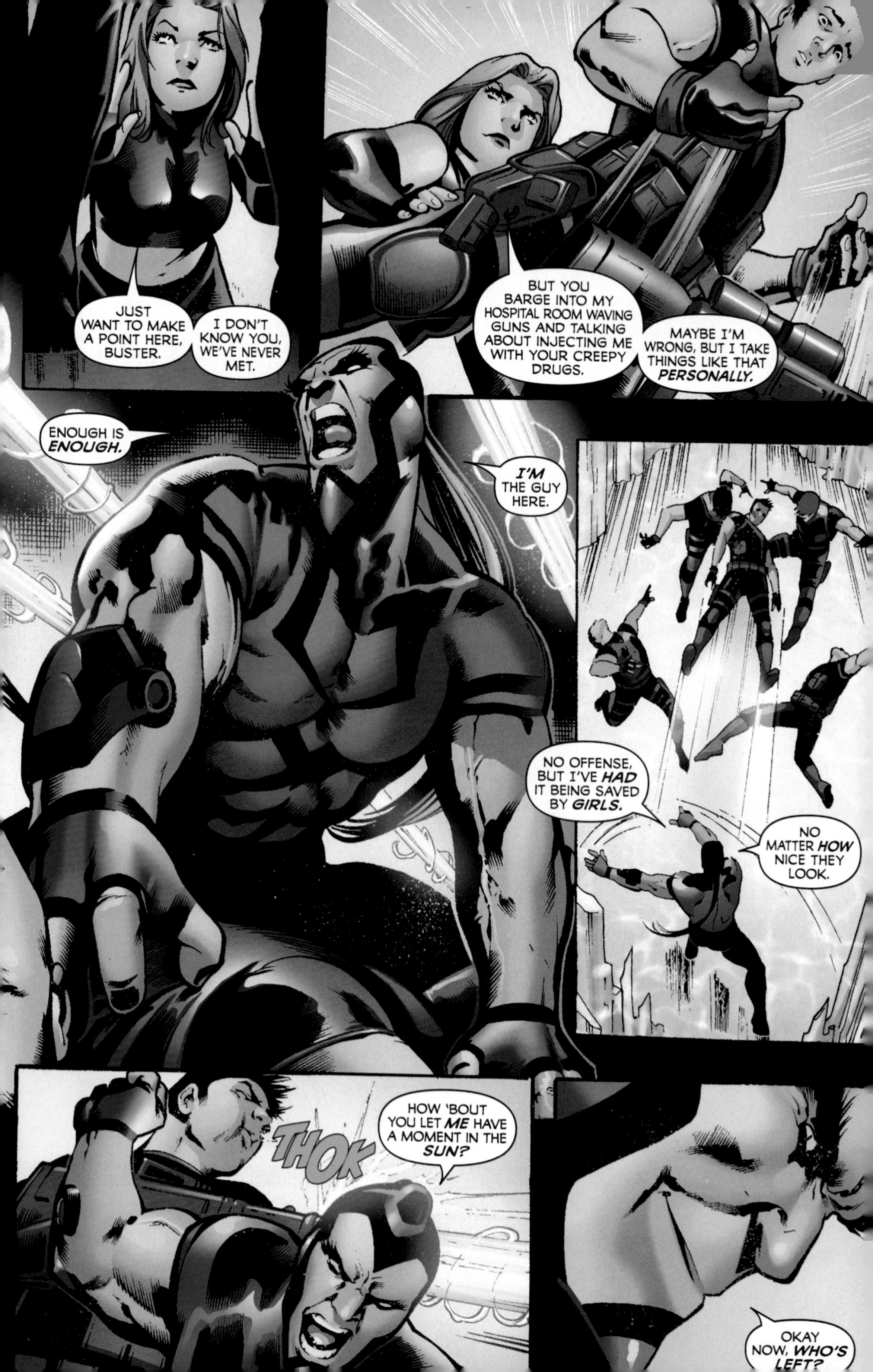
JUST WANT TO MAKE A POINT HERE, BUSTER.
I DON'T KNOW YOU, WE'VE NEVER MET.
BUT YOU BARGE INTO MY HOSPITAL ROOM WAVING GUNS AND TALKING ABOUT INJECTING ME WITH YOUR CREEPY DRUGS.
MAYBE I'M WRONG, BUT I TAKE THINGS LIKE THAT *PERSONALLY.*
ENOUGH IS *ENOUGH.*
I'M THE GUY HERE.
NO OFFENSE, BUT I'VE *HAD* IT BEING SAVED BY *GIRLS.*
NO MATTER *HOW* NICE THEY LOOK.
HOW 'BOUT YOU LET *ME* HAVE A MOMENT IN THE *SUN?*
THOK
OKAY NOW, *WHO'S LEFT?*

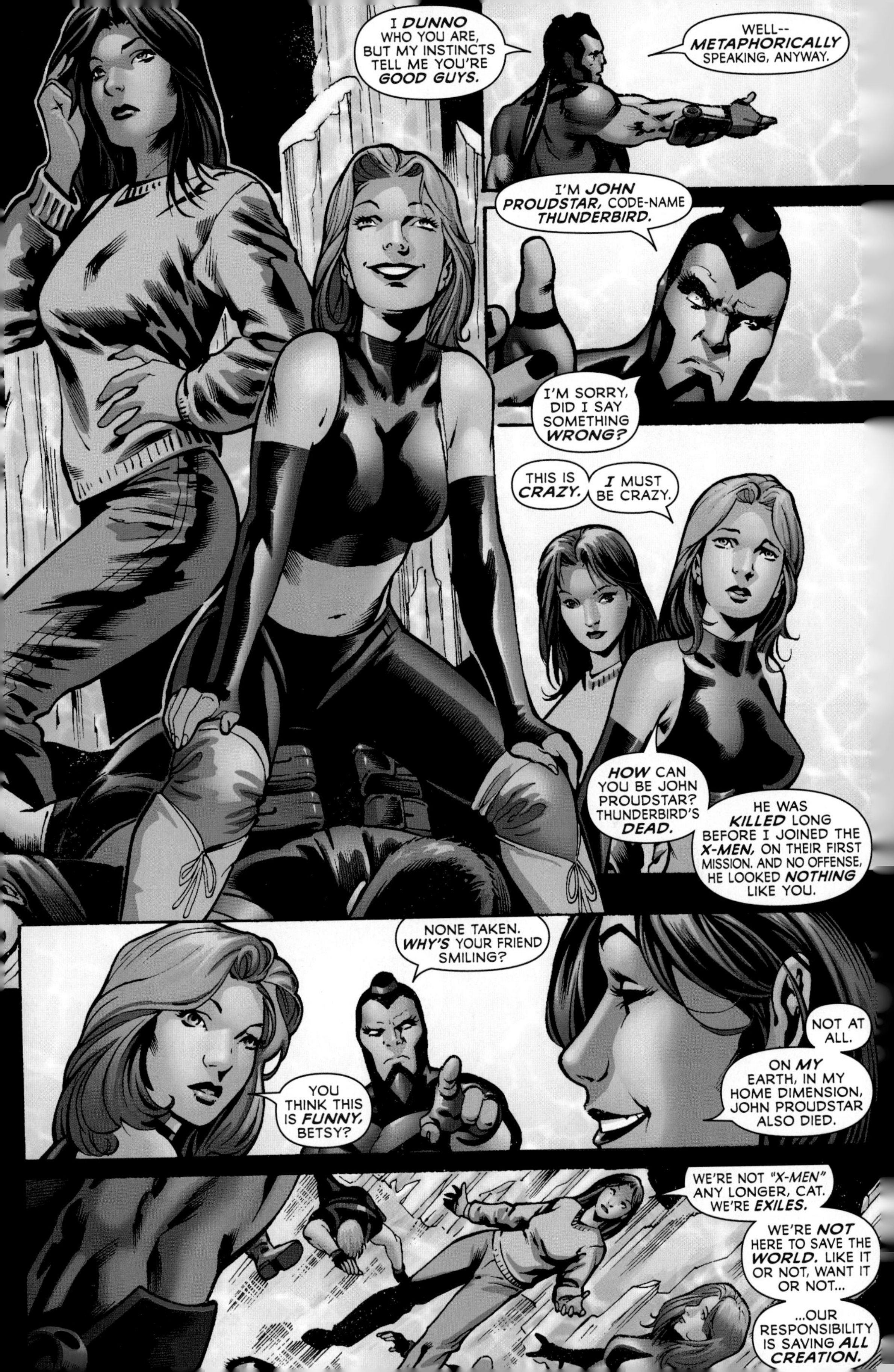
I DUNNO WHO YOU ARE, BUT MY INSTINCTS TELL ME YOU'RE GOOD GUYS.
WELL-- METAPHORICALLY SPEAKING, ANYWAY.
I'M JOHN PROUDSTAR, CODE-NAME THUNDERBIRD.
I'M SORRY, DID I SAY SOMETHING WRONG?
THIS IS CRAZY.
I MUST BE CRAZY.
HOW CAN YOU BE JOHN PROUDSTAR? THUNDERBIRD'S DEAD.
HE WAS KILLED LONG BEFORE I JOINED THE X-MEN, ON THEIR FIRST MISSION. AND NO OFFENSE, HE LOOKED NOTHING LIKE YOU.
NONE TAKEN. WHY'S YOUR FRIEND SMILING?
YOU THINK THIS IS FUNNY, BETSY?
NOT AT ALL.
ON MY EARTH, IN MY HOME DIMENSION, JOHN PROUDSTAR ALSO DIED.
WE'RE NOT "X-MEN" ANY LONGER, CAT. WE'RE EXILES.
WE'RE NOT HERE TO SAVE THE WORLD. LIKE IT OR NOT, WANT IT OR NOT...
...OUR RESPONSIBILITY IS SAVING ALL CREATION.

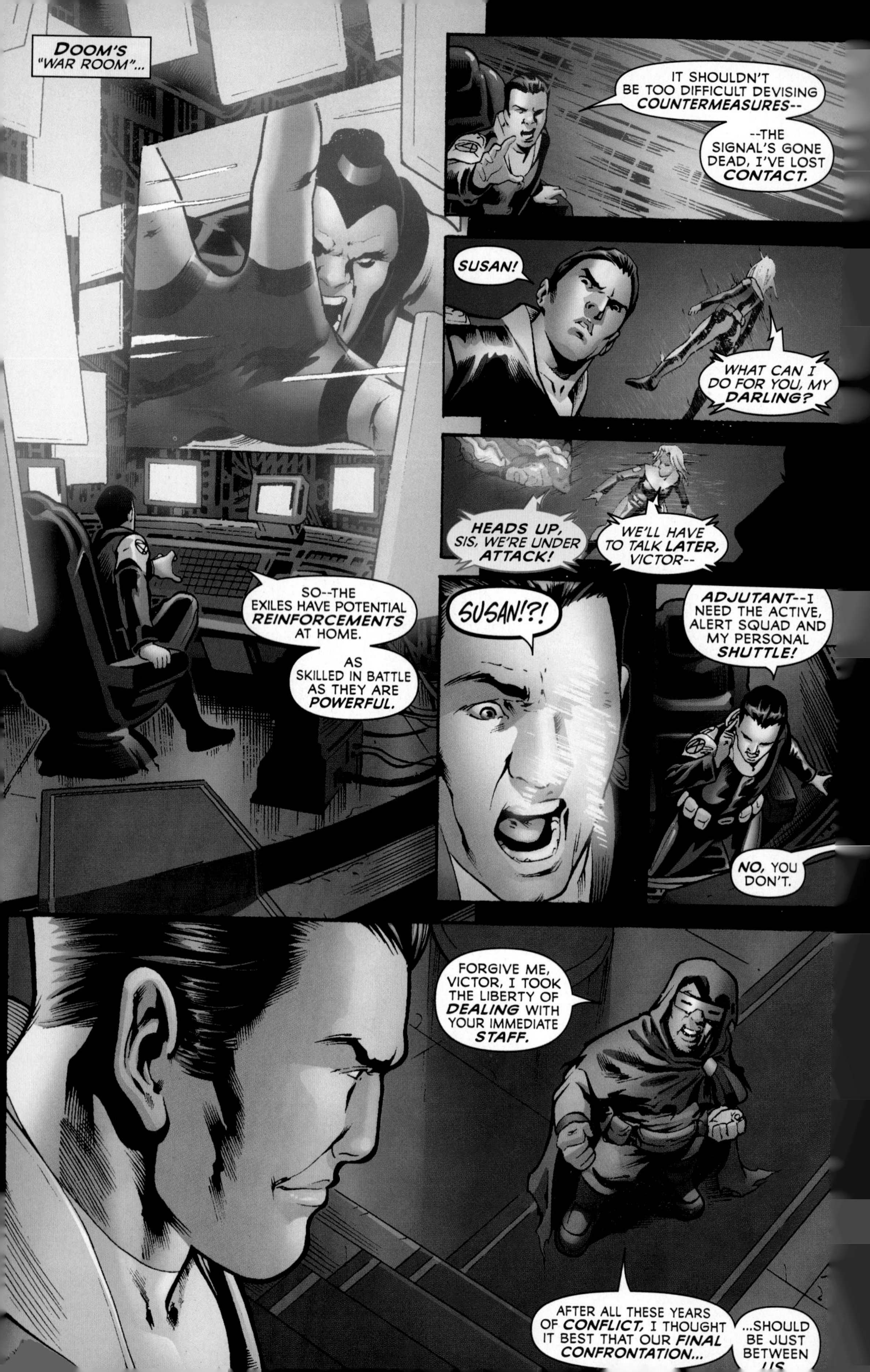
DOOM'S "WAR ROOM"...
SO--THE EXILES HAVE POTENTIAL REINFORCEMENTS AT HOME.
AS SKILLED IN BATTLE AS THEY ARE POWERFUL.
IT SHOULDN'T BE TOO DIFFICULT DEVISING COUNTERMEASURES--
--THE SIGNAL'S GONE DEAD, I'VE LOST CONTACT.
SUSAN!
WHAT CAN I DO FOR YOU, MY DARLING?
HEADS UP, SIS, WE'RE UNDER ATTACK!
WE'LL HAVE TO TALK LATER, VICTOR--
SUSAN!?!
ADJUTANT--I NEED THE ACTIVE, ALERT SQUAD AND MY PERSONAL SHUTTLE!
NO, YOU DON'T.
FORGIVE ME, VICTOR, I TOOK THE LIBERTY OF DEALING WITH YOUR IMMEDIATE STAFF.
AFTER ALL THESE YEARS OF CONFLICT, I THOUGHT IT BEST THAT OUR FINAL CONFRONTATION...
...SHOULD BE JUST BETWEEN US.

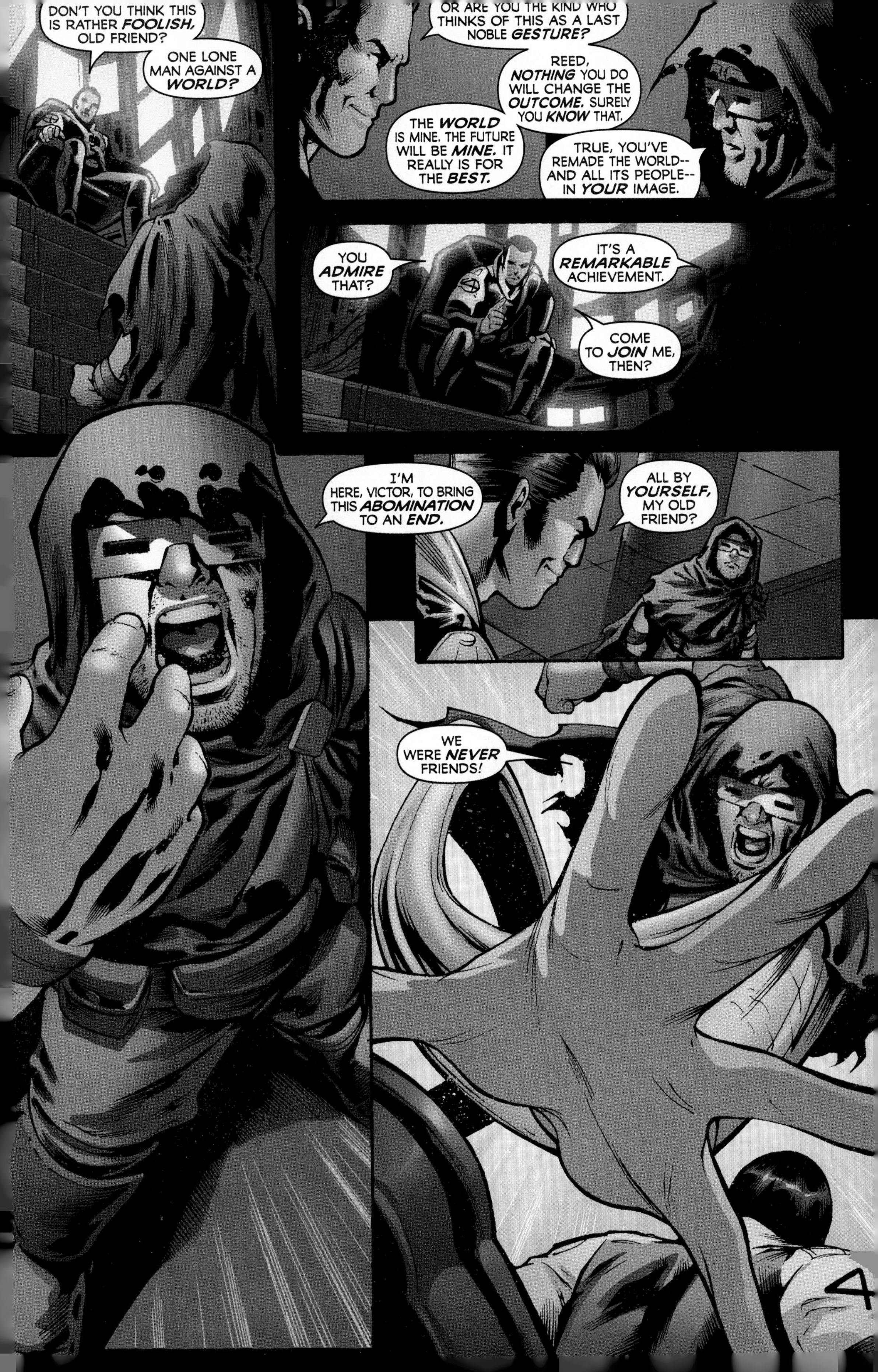

DON'T YOU THINK THIS IS RATHER FOOLISH, OLD FRIEND?
ONE LONE MAN AGAINST A WORLD?
OR ARE YOU THE KIND WHO THINKS OF THIS AS A LAST NOBLE GESTURE?
REED, NOTHING YOU DO WILL CHANGE THE OUTCOME. SURELY YOU KNOW THAT.
THE WORLD IS MINE. THE FUTURE WILL BE MINE. IT REALLY IS FOR THE BEST.
TRUE, YOU'VE REMADE THE WORLD-- AND ALL ITS PEOPLE-- IN YOUR IMAGE.
YOU ADMIRE THAT?
IT'S A REMARKABLE ACHIEVEMENT.
COME TO JOIN ME, THEN?
I'M HERE, VICTOR, TO BRING THIS ABOMINATION TO AN END.
ALL BY YOURSELF, MY OLD FRIEND?
WE WERE NEVER FRIENDS!

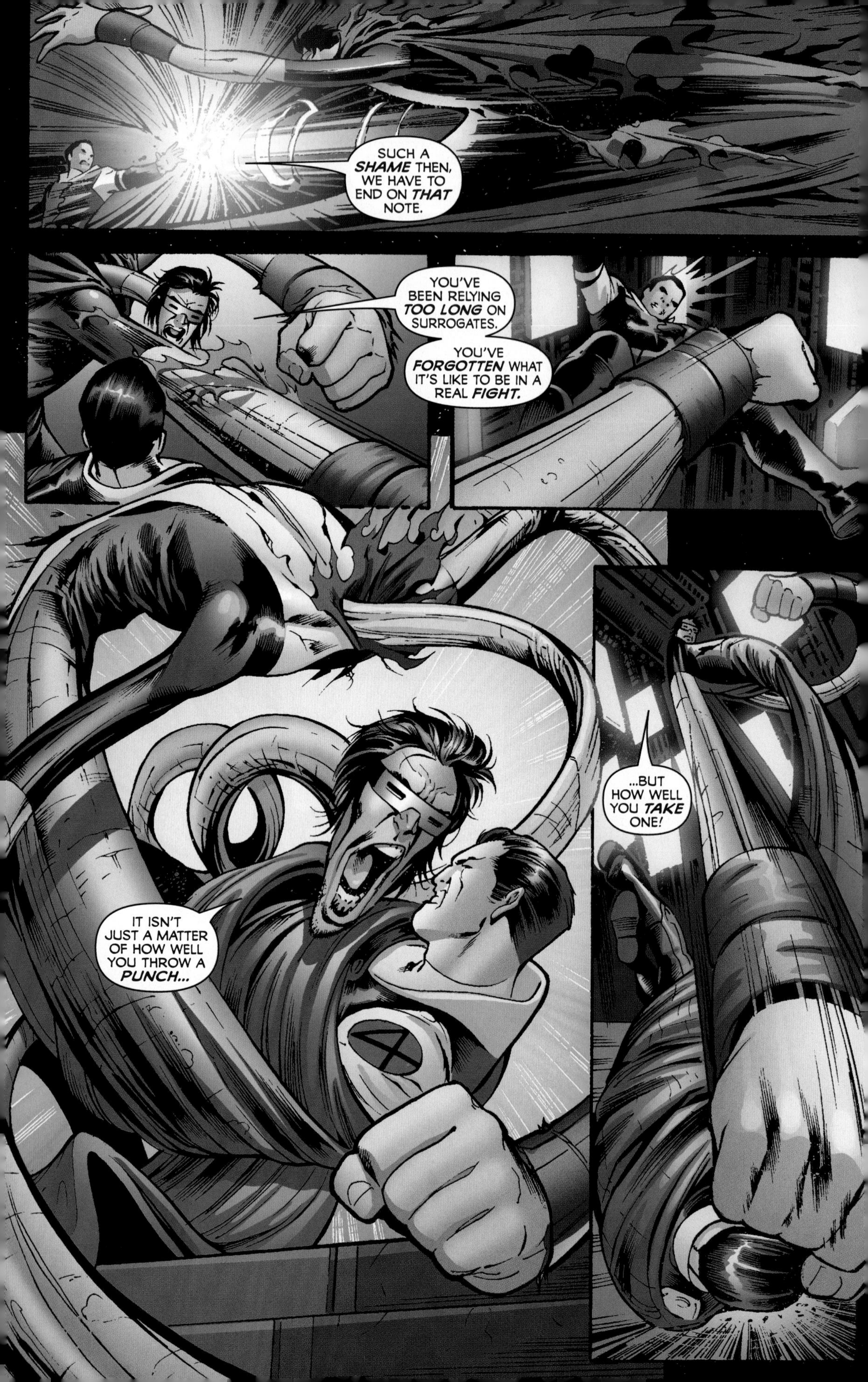

SUCH A *SHAME* THEN, WE HAVE TO END ON *THAT* NOTE.
YOU'VE BEEN RELYING *TOO LONG* ON SURROGATES.
YOU'VE *FORGOTTEN* WHAT IT'S LIKE TO BE IN A REAL *FIGHT.*
IT ISN'T JUST A MATTER OF HOW WELL YOU THROW A *PUNCH...*
...BUT HOW WELL YOU *TAKE* ONE!

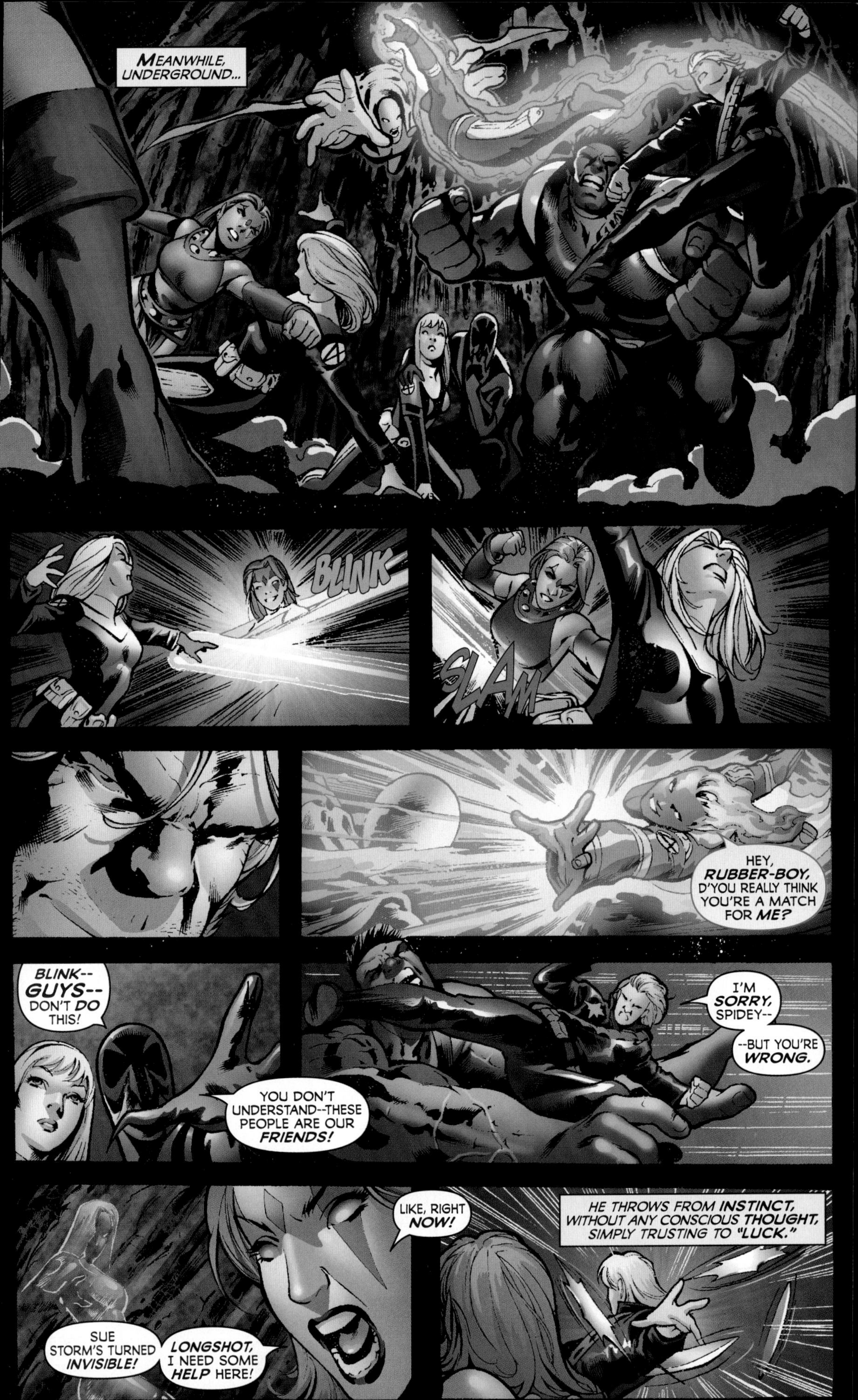
MEANWHILE, UNDERGROUND...
BLINK
SLAM
HEY, RUBBER-BOY, D'YOU REALLY THINK YOU'RE A MATCH FOR ME?
BLINK-- GUYS-- DON'T DO THIS!
YOU DON'T UNDERSTAND--THESE PEOPLE ARE OUR FRIENDS!
I'M SORRY, SPIDEY--
--BUT YOU'RE WRONG.
SUE STORM'S TURNED INVISIBLE!
LONGSHOT, I NEED SOME HELP HERE!
LIKE, RIGHT NOW!
HE THROWS FROM INSTINCT, WITHOUT ANY CONSCIOUS THOUGHT, SIMPLY TRUSTING TO "LUCK."

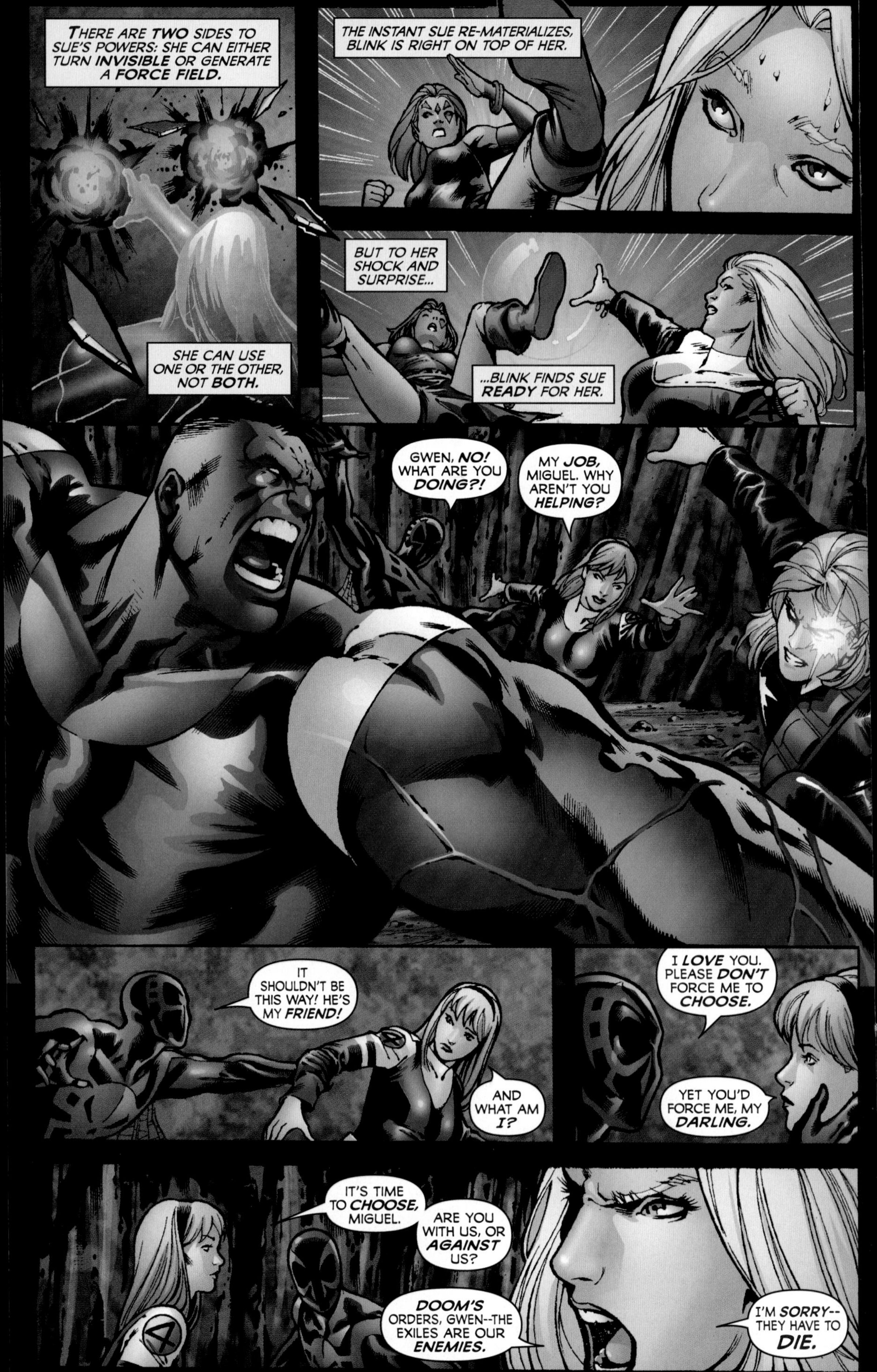
THERE ARE TWO SIDES TO SUE'S POWERS: SHE CAN EITHER TURN INVISIBLE OR GENERATE A FORCE FIELD.
SHE CAN USE ONE OR THE OTHER, NOT BOTH.
THE INSTANT SUE RE-MATERIALIZES, BLINK IS RIGHT ON TOP OF HER.
BUT TO HER SHOCK AND SURPRISE...
...BLINK FINDS SUE READY FOR HER.
GWEN, NO! WHAT ARE YOU DOING?!
MY JOB, MIGUEL. WHY AREN'T YOU HELPING?
IT SHOULDN'T BE THIS WAY! HE'S MY FRIEND!
AND WHAT AM I?
I LOVE YOU. PLEASE DON'T FORCE ME TO CHOOSE.
YET YOU'D FORCE ME, MY DARLING.
IT'S TIME TO CHOOSE, MIGUEL.
ARE YOU WITH US, OR AGAINST US?
DOOM'S ORDERS, GWEN--THE EXILES ARE OUR ENEMIES.
I'M SORRY-- THEY HAVE TO DIE.

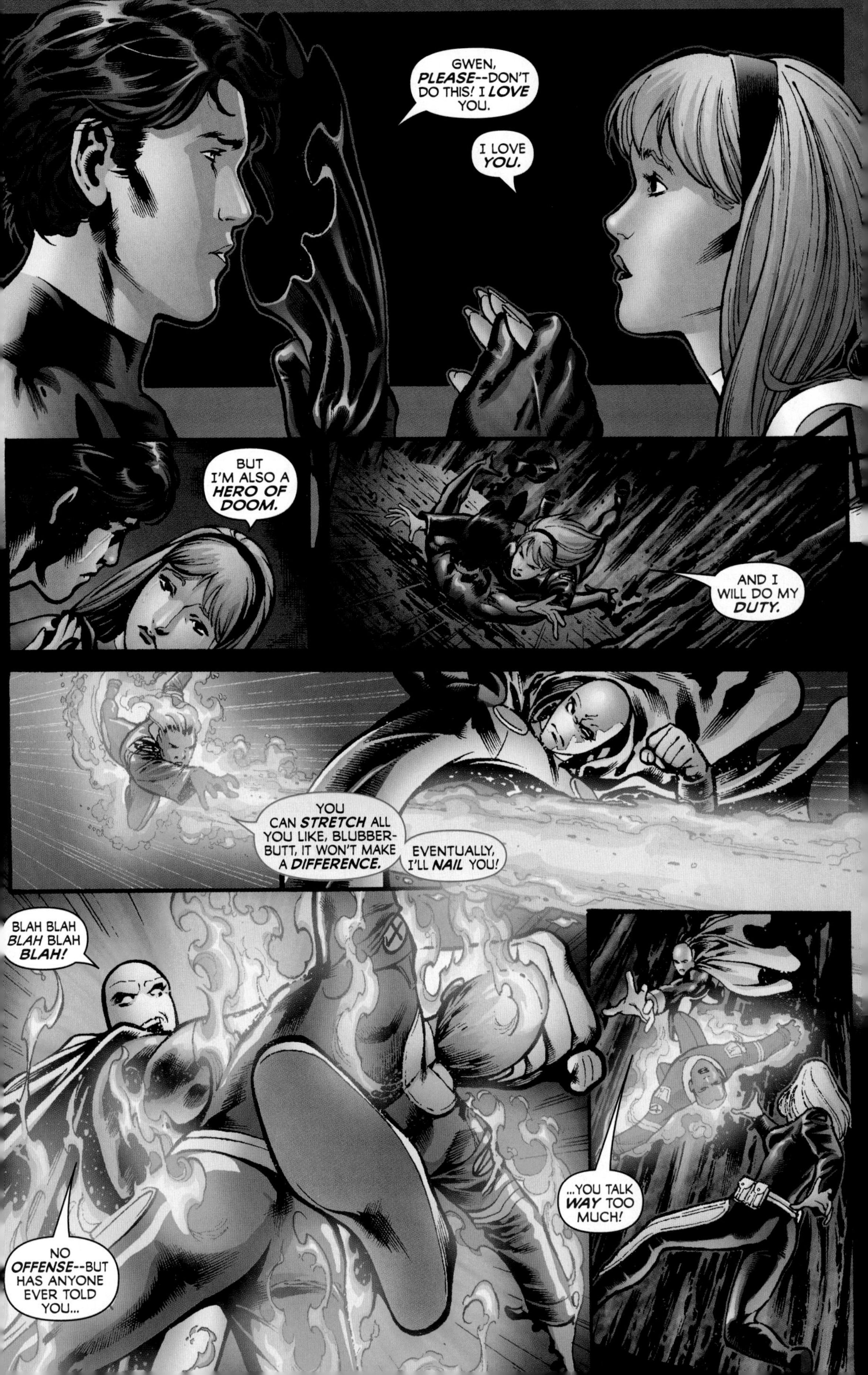
GWEN, PLEASE--DON'T DO THIS! I LOVE YOU.
I LOVE YOU.
BUT I'M ALSO A HERO OF DOOM.
AND I WILL DO MY DUTY.
YOU CAN STRETCH ALL YOU LIKE, BLUBBER-BUTT, IT WON'T MAKE A DIFFERENCE.
EVENTUALLY, I'LL NAIL YOU!
BLAH BLAH BLAH BLAH BLAH!
NO OFFENSE--BUT HAS ANYONE EVER TOLD YOU...
...YOU TALK WAY TOO MUCH!

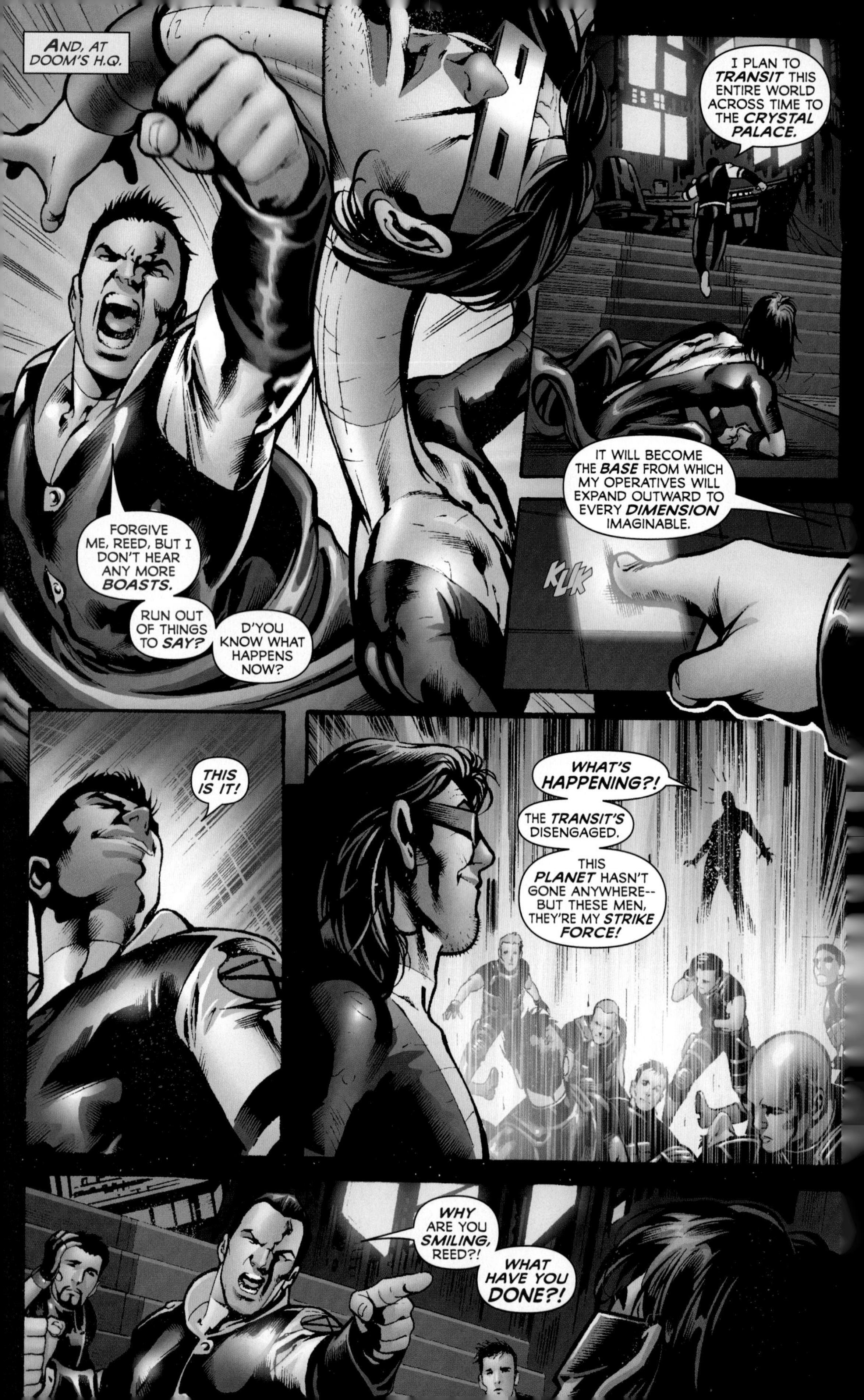
AND, AT DOOM'S H.Q.
I PLAN TO TRANSIT THIS ENTIRE WORLD ACROSS TIME TO THE CRYSTAL PALACE.
IT WILL BECOME THE BASE FROM WHICH MY OPERATIVES WILL EXPAND OUTWARD TO EVERY DIMENSION IMAGINABLE.
KLIK
FORGIVE ME, REED, BUT I DON'T HEAR ANY MORE BOASTS.
RUN OUT OF THINGS TO SAY?
D'YOU KNOW WHAT HAPPENS NOW?
THIS IS IT!
WHAT'S HAPPENING?!
THE TRANSIT'S DISENGAGED.
THIS PLANET HASN'T GONE ANYWHERE-- BUT THESE MEN, THEY'RE MY STRIKE FORCE!
WHY ARE YOU SMILING, REED?!
WHAT HAVE YOU DONE?!

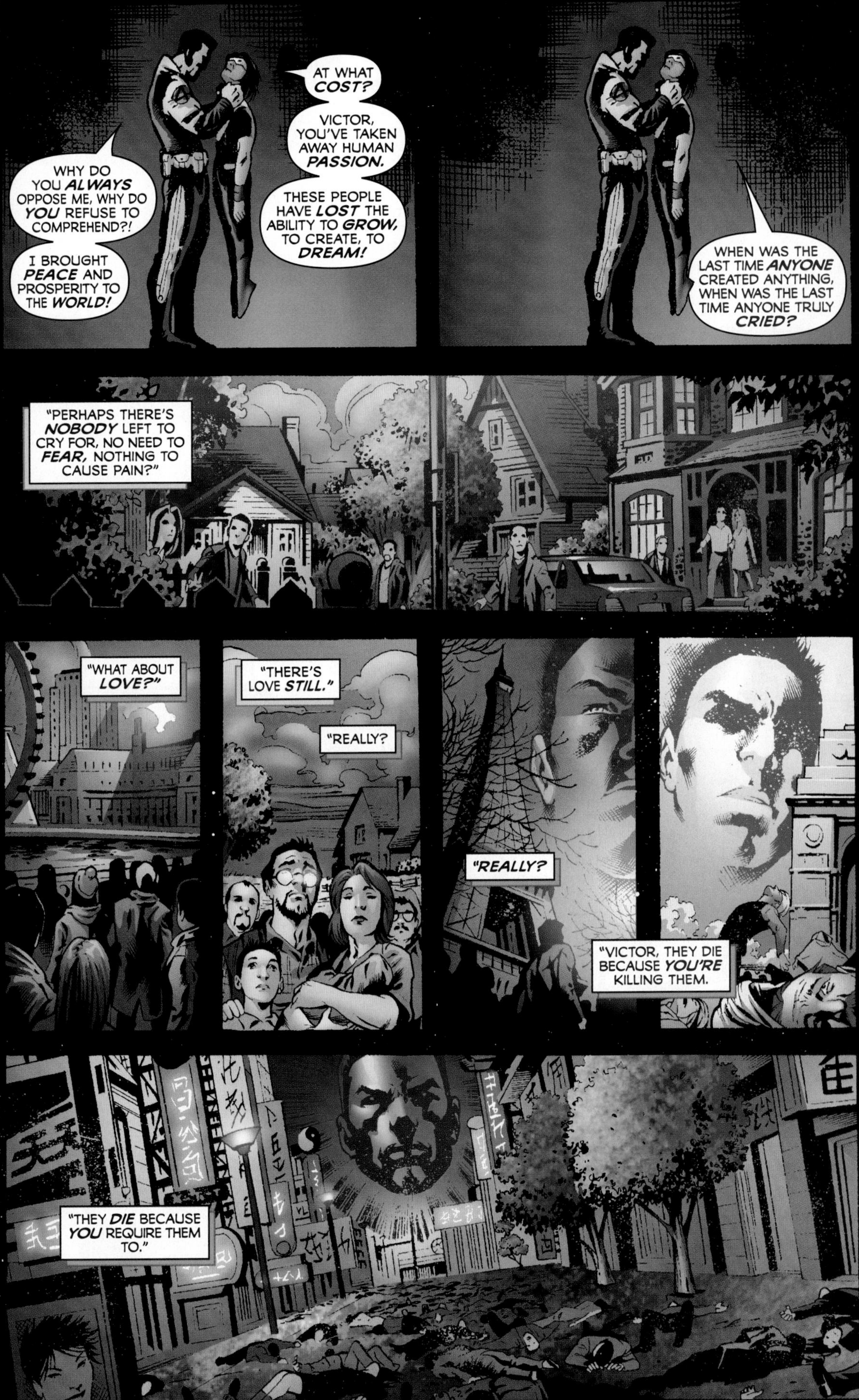
WHY DO YOU ALWAYS OPPOSE ME, WHY DO YOU REFUSE TO COMPREHEND?!
I BROUGHT PEACE AND PROSPERITY TO THE WORLD!
AT WHAT COST?
VICTOR, YOU'VE TAKEN AWAY HUMAN PASSION.
THESE PEOPLE HAVE LOST THE ABILITY TO GROW, TO CREATE, TO DREAM!
WHEN WAS THE LAST TIME ANYONE CREATED ANYTHING, WHEN WAS THE LAST TIME ANYONE TRULY CRIED?
"PERHAPS THERE'S NOBODY LEFT TO CRY FOR, NO NEED TO FEAR, NOTHING TO CAUSE PAIN?"
"WHAT ABOUT LOVE?"
"THERE'S LOVE STILL."
"REALLY?
"REALLY?
"VICTOR, THEY DIE BECAUSE YOU'RE KILLING THEM.
"THEY DIE BECAUSE YOU REQUIRE THEM TO."

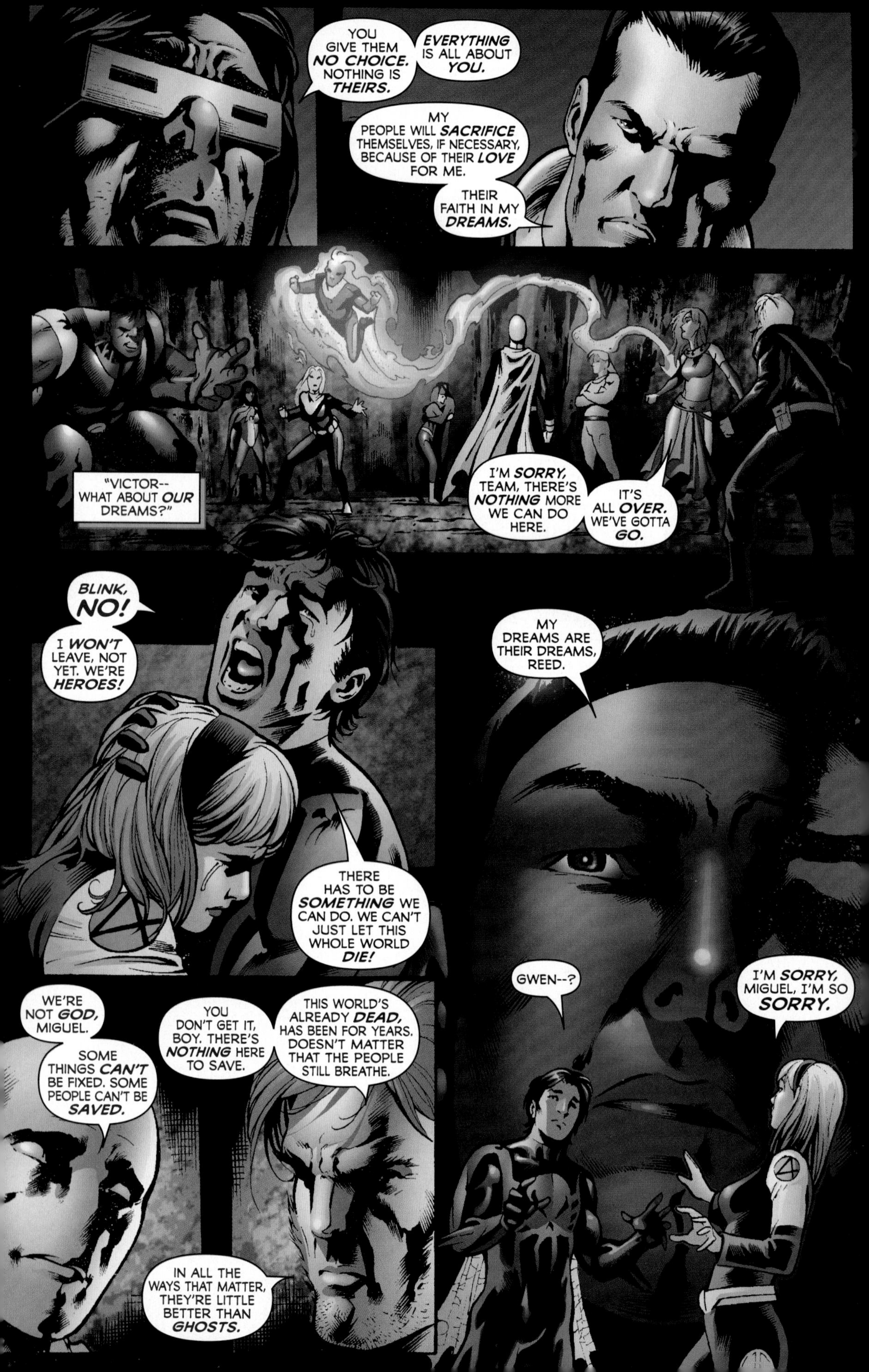
YOU GIVE THEM NO CHOICE. NOTHING IS THEIRS.
EVERYTHING IS ALL ABOUT YOU.
MY PEOPLE WILL SACRIFICE THEMSELVES, IF NECESSARY, BECAUSE OF THEIR LOVE FOR ME.
THEIR FAITH IN MY DREAMS.
"VICTOR-- WHAT ABOUT OUR DREAMS?"
I'M SORRY, TEAM, THERE'S NOTHING MORE WE CAN DO HERE.
IT'S ALL OVER. WE'VE GOTTA GO.
BLINK, NO!
I WON'T LEAVE, NOT YET. WE'RE HEROES!
THERE HAS TO BE SOMETHING WE CAN DO. WE CAN'T JUST LET THIS WHOLE WORLD DIE!
MY DREAMS ARE THEIR DREAMS, REED.
WE'RE NOT GOD, MIGUEL.
SOME THINGS CAN'T BE FIXED. SOME PEOPLE CAN'T BE SAVED.
YOU DON'T GET IT, BOY. THERE'S NOTHING HERE TO SAVE.
THIS WORLD'S ALREADY DEAD, HAS BEEN FOR YEARS. DOESN'T MATTER THAT THE PEOPLE STILL BREATHE.
IN ALL THE WAYS THAT MATTER, THEY'RE LITTLE BETTER THAN GHOSTS.
GWEN--?
I'M SORRY, MIGUEL, I'M SO SORRY.

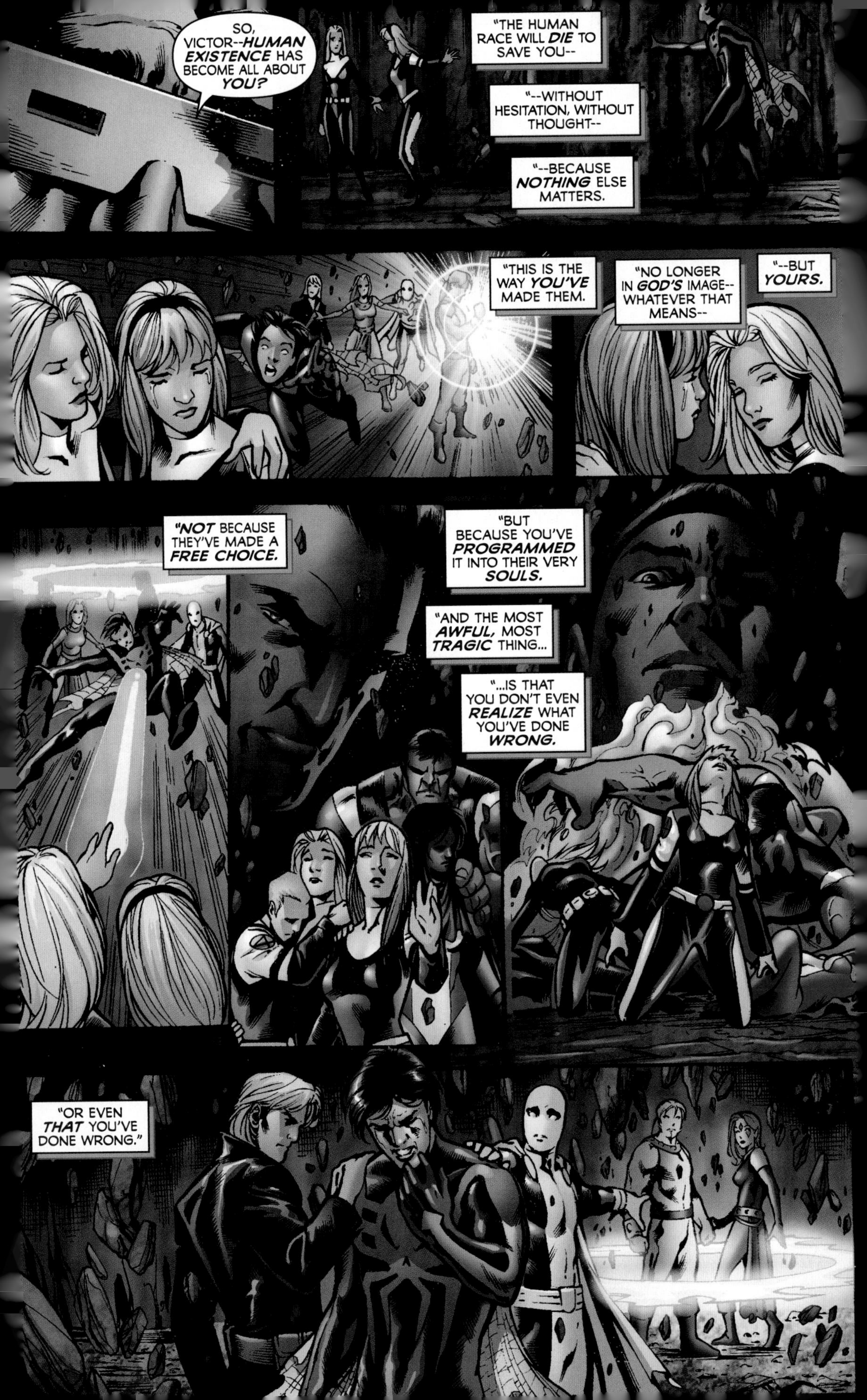
SO, VICTOR--HUMAN EXISTENCE HAS BECOME ALL ABOUT YOU?
"THE HUMAN RACE WILL DIE TO SAVE YOU--
"--WITHOUT HESITATION, WITHOUT THOUGHT--
"--BECAUSE NOTHING ELSE MATTERS.
"THIS IS THE WAY YOU'VE MADE THEM.
"NO LONGER IN GOD'S IMAGE--WHATEVER THAT MEANS--
"--BUT YOURS.
"NOT BECAUSE THEY'VE MADE A FREE CHOICE.
"BUT BECAUSE YOU'VE PROGRAMMED IT INTO THEIR VERY SOULS.
"AND THE MOST AWFUL, MOST TRAGIC THING...
"...IS THAT YOU DON'T EVEN REALIZE WHAT YOU'VE DONE WRONG.
"OR EVEN THAT YOU'VE DONE WRONG."

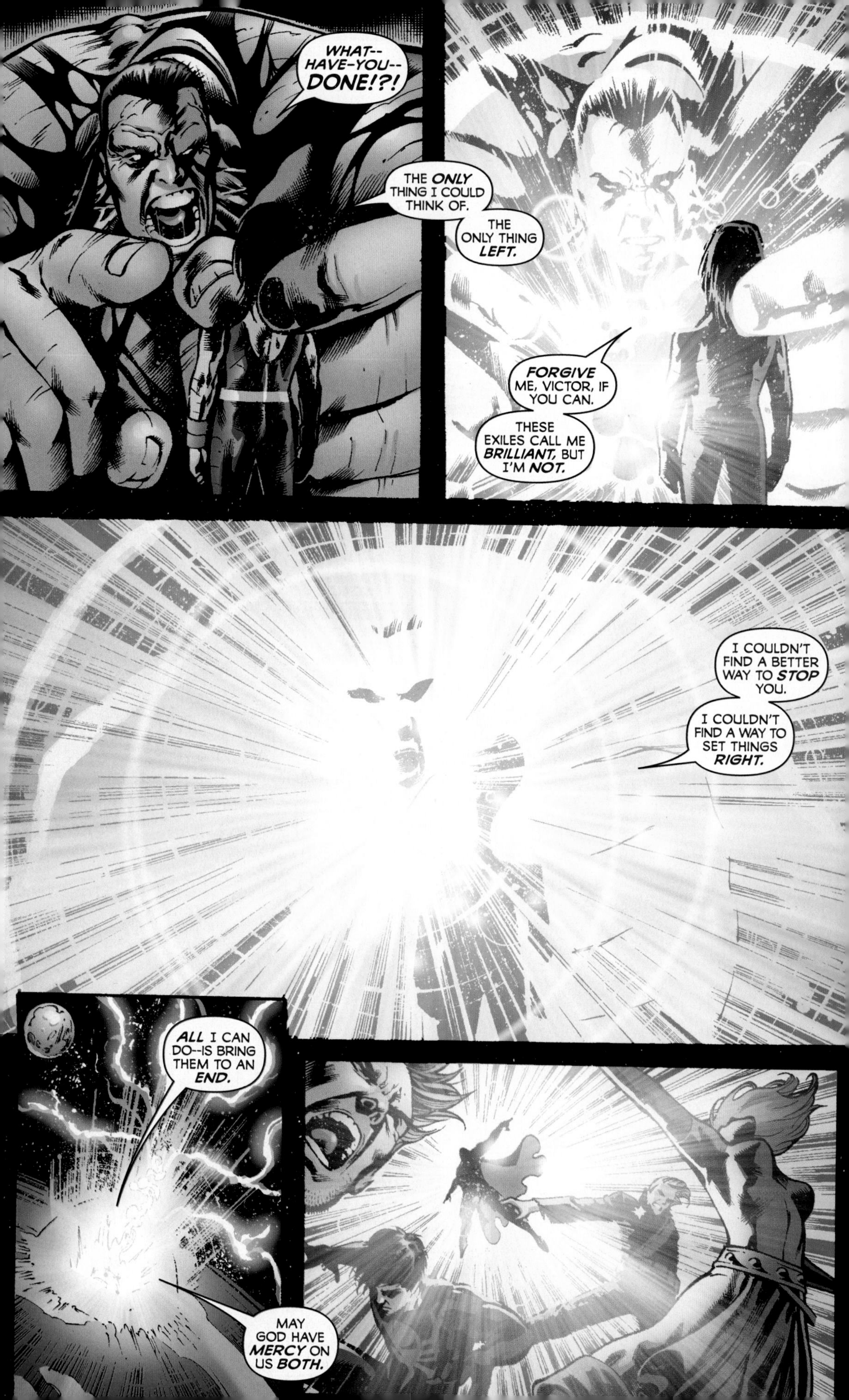
WHAT-- HAVE-YOU-- DONE!?!
THE ONLY THING I COULD THINK OF.
THE ONLY THING LEFT.
FORGIVE ME, VICTOR, IF YOU CAN.
THESE EXILES CALL ME BRILLIANT, BUT I'M NOT.
I COULDN'T FIND A BETTER WAY TO STOP YOU.
I COULDN'T FIND A WAY TO SET THINGS RIGHT.
ALL I CAN DO--IS BRING THEM TO AN END.
MAY GOD HAVE MERCY ON US BOTH.

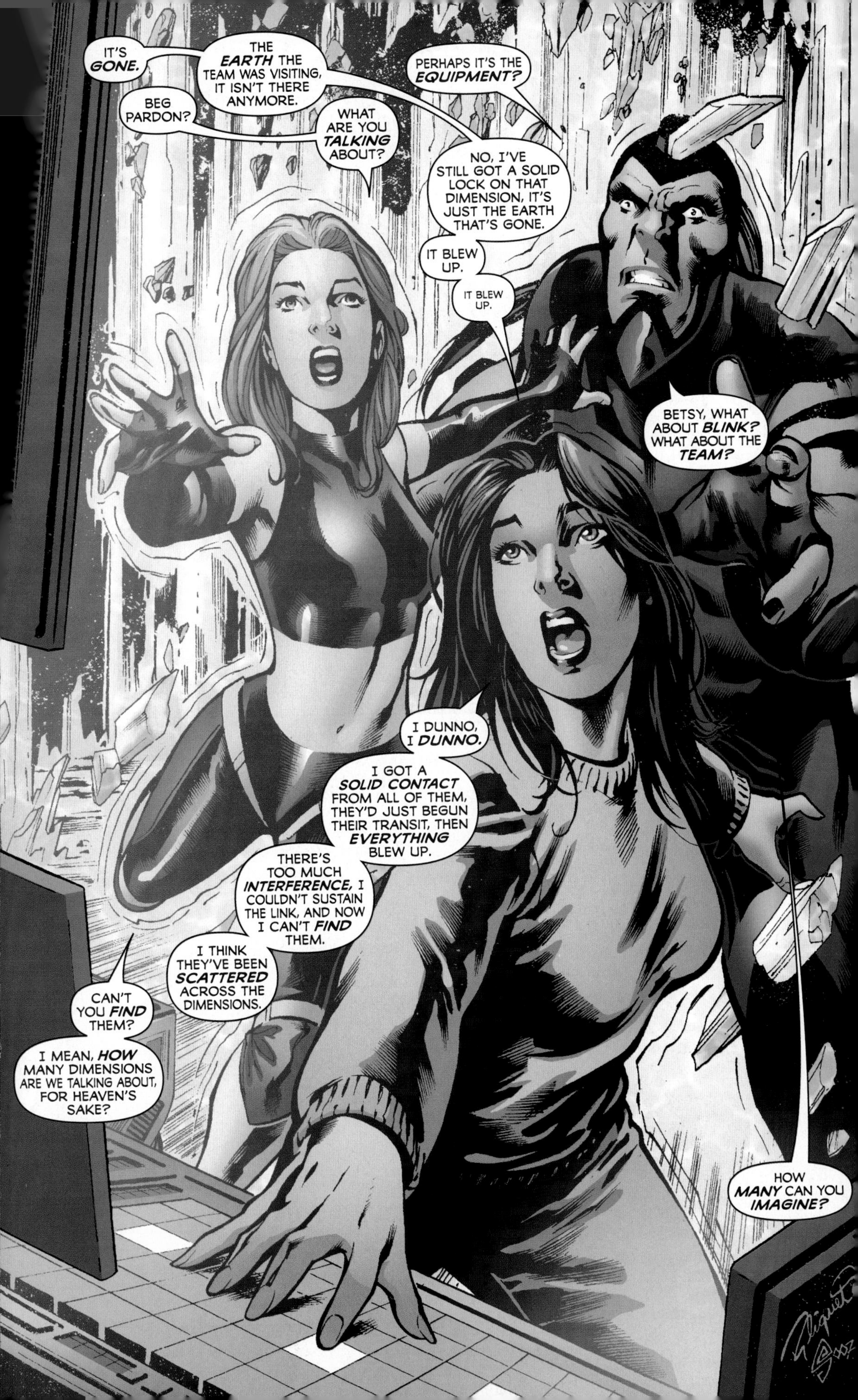
IT'S GONE.
THE EARTH THE TEAM WAS VISITING, IT ISN'T THERE ANYMORE.
BEG PARDON?
WHAT ARE YOU TALKING ABOUT?
PERHAPS IT'S THE EQUIPMENT?
NO, I'VE STILL GOT A SOLID LOCK ON THAT DIMENSION, IT'S JUST THE EARTH THAT'S GONE.
IT BLEW UP.
IT BLEW UP.
BETSY, WHAT ABOUT BLINK? WHAT ABOUT THE TEAM?
I DUNNO, I DUNNO.
I GOT A SOLID CONTACT FROM ALL OF THEM, THEY'D JUST BEGUN THEIR TRANSIT, THEN EVERYTHING BLEW UP.
THERE'S TOO MUCH INTERFERENCE, I COULDN'T SUSTAIN THE LINK, AND NOW I CAN'T FIND THEM.
I THINK THEY'VE BEEN SCATTERED ACROSS THE DIMENSIONS.
CAN'T YOU FIND THEM?
I MEAN, HOW MANY DIMENSIONS ARE WE TALKING ABOUT, FOR HEAVEN'S SAKE?
HOW MANY CAN YOU IMAGINE?

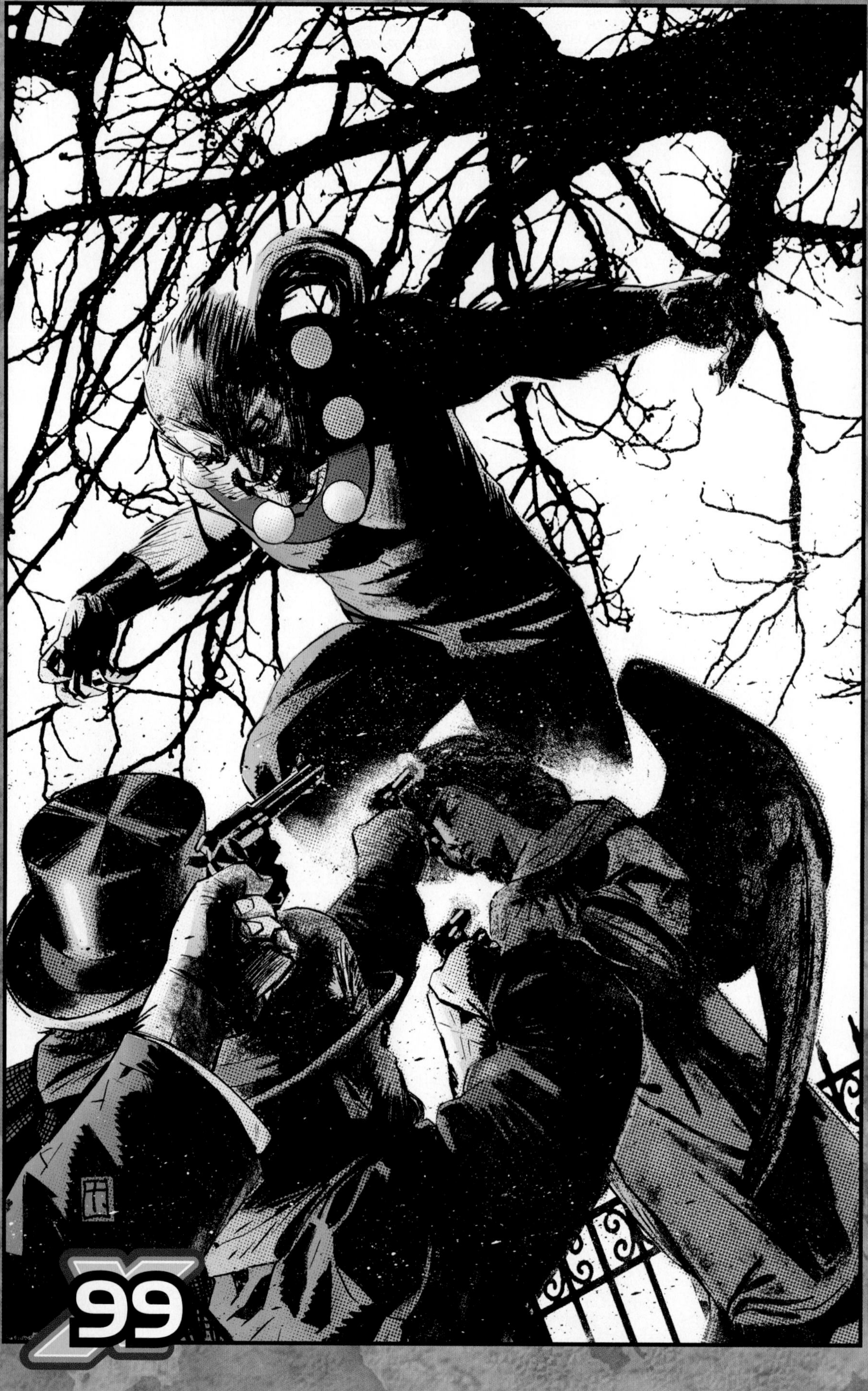

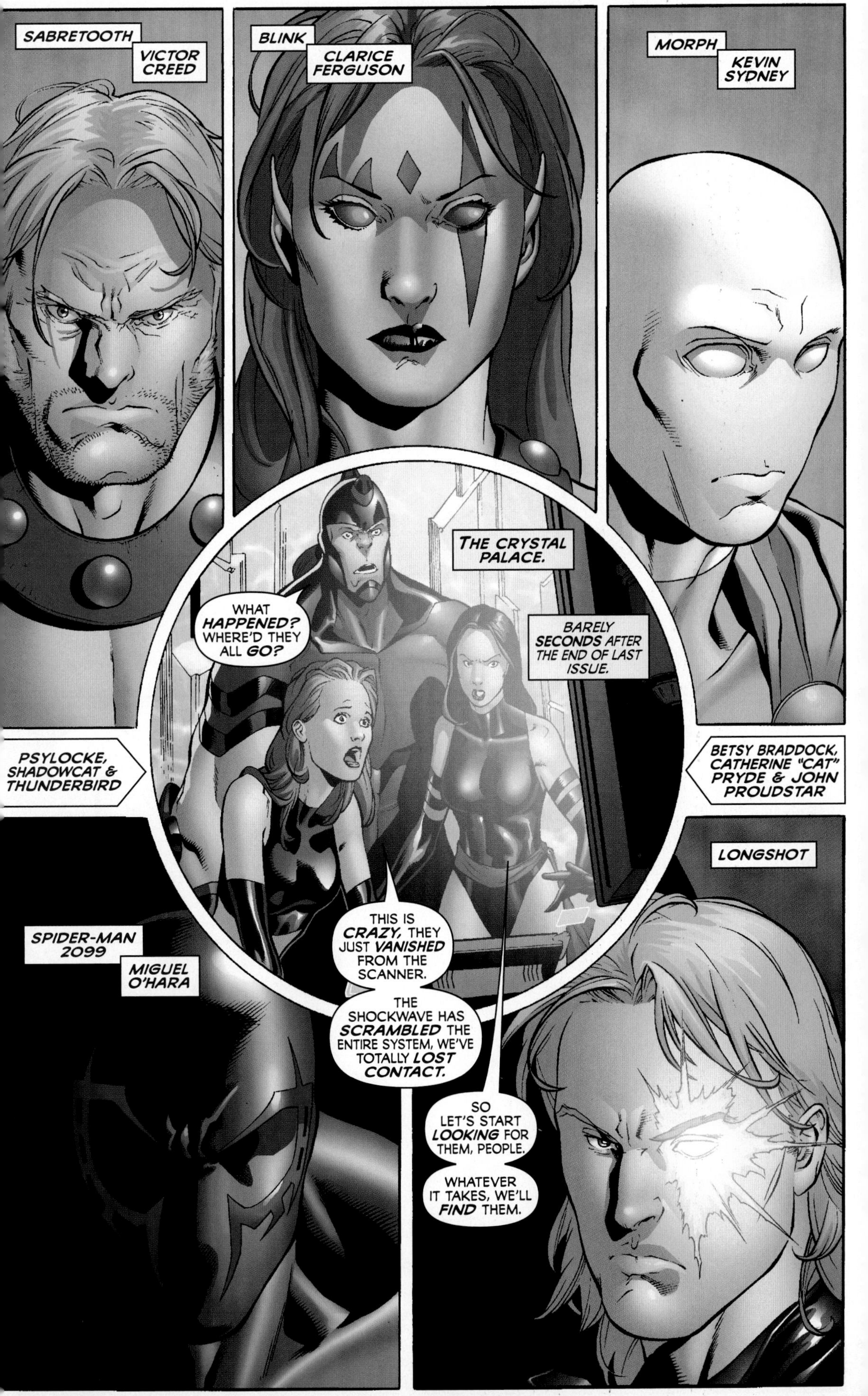
SABRETOOTH
VICTOR CREED
BLINK
CLARICE FERGUSON
MORPH
KEVIN SYDNEY
THE CRYSTAL PALACE.
BARELY SECONDS AFTER THE END OF LAST ISSUE.
WHAT HAPPENED? WHERE'D THEY ALL GO?
PSYLOCKE, SHADOWCAT & THUNDERBIRD
BETSY BRADDOCK, CATHERINE "CAT" PRYDE & JOHN PROUDSTAR
THIS IS CRAZY, THEY JUST VANISHED FROM THE SCANNER.
THE SHOCKWAVE HAS SCRAMBLED THE ENTIRE SYSTEM, WE'VE TOTALLY LOST CONTACT.
SO LET'S START LOOKING FOR THEM, PEOPLE.
WHATEVER IT TAKES, WE'LL FIND THEM.
LONGSHOT
SPIDER-MAN 2099
MIGUEL O'HARA

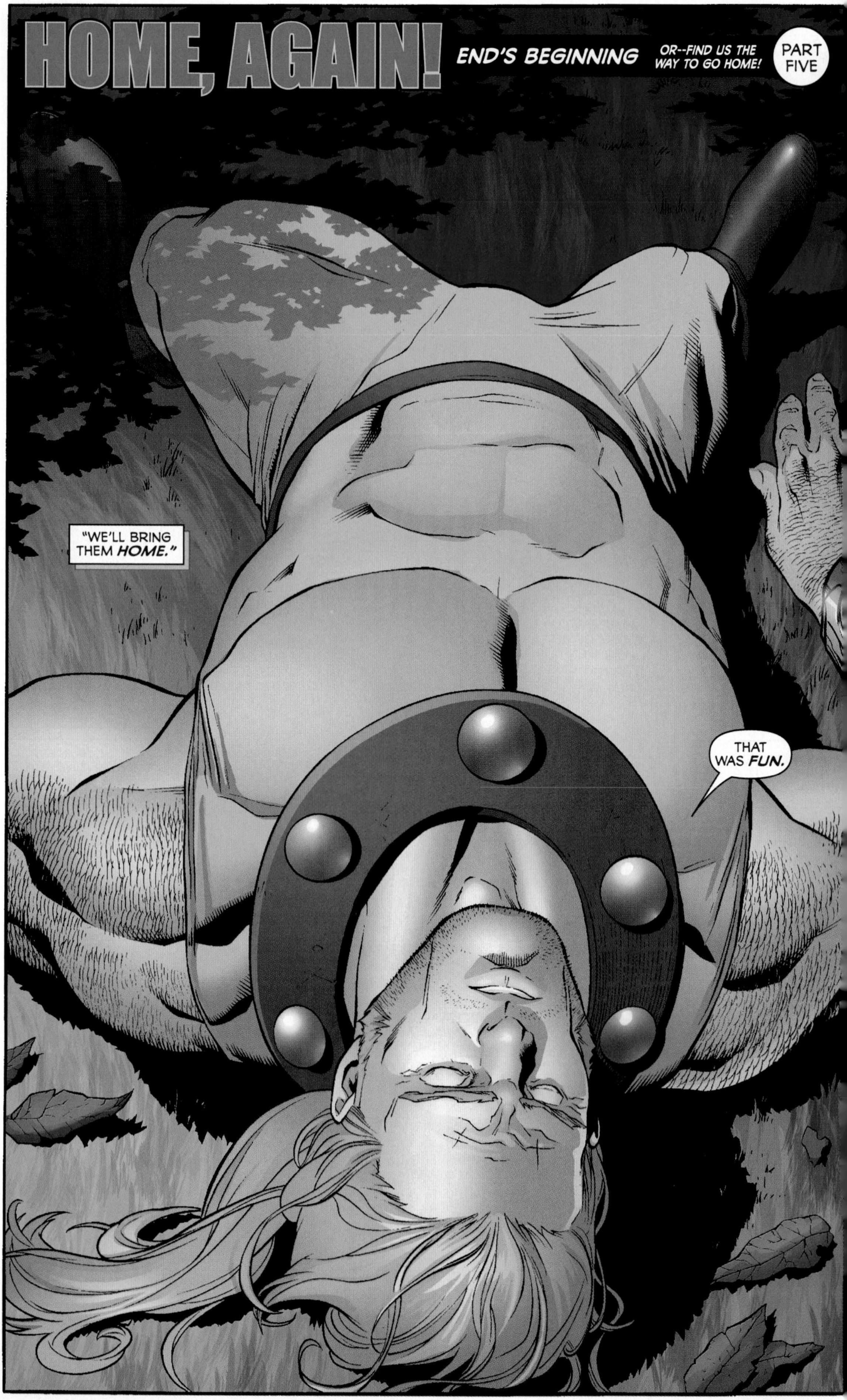
HOME, AGAIN!
END'S BEGINNING
OR--FIND US THE WAY TO GO HOME!
PART FIVE
"WE'LL BRING THEM HOME."
THAT WAS FUN.

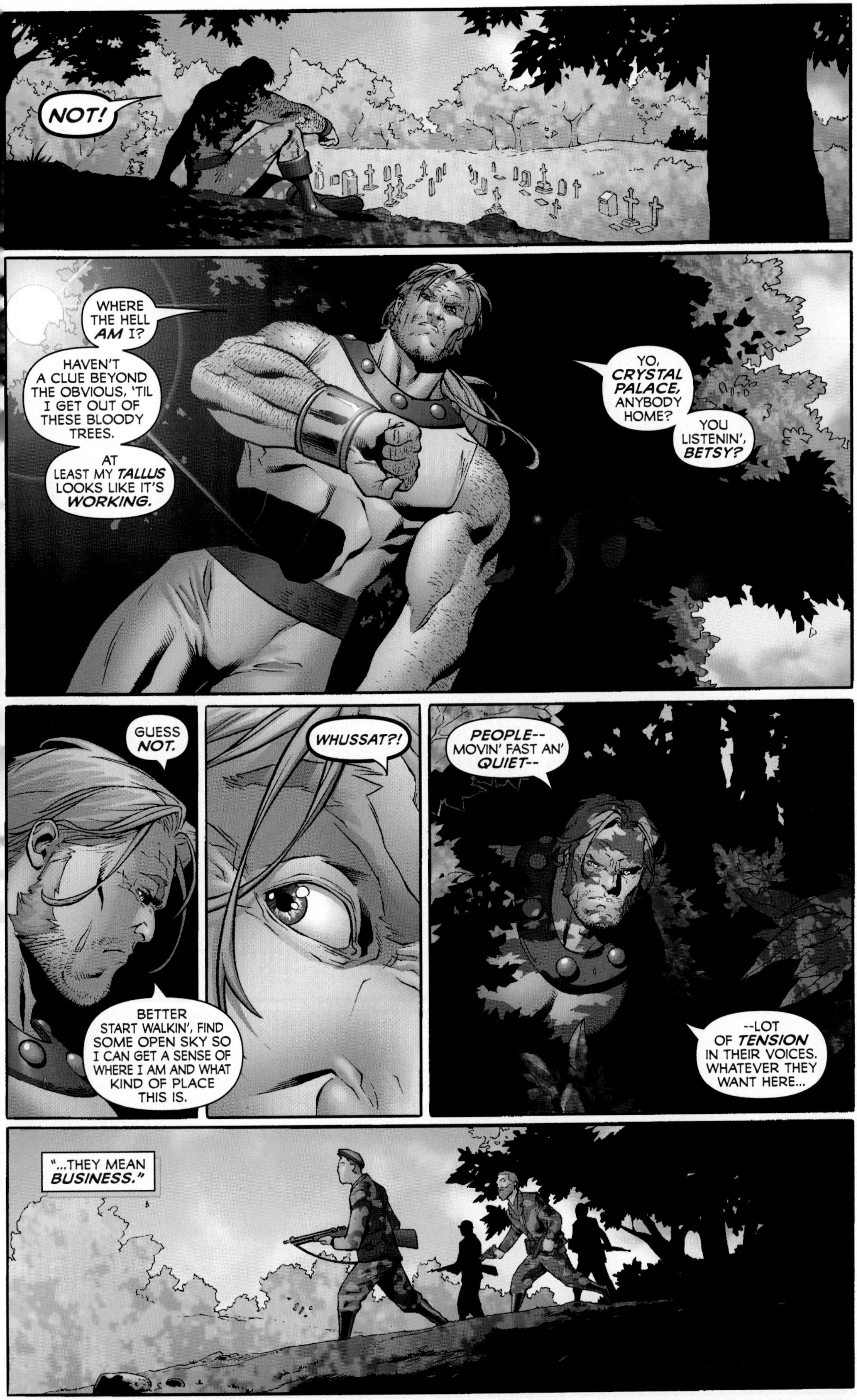
NOT!
WHERE THE HELL AM I?
HAVEN'T A CLUE BEYOND THE OBVIOUS, 'TIL I GET OUT OF THESE BLOODY TREES.
AT LEAST MY TALLUS LOOKS LIKE IT'S WORKING.
YO, CRYSTAL PALACE, ANYBODY HOME?
YOU LISTENIN', BETSY?
GUESS NOT.
BETTER START WALKIN', FIND SOME OPEN SKY SO I CAN GET A SENSE OF WHERE I AM AND WHAT KIND OF PLACE THIS IS.
WHUSSAT?!
PEOPLE-- MOVIN' FAST AN' QUIET--
--LOT OF TENSION IN THEIR VOICES. WHATEVER THEY WANT HERE...
"...THEY MEAN BUSINESS."

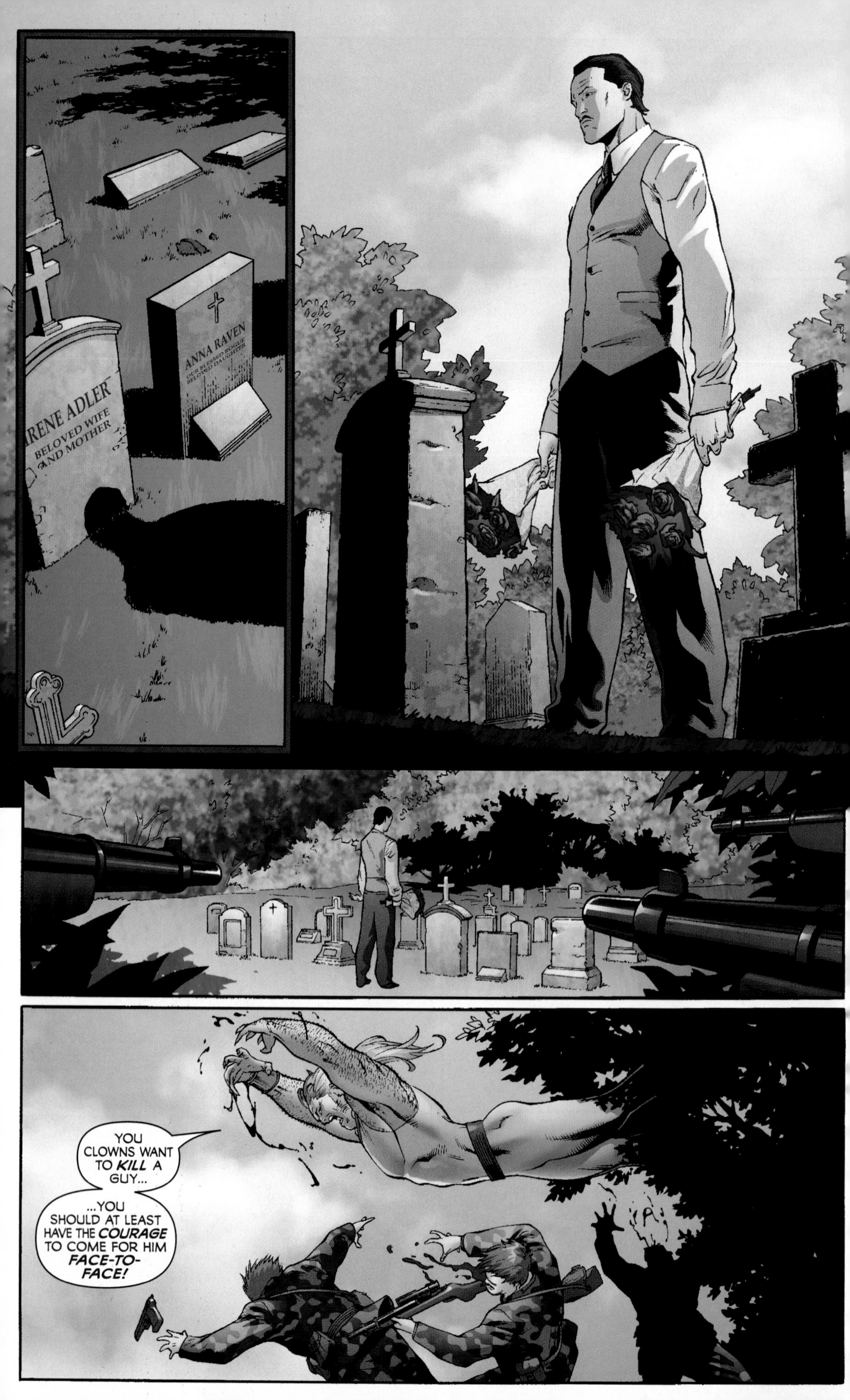
RENE ADLER
BELOVED WIFE
AND MOTHER
ANNA RAVEN
OUR BLESSED ROGUE
BELOVED DAUGHTER
YOU CLOWNS WANT TO *KILL* A GUY...
...YOU SHOULD AT LEAST HAVE THE *COURAGE* TO COME FOR HIM *FACE-TO-FACE!*

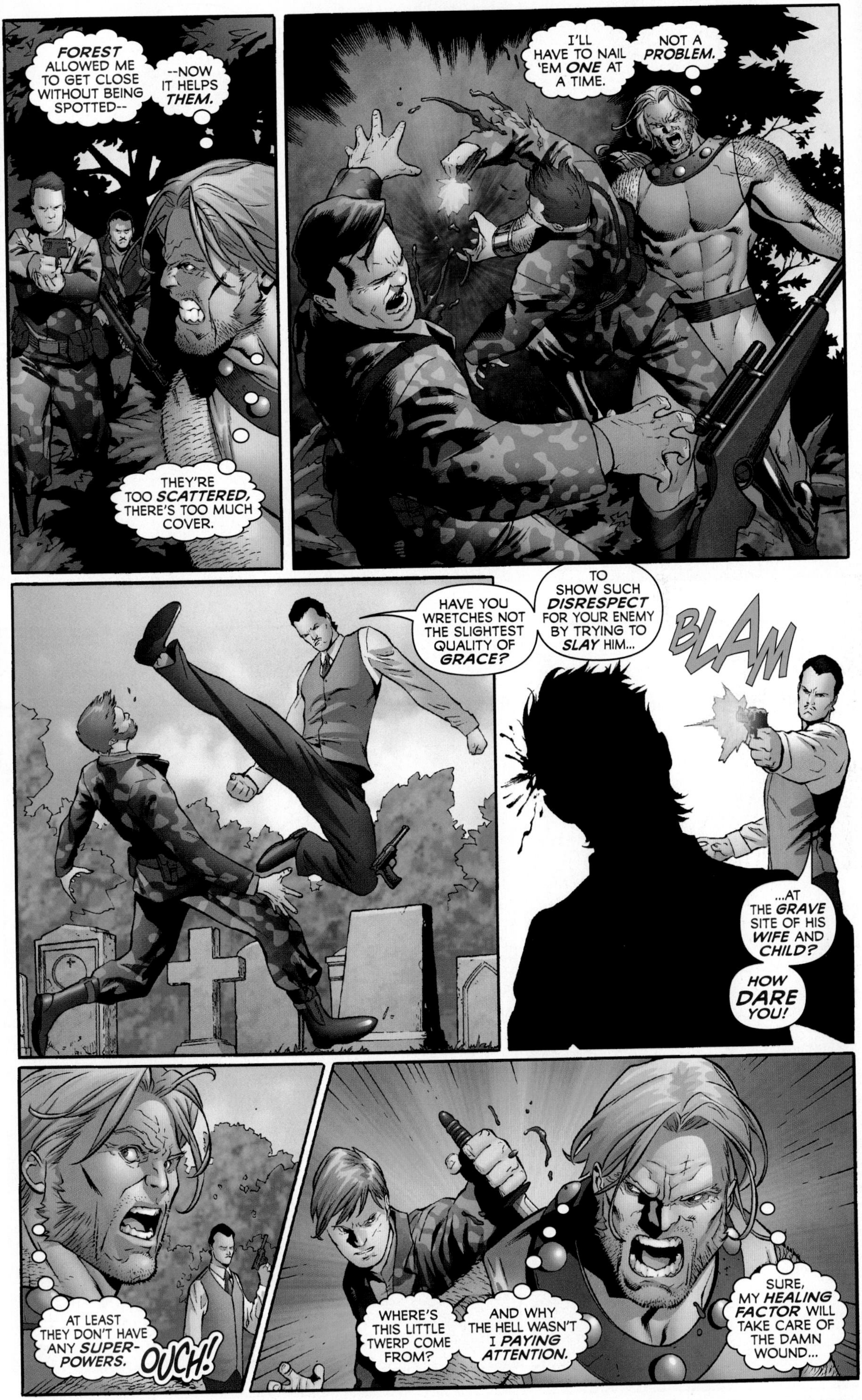
FOREST ALLOWED ME TO GET CLOSE WITHOUT BEING SPOTTED--
--NOW IT HELPS THEM.
THEY'RE TOO SCATTERED, THERE'S TOO MUCH COVER.
I'LL HAVE TO NAIL 'EM ONE AT A TIME.
NOT A PROBLEM.
HAVE YOU WRETCHES NOT THE SLIGHTEST QUALITY OF GRACE?
TO SHOW SUCH DISRESPECT FOR YOUR ENEMY BY TRYING TO SLAY HIM...
BLAM
...AT THE GRAVE SITE OF HIS WIFE AND CHILD?
HOW DARE YOU!
AT LEAST THEY DON'T HAVE ANY SUPER-POWERS.
OUCH!
WHERE'S THIS LITTLE TWERP COME FROM?
AND WHY THE HELL WASN'T I PAYING ATTENTION.
SURE, MY HEALING FACTOR WILL TAKE CARE OF THE DAMN WOUND...

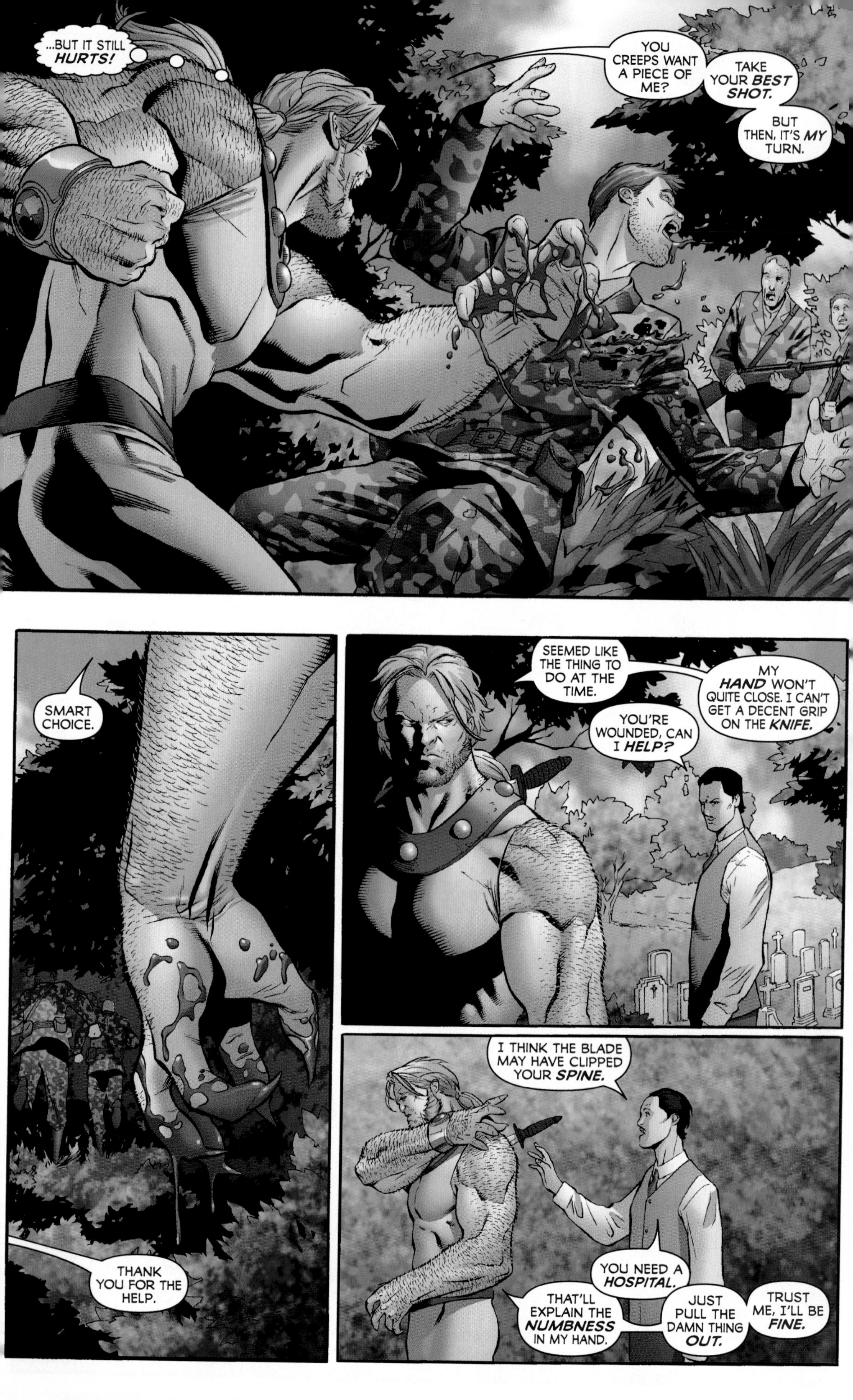
...BUT IT STILL *HURTS!*
YOU CREEPS WANT A PIECE OF ME?
TAKE YOUR *BEST SHOT.*
BUT THEN, IT'S *MY* TURN.
SMART CHOICE.
THANK YOU FOR THE HELP.
SEEMED LIKE THE THING TO DO AT THE TIME.
MY *HAND* WON'T QUITE CLOSE. I CAN'T GET A DECENT GRIP ON THE *KNIFE.*
YOU'RE WOUNDED, CAN I *HELP?*
I THINK THE BLADE MAY HAVE CLIPPED YOUR *SPINE.*
THAT'LL EXPLAIN THE *NUMBNESS* IN MY HAND.
YOU NEED A *HOSPITAL.*
JUST PULL THE DAMN THING *OUT.*
TRUST ME, I'LL BE *FINE.*

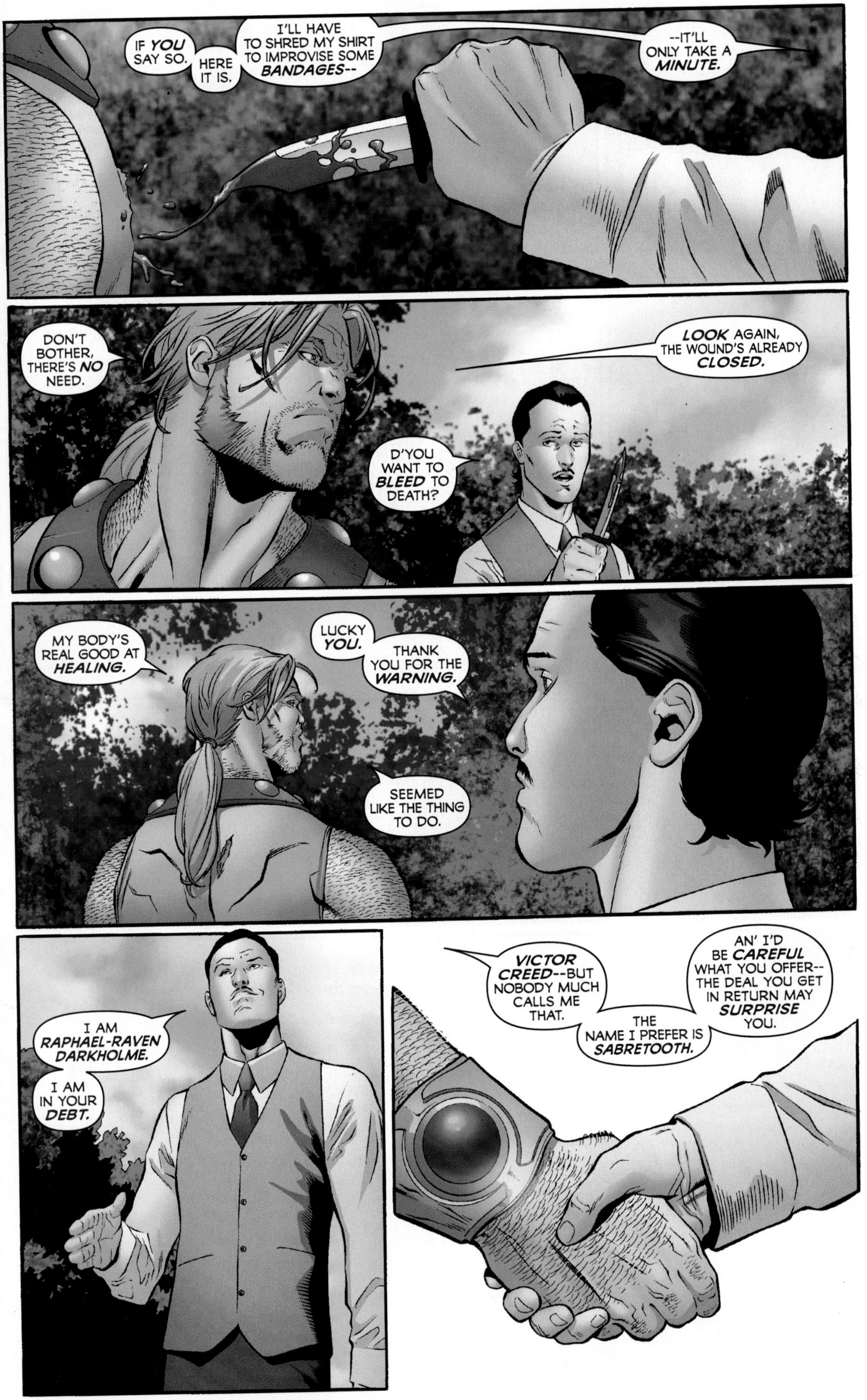
IF *YOU* SAY SO.
HERE IT IS.
I'LL HAVE TO SHRED MY SHIRT TO IMPROVISE SOME *BANDAGES*--
--IT'LL ONLY TAKE A *MINUTE.*
DON'T BOTHER, THERE'S *NO* NEED.
D'YOU WANT TO *BLEED* TO DEATH?
LOOK AGAIN, THE WOUND'S ALREADY *CLOSED.*
MY BODY'S REAL GOOD AT *HEALING.*
LUCKY *YOU.*
THANK YOU FOR THE *WARNING.*
SEEMED LIKE THE THING TO DO.
I AM *RAPHAEL-RAVEN DARKHOLME.*
I AM IN YOUR *DEBT.*
VICTOR CREED--BUT NOBODY MUCH CALLS ME THAT.
THE NAME I PREFER IS *SABRETOOTH.*
AN' I'D BE *CAREFUL* WHAT YOU OFFER-- THE DEAL YOU GET IN RETURN MAY *SURPRISE* YOU.

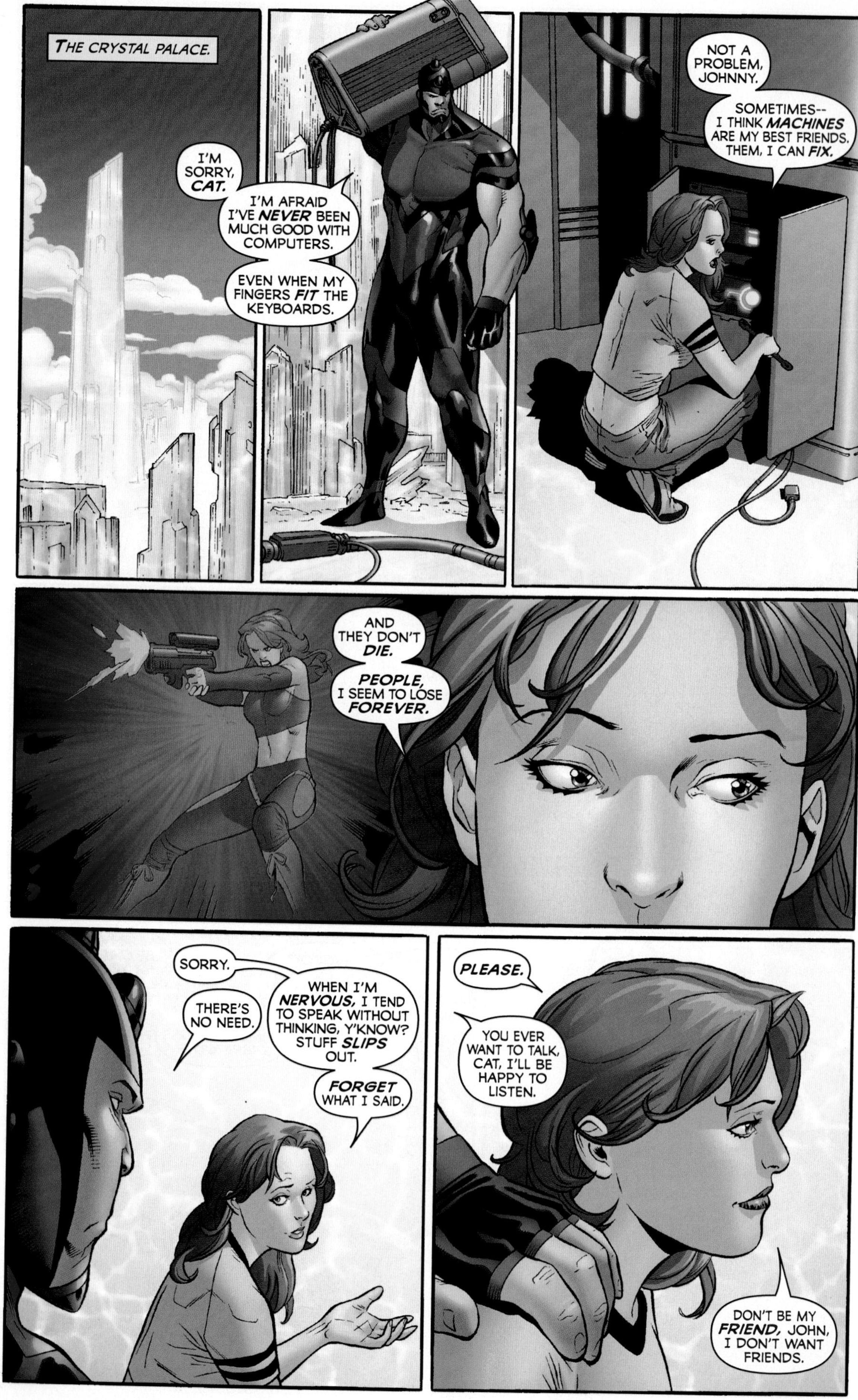

THE CRYSTAL PALACE.
I'M SORRY, CAT.
I'M AFRAID I'VE NEVER BEEN MUCH GOOD WITH COMPUTERS.
EVEN WHEN MY FINGERS FIT THE KEYBOARDS.
NOT A PROBLEM, JOHNNY.
SOMETIMES-- I THINK MACHINES ARE MY BEST FRIENDS. THEM, I CAN FIX.
AND THEY DON'T DIE.
PEOPLE, I SEEM TO LOSE FOREVER.
SORRY.
WHEN I'M NERVOUS, I TEND TO SPEAK WITHOUT THINKING, Y'KNOW? STUFF SLIPS OUT.
THERE'S NO NEED.
FORGET WHAT I SAID.
PLEASE.
YOU EVER WANT TO TALK, CAT, I'LL BE HAPPY TO LISTEN.
DON'T BE MY FRIEND, JOHN. I DON'T WANT FRIENDS.

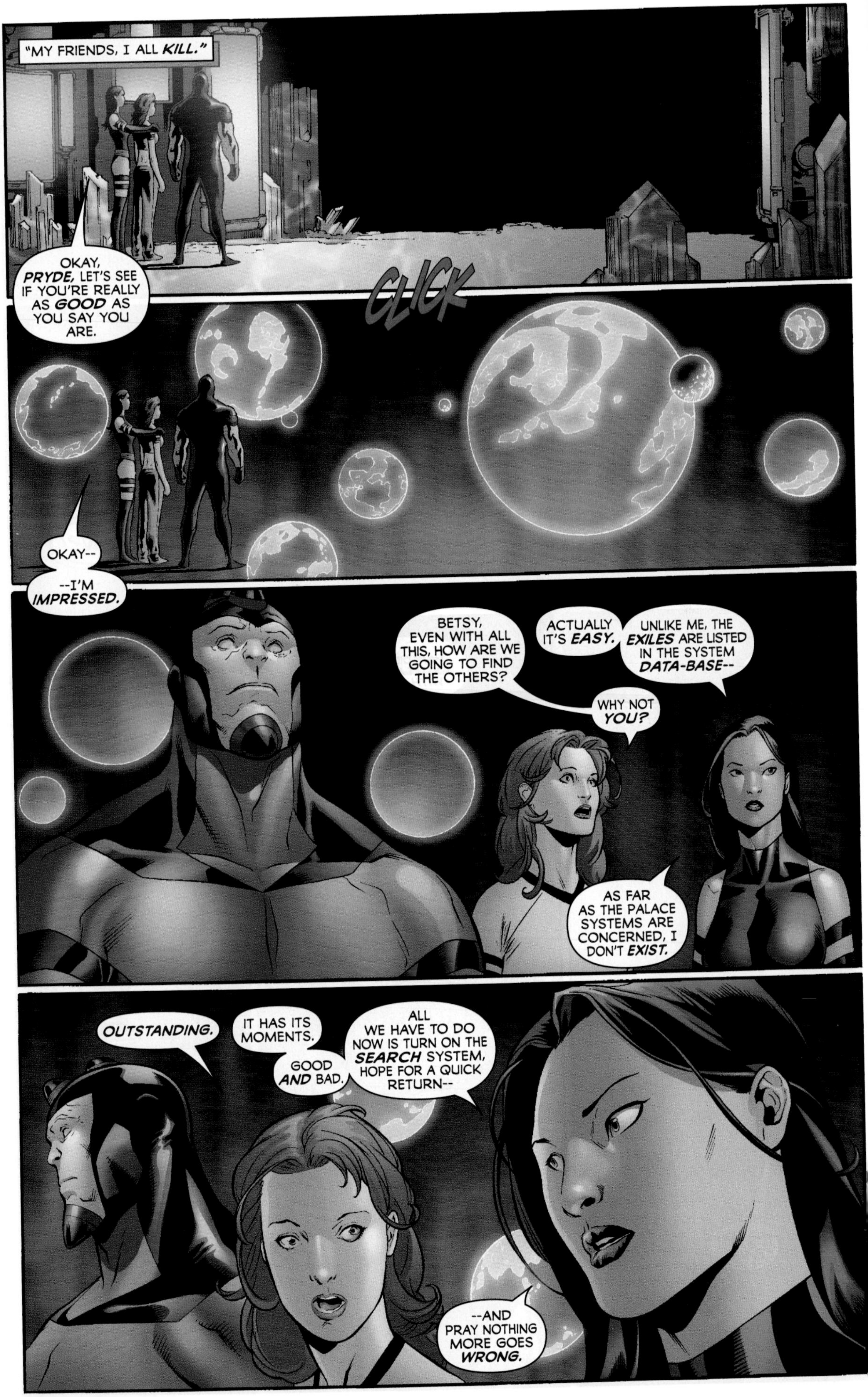
"MY FRIENDS, I ALL KILL."
OKAY, PRYDE, LET'S SEE IF YOU'RE REALLY AS GOOD AS YOU SAY YOU ARE.
CLICK
OKAY--
--I'M IMPRESSED.
BETSY, EVEN WITH ALL THIS, HOW ARE WE GOING TO FIND THE OTHERS?
ACTUALLY IT'S EASY.
UNLIKE ME, THE EXILES ARE LISTED IN THE SYSTEM DATA-BASE--
WHY NOT YOU?
AS FAR AS THE PALACE SYSTEMS ARE CONCERNED, I DON'T EXIST.
OUTSTANDING.
IT HAS ITS MOMENTS.
GOOD AND BAD.
ALL WE HAVE TO DO NOW IS TURN ON THE SEARCH SYSTEM, HOPE FOR A QUICK RETURN--
--AND PRAY NOTHING MORE GOES WRONG.

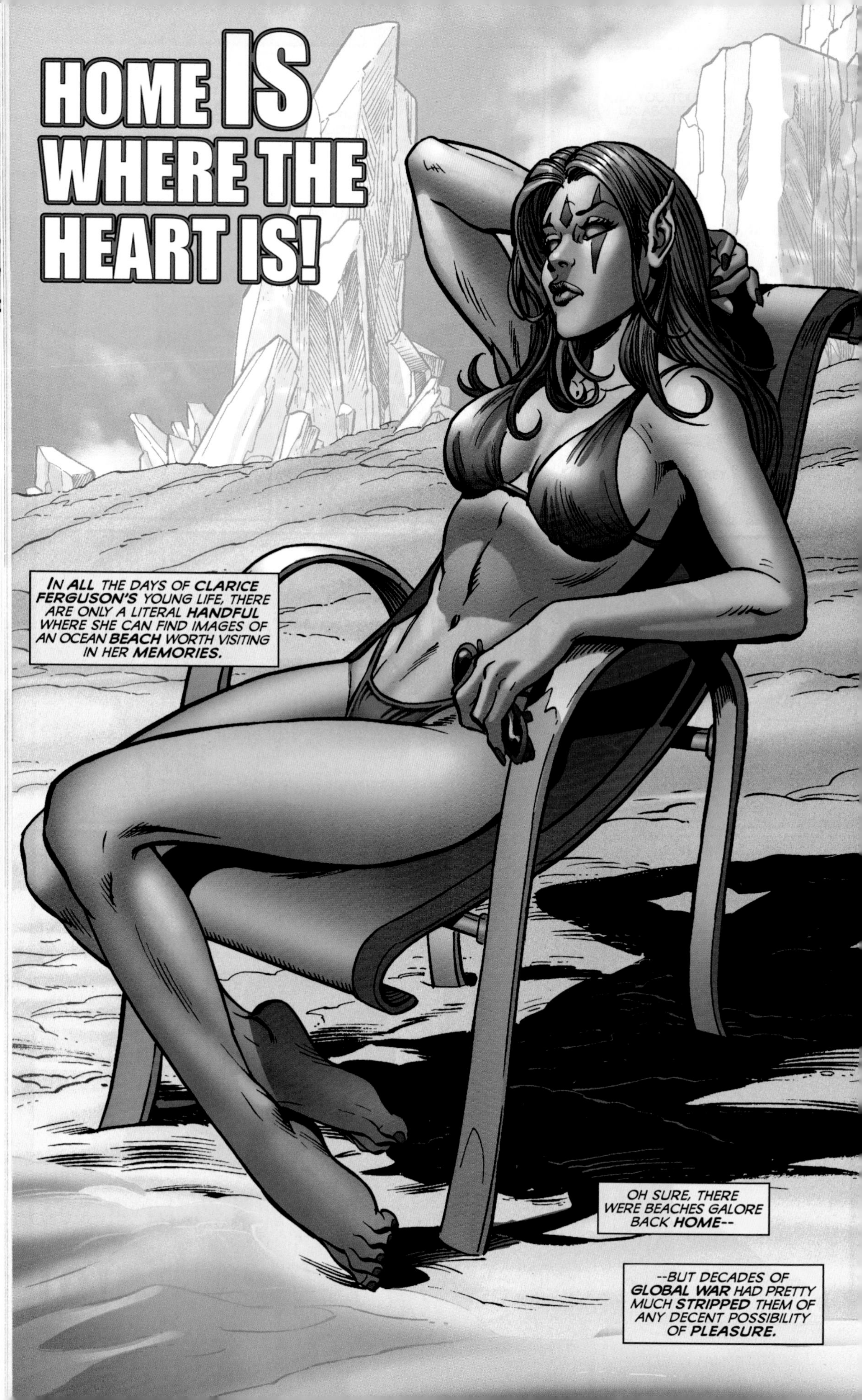
HOME IS WHERE THE HEART IS!
IN ALL THE DAYS OF CLARICE FERGUSON'S YOUNG LIFE, THERE ARE ONLY A LITERAL HANDFUL WHERE SHE CAN FIND IMAGES OF AN OCEAN BEACH WORTH VISITING IN HER MEMORIES.
OH SURE, THERE WERE BEACHES GALORE BACK HOME--
--BUT DECADES OF GLOBAL WAR HAD PRETTY MUCH STRIPPED THEM OF ANY DECENT POSSIBILITY OF PLEASURE.

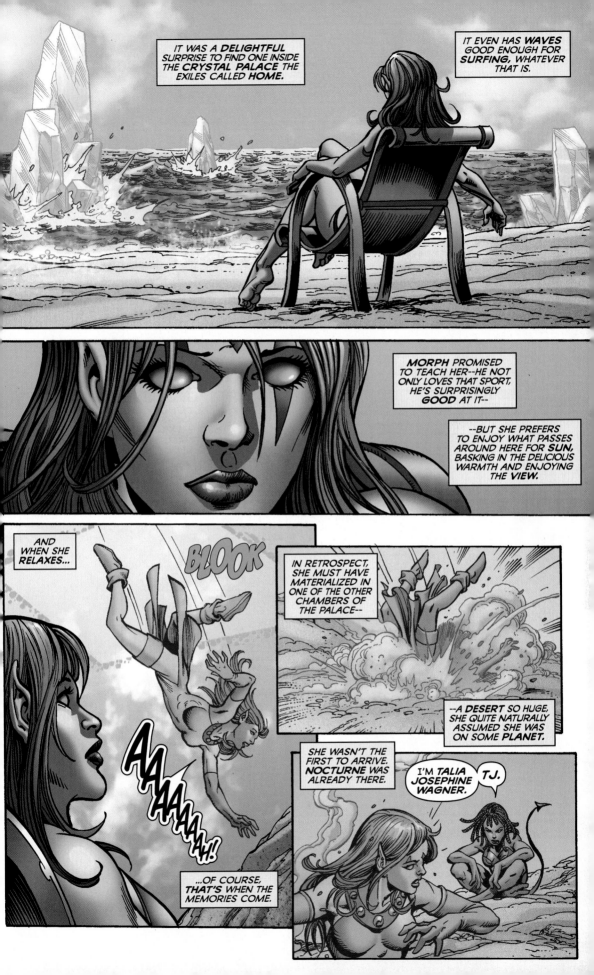

IT WAS A **DELIGHTFUL** SURPRISE TO FIND ONE INSIDE THE **CRYSTAL PALACE** THE EXILES CALLED **HOME**.

IT EVEN HAS **WAVES** GOOD ENOUGH FOR **SURFING**, WHATEVER THAT IS.

MORPH PROMISED TO TEACH HER--HE NOT ONLY LOVES THAT SPORT, HE'S SURPRISINGLY **GOOD** AT IT--

--BUT SHE PREFERS TO ENJOY WHAT PASSES AROUND HERE FOR **SUN**, BASKING IN THE DELICIOUS WARMTH AND ENJOYING THE **VIEW**.

AND WHEN SHE RELAXES...

BLOOK

AAAAAAAH!

IN RETROSPECT, SHE MUST HAVE MATERIALIZED IN ONE OF THE OTHER CHAMBERS OF THE PALACE--

--A **DESERT** SO HUGE, SHE QUITE NATURALLY ASSUMED SHE WAS ON SOME **PLANET**.

...OF COURSE, **THAT'S** WHEN THE MEMORIES COME.

SHE WASN'T THE FIRST TO ARRIVE. **NOCTURNE** WAS ALREADY THERE.

I'M **TALIA JOSEPHINE WAGNER**.

T.J.

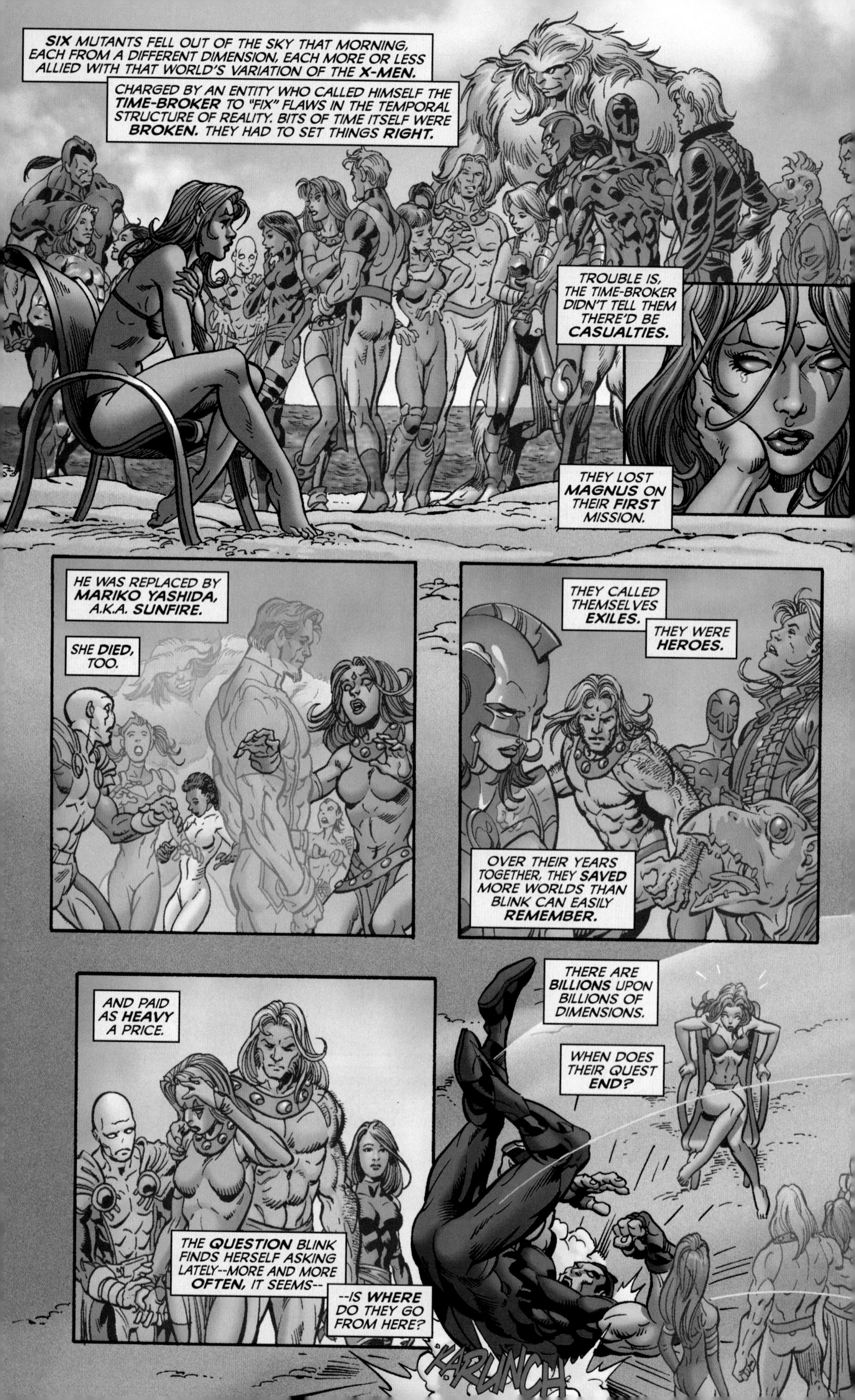

SIX MUTANTS FELL OUT OF THE SKY THAT MORNING, EACH FROM A DIFFERENT DIMENSION, EACH MORE OR LESS ALLIED WITH THAT WORLD'S VARIATION OF THE X-MEN.
CHARGED BY AN ENTITY WHO CALLED HIMSELF THE TIME-BROKER TO "FIX" FLAWS IN THE TEMPORAL STRUCTURE OF REALITY. BITS OF TIME ITSELF WERE BROKEN. THEY HAD TO SET THINGS RIGHT.
TROUBLE IS, THE TIME-BROKER DIDN'T TELL THEM THERE'D BE CASUALTIES.
THEY LOST MAGNUS ON THEIR FIRST MISSION.
HE WAS REPLACED BY MARIKO YASHIDA, A.K.A. SUNFIRE.
SHE DIED, TOO.
THEY CALLED THEMSELVES EXILES.
THEY WERE HEROES.
OVER THEIR YEARS TOGETHER, THEY SAVED MORE WORLDS THAN BLINK CAN EASILY REMEMBER.
AND PAID AS HEAVY A PRICE.
THERE ARE BILLIONS UPON BILLIONS OF DIMENSIONS.
WHEN DOES THEIR QUEST END?
THE QUESTION BLINK FINDS HERSELF ASKING LATELY--MORE AND MORE OFTEN, IT SEEMS--
--IS WHERE DO THEY GO FROM HERE?
KARUNCH

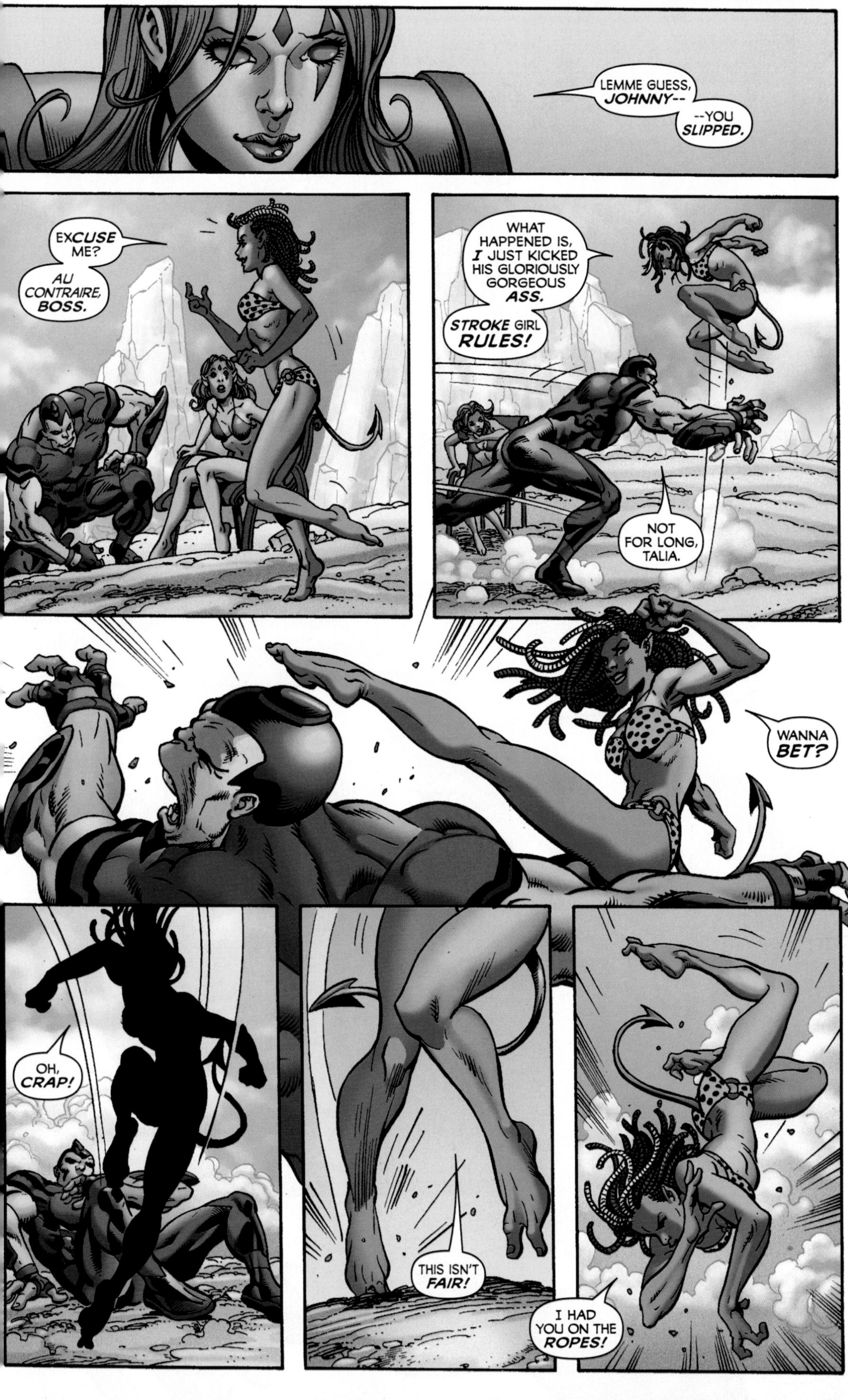
LEMME GUESS, JOHNNY--
--YOU SLIPPED.
EXCUSE ME?
AU CONTRAIRE, BOSS.
WHAT HAPPENED IS, I JUST KICKED HIS GLORIOUSLY GORGEOUS ASS.
STROKE GIRL RULES!
NOT FOR LONG, TALIA.
WANNA BET?
OH, CRAP!
THIS ISN'T FAIR!
I HAD YOU ON THE ROPES!

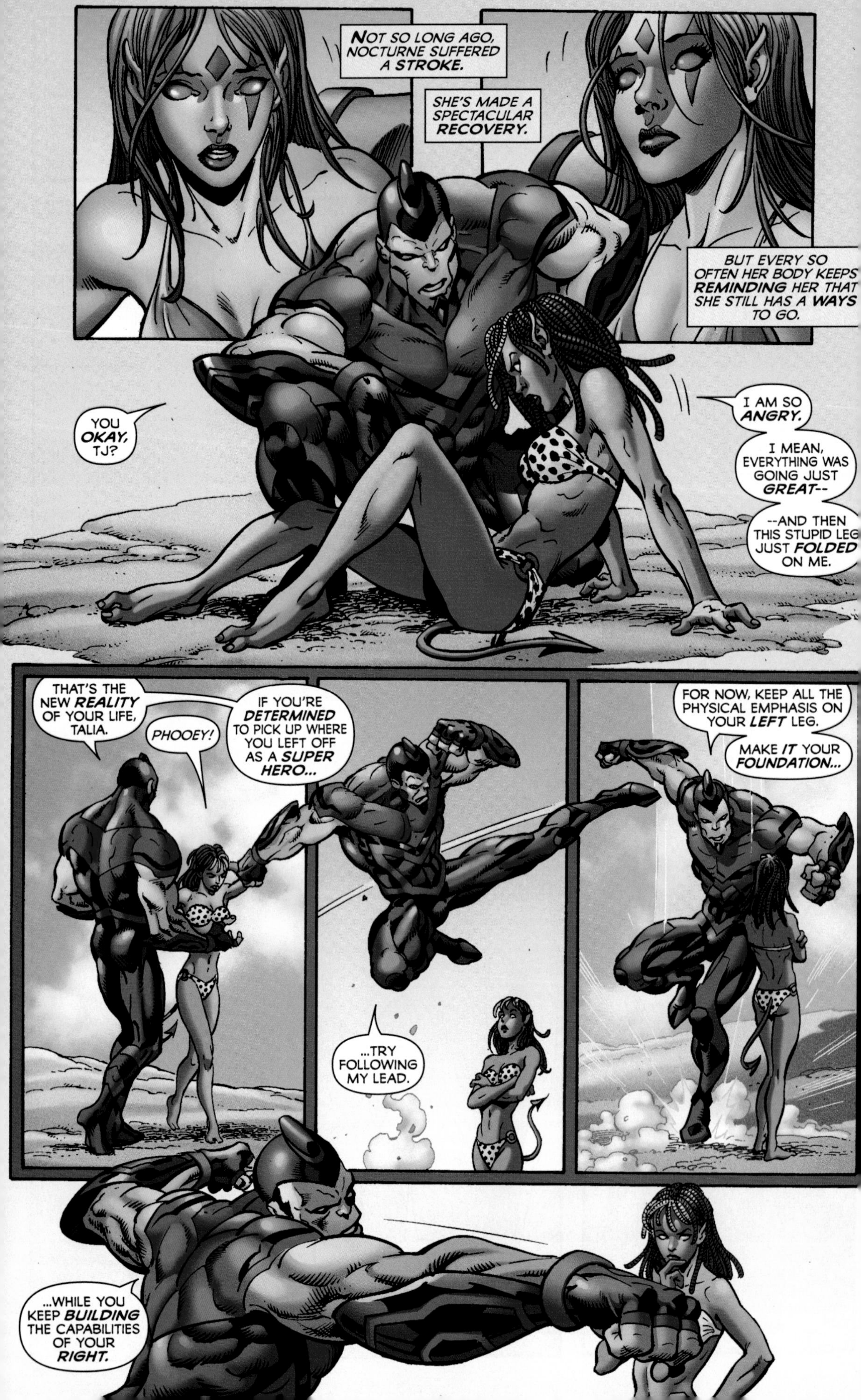
NOT SO LONG AGO, NOCTURNE SUFFERED A STROKE.
SHE'S MADE A SPECTACULAR RECOVERY.
BUT EVERY SO OFTEN HER BODY KEEPS REMINDING HER THAT SHE STILL HAS A WAYS TO GO.
YOU OKAY, TJ?
I AM SO ANGRY.
I MEAN, EVERYTHING WAS GOING JUST GREAT--
--AND THEN THIS STUPID LEG JUST FOLDED ON ME.
THAT'S THE NEW REALITY OF YOUR LIFE, TALIA.
PHOOEY!
IF YOU'RE DETERMINED TO PICK UP WHERE YOU LEFT OFF AS A SUPER HERO...
...TRY FOLLOWING MY LEAD.
FOR NOW, KEEP ALL THE PHYSICAL EMPHASIS ON YOUR LEFT LEG.
MAKE IT YOUR FOUNDATION...
...WHILE YOU KEEP BUILDING THE CAPABILITIES OF YOUR RIGHT.

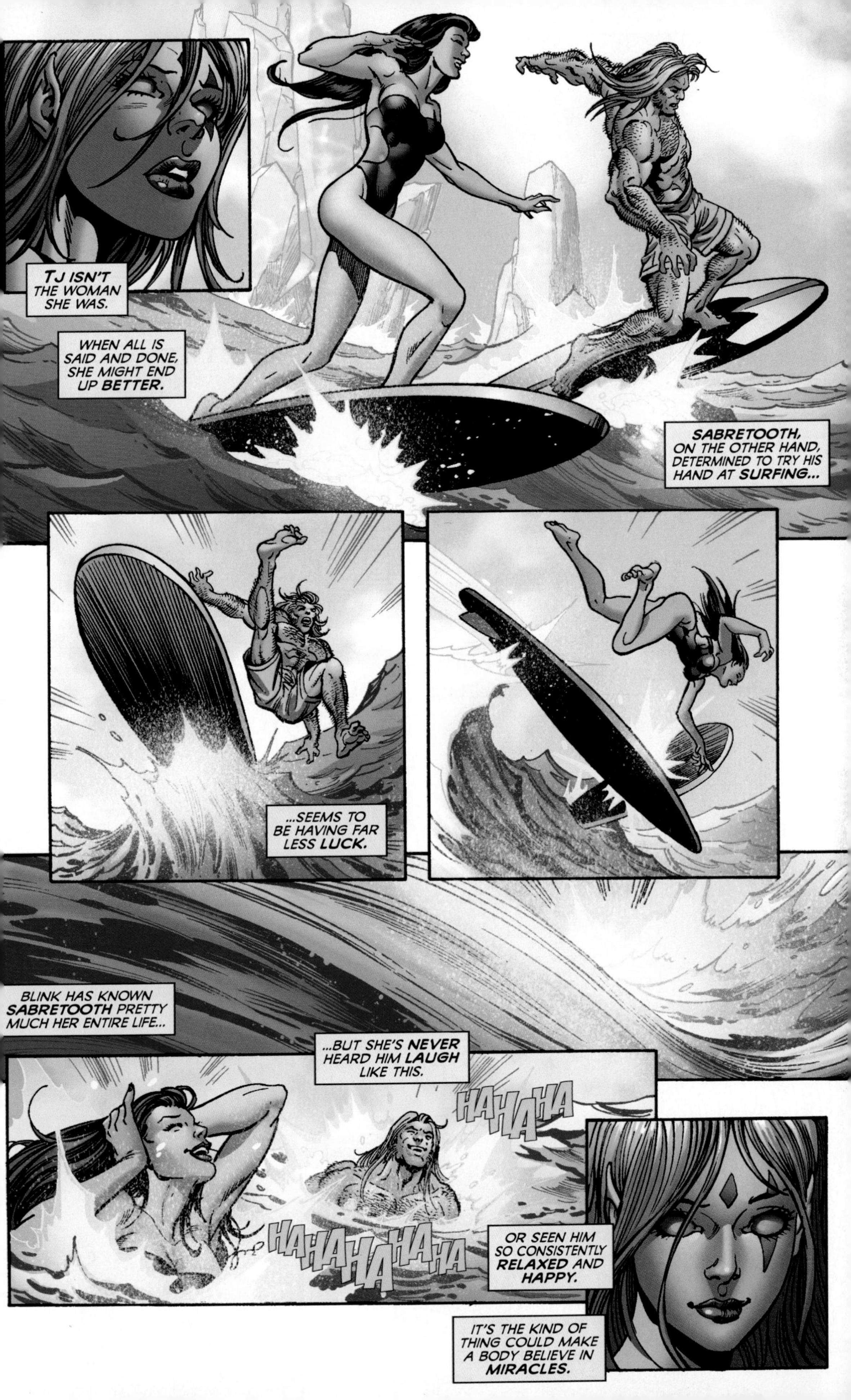
TJ ISN'T THE WOMAN SHE WAS.
WHEN ALL IS SAID AND DONE, SHE MIGHT END UP BETTER.
SABRETOOTH, ON THE OTHER HAND, DETERMINED TO TRY HIS HAND AT SURFING...
...SEEMS TO BE HAVING FAR LESS LUCK.
BLINK HAS KNOWN SABRETOOTH PRETTY MUCH HER ENTIRE LIFE...
...BUT SHE'S NEVER HEARD HIM LAUGH LIKE THIS.
HAHAHA
HAHAHAHAHAHA
OR SEEN HIM SO CONSISTENTLY RELAXED AND HAPPY.
IT'S THE KIND OF THING COULD MAKE A BODY BELIEVE IN MIRACLES.

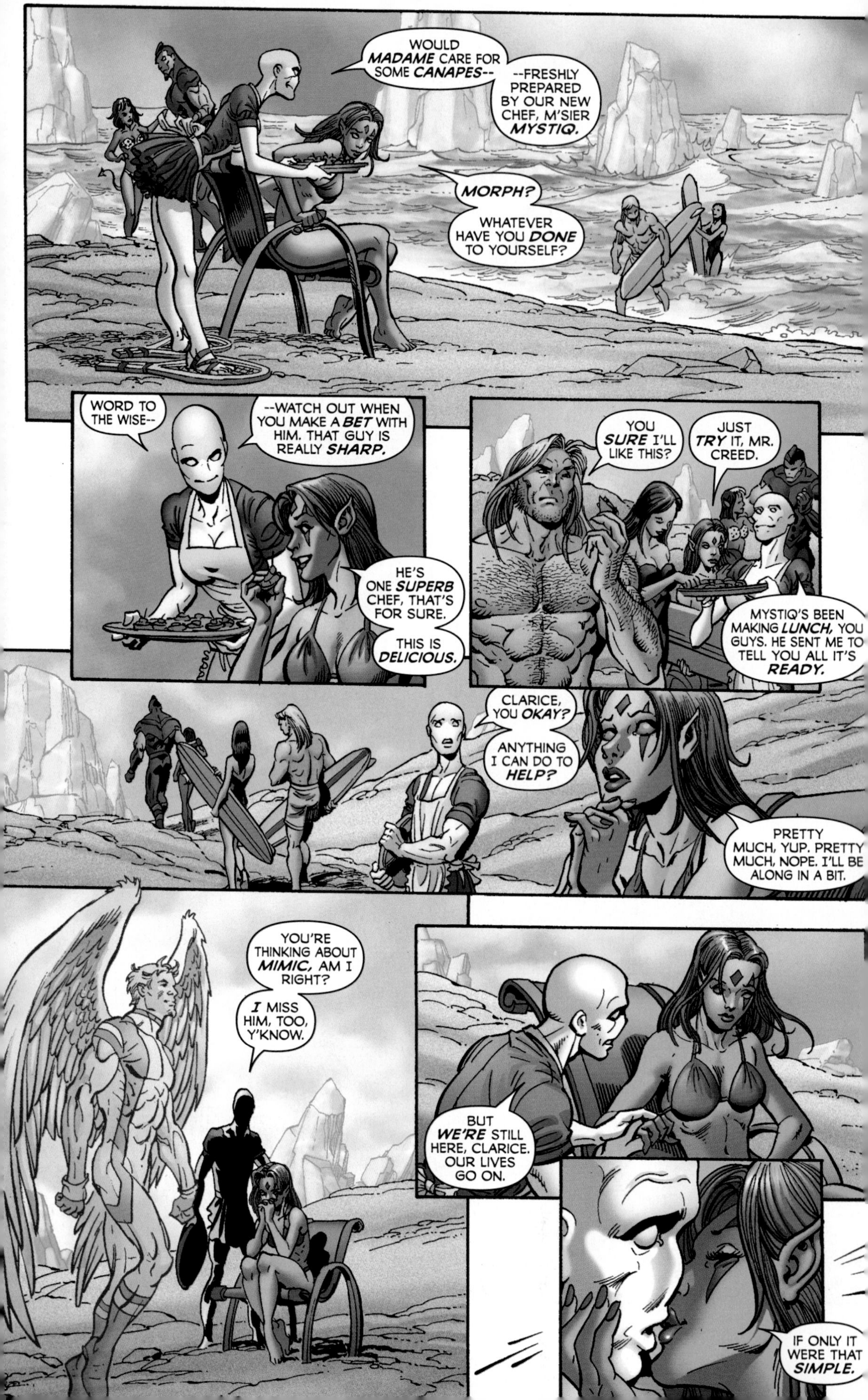
WOULD MADAME CARE FOR SOME CANAPES--
--FRESHLY PREPARED BY OUR NEW CHEF, M'SIER MYSTIQ.
MORPH?
WHATEVER HAVE YOU DONE TO YOURSELF?
WORD TO THE WISE--
--WATCH OUT WHEN YOU MAKE A BET WITH HIM. THAT GUY IS REALLY SHARP.
HE'S ONE SUPERB CHEF, THAT'S FOR SURE.
THIS IS DELICIOUS.
YOU SURE I'LL LIKE THIS?
JUST TRY IT, MR. CREED.
MYSTIQ'S BEEN MAKING LUNCH, YOU GUYS. HE SENT ME TO TELL YOU ALL IT'S READY.
CLARICE, YOU OKAY?
ANYTHING I CAN DO TO HELP?
PRETTY MUCH, YUP. PRETTY MUCH, NOPE. I'LL BE ALONG IN A BIT.
YOU'RE THINKING ABOUT MIMIC, AM I RIGHT?
I MISS HIM, TOO, Y'KNOW.
BUT WE'RE STILL HERE, CLARICE. OUR LIVES GO ON.
IF ONLY IT WERE THAT SIMPLE.

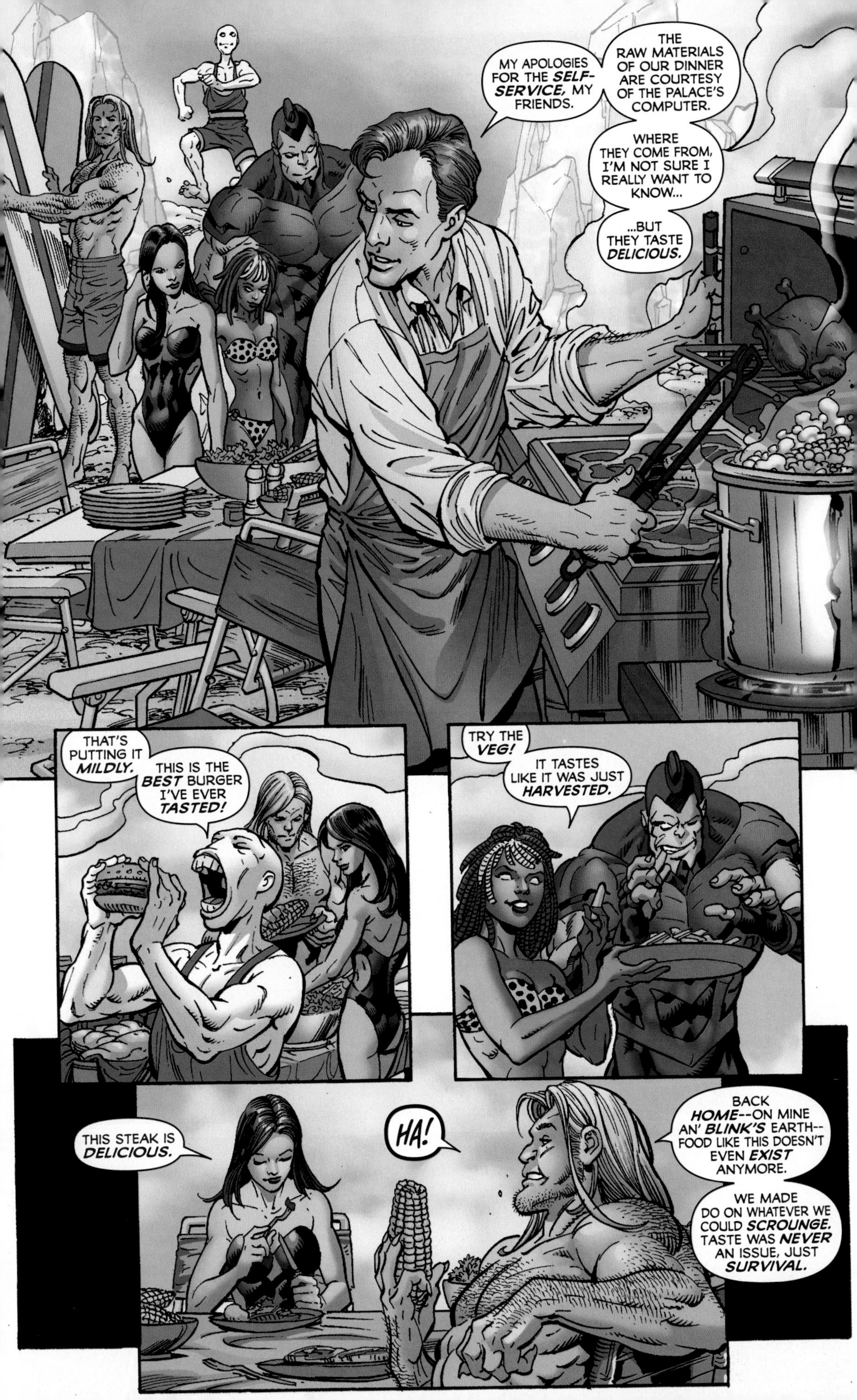
MY APOLOGIES FOR THE SELF-SERVICE, MY FRIENDS.
THE RAW MATERIALS OF OUR DINNER ARE COURTESY OF THE PALACE'S COMPUTER.
WHERE THEY COME FROM, I'M NOT SURE I REALLY WANT TO KNOW...
...BUT THEY TASTE DELICIOUS.
THAT'S PUTTING IT MILDLY.
THIS IS THE BEST BURGER I'VE EVER TASTED!
TRY THE VEG!
IT TASTES LIKE IT WAS JUST HARVESTED.
THIS STEAK IS DELICIOUS.
HA!
BACK HOME--ON MINE AN' BLINK'S EARTH--FOOD LIKE THIS DOESN'T EVEN EXIST ANYMORE.
WE MADE DO ON WHATEVER WE COULD SCROUNGE. TASTE WAS NEVER AN ISSUE, JUST SURVIVAL.

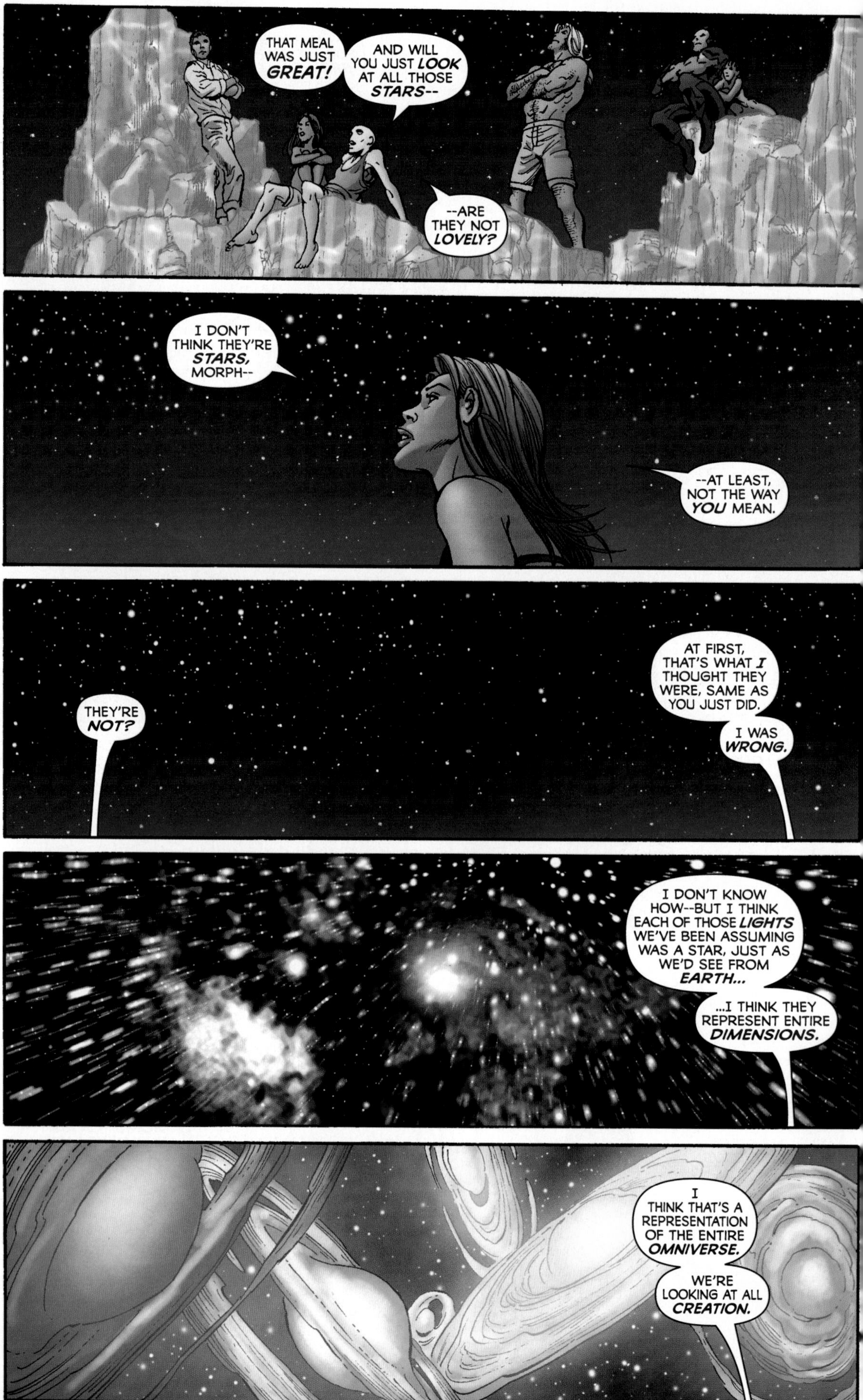
THAT MEAL WAS JUST *GREAT!*
AND WILL YOU JUST *LOOK* AT ALL THOSE *STARS*--
--ARE THEY NOT *LOVELY?*
I DON'T THINK THEY'RE *STARS,* MORPH--
--AT LEAST, NOT THE WAY *YOU* MEAN.
THEY'RE *NOT?*
AT FIRST, THAT'S WHAT *I* THOUGHT THEY WERE, SAME AS YOU JUST DID.
I WAS *WRONG.*
I DON'T KNOW HOW--BUT I THINK EACH OF THOSE *LIGHTS* WE'VE BEEN ASSUMING WAS A STAR, JUST AS WE'D SEE FROM *EARTH...*
...I THINK THEY REPRESENT ENTIRE *DIMENSIONS.*
I THINK THAT'S A REPRESENTATION OF THE ENTIRE *OMNIVERSE.*
WE'RE LOOKING AT ALL *CREATION.*

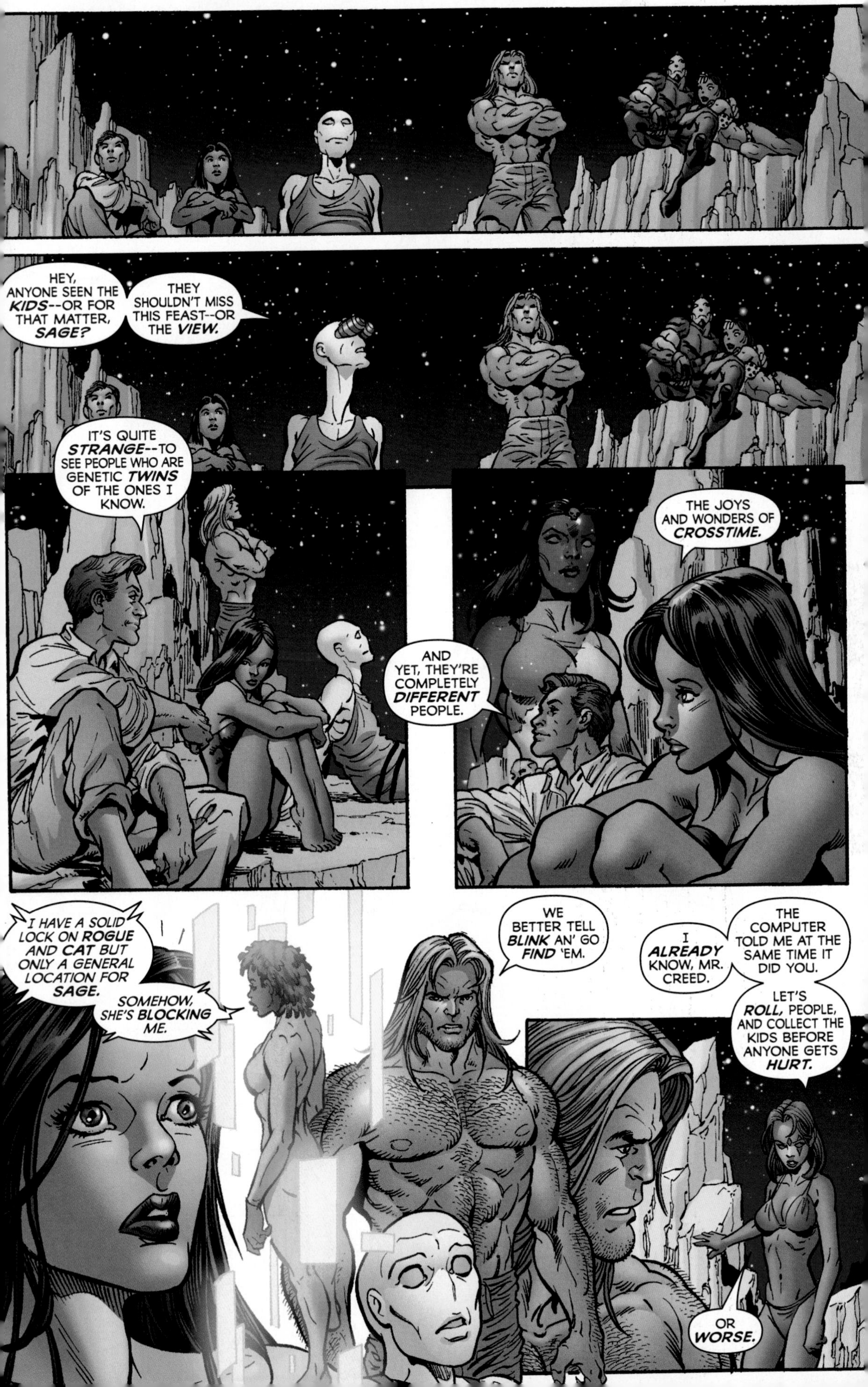
HEY, ANYONE SEEN THE KIDS--OR FOR THAT MATTER, SAGE?
THEY SHOULDN'T MISS THIS FEAST--OR THE VIEW.
IT'S QUITE STRANGE--TO SEE PEOPLE WHO ARE GENETIC TWINS OF THE ONES I KNOW.
AND YET, THEY'RE COMPLETELY DIFFERENT PEOPLE.
THE JOYS AND WONDERS OF CROSSTIME.
I HAVE A SOLID LOCK ON ROGUE AND CAT BUT ONLY A GENERAL LOCATION FOR SAGE.
SOMEHOW, SHE'S BLOCKING ME.
WE BETTER TELL BLINK AN' GO FIND 'EM.
I ALREADY KNOW, MR. CREED.
THE COMPUTER TOLD ME AT THE SAME TIME IT DID YOU.
LET'S ROLL, PEOPLE, AND COLLECT THE KIDS BEFORE ANYONE GETS HURT.
OR WORSE.

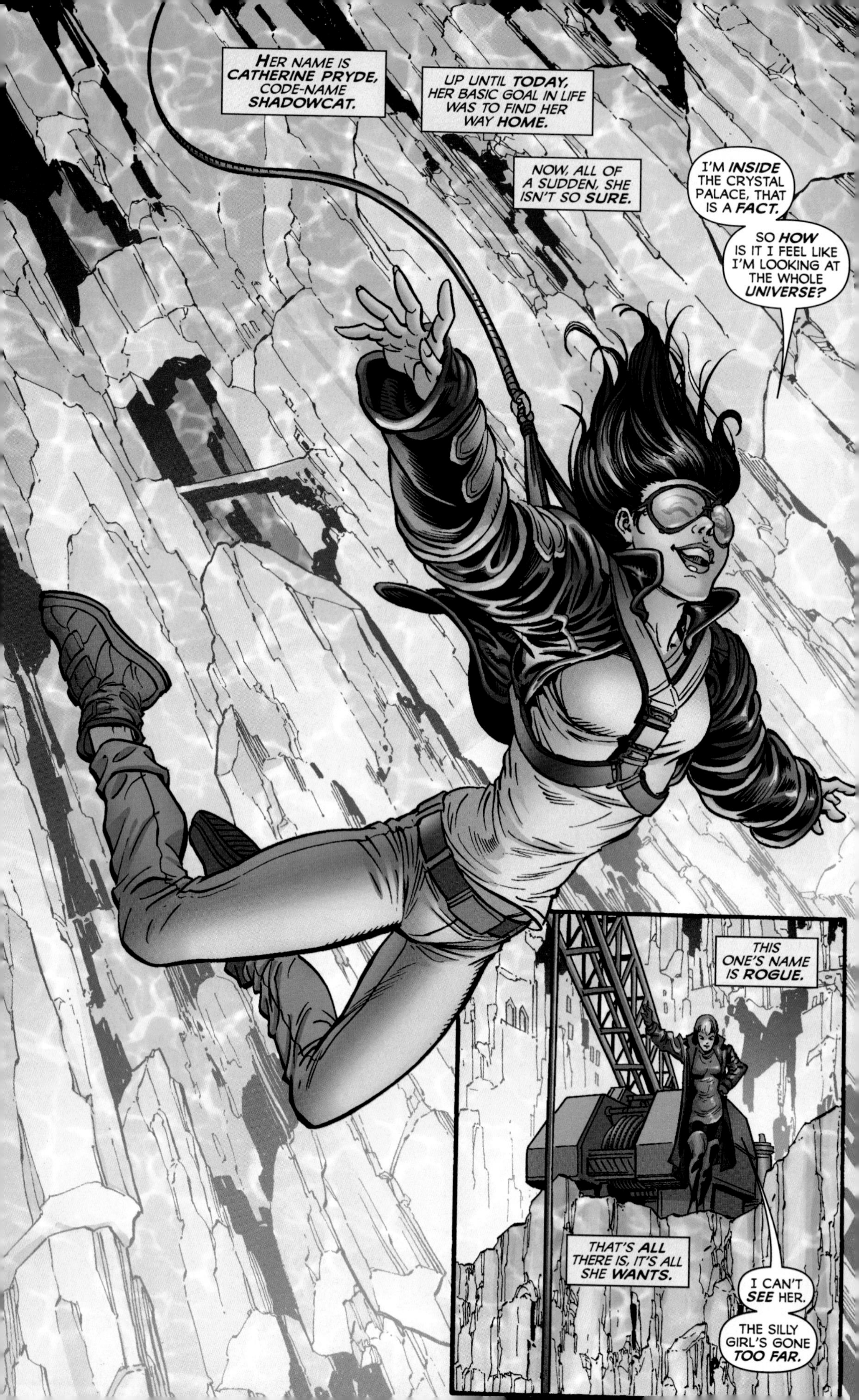
HER NAME IS CATHERINE PRYDE, CODE-NAME SHADOWCAT.
UP UNTIL TODAY, HER BASIC GOAL IN LIFE WAS TO FIND HER WAY HOME.
NOW, ALL OF A SUDDEN, SHE ISN'T SO SURE.
I'M INSIDE THE CRYSTAL PALACE, THAT IS A FACT.
SO HOW IS IT I FEEL LIKE I'M LOOKING AT THE WHOLE UNIVERSE?
THIS ONE'S NAME IS ROGUE.
THAT'S ALL THERE IS, IT'S ALL SHE WANTS.
I CAN'T SEE HER.
THE SILLY GIRL'S GONE TOO FAR.

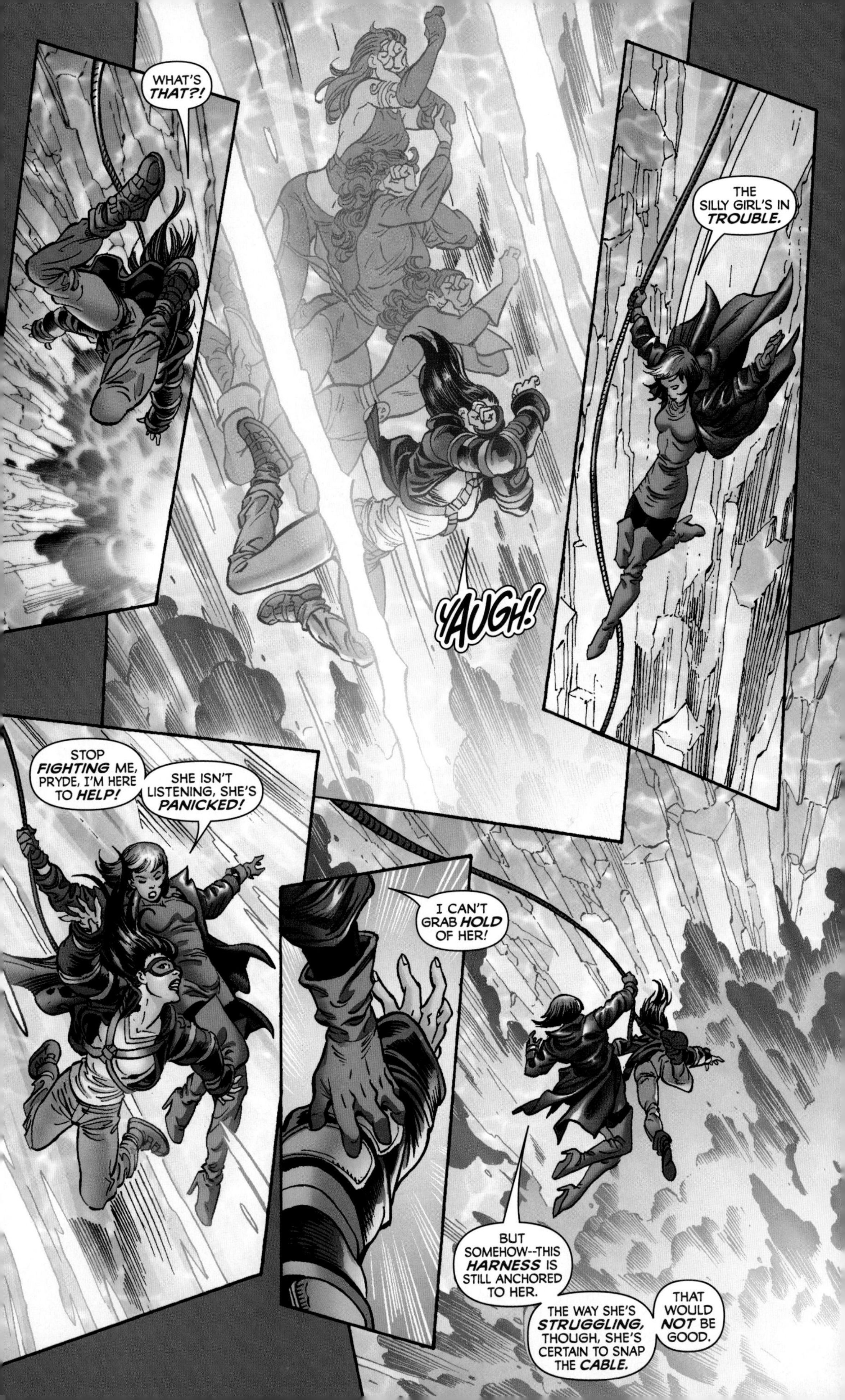
WHAT'S THAT?!
THE SILLY GIRL'S IN TROUBLE.
YAUGH!
STOP FIGHTING ME, PRYDE, I'M HERE TO HELP!
SHE ISN'T LISTENING, SHE'S PANICKED!
I CAN'T GRAB HOLD OF HER!
BUT SOMEHOW--THIS HARNESS IS STILL ANCHORED TO HER.
THE WAY SHE'S STRUGGLING, THOUGH, SHE'S CERTAIN TO SNAP THE CABLE.
THAT WOULD NOT BE GOOD.

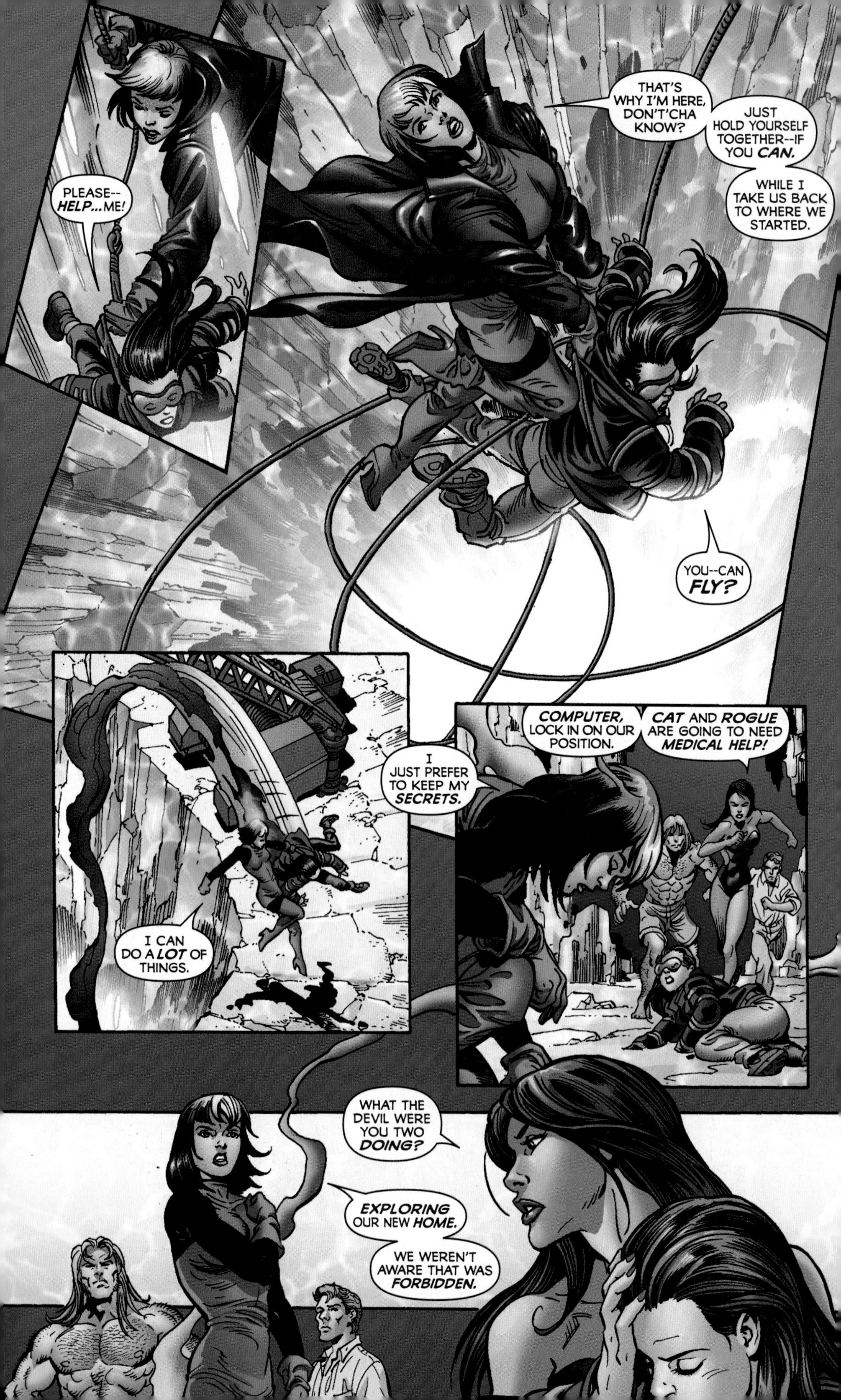
PLEASE-- HELP...ME!
THAT'S WHY I'M HERE, DON'T'CHA KNOW?
JUST HOLD YOURSELF TOGETHER--IF YOU CAN.
WHILE I TAKE US BACK TO WHERE WE STARTED.
YOU--CAN FLY?
I JUST PREFER TO KEEP MY SECRETS.
I CAN DO A LOT OF THINGS.
COMPUTER, LOCK IN ON OUR POSITION.
CAT AND ROGUE ARE GOING TO NEED MEDICAL HELP!
WHAT THE DEVIL WERE YOU TWO DOING?
EXPLORING OUR NEW HOME.
WE WEREN'T AWARE THAT WAS FORBIDDEN.

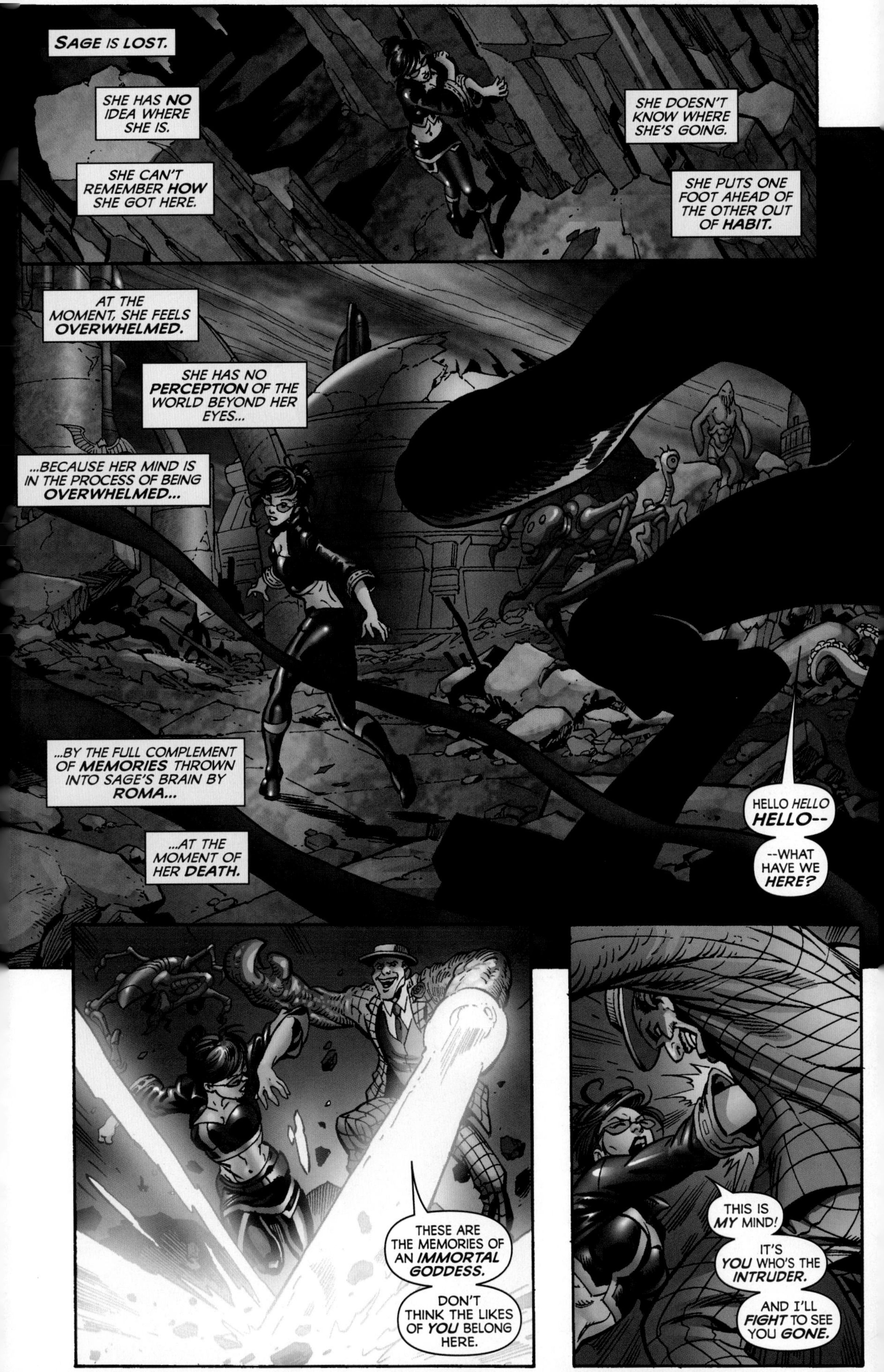
SAGE IS LOST.
SHE HAS NO IDEA WHERE SHE IS.
SHE CAN'T REMEMBER HOW SHE GOT HERE.
SHE DOESN'T KNOW WHERE SHE'S GOING.
SHE PUTS ONE FOOT AHEAD OF THE OTHER OUT OF HABIT.
AT THE MOMENT, SHE FEELS OVERWHELMED.
SHE HAS NO PERCEPTION OF THE WORLD BEYOND HER EYES...
...BECAUSE HER MIND IS IN THE PROCESS OF BEING OVERWHELMED...
...BY THE FULL COMPLEMENT OF MEMORIES THROWN INTO SAGE'S BRAIN BY ROMA...
...AT THE MOMENT OF HER DEATH.
HELLO HELLO HELLO--
--WHAT HAVE WE HERE?
THESE ARE THE MEMORIES OF AN IMMORTAL GODDESS.
DON'T THINK THE LIKES OF YOU BELONG HERE.
THIS IS MY MIND!
IT'S YOU WHO'S THE INTRUDER.
AND I'LL FIGHT TO SEE YOU GONE.

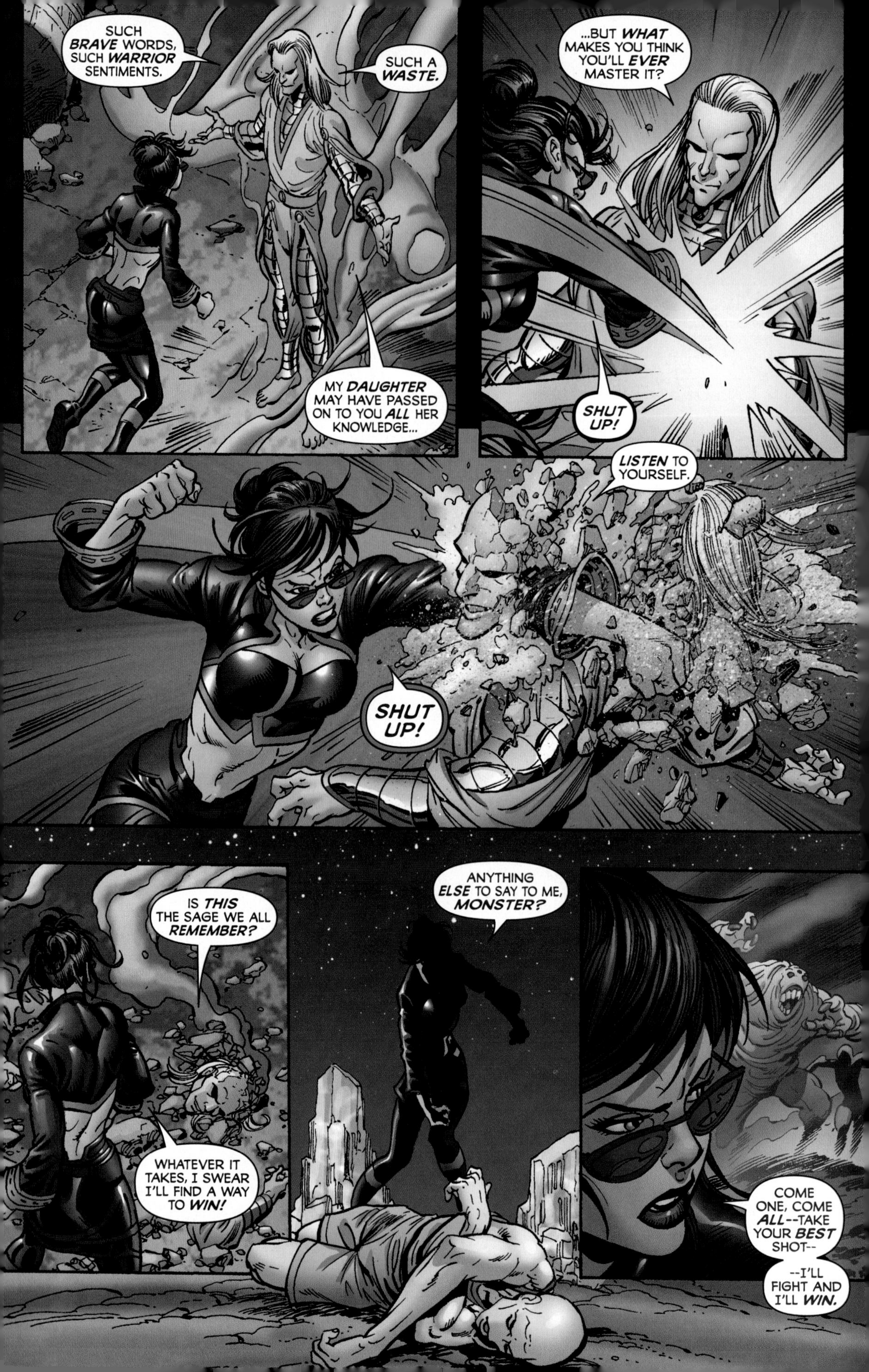

SUCH BRAVE WORDS, SUCH WARRIOR SENTIMENTS.
SUCH A WASTE.
MY DAUGHTER MAY HAVE PASSED ON TO YOU ALL HER KNOWLEDGE...
...BUT WHAT MAKES YOU THINK YOU'LL EVER MASTER IT?
SHUT UP!
LISTEN TO YOURSELF.
SHUT UP!
IS THIS THE SAGE WE ALL REMEMBER?
WHATEVER IT TAKES, I SWEAR I'LL FIND A WAY TO WIN!
ANYTHING ELSE TO SAY TO ME, MONSTER?
COME ONE, COME ALL--TAKE YOUR BEST SHOT--
--I'LL FIGHT AND I'LL WIN.

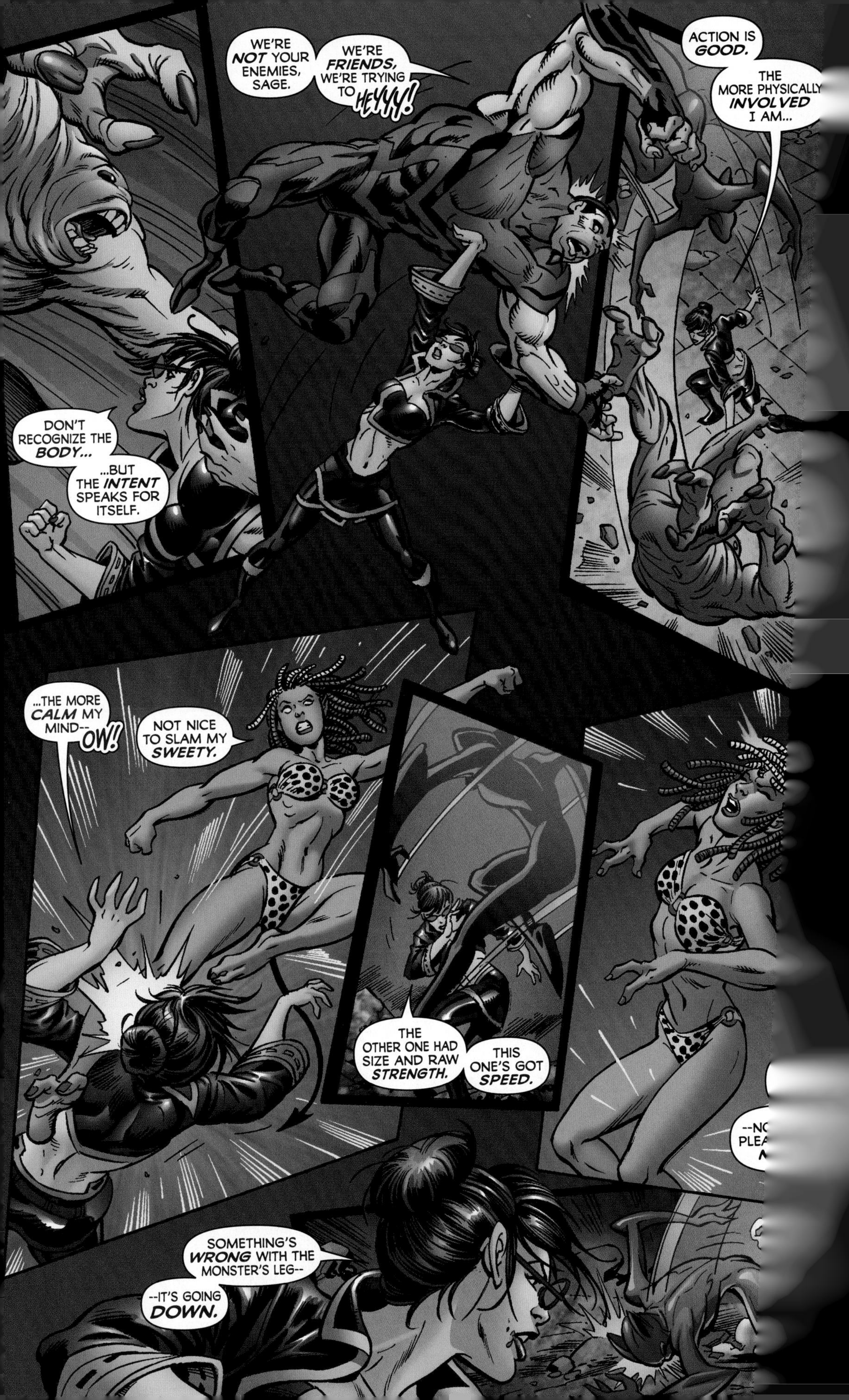
DON'T RECOGNIZE THE BODY...
...BUT THE INTENT SPEAKS FOR ITSELF.
WE'RE NOT YOUR ENEMIES, SAGE.
WE'RE FRIENDS, WE'RE TRYING TO HEYYY!
ACTION IS GOOD.
THE MORE PHYSICALLY INVOLVED I AM...
...THE MORE CALM MY MIND--OW!
NOT NICE TO SLAM MY SWEETY.
THE OTHER ONE HAD SIZE AND RAW STRENGTH.
THIS ONE'S GOT SPEED.
SOMETHING'S WRONG WITH THE MONSTER'S LEG--
--IT'S GOING DOWN.

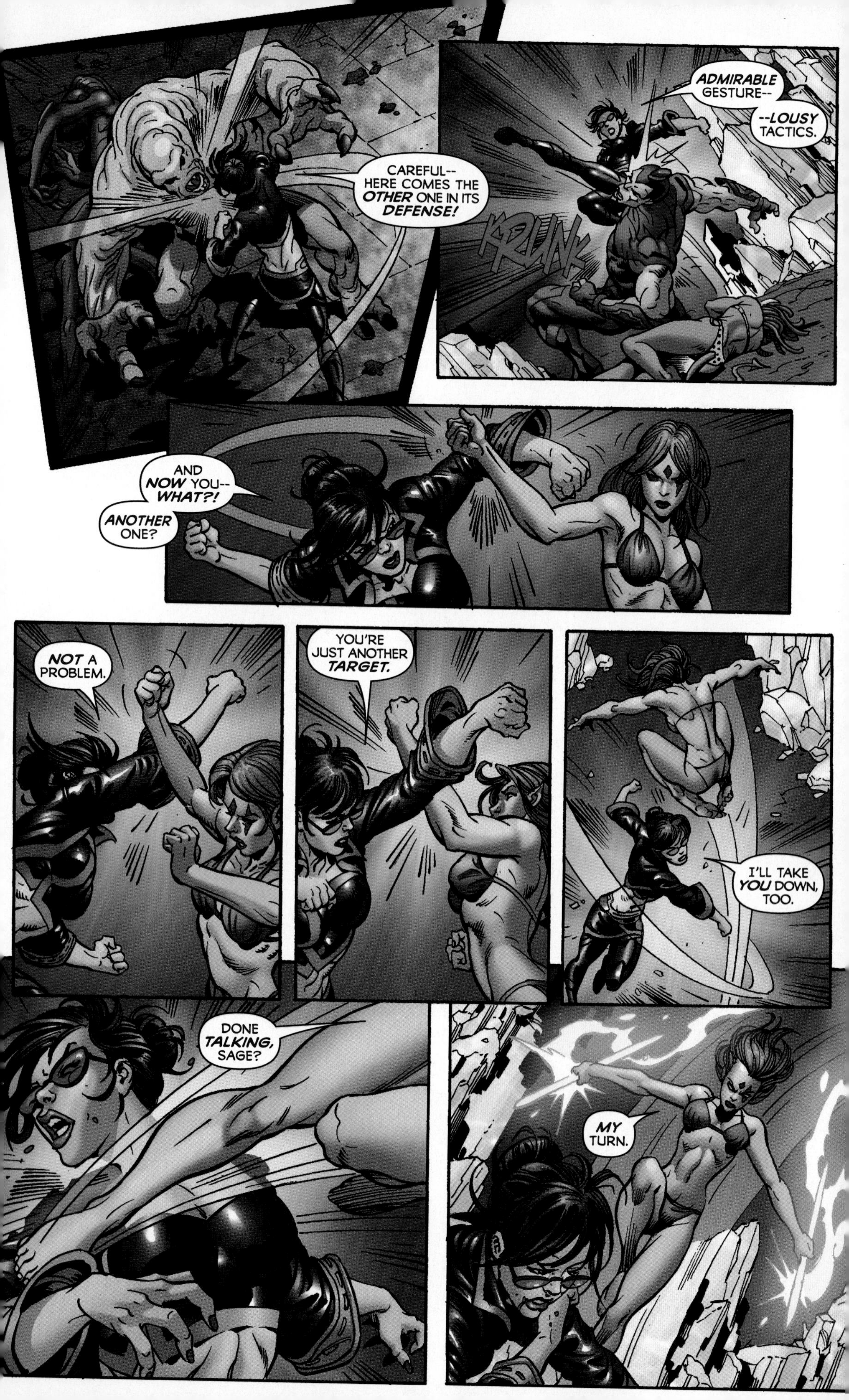
CAREFUL--
HERE COMES THE
OTHER ONE IN ITS
DEFENSE!
ADMIRABLE
GESTURE--
--LOUSY
TACTICS.
KRUNK
AND
NOW YOU--
WHAT?!
ANOTHER
ONE?
NOT A
PROBLEM.
YOU'RE
JUST ANOTHER
TARGET.
I'LL TAKE
YOU DOWN,
TOO.
DONE
TALKING,
SAGE?
MY
TURN.

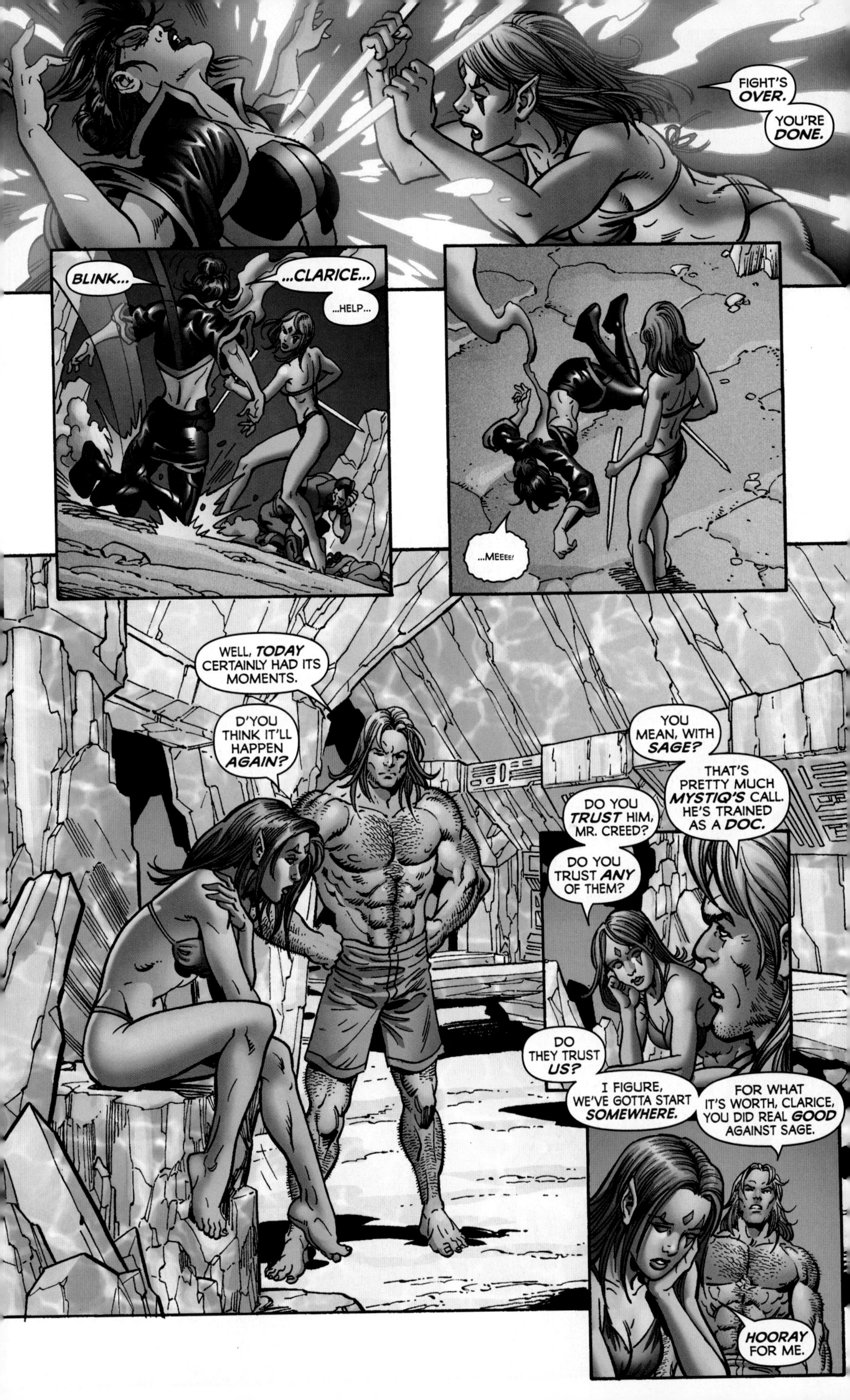
FIGHT'S OVER.
YOU'RE DONE.
BLINK...
...CLARICE...
...HELP...
...MEEEE!
WELL, TODAY CERTAINLY HAD ITS MOMENTS.
D'YOU THINK IT'LL HAPPEN AGAIN?
YOU MEAN, WITH SAGE?
THAT'S PRETTY MUCH MYSTIQ'S CALL. HE'S TRAINED AS A DOC.
DO YOU TRUST HIM, MR. CREED?
DO YOU TRUST ANY OF THEM?
DO THEY TRUST US?
I FIGURE, WE'VE GOTTA START SOMEWHERE.
FOR WHAT IT'S WORTH, CLARICE, YOU DID REAL GOOD AGAINST SAGE.
HOORAY FOR ME.

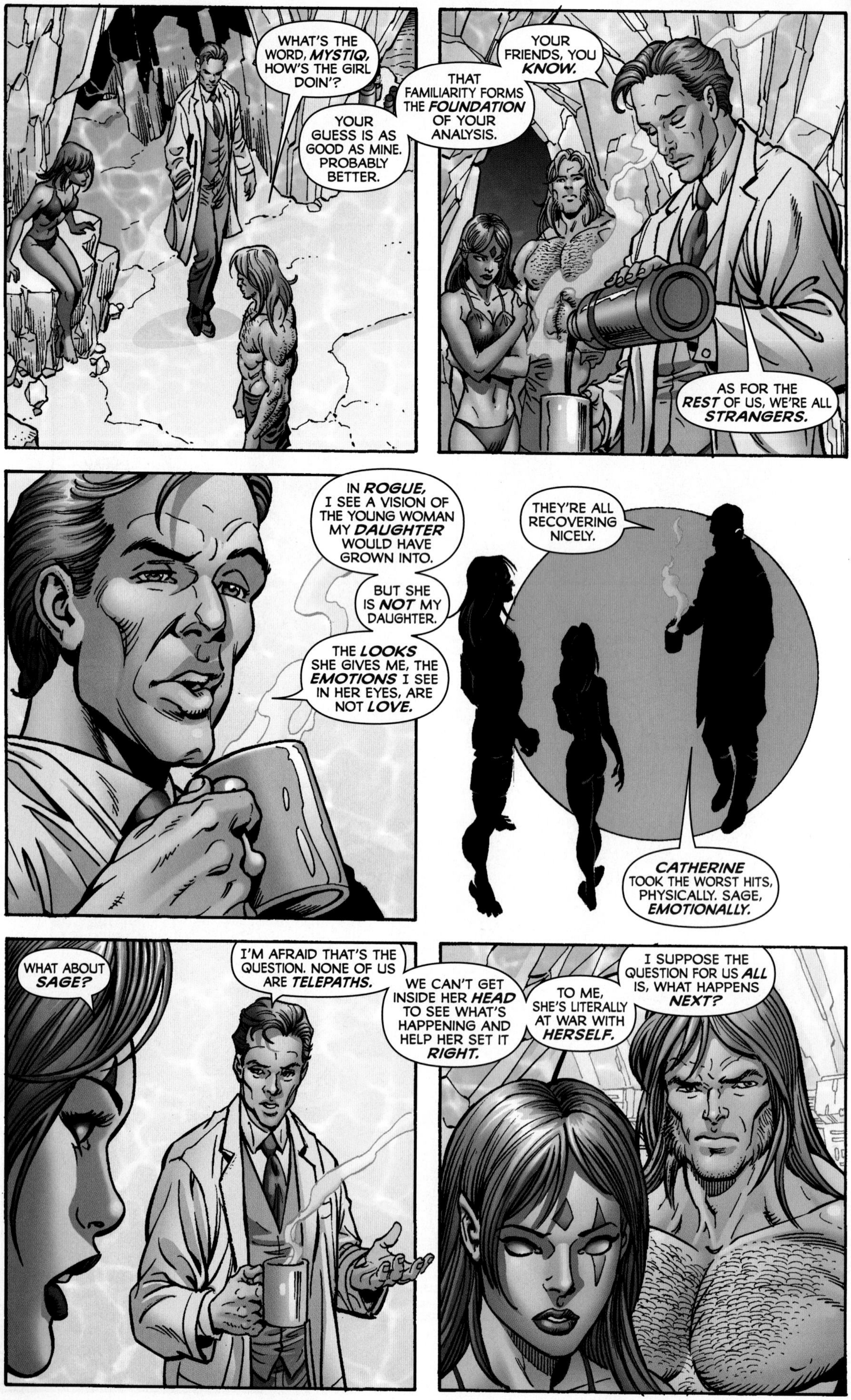
WHAT'S THE WORD, MYSTIQ, HOW'S THE GIRL DOIN'?
YOUR GUESS IS AS GOOD AS MINE. PROBABLY BETTER.
THAT FAMILIARITY FORMS THE FOUNDATION OF YOUR ANALYSIS.
YOUR FRIENDS, YOU KNOW.
AS FOR THE REST OF US, WE'RE ALL STRANGERS.
IN ROGUE, I SEE A VISION OF THE YOUNG WOMAN MY DAUGHTER WOULD HAVE GROWN INTO.
BUT SHE IS NOT MY DAUGHTER.
THE LOOKS SHE GIVES ME, THE EMOTIONS I SEE IN HER EYES, ARE NOT LOVE.
THEY'RE ALL RECOVERING NICELY.
CATHERINE TOOK THE WORST HITS, PHYSICALLY. SAGE, EMOTIONALLY.
WHAT ABOUT SAGE?
I'M AFRAID THAT'S THE QUESTION. NONE OF US ARE TELEPATHS.
WE CAN'T GET INSIDE HER HEAD TO SEE WHAT'S HAPPENING AND HELP HER SET IT RIGHT.
TO ME, SHE'S LITERALLY AT WAR WITH HERSELF.
I SUPPOSE THE QUESTION FOR US ALL IS, WHAT HAPPENS NEXT?

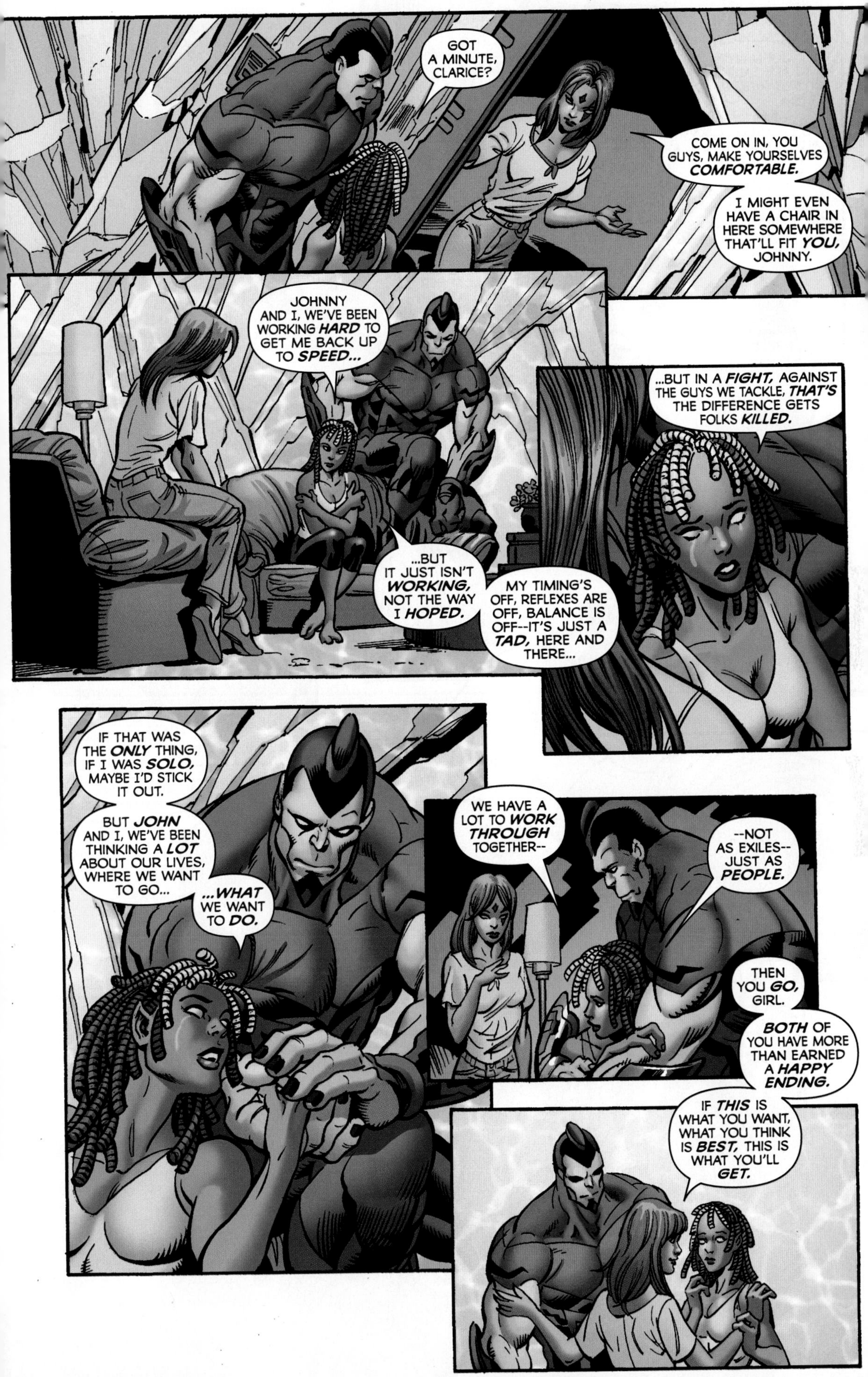
GOT A MINUTE, CLARICE?
COME ON IN, YOU GUYS, MAKE YOURSELVES COMFORTABLE.
I MIGHT EVEN HAVE A CHAIR IN HERE SOMEWHERE THAT'LL FIT YOU, JOHNNY.
JOHNNY AND I, WE'VE BEEN WORKING HARD TO GET ME BACK UP TO SPEED...
...BUT IT JUST ISN'T WORKING, NOT THE WAY I HOPED.
MY TIMING'S OFF, REFLEXES ARE OFF, BALANCE IS OFF--IT'S JUST A TAD, HERE AND THERE...
...BUT IN A FIGHT, AGAINST THE GUYS WE TACKLE, THAT'S THE DIFFERENCE GETS FOLKS KILLED.
IF THAT WAS THE ONLY THING, IF I WAS SOLO, MAYBE I'D STICK IT OUT.
BUT JOHN AND I, WE'VE BEEN THINKING A LOT ABOUT OUR LIVES, WHERE WE WANT TO GO...
...WHAT WE WANT TO DO.
WE HAVE A LOT TO WORK THROUGH TOGETHER--
--NOT AS EXILES-- JUST AS PEOPLE.
THEN YOU GO, GIRL.
BOTH OF YOU HAVE MORE THAN EARNED A HAPPY ENDING.
IF THIS IS WHAT YOU WANT, WHAT YOU THINK IS BEST, THIS IS WHAT YOU'LL GET.

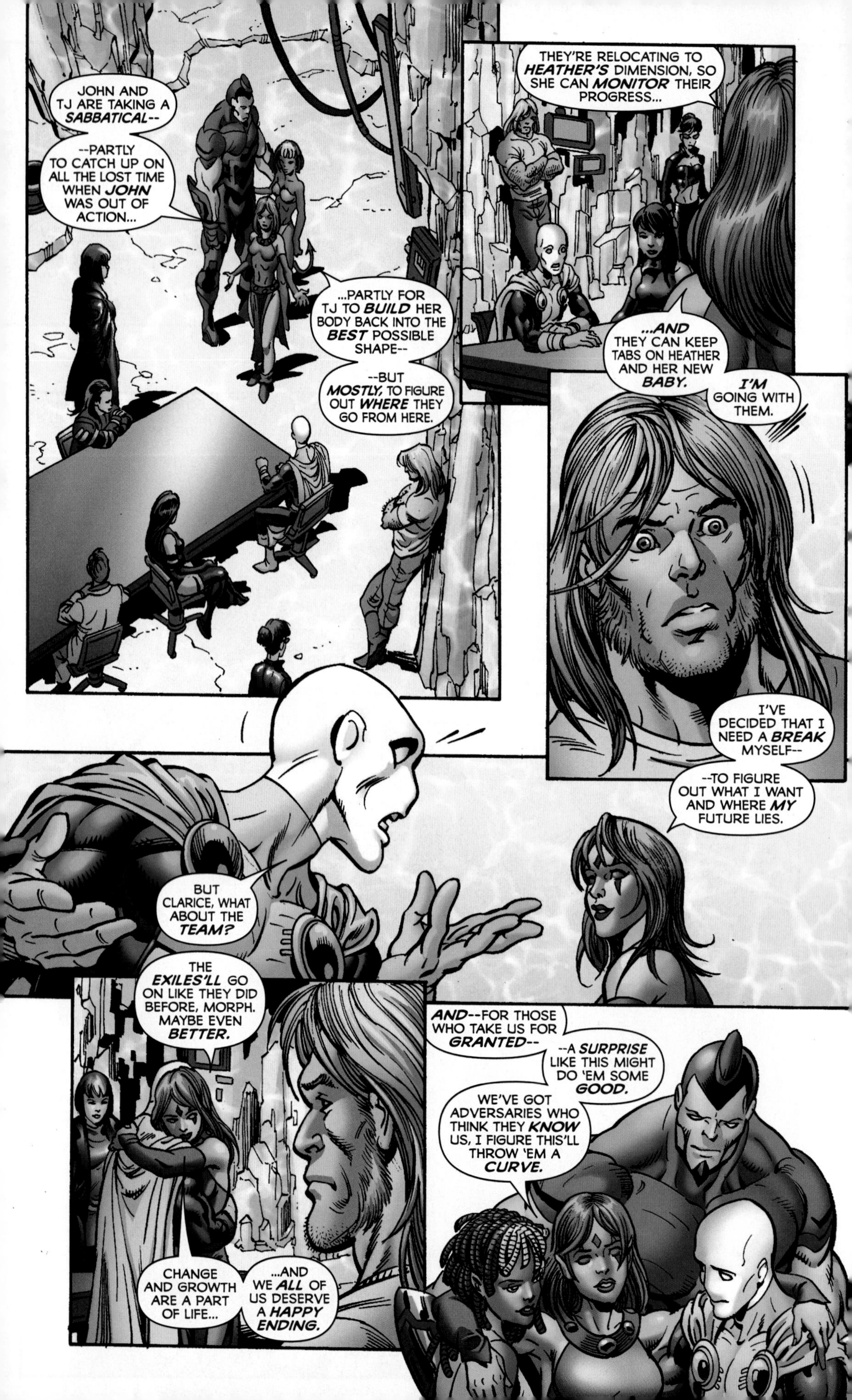
JOHN AND TJ ARE TAKING A SABBATICAL--
--PARTLY TO CATCH UP ON ALL THE LOST TIME WHEN JOHN WAS OUT OF ACTION...
...PARTLY FOR TJ TO BUILD HER BODY BACK INTO THE BEST POSSIBLE SHAPE--
--BUT MOSTLY, TO FIGURE OUT WHERE THEY GO FROM HERE.
THEY'RE RELOCATING TO HEATHER'S DIMENSION, SO SHE CAN MONITOR THEIR PROGRESS...
...AND THEY CAN KEEP TABS ON HEATHER AND HER NEW BABY.
I'M GOING WITH THEM.
I'VE DECIDED THAT I NEED A BREAK MYSELF--
--TO FIGURE OUT WHAT I WANT AND WHERE MY FUTURE LIES.
BUT CLARICE, WHAT ABOUT THE TEAM?
THE EXILES'LL GO ON LIKE THEY DID BEFORE, MORPH. MAYBE EVEN BETTER.
CHANGE AND GROWTH ARE A PART OF LIFE...
...AND WE ALL OF US DESERVE A HAPPY ENDING.
AND--FOR THOSE WHO TAKE US FOR GRANTED--
--A SURPRISE LIKE THIS MIGHT DO 'EM SOME GOOD.
WE'VE GOT ADVERSARIES WHO THINK THEY KNOW US, I FIGURE THIS'LL THROW 'EM A CURVE.

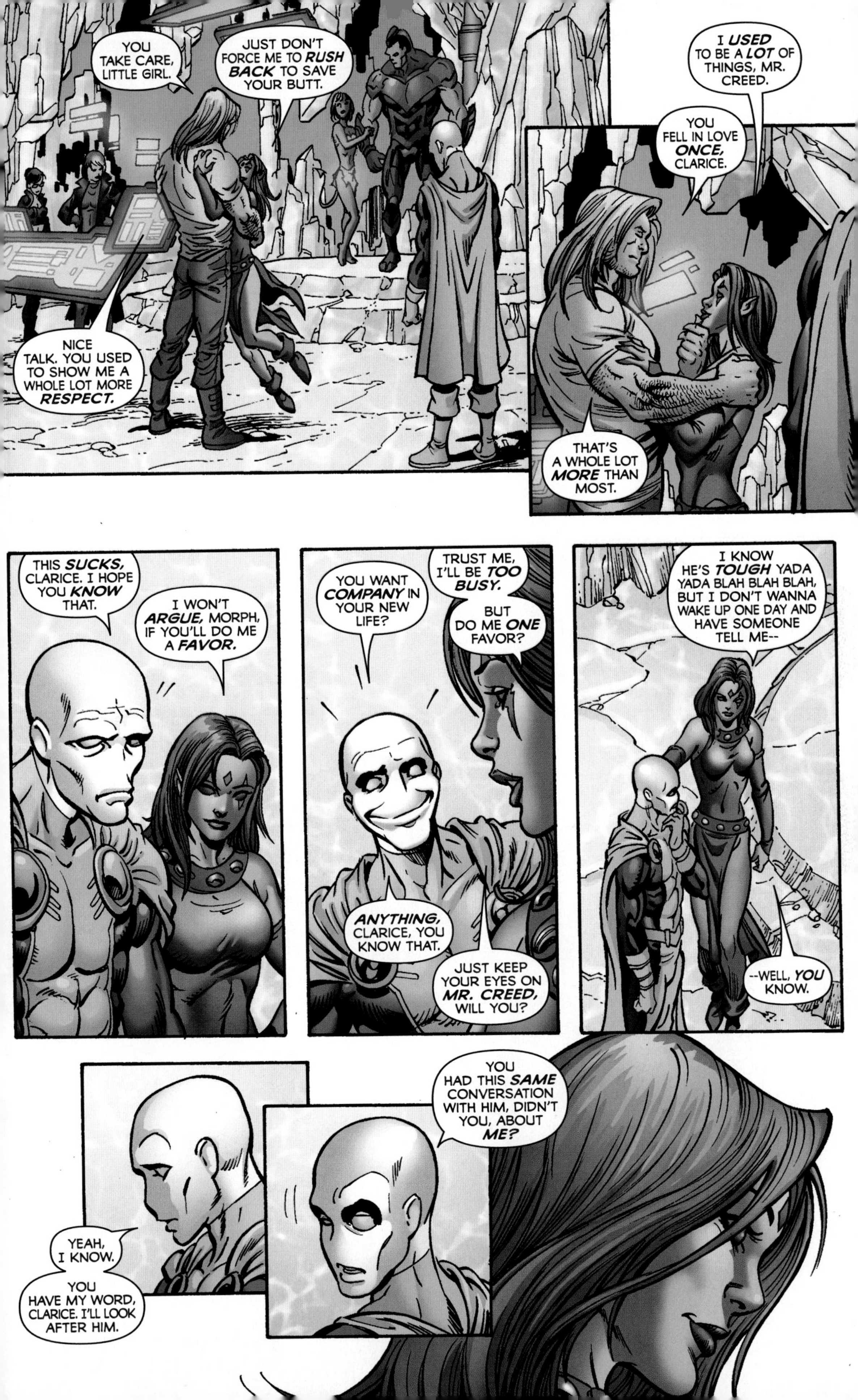
YOU TAKE CARE, LITTLE GIRL.
JUST DON'T FORCE ME TO RUSH BACK TO SAVE YOUR BUTT.
NICE TALK. YOU USED TO SHOW ME A WHOLE LOT MORE RESPECT.
I USED TO BE A LOT OF THINGS, MR. CREED.
YOU FELL IN LOVE ONCE, CLARICE.
THAT'S A WHOLE LOT MORE THAN MOST.
THIS SUCKS, CLARICE. I HOPE YOU KNOW THAT.
I WON'T ARGUE, MORPH, IF YOU'LL DO ME A FAVOR.
YOU WANT COMPANY IN YOUR NEW LIFE?
TRUST ME, I'LL BE TOO BUSY.
BUT DO ME ONE FAVOR?
ANYTHING, CLARICE, YOU KNOW THAT.
JUST KEEP YOUR EYES ON MR. CREED, WILL YOU?
I KNOW HE'S TOUGH YADA YADA BLAH BLAH BLAH, BUT I DON'T WANNA WAKE UP ONE DAY AND HAVE SOMEONE TELL ME--
--WELL, YOU KNOW.
YEAH, I KNOW.
YOU HAVE MY WORD, CLARICE. I'LL LOOK AFTER HIM.
YOU HAD THIS SAME CONVERSATION WITH HIM, DIDN'T YOU, ABOUT ME?

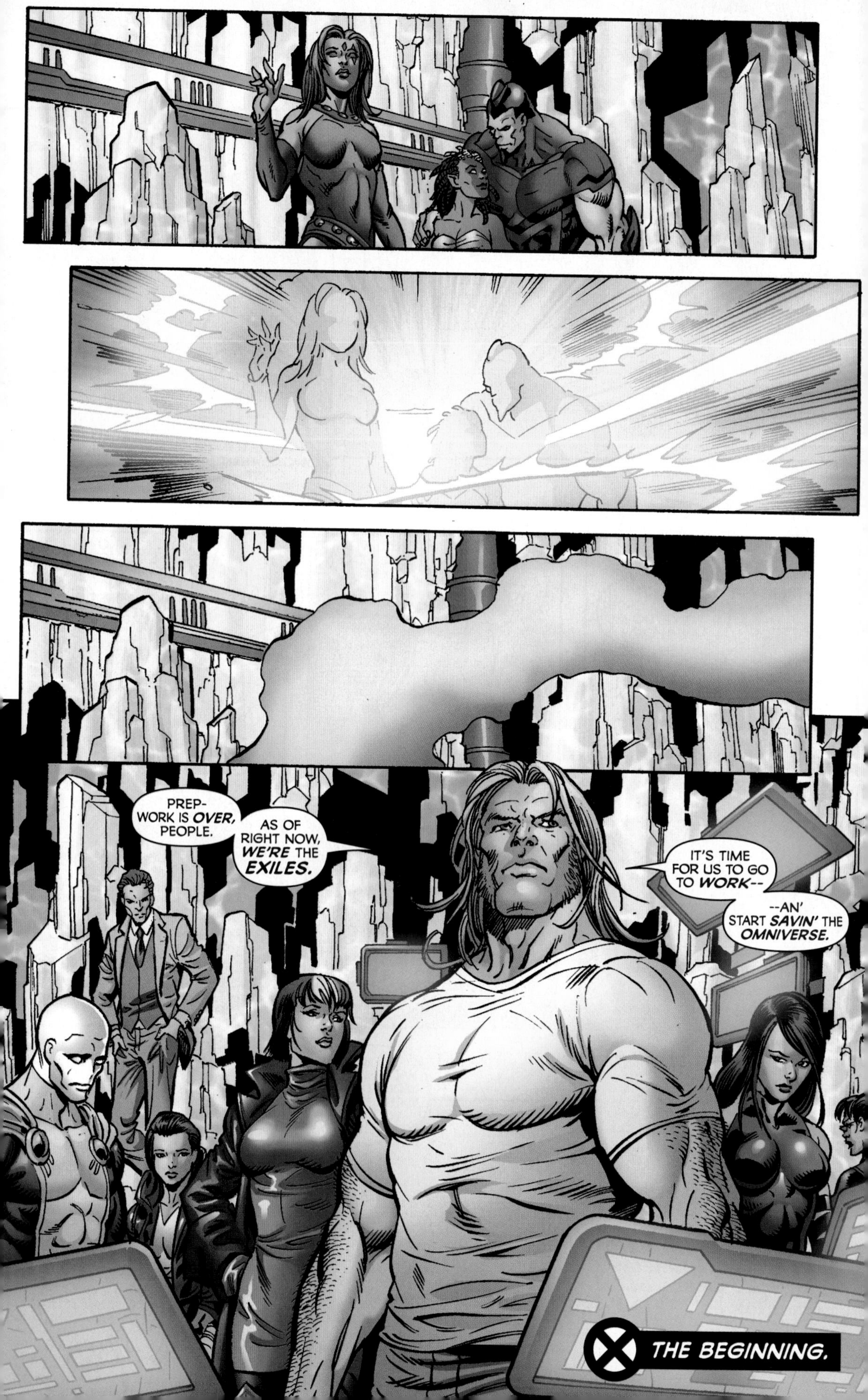
PREP-WORK IS OVER, PEOPLE.
AS OF RIGHT NOW, WE'RE THE EXILES.
IT'S TIME FOR US TO GO TO WORK--
--AN' START SAVIN' THE OMNIVERSE.
THE BEGINNING.

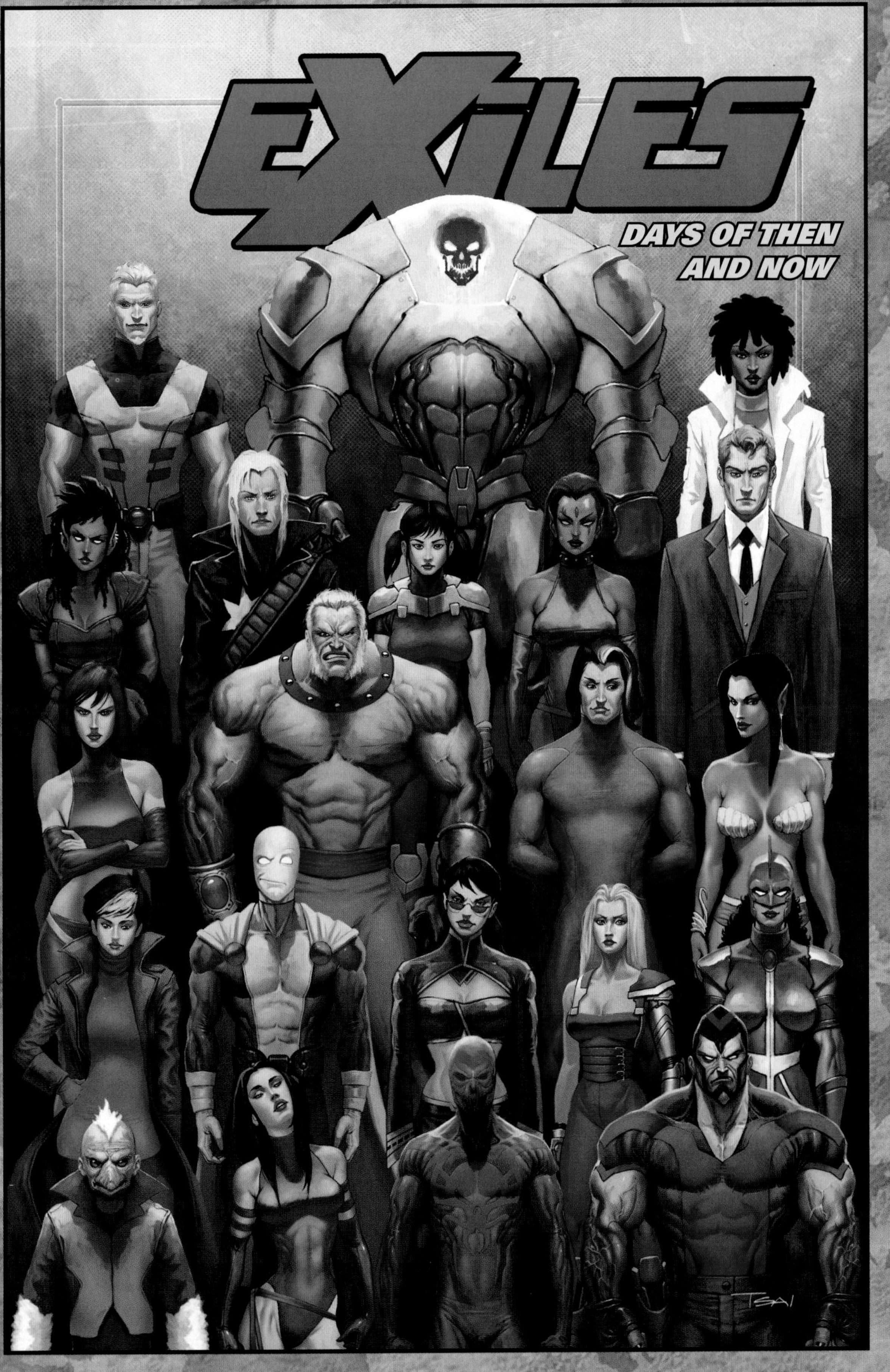
EXILES
DAYS OF THEN AND NOW
TSAI

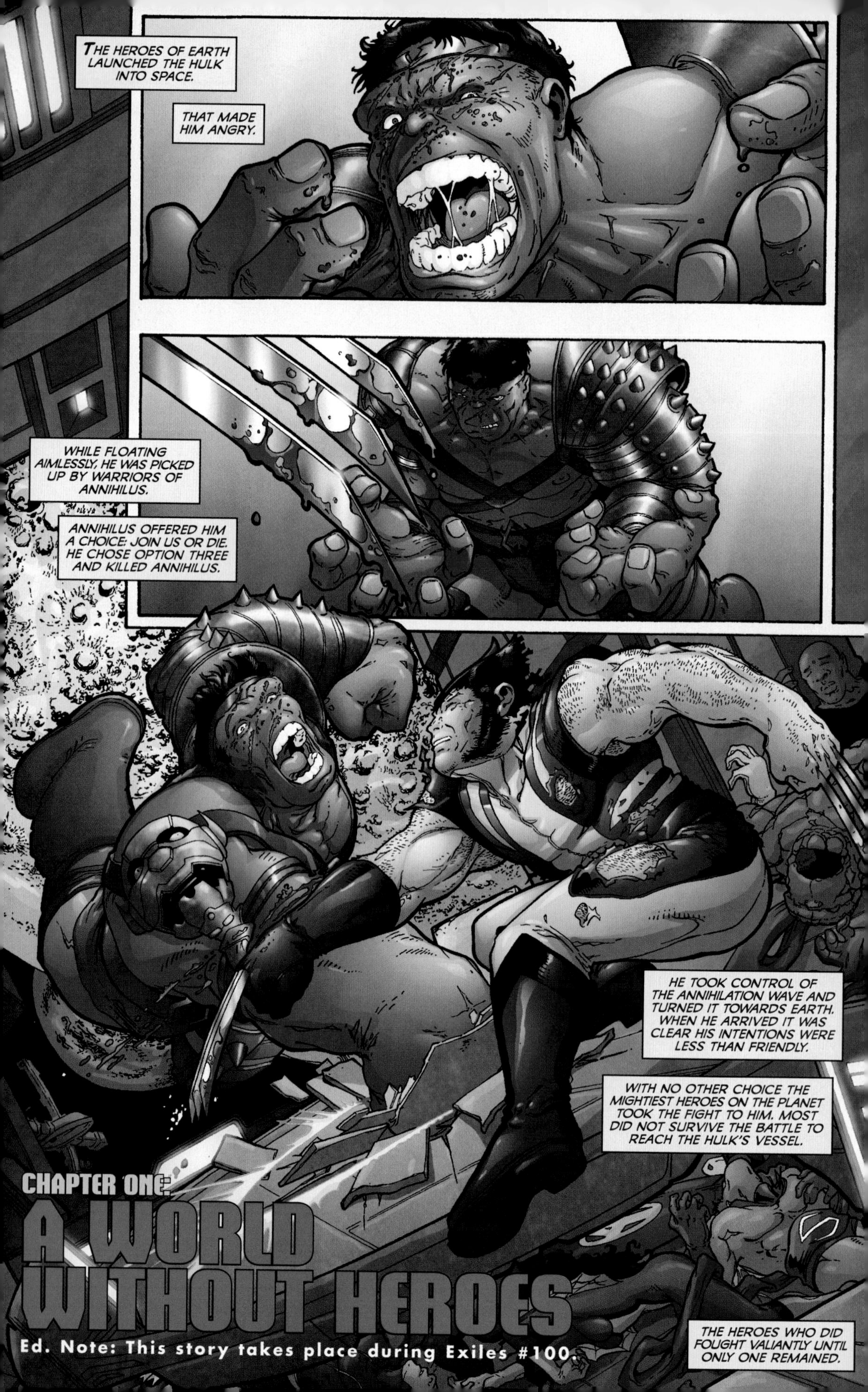
THE HEROES OF EARTH LAUNCHED THE HULK INTO SPACE.
THAT MADE HIM ANGRY.
WHILE FLOATING AIMLESSLY, HE WAS PICKED UP BY WARRIORS OF ANNIHILUS.
ANNIHILUS OFFERED HIM A CHOICE: JOIN US OR DIE. HE CHOSE OPTION THREE AND KILLED ANNIHILUS.
HE TOOK CONTROL OF THE ANNIHILATION WAVE AND TURNED IT TOWARDS EARTH. WHEN HE ARRIVED IT WAS CLEAR HIS INTENTIONS WERE LESS THAN FRIENDLY.
WITH NO OTHER CHOICE THE MIGHTIEST HEROES ON THE PLANET TOOK THE FIGHT TO HIM. MOST DID NOT SURVIVE THE BATTLE TO REACH THE HULK'S VESSEL.
CHAPTER ONE:
A WORLD WITHOUT HEROES
Ed. Note: This story takes place during Exiles #100.
THE HEROES WHO DID FOUGHT VALIANTLY UNTIL ONLY ONE REMAINED.

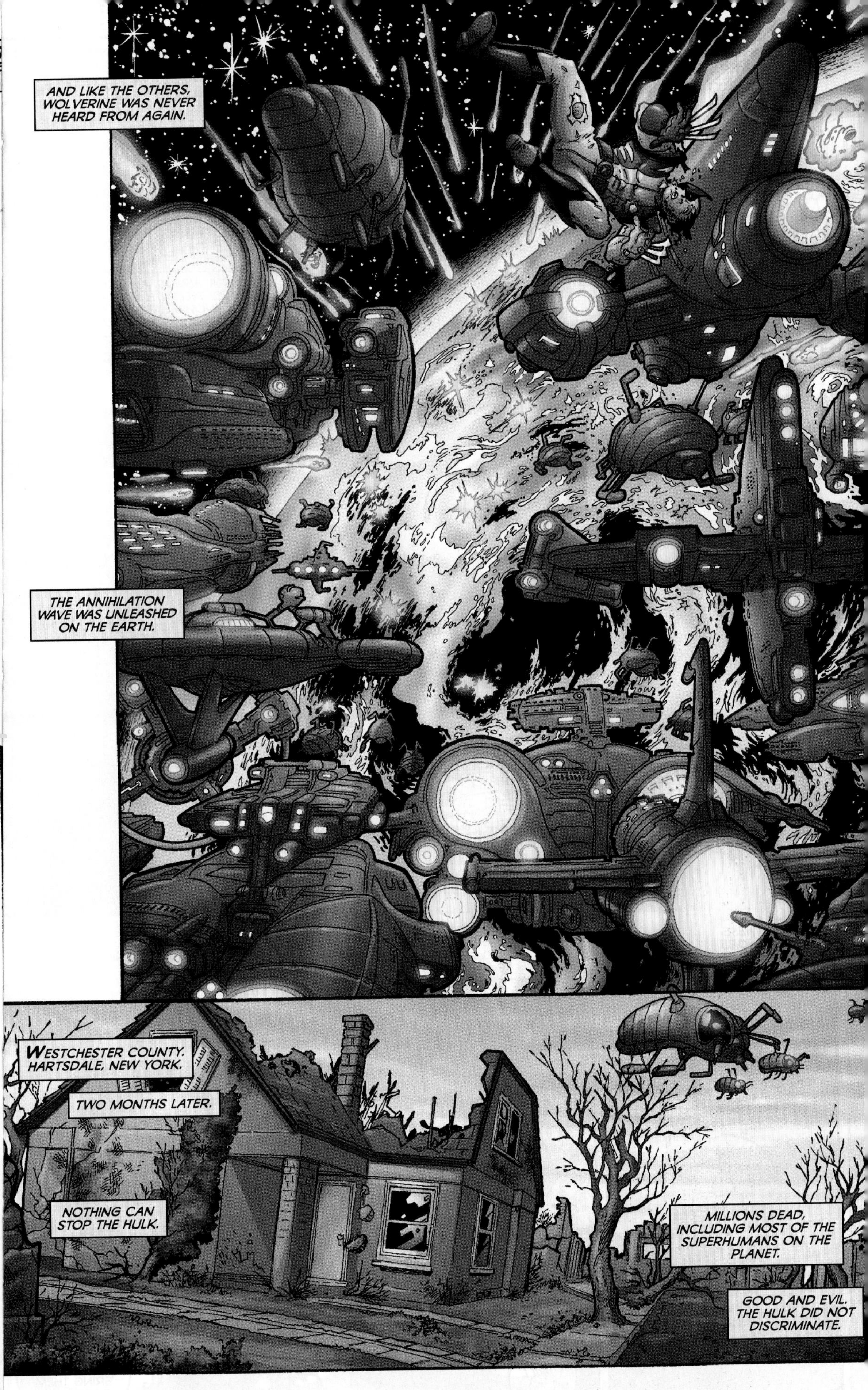
AND LIKE THE OTHERS, WOLVERINE WAS NEVER HEARD FROM AGAIN.
THE ANNIHILATION WAVE WAS UNLEASHED ON THE EARTH.
WESTCHESTER COUNTY. HARTSDALE, NEW YORK.
TWO MONTHS LATER.
NOTHING CAN STOP THE HULK.
MILLIONS DEAD, INCLUDING MOST OF THE SUPERHUMANS ON THE PLANET.
GOOD AND EVIL. THE HULK DID NOT DISCRIMINATE.

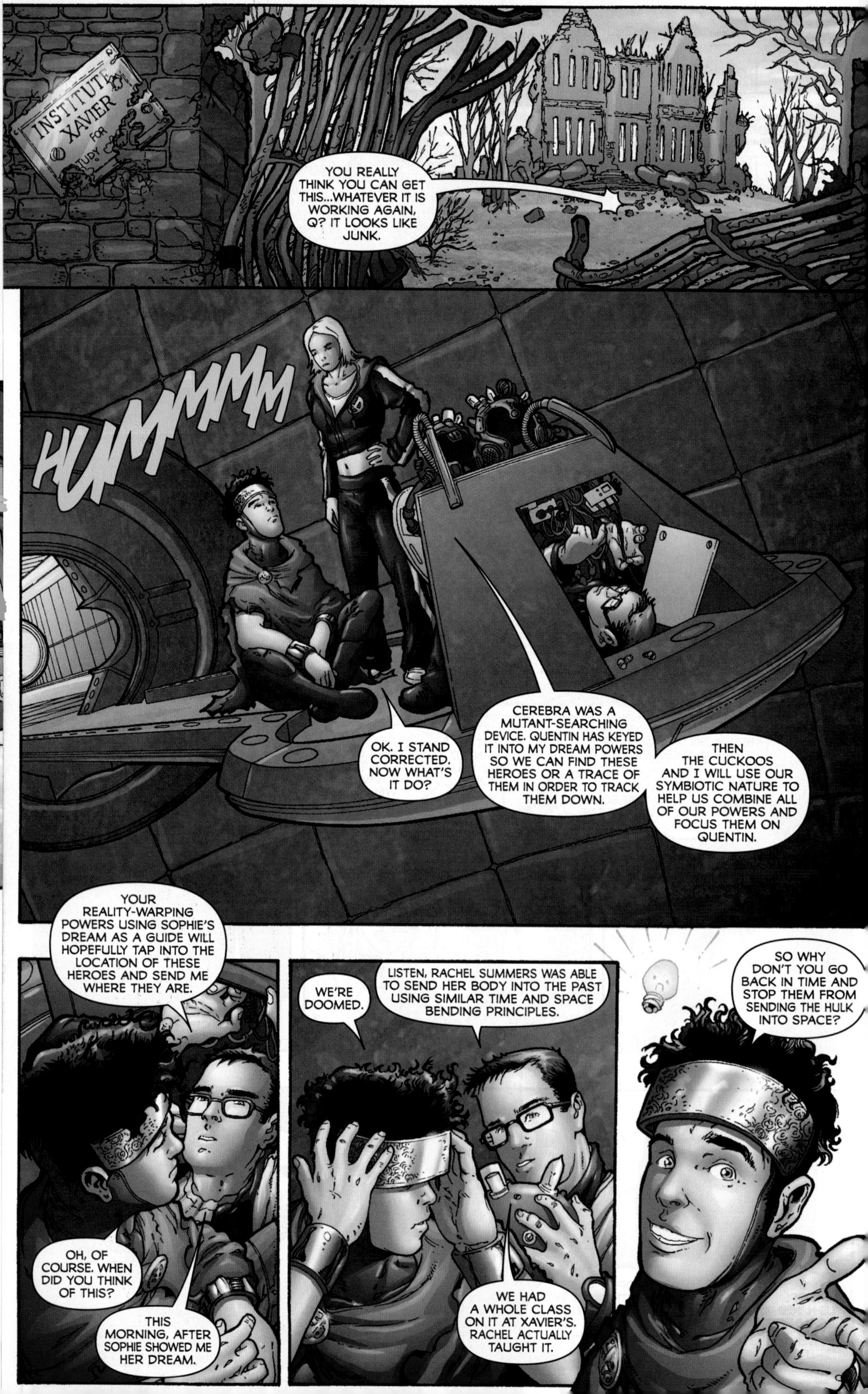
INSTITUTE XAVIER FOR
YOU REALLY THINK YOU CAN GET THIS...WHATEVER IT IS WORKING AGAIN, Q? IT LOOKS LIKE JUNK.
HUMMMMM
OK. I STAND CORRECTED. NOW WHAT'S IT DO?
CEREBRA WAS A MUTANT-SEARCHING DEVICE. QUENTIN HAS KEYED IT INTO MY DREAM POWERS SO WE CAN FIND THESE HEROES OR A TRACE OF THEM IN ORDER TO TRACK THEM DOWN.
THEN THE CUCKOOS AND I WILL USE OUR SYMBIOTIC NATURE TO HELP US COMBINE ALL OF OUR POWERS AND FOCUS THEM ON QUENTIN.
YOUR REALITY-WARPING POWERS USING SOPHIE'S DREAM AS A GUIDE WILL HOPEFULLY TAP INTO THE LOCATION OF THESE HEROES AND SEND ME WHERE THEY ARE.
OH, OF COURSE. WHEN DID YOU THINK OF THIS?
THIS MORNING, AFTER SOPHIE SHOWED ME HER DREAM.
WE'RE DOOMED.
LISTEN, RACHEL SUMMERS WAS ABLE TO SEND HER BODY INTO THE PAST USING SIMILAR TIME AND SPACE BENDING PRINCIPLES.
WE HAD A WHOLE CLASS ON IT AT XAVIER'S. RACHEL ACTUALLY TAUGHT IT.
SO WHY DON'T YOU GO BACK IN TIME AND STOP THEM FROM SENDING THE HULK INTO SPACE?

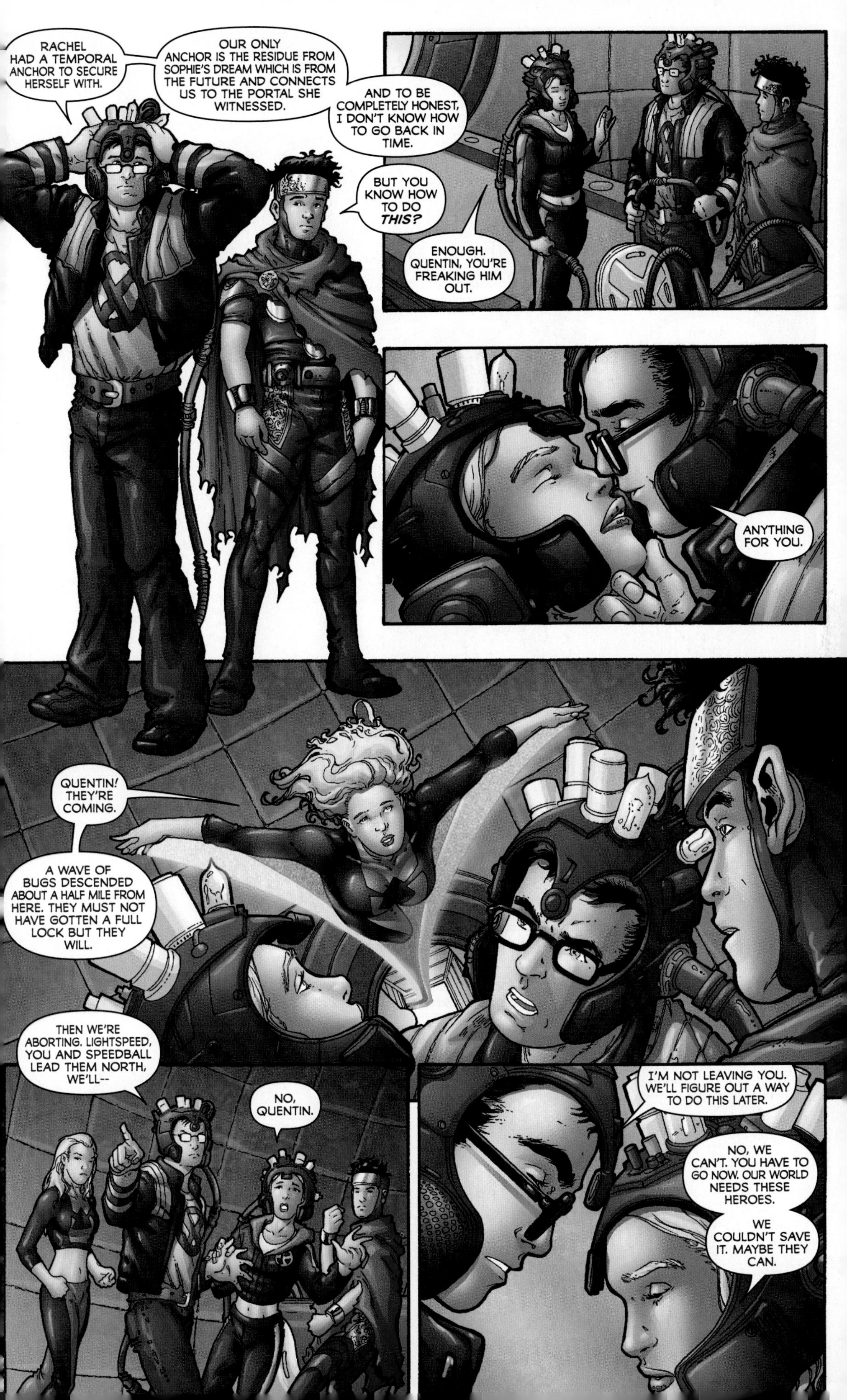
RACHEL HAD A TEMPORAL ANCHOR TO SECURE HERSELF WITH.
OUR ONLY ANCHOR IS THE RESIDUE FROM SOPHIE'S DREAM WHICH IS FROM THE FUTURE AND CONNECTS US TO THE PORTAL SHE WITNESSED.
AND TO BE COMPLETELY HONEST, I DON'T KNOW HOW TO GO BACK IN TIME.
BUT YOU KNOW HOW TO DO *THIS?*
ENOUGH. QUENTIN, YOU'RE FREAKING HIM OUT.
ANYTHING FOR YOU.
QUENTIN! THEY'RE COMING.
A WAVE OF BUGS DESCENDED ABOUT A HALF MILE FROM HERE. THEY MUST NOT HAVE GOTTEN A FULL LOCK BUT THEY WILL.
THEN WE'RE ABORTING. LIGHTSPEED, YOU AND SPEEDBALL LEAD THEM NORTH, WE'LL--
NO, QUENTIN.
I'M NOT LEAVING YOU. WE'LL FIGURE OUT A WAY TO DO THIS LATER.
NO, WE CAN'T. YOU HAVE TO GO NOW. OUR WORLD NEEDS THESE HEROES.
WE COULDN'T SAVE IT. MAYBE THEY CAN.

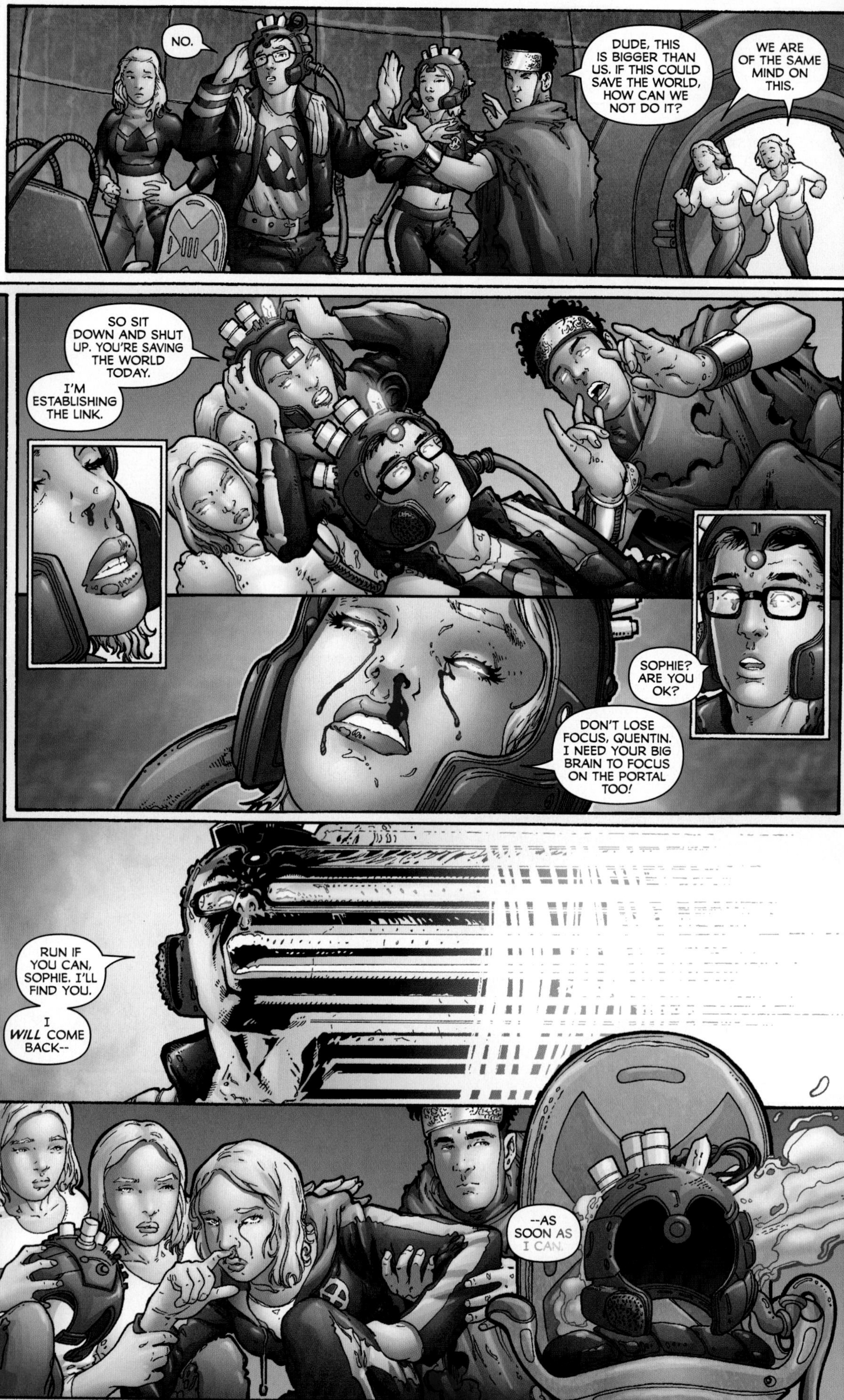
NO.
DUDE, THIS IS BIGGER THAN US. IF THIS COULD SAVE THE WORLD, HOW CAN WE NOT DO IT?
WE ARE OF THE SAME MIND ON THIS.
SO SIT DOWN AND SHUT UP. YOU'RE SAVING THE WORLD TODAY.
I'M ESTABLISHING THE LINK.
SOPHIE? ARE YOU OK?
DON'T LOSE FOCUS, QUENTIN. I NEED YOUR BIG BRAIN TO FOCUS ON THE PORTAL TOO!
RUN IF YOU CAN, SOPHIE. I'LL FIND YOU.
I *WILL* COME BACK--
--AS SOON AS I CAN.

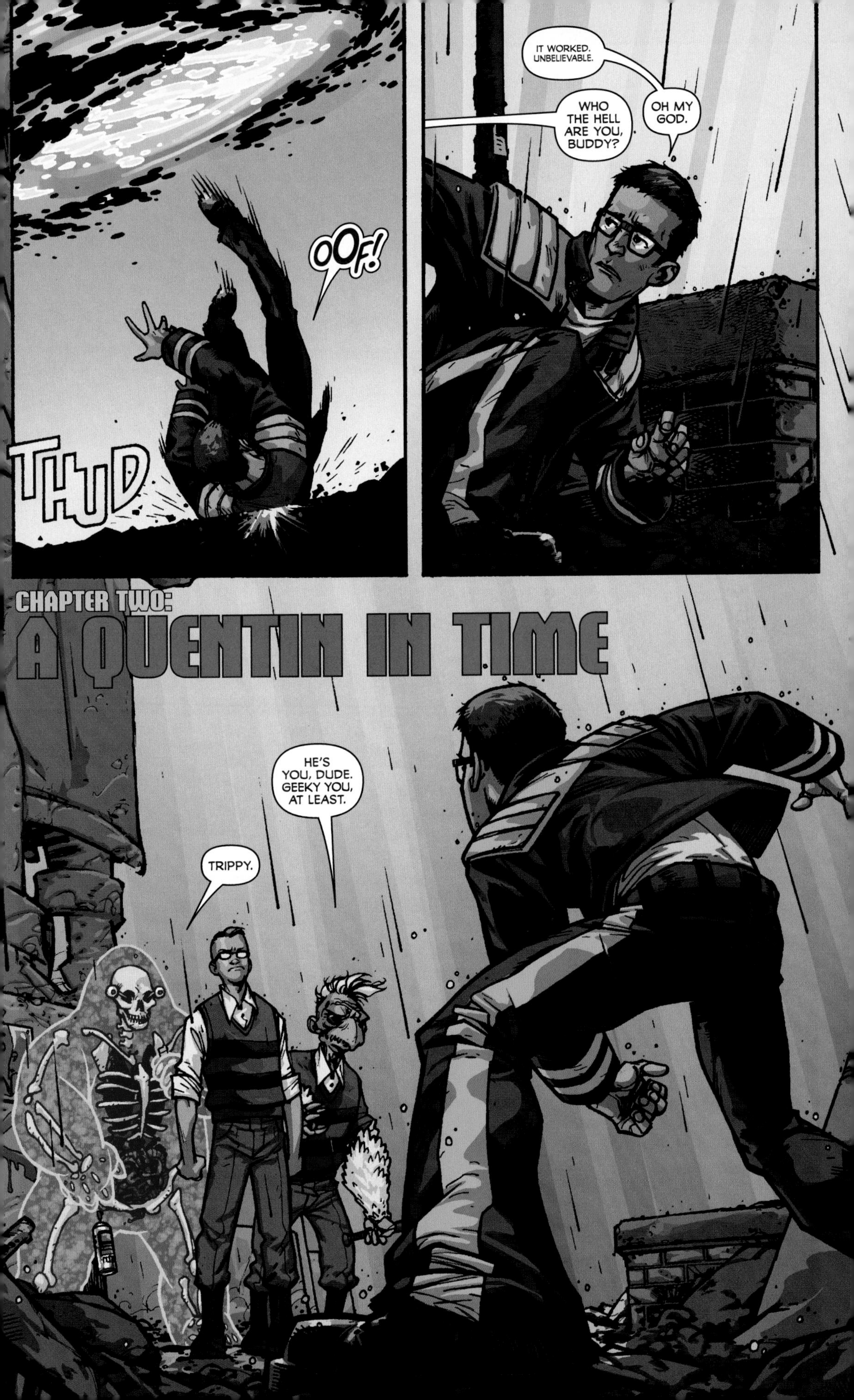
OOF!
THUD
IT WORKED. UNBELIEVABLE.
OH MY GOD.
WHO THE HELL ARE YOU, BUDDY?
CHAPTER TWO:
A QUENTIN IN TIME
HE'S YOU, DUDE. GEEKY YOU, AT LEAST.
TRIPPY.

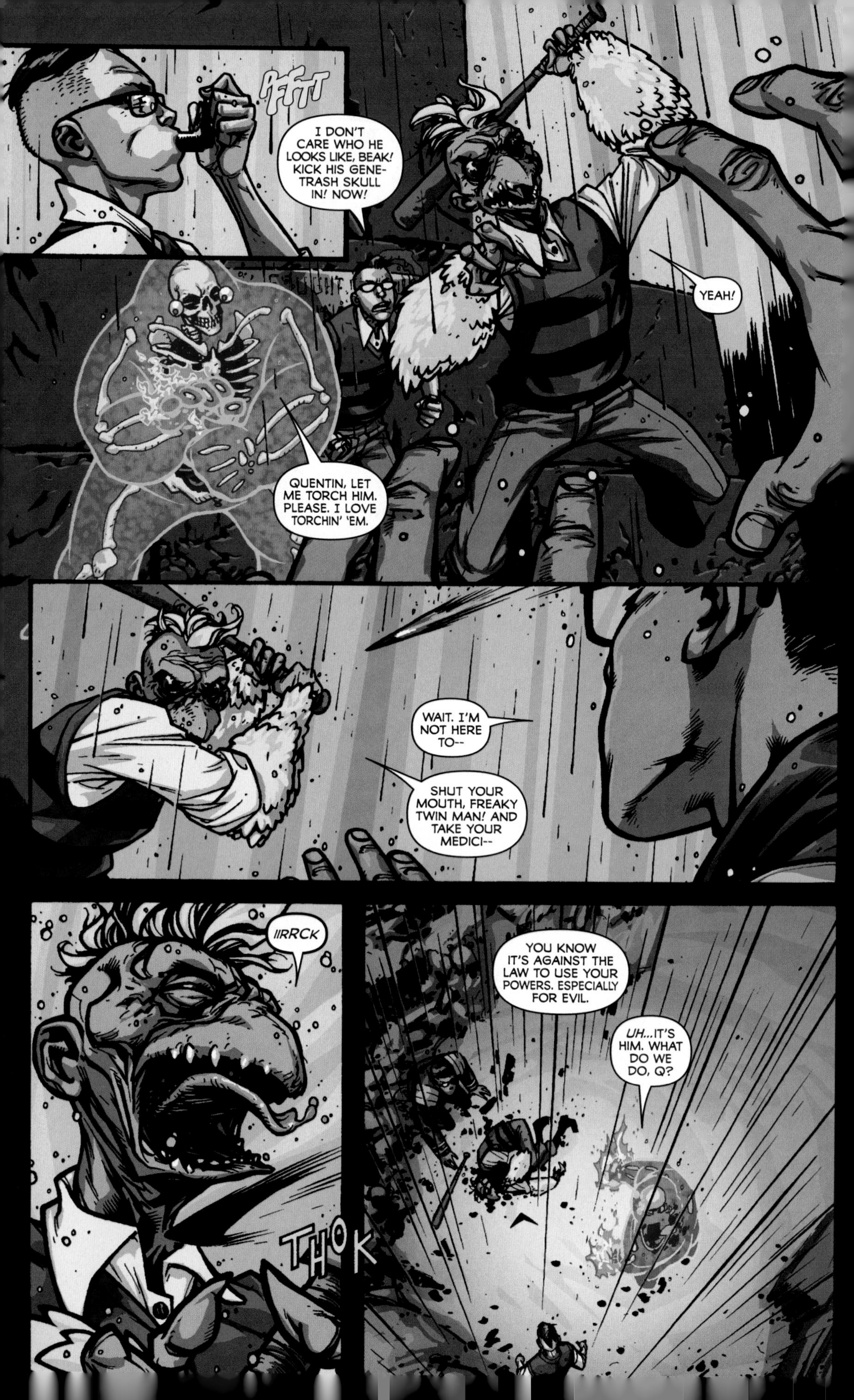
PFFTT
I DON'T CARE WHO HE LOOKS LIKE, BEAK! KICK HIS GENE-TRASH SKULL IN! NOW!
YEAH!
QUENTIN, LET ME TORCH HIM. PLEASE. I LOVE TORCHIN' 'EM.
WAIT. I'M NOT HERE TO--
SHUT YOUR MOUTH, FREAKY TWIN MAN! AND TAKE YOUR MEDICI--
IIRRCK
THOK
YOU KNOW IT'S AGAINST THE LAW TO USE YOUR POWERS. ESPECIALLY FOR EVIL.
UH...IT'S HIM. WHAT DO WE DO, Q?

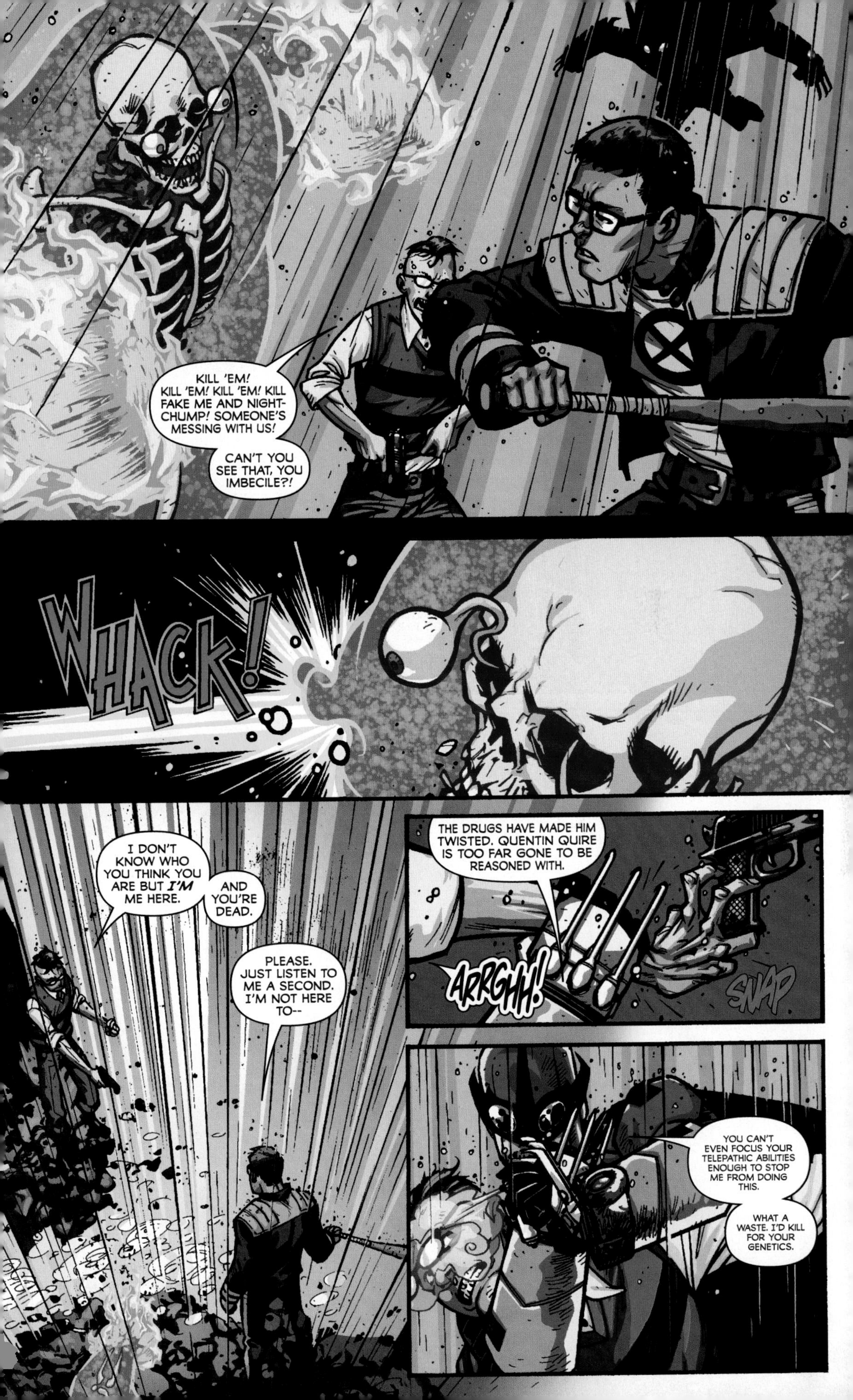

KILL 'EM! KILL 'EM! KILL 'EM! KILL FAKE ME AND NIGHT-CHUMP! SOMEONE'S MESSING WITH US!
CAN'T YOU SEE THAT, YOU IMBECILE?!
WHACK!
I DON'T KNOW WHO YOU THINK YOU ARE BUT I'M ME HERE.
AND YOU'RE DEAD.
PLEASE. JUST LISTEN TO ME A SECOND. I'M NOT HERE TO--
THE DRUGS HAVE MADE HIM TWISTED. QUENTIN QUIRE IS TOO FAR GONE TO BE REASONED WITH.
ARRGHH!
SNAP
YOU CAN'T EVEN FOCUS YOUR TELEPATHIC ABILITIES ENOUGH TO STOP ME FROM DOING THIS.
WHAT A WASTE. I'D KILL FOR YOUR GENETICS.

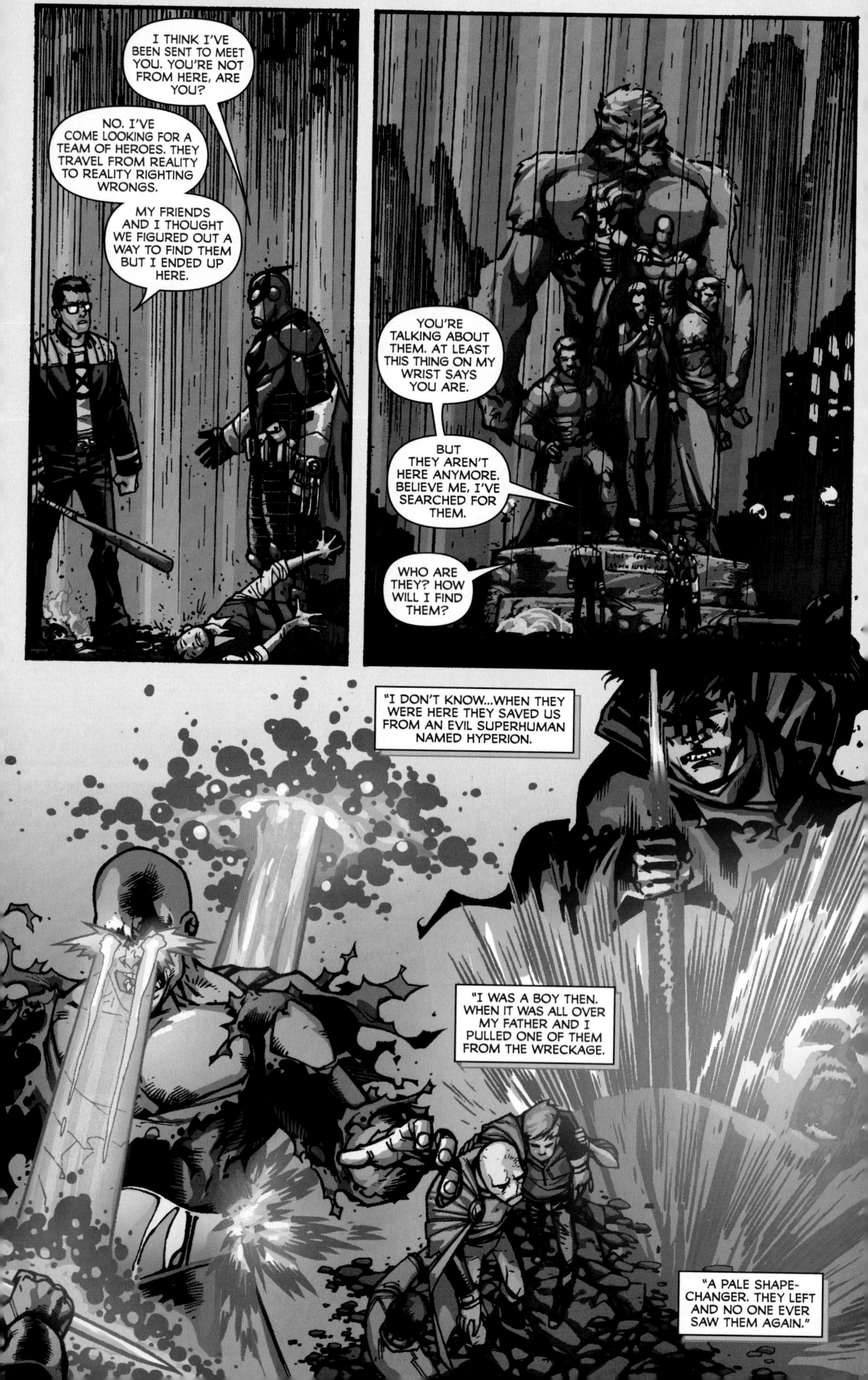
I THINK I'VE BEEN SENT TO MEET YOU. YOU'RE NOT FROM HERE, ARE YOU?
NO. I'VE COME LOOKING FOR A TEAM OF HEROES. THEY TRAVEL FROM REALITY TO REALITY RIGHTING WRONGS.
MY FRIENDS AND I THOUGHT WE FIGURED OUT A WAY TO FIND THEM BUT I ENDED UP HERE.
YOU'RE TALKING ABOUT THEM. AT LEAST THIS THING ON MY WRIST SAYS YOU ARE.
BUT THEY AREN'T HERE ANYMORE. BELIEVE ME, I'VE SEARCHED FOR THEM.
WHO ARE THEY? HOW WILL I FIND THEM?
"I DON'T KNOW...WHEN THEY WERE HERE THEY SAVED US FROM AN EVIL SUPERHUMAN NAMED HYPERION.
"I WAS A BOY THEN. WHEN IT WAS ALL OVER MY FATHER AND I PULLED ONE OF THEM FROM THE WRECKAGE.
"A PALE SHAPE-CHANGER. THEY LEFT AND NO ONE EVER SAW THEM AGAIN."

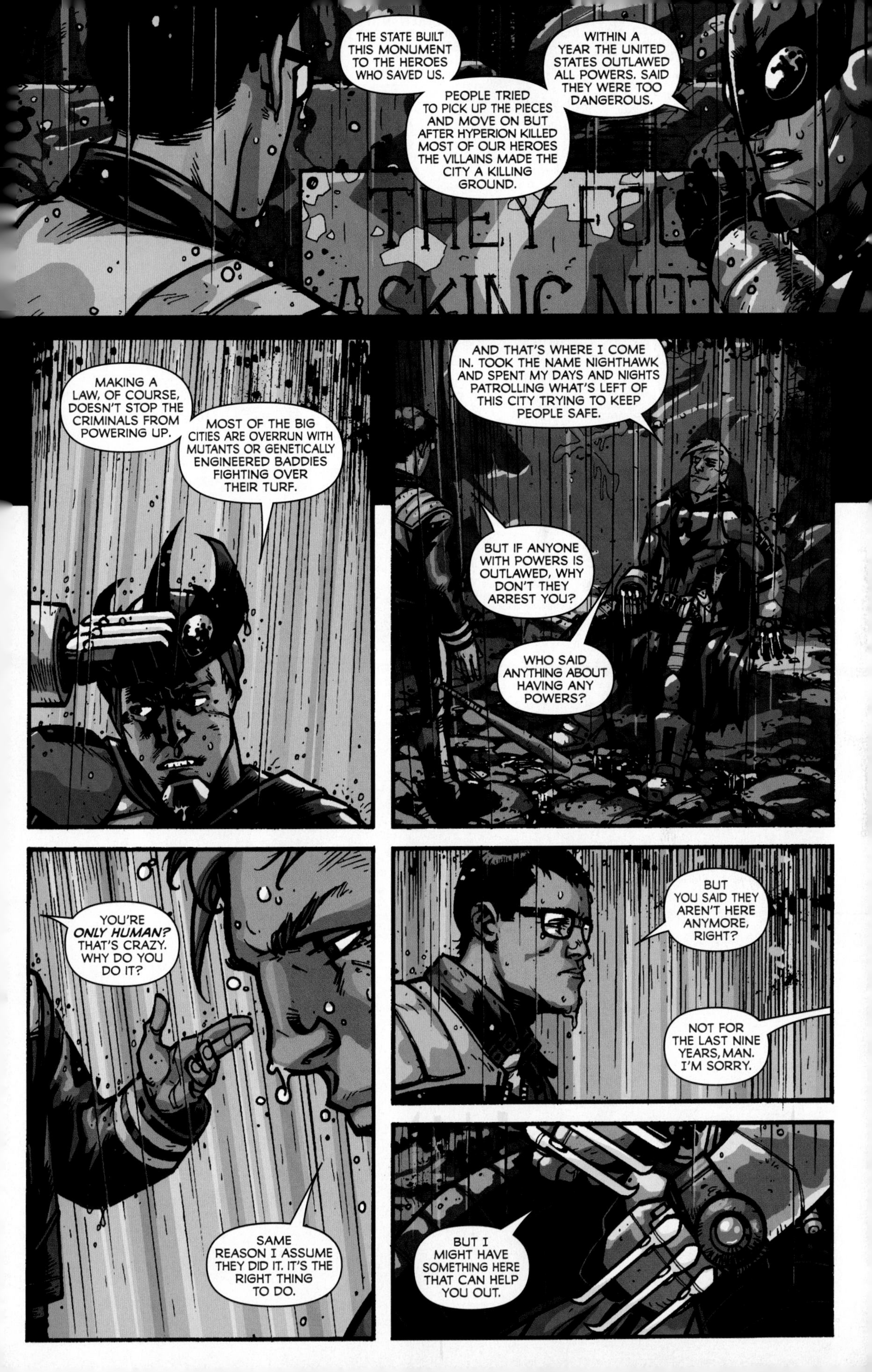
THE STATE BUILT THIS MONUMENT TO THE HEROES WHO SAVED US.
PEOPLE TRIED TO PICK UP THE PIECES AND MOVE ON BUT AFTER HYPERION KILLED MOST OF OUR HEROES THE VILLAINS MADE THE CITY A KILLING GROUND.
WITHIN A YEAR THE UNITED STATES OUTLAWED ALL POWERS. SAID THEY WERE TOO DANGEROUS.
THEY FOU
ASKING NOT
MAKING A LAW, OF COURSE, DOESN'T STOP THE CRIMINALS FROM POWERING UP.
MOST OF THE BIG CITIES ARE OVERRUN WITH MUTANTS OR GENETICALLY ENGINEERED BADDIES FIGHTING OVER THEIR TURF.
AND THAT'S WHERE I COME IN. TOOK THE NAME NIGHTHAWK AND SPENT MY DAYS AND NIGHTS PATROLLING WHAT'S LEFT OF THIS CITY TRYING TO KEEP PEOPLE SAFE.
BUT IF ANYONE WITH POWERS IS OUTLAWED, WHY DON'T THEY ARREST YOU?
WHO SAID ANYTHING ABOUT HAVING ANY POWERS?
YOU'RE *ONLY HUMAN?* THAT'S CRAZY. WHY DO YOU DO IT?
SAME REASON I ASSUME THEY DID IT. IT'S THE RIGHT THING TO DO.
BUT YOU SAID THEY AREN'T HERE ANYMORE, RIGHT?
NOT FOR THE LAST NINE YEARS, MAN. I'M SORRY.
BUT I MIGHT HAVE SOMETHING HERE THAT CAN HELP YOU OUT.

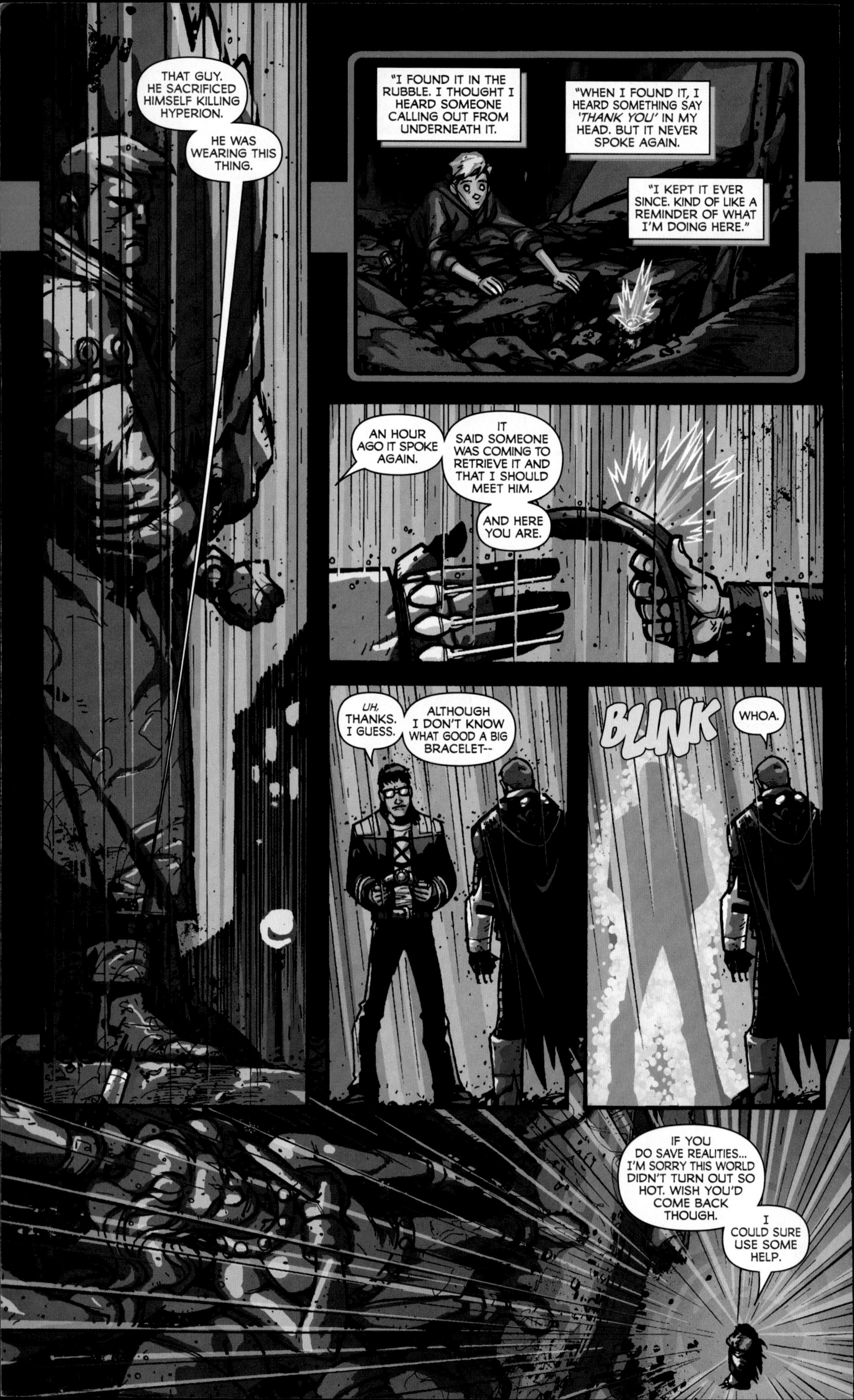
THAT GUY. HE SACRIFICED HIMSELF KILLING HYPERION.
HE WAS WEARING THIS THING.
"I FOUND IT IN THE RUBBLE. I THOUGHT I HEARD SOMEONE CALLING OUT FROM UNDERNEATH IT.
"WHEN I FOUND IT, I HEARD SOMETHING SAY *'THANK YOU'* IN MY HEAD. BUT IT NEVER SPOKE AGAIN.
"I KEPT IT EVER SINCE. KIND OF LIKE A REMINDER OF WHAT I'M DOING HERE."
AN HOUR AGO IT SPOKE AGAIN.
IT SAID SOMEONE WAS COMING TO RETRIEVE IT AND THAT I SHOULD MEET HIM.
AND HERE YOU ARE.
UH, THANKS. I GUESS.
ALTHOUGH I DON'T KNOW WHAT GOOD A BIG BRACELET--
BLINK
WHOA.
IF YOU DO SAVE REALITIES... I'M SORRY THIS WORLD DIDN'T TURN OUT SO HOT. WISH YOU'D COME BACK THOUGH.
I COULD SURE USE SOME HELP.

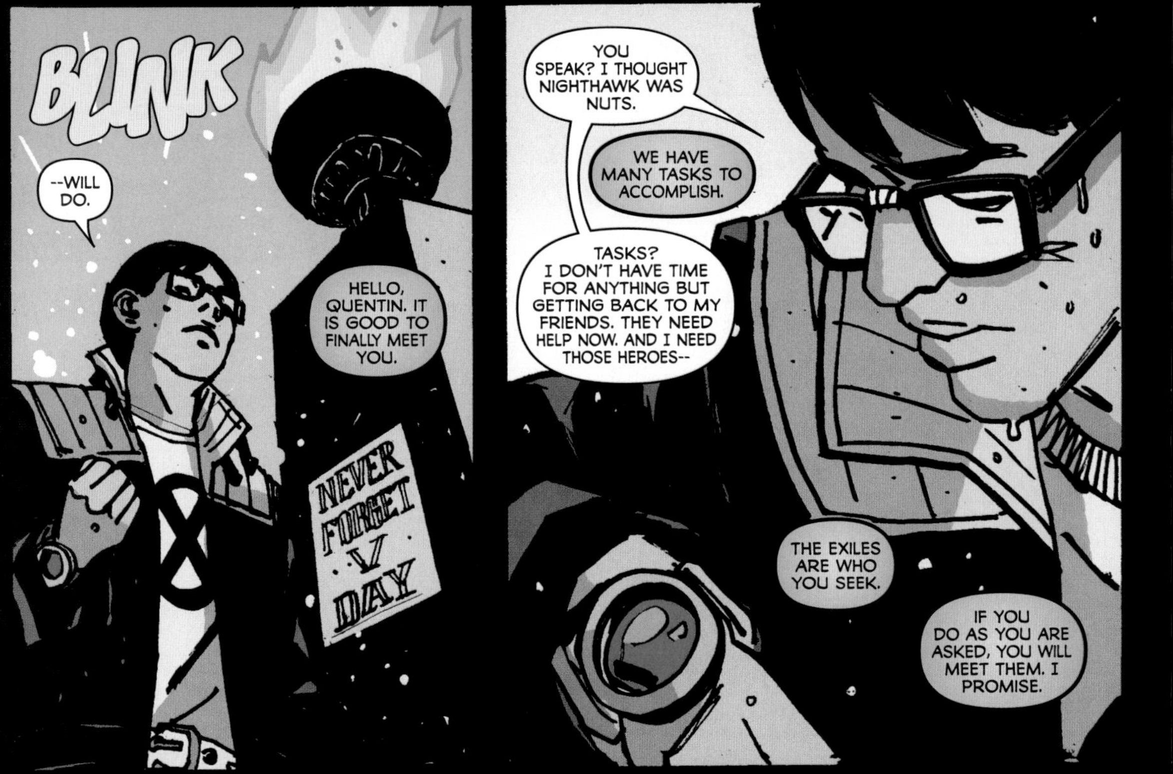
BLINK
--WILL DO.
HELLO, QUENTIN. IT IS GOOD TO FINALLY MEET YOU.
NEVER FORGET V DAY
YOU SPEAK? I THOUGHT NIGHTHAWK WAS NUTS.
WE HAVE MANY TASKS TO ACCOMPLISH.
TASKS? I DON'T HAVE TIME FOR ANYTHING BUT GETTING BACK TO MY FRIENDS. THEY NEED HELP NOW. AND I NEED THOSE HEROES--
THE EXILES ARE WHO YOU SEEK.
IF YOU DO AS YOU ARE ASKED, YOU WILL MEET THEM. I PROMISE.

CHAPTER THREE:

LEGACY

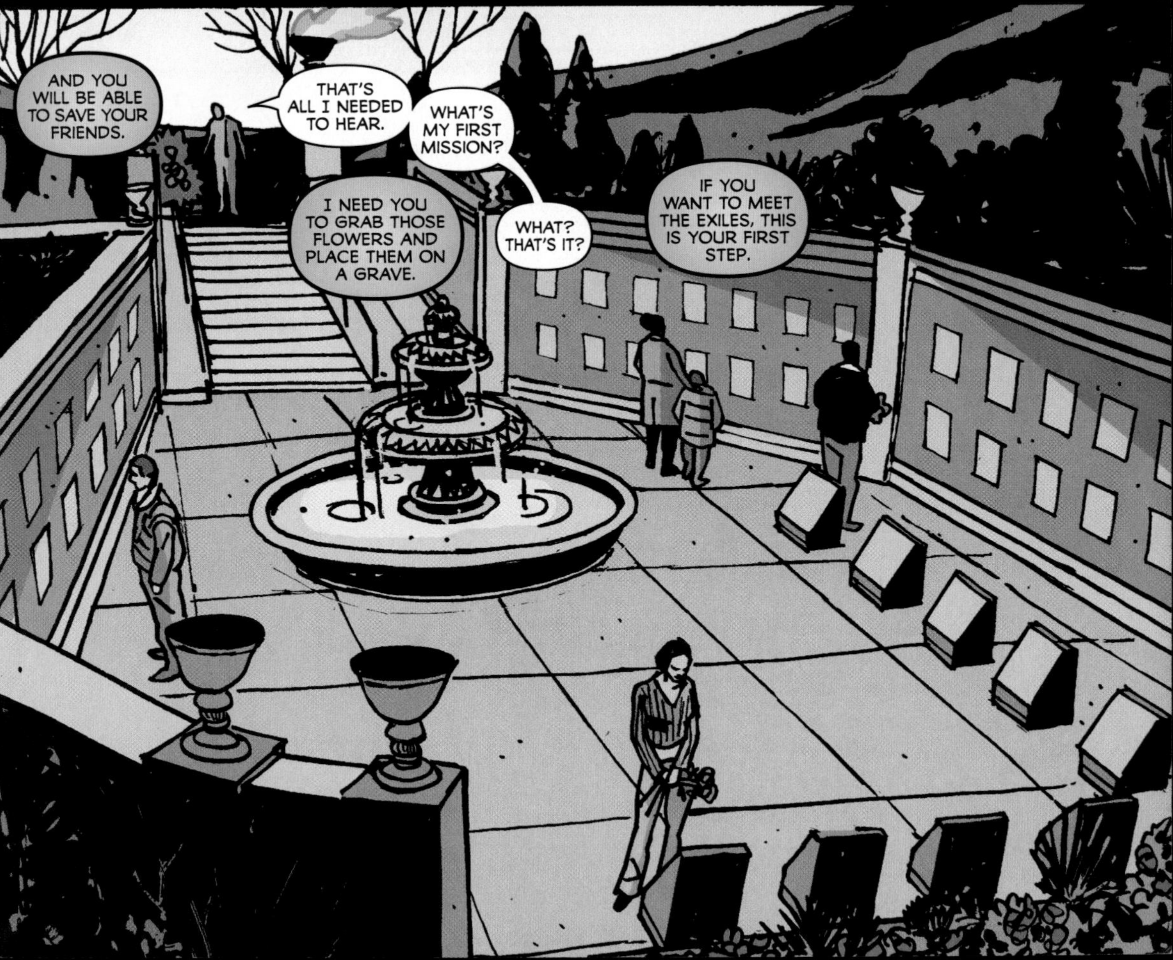
AND YOU WILL BE ABLE TO SAVE YOUR FRIENDS.
THAT'S ALL I NEEDED TO HEAR.
WHAT'S MY FIRST MISSION?
I NEED YOU TO GRAB THOSE FLOWERS AND PLACE THEM ON A GRAVE.
WHAT? THAT'S IT?
IF YOU WANT TO MEET THE EXILES, THIS IS YOUR FIRST STEP.

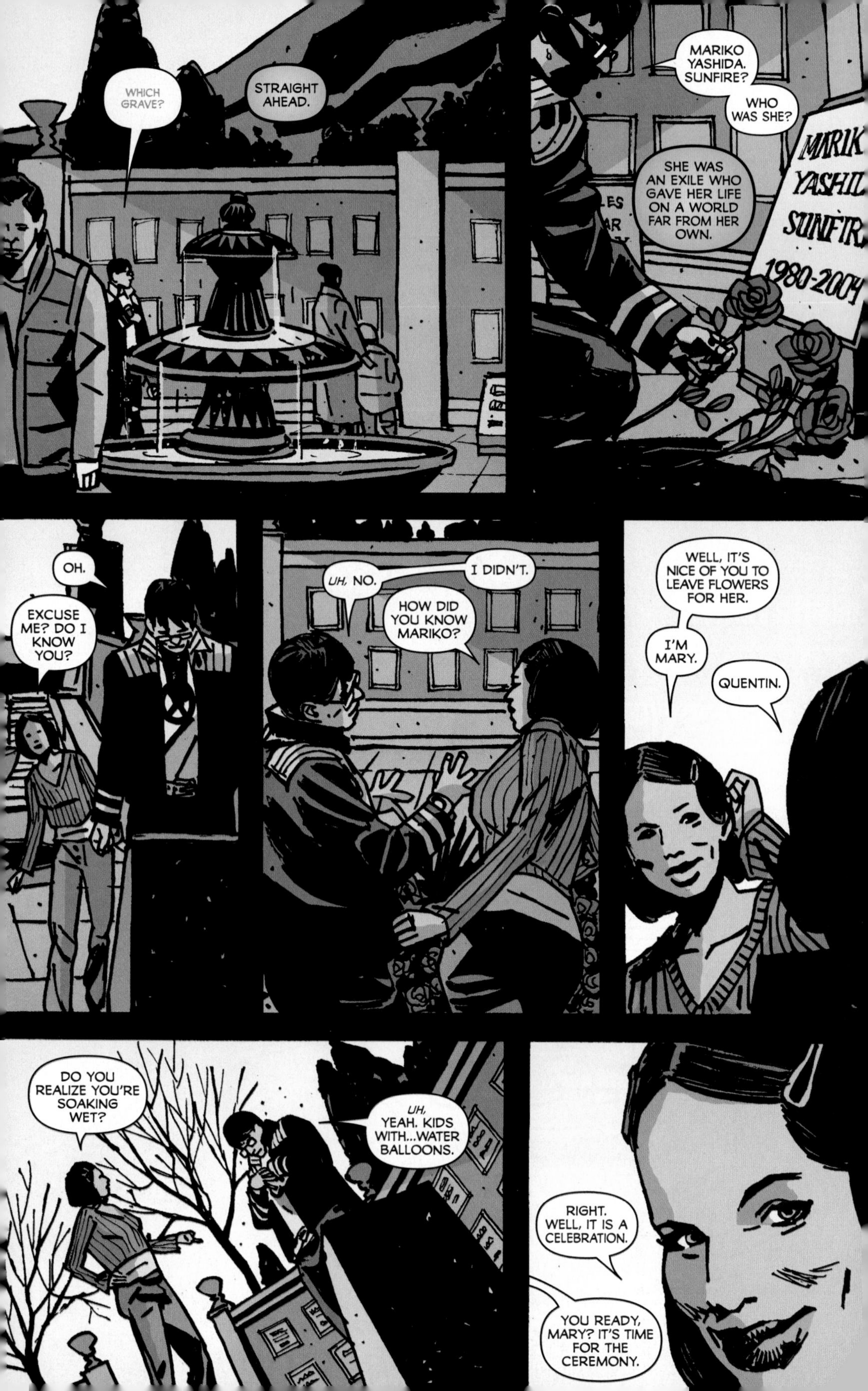
WHICH GRAVE?
STRAIGHT AHEAD.
MARIKO YASHIDA. SUNFIRE?
WHO WAS SHE?
SHE WAS AN EXILE WHO GAVE HER LIFE ON A WORLD FAR FROM HER OWN.
MARIK
YASHIL
SUNFIR
1980-2004
OH.
EXCUSE ME? DO I KNOW YOU?
UH, NO.
I DIDN'T.
HOW DID YOU KNOW MARIKO?
WELL, IT'S NICE OF YOU TO LEAVE FLOWERS FOR HER.
I'M MARY.
QUENTIN.
DO YOU REALIZE YOU'RE SOAKING WET?
UH, YEAH. KIDS WITH...WATER BALLOONS.
RIGHT. WELL, IT IS A CELEBRATION.
YOU READY, MARY? IT'S TIME FOR THE CEREMONY.

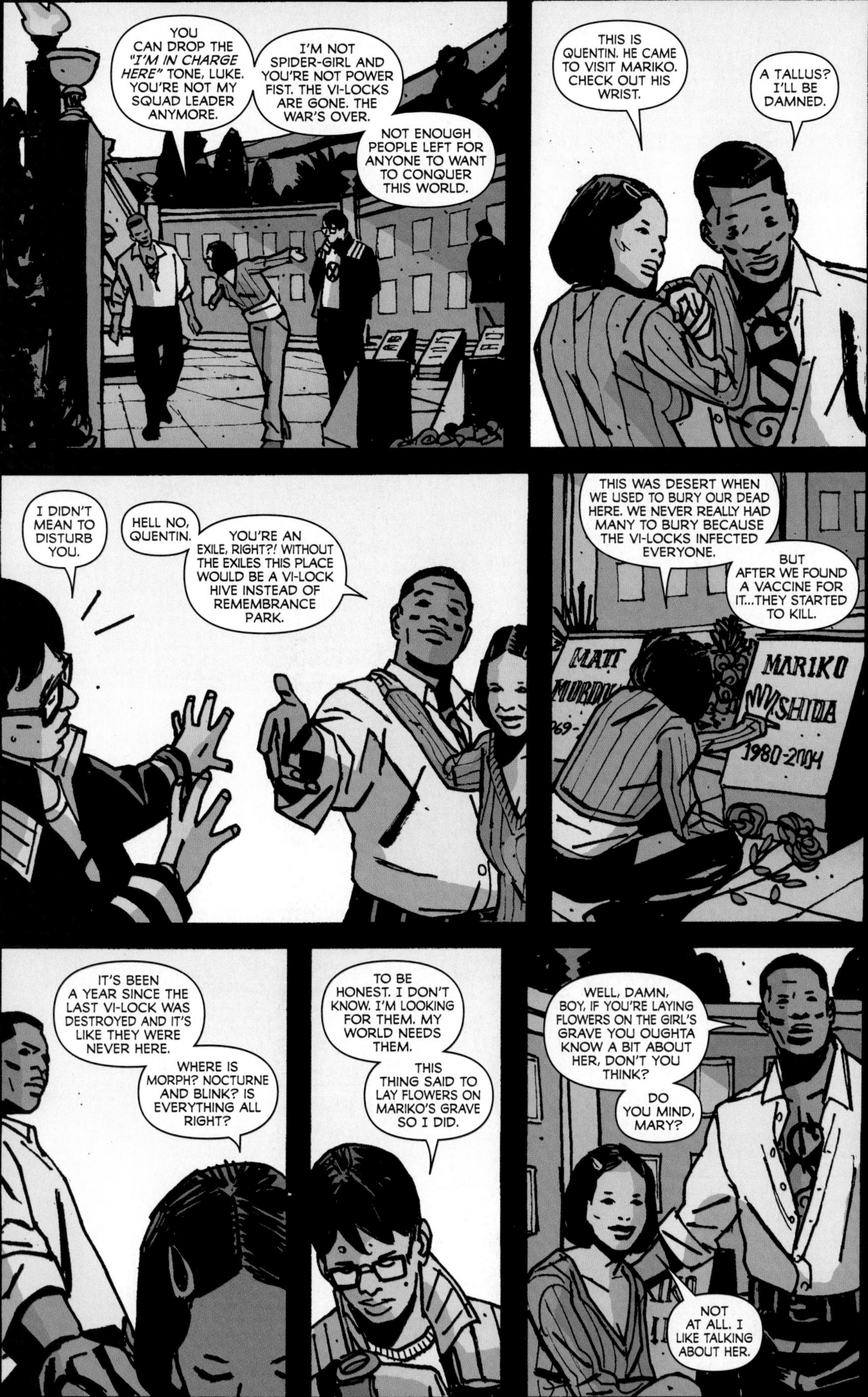
YOU CAN DROP THE *"I'M IN CHARGE HERE"* TONE, LUKE. YOU'RE NOT MY SQUAD LEADER ANYMORE.
I'M NOT SPIDER-GIRL AND YOU'RE NOT POWER FIST. THE VI-LOCKS ARE GONE. THE WAR'S OVER.
NOT ENOUGH PEOPLE LEFT FOR ANYONE TO WANT TO CONQUER THIS WORLD.
THIS IS QUENTIN. HE CAME TO VISIT MARIKO. CHECK OUT HIS WRIST.
A TALLUS? I'LL BE DAMNED.
I DIDN'T MEAN TO DISTURB YOU.
HELL NO, QUENTIN.
YOU'RE AN EXILE, RIGHT?! WITHOUT THE EXILES THIS PLACE WOULD BE A VI-LOCK HIVE INSTEAD OF REMEMBRANCE PARK.
THIS WAS DESERT WHEN WE USED TO BURY OUR DEAD HERE. WE NEVER REALLY HAD MANY TO BURY BECAUSE THE VI-LOCKS INFECTED EVERYONE.
BUT AFTER WE FOUND A VACCINE FOR IT...THEY STARTED TO KILL.
MATT MURDO
MARIKO SHIDA
1980-2004
IT'S BEEN A YEAR SINCE THE LAST VI-LOCK WAS DESTROYED AND IT'S LIKE THEY WERE NEVER HERE.
WHERE IS MORPH? NOCTURNE AND BLINK? IS EVERYTHING ALL RIGHT?
TO BE HONEST. I DON'T KNOW. I'M LOOKING FOR THEM. MY WORLD NEEDS THEM.
THIS THING SAID TO LAY FLOWERS ON MARIKO'S GRAVE SO I DID.
WELL, DAMN, BOY, IF YOU'RE LAYING FLOWERS ON THE GIRL'S GRAVE YOU OUGHTA KNOW A BIT ABOUT HER, DON'T YOU THINK?
DO YOU MIND, MARY?
NOT AT ALL. I LIKE TALKING ABOUT HER.

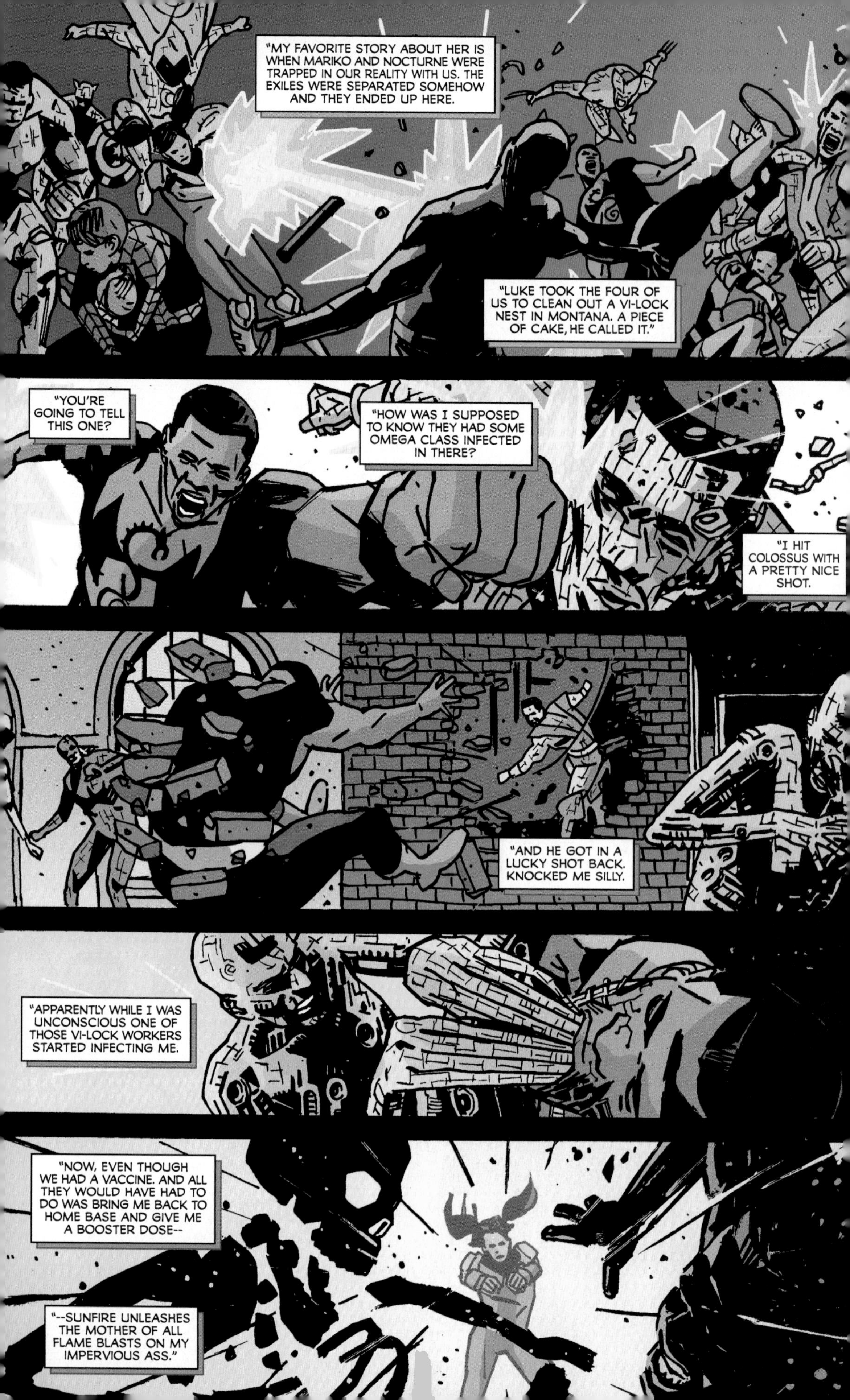
"MY FAVORITE STORY ABOUT HER IS WHEN MARIKO AND NOCTURNE WERE TRAPPED IN OUR REALITY WITH US. THE EXILES WERE SEPARATED SOMEHOW AND THEY ENDED UP HERE.
"LUKE TOOK THE FOUR OF US TO CLEAN OUT A VI-LOCK NEST IN MONTANA. A PIECE OF CAKE, HE CALLED IT."
"YOU'RE GOING TO TELL THIS ONE?
"HOW WAS I SUPPOSED TO KNOW THEY HAD SOME OMEGA CLASS INFECTED IN THERE?
"I HIT COLOSSUS WITH A PRETTY NICE SHOT.
"AND HE GOT IN A LUCKY SHOT BACK. KNOCKED ME SILLY.
"APPARENTLY WHILE I WAS UNCONSCIOUS ONE OF THOSE VI-LOCK WORKERS STARTED INFECTING ME.
"NOW, EVEN THOUGH WE HAD A VACCINE. AND ALL THEY WOULD HAVE HAD TO DO WAS BRING ME BACK TO HOME BASE AND GIVE ME A BOOSTER DOSE--
"--SUNFIRE UNLEASHES THE MOTHER OF ALL FLAME BLASTS ON MY IMPERVIOUS ASS."

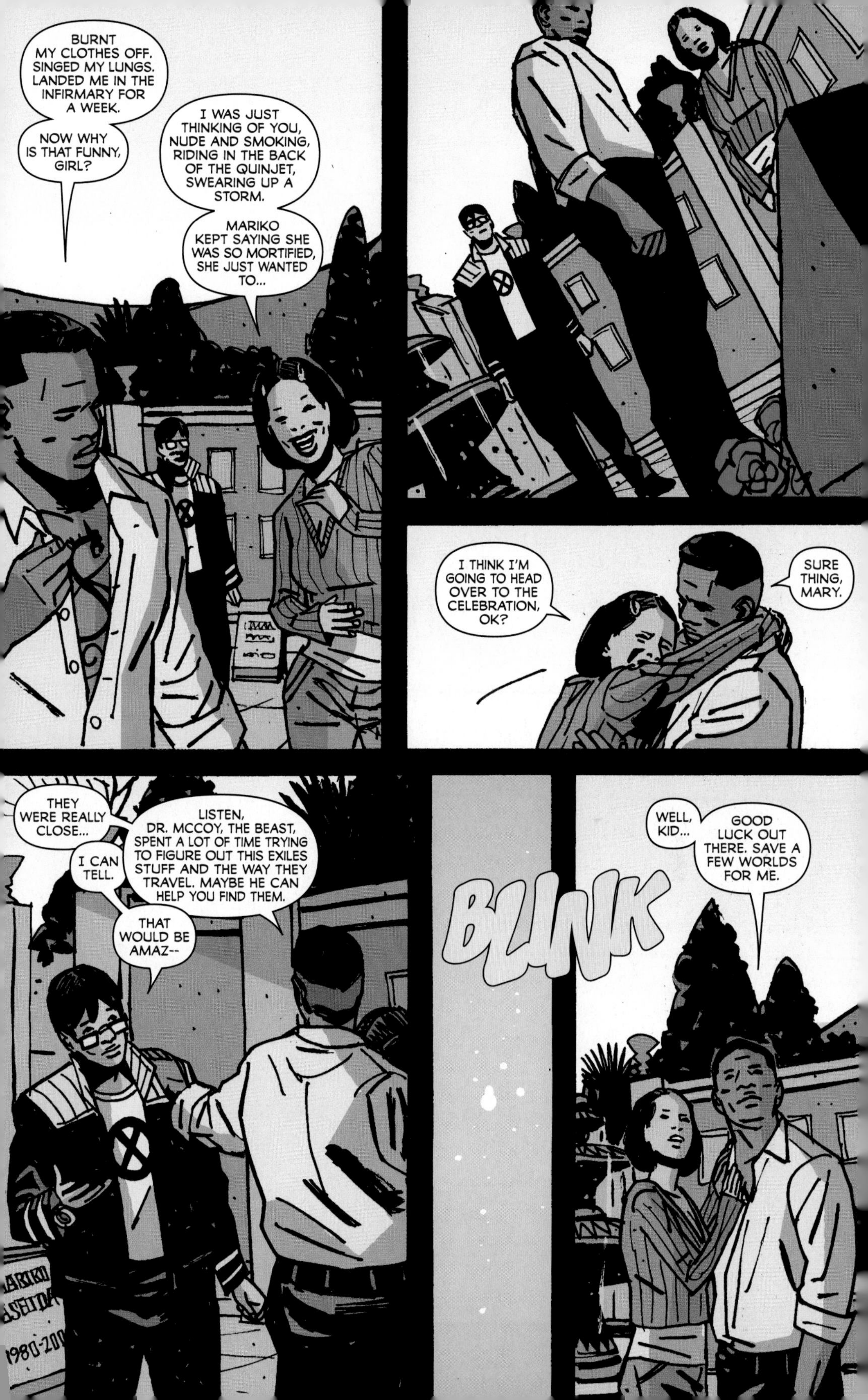
BURNT MY CLOTHES OFF. SINGED MY LUNGS. LANDED ME IN THE INFIRMARY FOR A WEEK.
NOW WHY IS THAT FUNNY, GIRL?
I WAS JUST THINKING OF YOU, NUDE AND SMOKING, RIDING IN THE BACK OF THE QUINJET, SWEARING UP A STORM.
MARIKO KEPT SAYING SHE WAS SO MORTIFIED, SHE JUST WANTED TO...
I THINK I'M GOING TO HEAD OVER TO THE CELEBRATION, OK?
SURE THING, MARY.
THEY WERE REALLY CLOSE...
I CAN TELL.
LISTEN, DR. MCCOY, THE BEAST, SPENT A LOT OF TIME TRYING TO FIGURE OUT THIS EXILES STUFF AND THE WAY THEY TRAVEL. MAYBE HE CAN HELP YOU FIND THEM.
THAT WOULD BE AMAZ--
BLINK
WELL, KID...
GOOD LUCK OUT THERE. SAVE A FEW WORLDS FOR ME.

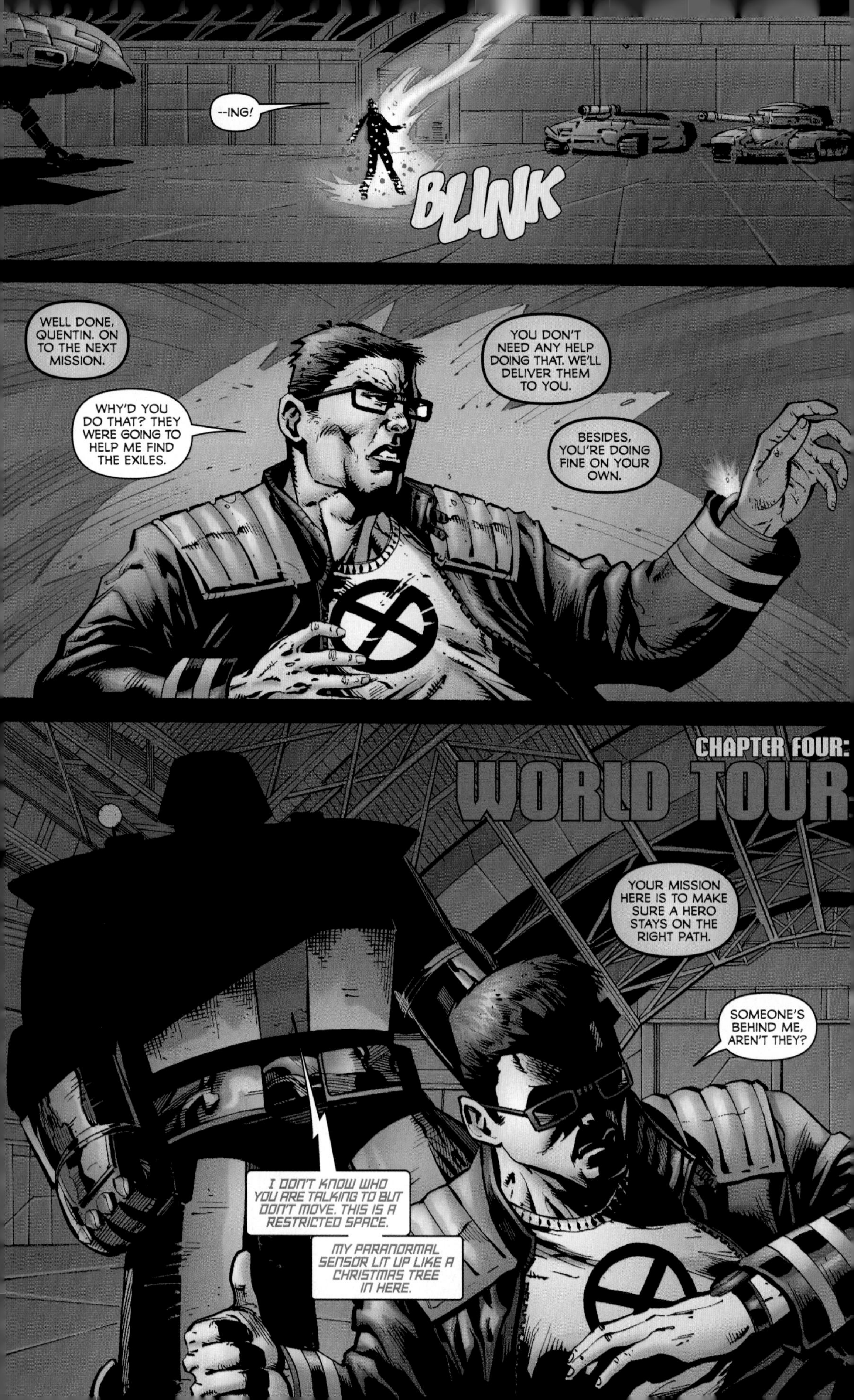

--ING!
BLINK
WELL DONE, QUENTIN. ON TO THE NEXT MISSION.
WHY'D YOU DO THAT? THEY WERE GOING TO HELP ME FIND THE EXILES.
YOU DON'T NEED ANY HELP DOING THAT. WE'LL DELIVER THEM TO YOU.
BESIDES, YOU'RE DOING FINE ON YOUR OWN.
CHAPTER FOUR:
WORLD TOUR
YOUR MISSION HERE IS TO MAKE SURE A HERO STAYS ON THE RIGHT PATH.
SOMEONE'S BEHIND ME, AREN'T THEY?
I DON'T KNOW WHO YOU ARE TALKING TO BUT DON'T MOVE. THIS IS A RESTRICTED SPACE.
MY PARANORMAL SENSOR LIT UP LIKE A CHRISTMAS TREE IN HERE.

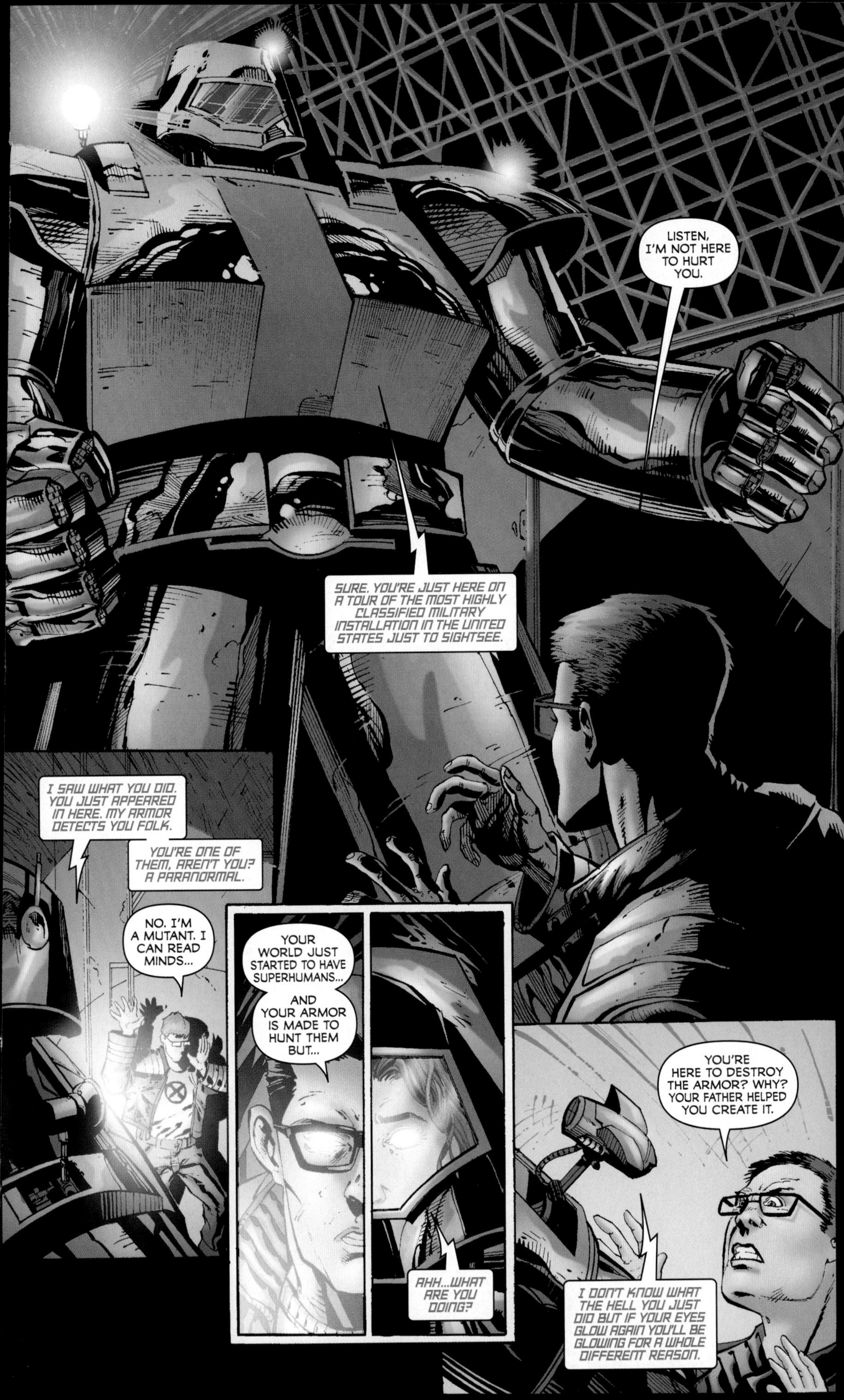
LISTEN, I'M NOT HERE TO HURT YOU.
SURE. YOU'RE JUST HERE ON A TOUR OF THE MOST HIGHLY CLASSIFIED MILITARY INSTALLATION IN THE UNITED STATES JUST TO SIGHTSEE.
I SAW WHAT YOU DID. YOU JUST APPEARED IN HERE. MY ARMOR DETECTS YOU FOLK.
YOU'RE ONE OF THEM, AREN'T YOU? A PARANORMAL.
NO. I'M A MUTANT. I CAN READ MINDS...
YOUR WORLD JUST STARTED TO HAVE SUPERHUMANS...
AND YOUR ARMOR IS MADE TO HUNT THEM BUT...
AHH...WHAT ARE YOU DOING?
YOU'RE HERE TO DESTROY THE ARMOR? WHY? YOUR FATHER HELPED YOU CREATE IT.
I DON'T KNOW WHAT THE HELL YOU JUST DID BUT IF YOUR EYES GLOW AGAIN YOU'LL BE GLOWING FOR A WHOLE DIFFERENT REASON.

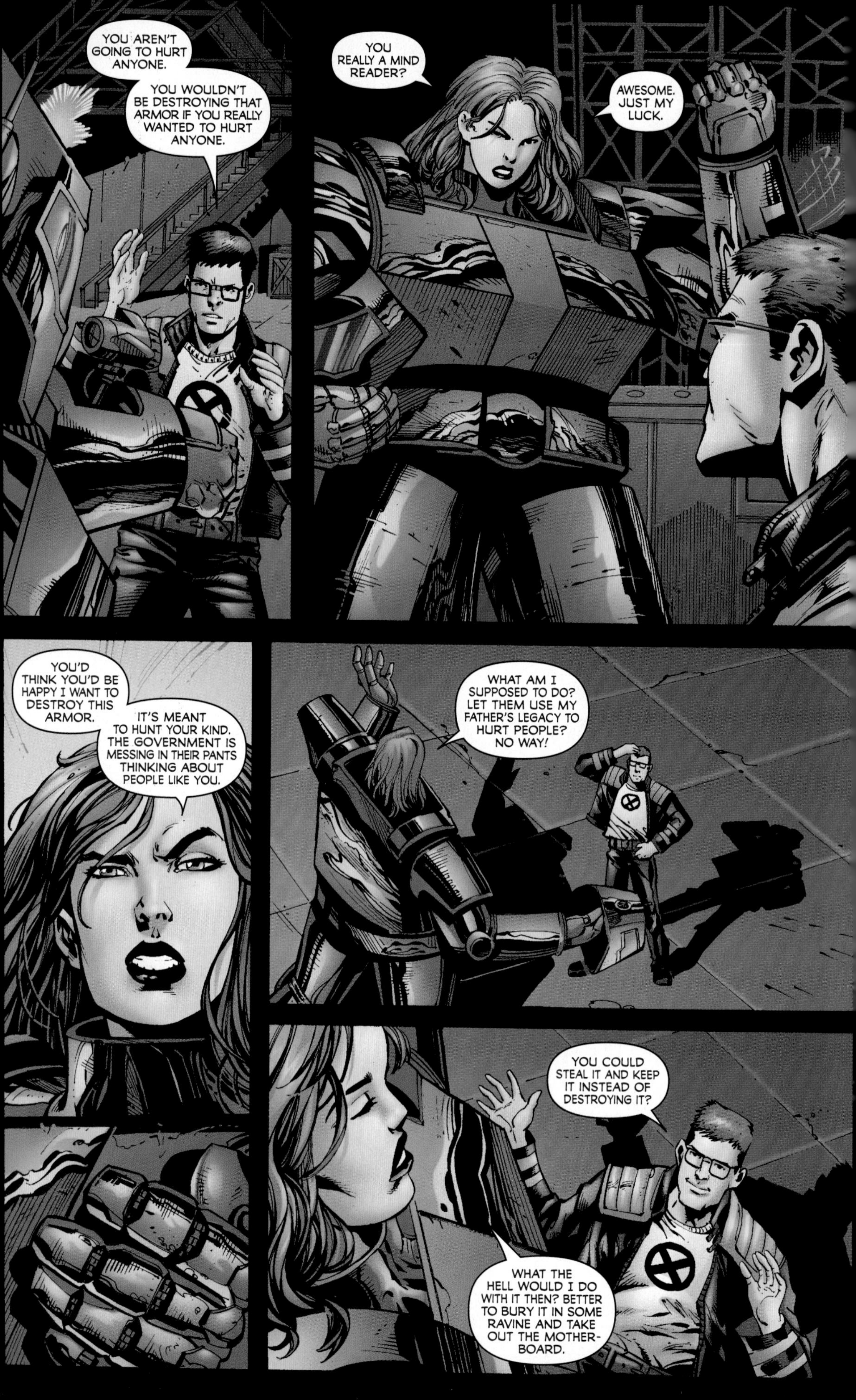
YOU AREN'T GOING TO HURT ANYONE.
YOU WOULDN'T BE DESTROYING THAT ARMOR IF YOU REALLY WANTED TO HURT ANYONE.
YOU REALLY A MIND READER?
AWESOME. JUST MY LUCK.
YOU'D THINK YOU'D BE HAPPY I WANT TO DESTROY THIS ARMOR.
IT'S MEANT TO HUNT YOUR KIND. THE GOVERNMENT IS MESSING IN THEIR PANTS THINKING ABOUT PEOPLE LIKE YOU.
WHAT AM I SUPPOSED TO DO? LET THEM USE MY FATHER'S LEGACY TO HURT PEOPLE? NO WAY!
YOU COULD STEAL IT AND KEEP IT INSTEAD OF DESTROYING IT?
WHAT THE HELL WOULD I DO WITH IT THEN? BETTER TO BURY IT IN SOME RAVINE AND TAKE OUT THE MOTHER-BOARD.

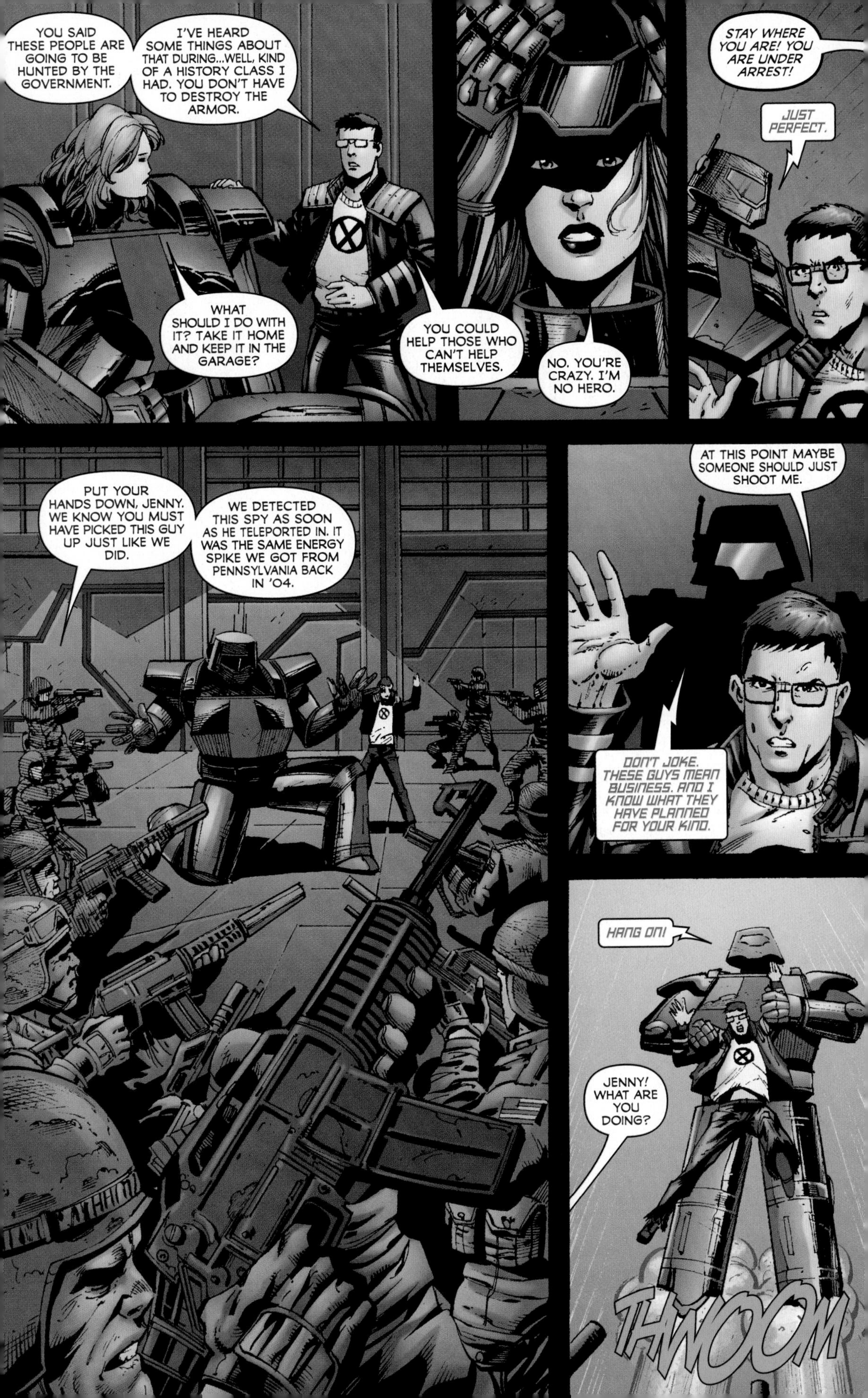
YOU SAID THESE PEOPLE ARE GOING TO BE HUNTED BY THE GOVERNMENT.
I'VE HEARD SOME THINGS ABOUT THAT DURING...WELL, KIND OF A HISTORY CLASS I HAD. YOU DON'T HAVE TO DESTROY THE ARMOR.
WHAT SHOULD I DO WITH IT? TAKE IT HOME AND KEEP IT IN THE GARAGE?
YOU COULD HELP THOSE WHO CAN'T HELP THEMSELVES.
NO. YOU'RE CRAZY. I'M NO HERO.
STAY WHERE YOU ARE! YOU ARE UNDER ARREST!
JUST PERFECT.
PUT YOUR HANDS DOWN, JENNY. WE KNOW YOU MUST HAVE PICKED THIS GUY UP JUST LIKE WE DID.
WE DETECTED THIS SPY AS SOON AS HE TELEPORTED IN. IT WAS THE SAME ENERGY SPIKE WE GOT FROM PENNSYLVANIA BACK IN '04.
AT THIS POINT MAYBE SOMEONE SHOULD JUST SHOOT ME.
DON'T JOKE. THESE GUYS MEAN BUSINESS. AND I KNOW WHAT THEY HAVE PLANNED FOR YOUR KIND.
HANG ON!
JENNY! WHAT ARE YOU DOING?
THWOOM

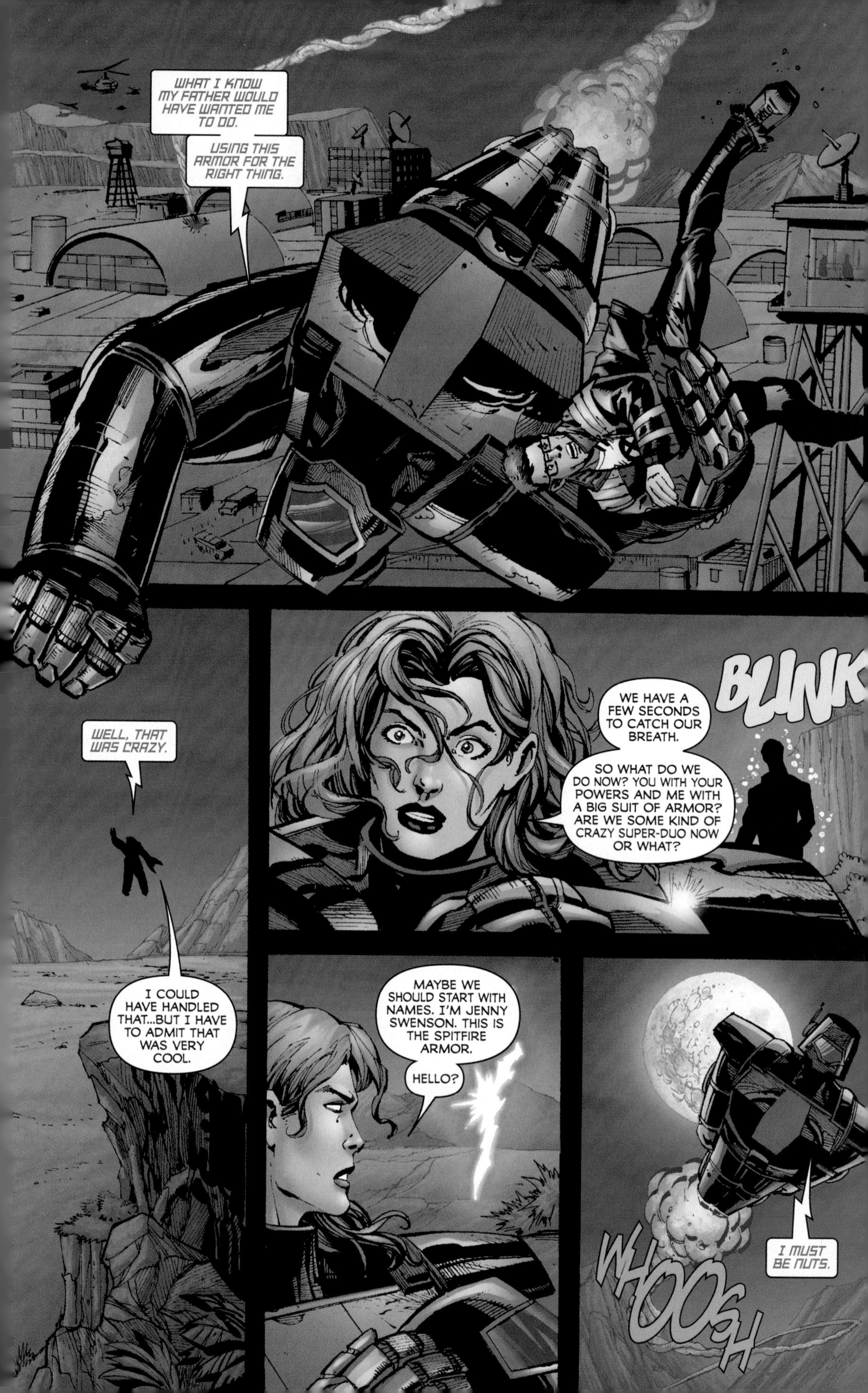
WHAT I KNOW MY FATHER WOULD HAVE WANTED ME TO DO.
USING THIS ARMOR FOR THE RIGHT THING.
WE HAVE A FEW SECONDS TO CATCH OUR BREATH.
SO WHAT DO WE DO NOW? YOU WITH YOUR POWERS AND ME WITH A BIG SUIT OF ARMOR? ARE WE SOME KIND OF CRAZY SUPER-DUO NOW OR WHAT?
BLINK
WELL, THAT WAS CRAZY.
I COULD HAVE HANDLED THAT...BUT I HAVE TO ADMIT THAT WAS VERY COOL.
MAYBE WE SHOULD START WITH NAMES. I'M JENNY SWENSON. THIS IS THE SPITFIRE ARMOR.
HELLO?
WHOOSH
I MUST BE NUTS.

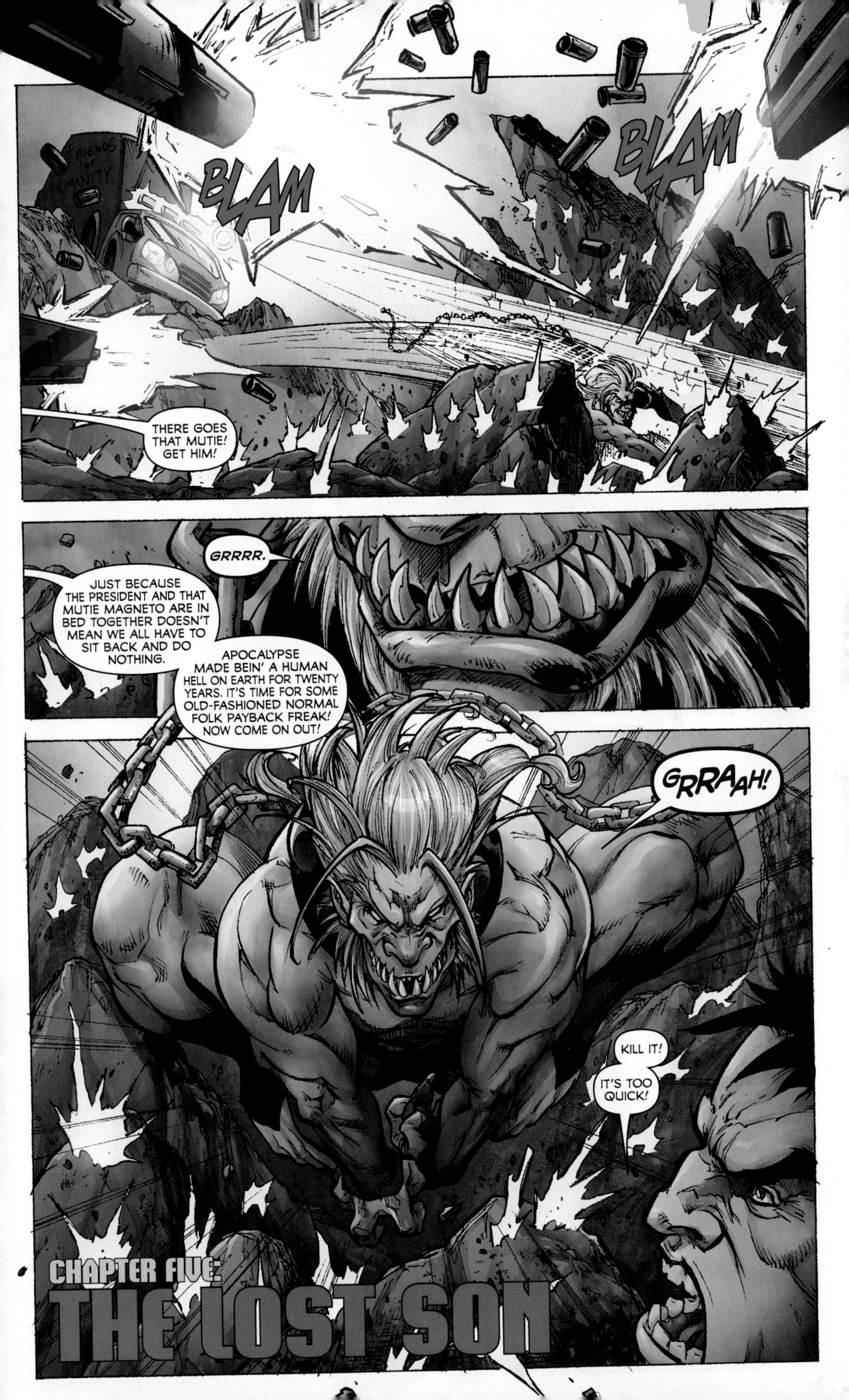
FRIENDS OF HUMANITY
BLAM
BLAM
THERE GOES THAT MUTIE! GET HIM!
GRRRR.
JUST BECAUSE THE PRESIDENT AND THAT MUTIE MAGNETO ARE IN BED TOGETHER DOESN'T MEAN WE ALL HAVE TO SIT BACK AND DO NOTHING.
APOCALYPSE MADE BEIN' A HUMAN HELL ON EARTH FOR TWENTY YEARS. IT'S TIME FOR SOME OLD-FASHIONED NORMAL FOLK PAYBACK FREAK! NOW COME ON OUT!
GRRAAH!
KILL IT!
IT'S TOO QUICK!
CHAPTER FIVE:
THE LOST SON

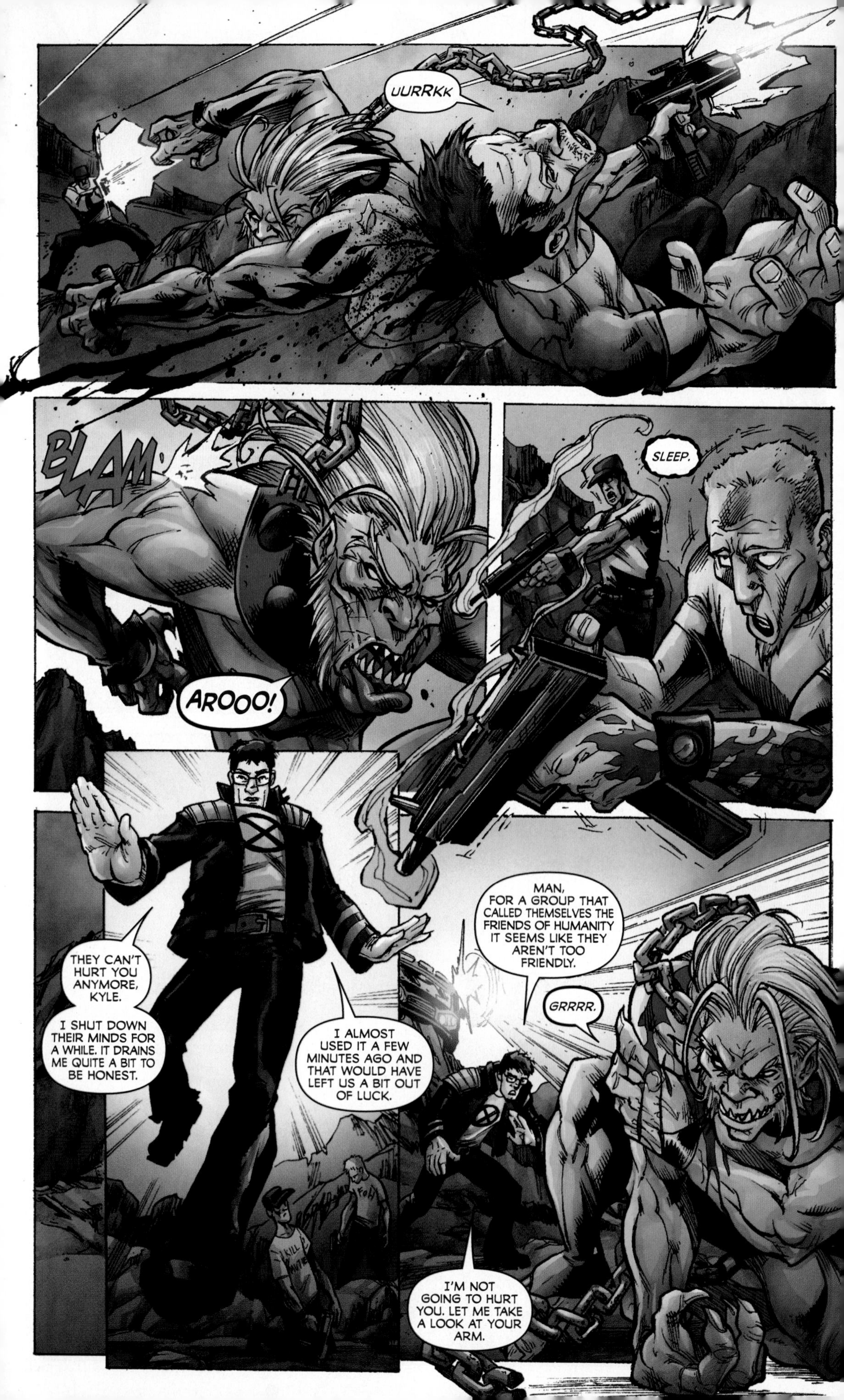

UURRKK
BLAM
AROOO!
SLEEP.
THEY CAN'T HURT YOU ANYMORE, KYLE.
I SHUT DOWN THEIR MINDS FOR A WHILE. IT DRAINS ME QUITE A BIT TO BE HONEST.
I ALMOST USED IT A FEW MINUTES AGO AND THAT WOULD HAVE LEFT US A BIT OUT OF LUCK.
MAN, FOR A GROUP THAT CALLED THEMSELVES THE FRIENDS OF HUMANITY IT SEEMS LIKE THEY AREN'T TOO FRIENDLY.
GRRRR.
I'M NOT GOING TO HURT YOU. LET ME TAKE A LOOK AT YOUR ARM.

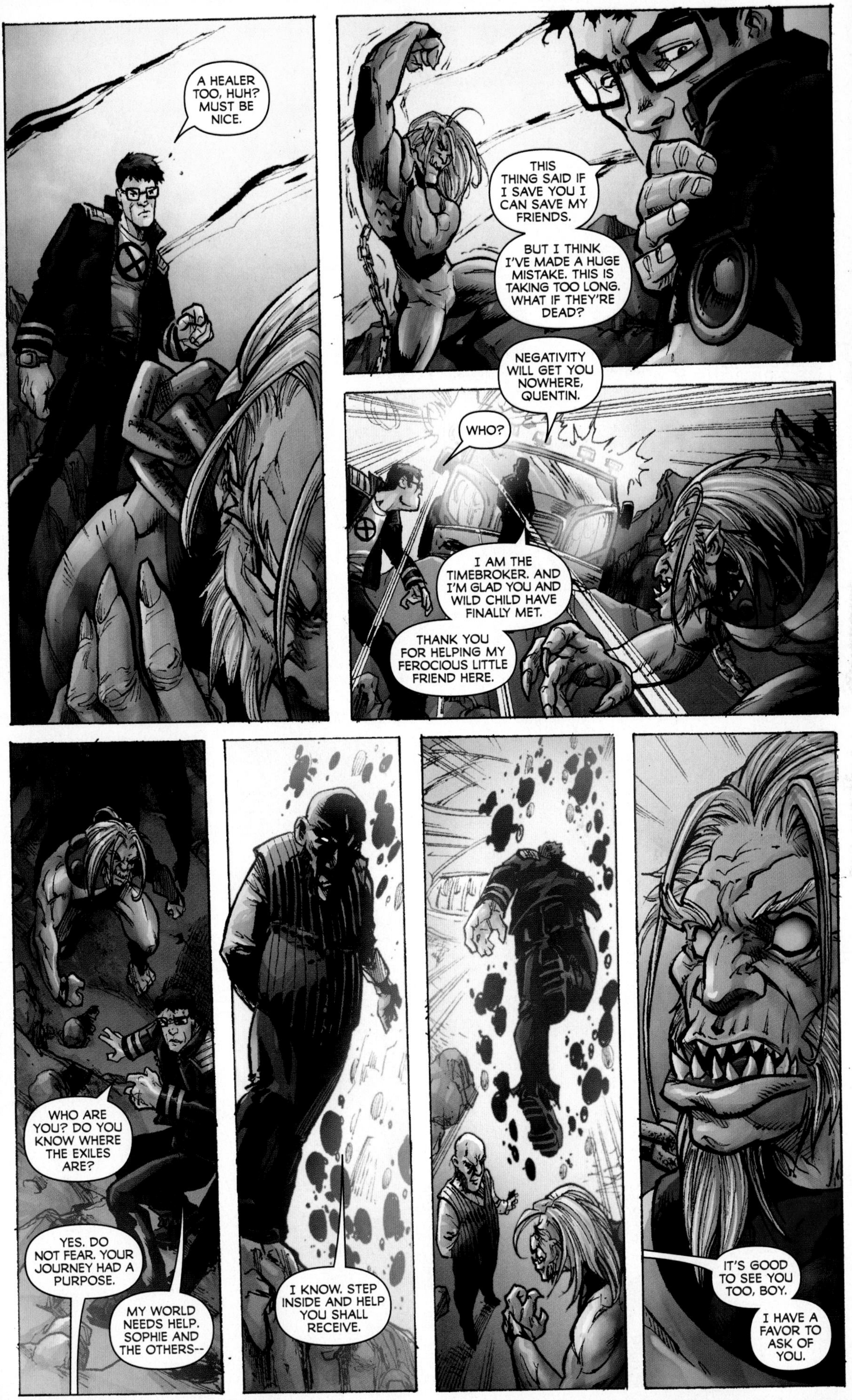
A HEALER TOO, HUH? MUST BE NICE.
THIS THING SAID IF I SAVE YOU I CAN SAVE MY FRIENDS.
BUT I THINK I'VE MADE A HUGE MISTAKE. THIS IS TAKING TOO LONG. WHAT IF THEY'RE DEAD?
NEGATIVITY WILL GET YOU NOWHERE, QUENTIN.
WHO?
I AM THE TIMEBROKER. AND I'M GLAD YOU AND WILD CHILD HAVE FINALLY MET.
THANK YOU FOR HELPING MY FEROCIOUS LITTLE FRIEND HERE.
WHO ARE YOU? DO YOU KNOW WHERE THE EXILES ARE?
YES. DO NOT FEAR. YOUR JOURNEY HAD A PURPOSE.
MY WORLD NEEDS HELP. SOPHIE AND THE OTHERS--
I KNOW. STEP INSIDE AND HELP YOU SHALL RECEIVE.
IT'S GOOD TO SEE YOU TOO, BOY.
I HAVE A FAVOR TO ASK OF YOU.

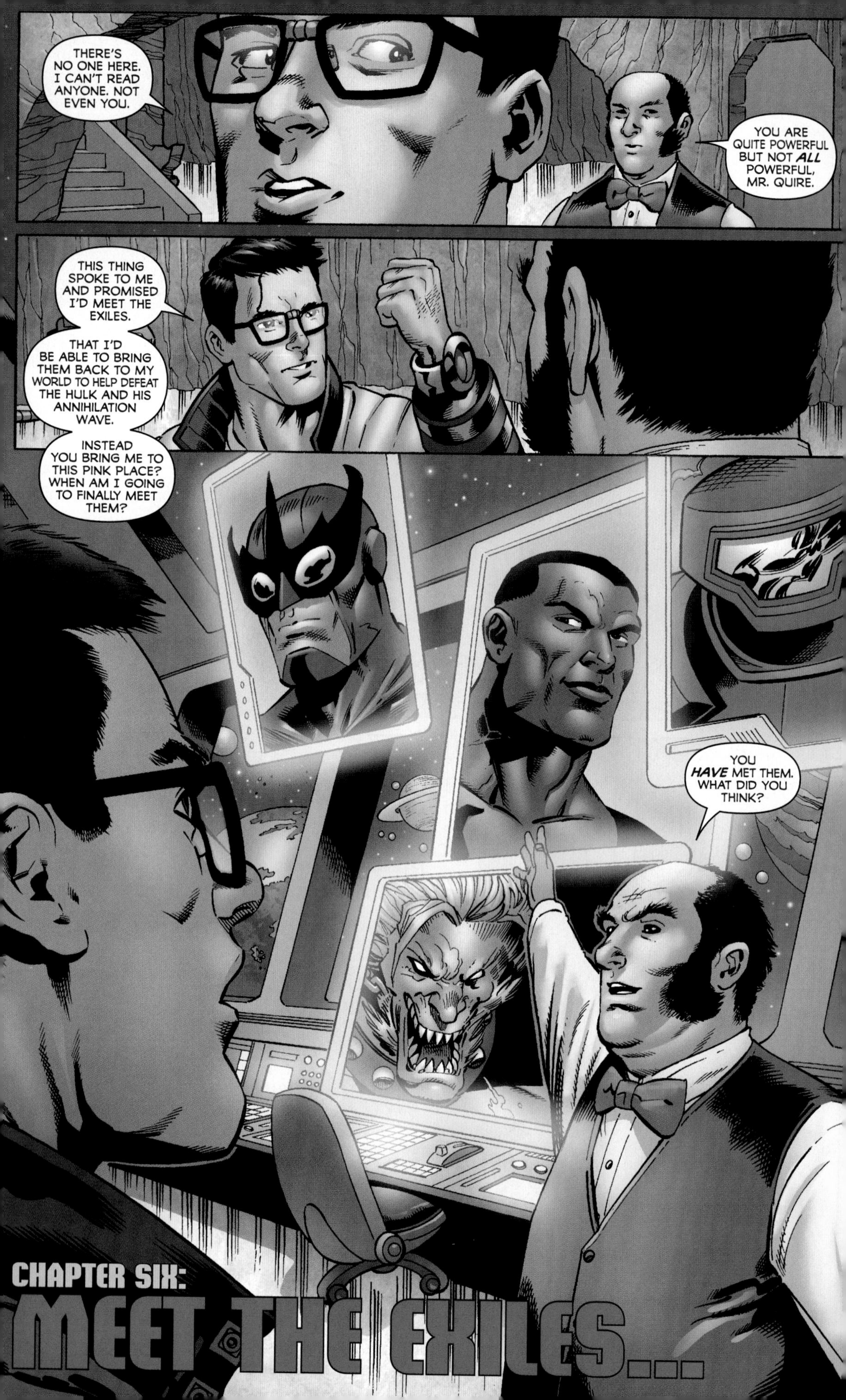
THERE'S NO ONE HERE. I CAN'T READ ANYONE. NOT EVEN YOU.
YOU ARE QUITE POWERFUL BUT NOT *ALL* POWERFUL, MR. QUIRE.
THIS THING SPOKE TO ME AND PROMISED I'D MEET THE EXILES.
THAT I'D BE ABLE TO BRING THEM BACK TO MY WORLD TO HELP DEFEAT THE HULK AND HIS ANNIHILATION WAVE.
INSTEAD YOU BRING ME TO THIS PINK PLACE? WHEN AM I GOING TO FINALLY MEET THEM?
YOU *HAVE* MET THEM. WHAT DID YOU THINK?
CHAPTER SIX:
MEET THE EXILES...

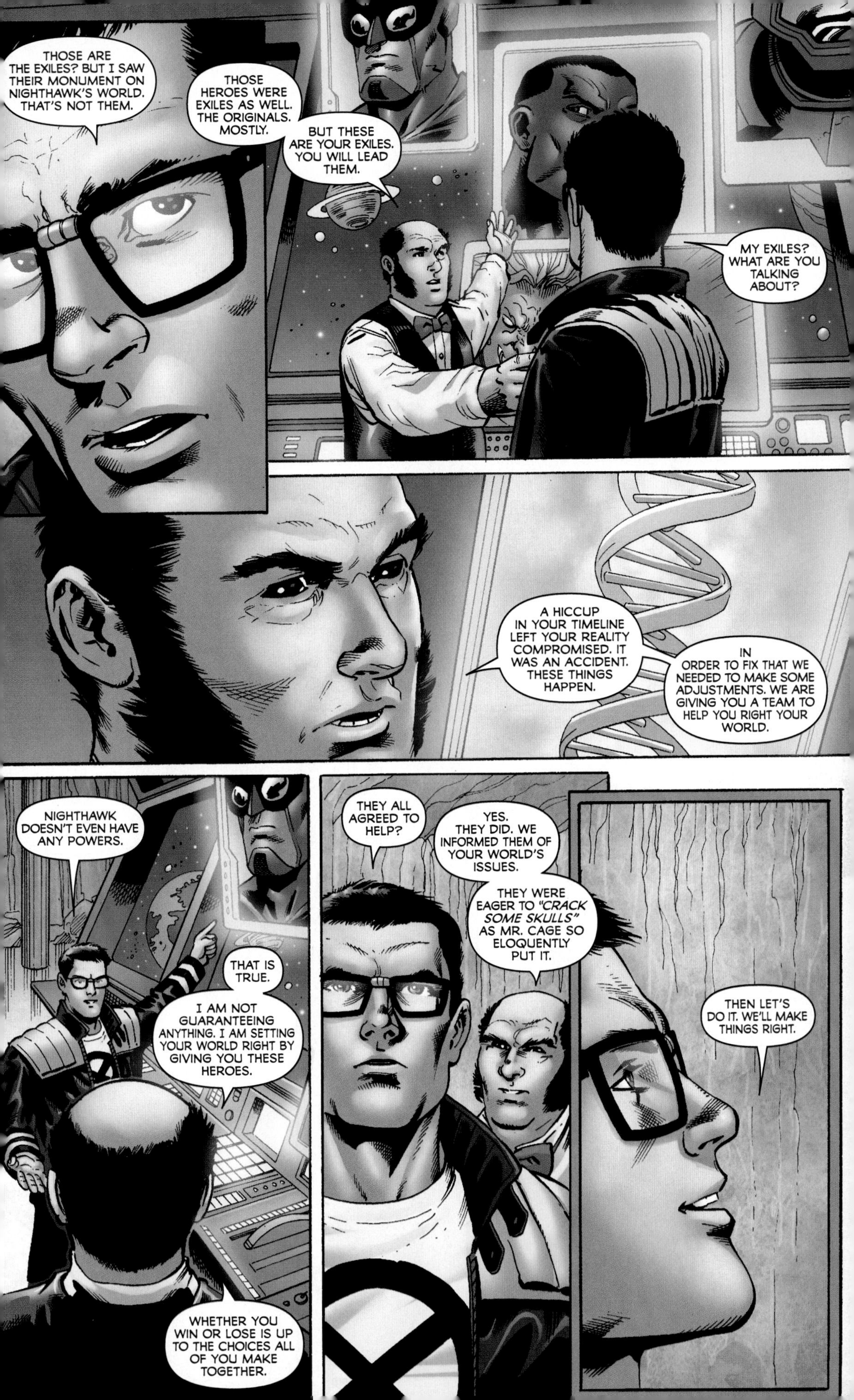
THOSE ARE THE EXILES? BUT I SAW THEIR MONUMENT ON NIGHTHAWK'S WORLD. THAT'S NOT THEM.
THOSE HEROES WERE EXILES AS WELL. THE ORIGINALS. MOSTLY.
BUT THESE ARE YOUR EXILES. YOU WILL LEAD THEM.
MY EXILES? WHAT ARE YOU TALKING ABOUT?
A HICCUP IN YOUR TIMELINE LEFT YOUR REALITY COMPROMISED. IT WAS AN ACCIDENT. THESE THINGS HAPPEN.
IN ORDER TO FIX THAT WE NEEDED TO MAKE SOME ADJUSTMENTS. WE ARE GIVING YOU A TEAM TO HELP YOU RIGHT YOUR WORLD.
NIGHTHAWK DOESN'T EVEN HAVE ANY POWERS.
THAT IS TRUE.
I AM NOT GUARANTEEING ANYTHING. I AM SETTING YOUR WORLD RIGHT BY GIVING YOU THESE HEROES.
WHETHER YOU WIN OR LOSE IS UP TO THE CHOICES ALL OF YOU MAKE TOGETHER.
THEY ALL AGREED TO HELP?
YES. THEY DID. WE INFORMED THEM OF YOUR WORLD'S ISSUES.
THEY WERE EAGER TO *"CRACK SOME SKULLS"* AS MR. CAGE SO ELOQUENTLY PUT IT.
THEN LET'S DO IT. WE'LL MAKE THINGS RIGHT.

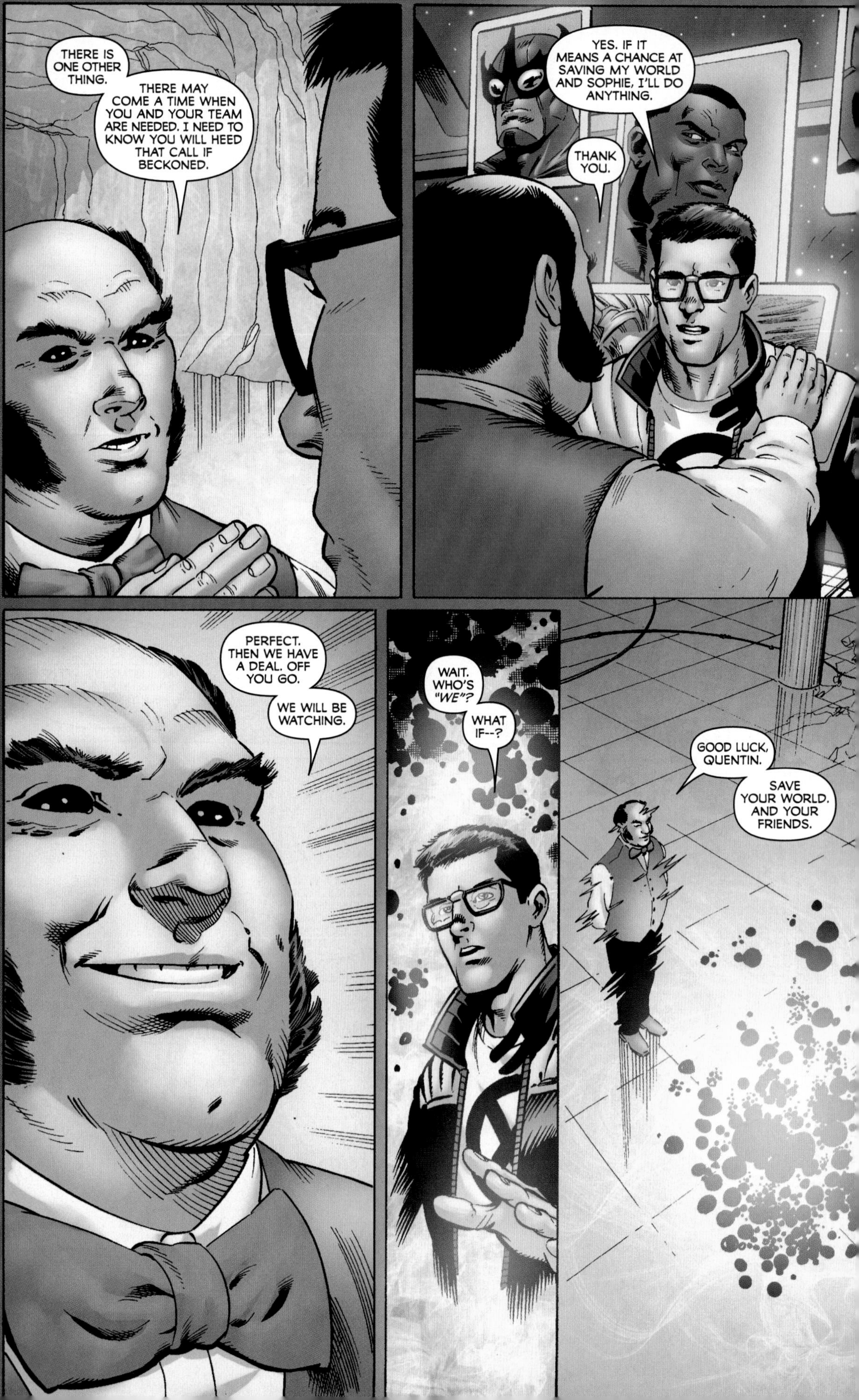
THERE IS ONE OTHER THING.
THERE MAY COME A TIME WHEN YOU AND YOUR TEAM ARE NEEDED. I NEED TO KNOW YOU WILL HEED THAT CALL IF BECKONED.
YES. IF IT MEANS A CHANCE AT SAVING MY WORLD AND SOPHIE, I'LL DO ANYTHING.
THANK YOU.
PERFECT. THEN WE HAVE A DEAL. OFF YOU GO.
WE WILL BE WATCHING.
WAIT. WHO'S *"WE"*?
WHAT IF--?
GOOD LUCK, QUENTIN.
SAVE YOUR WORLD. AND YOUR FRIENDS.

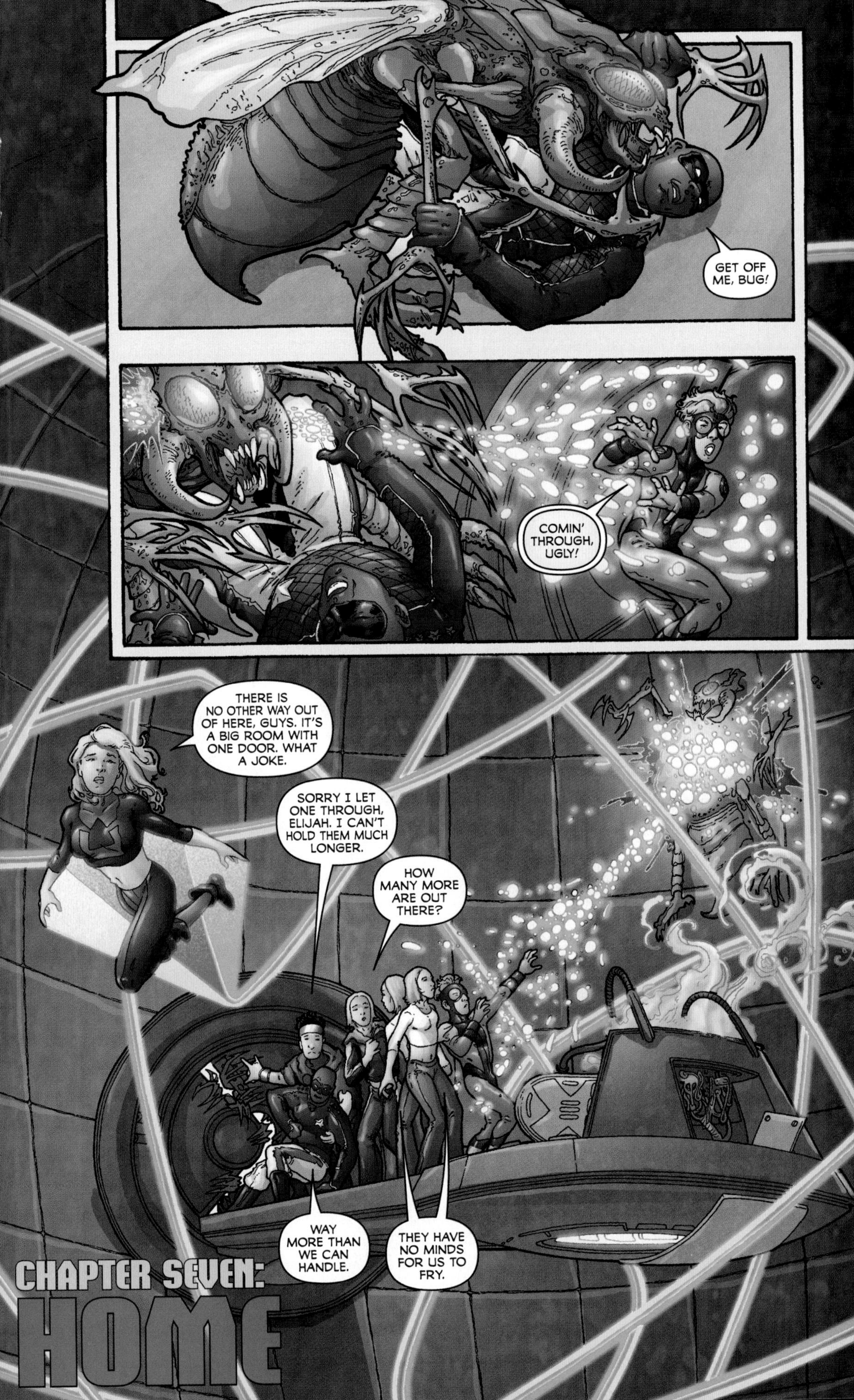
GET OFF ME, BUG!
COMIN' THROUGH, UGLY!
THERE IS NO OTHER WAY OUT OF HERE, GUYS. IT'S A BIG ROOM WITH ONE DOOR. WHAT A JOKE.
SORRY I LET ONE THROUGH, ELIJAH. I CAN'T HOLD THEM MUCH LONGER.
HOW MANY MORE ARE OUT THERE?
WAY MORE THAN WE CAN HANDLE.
THEY HAVE NO MINDS FOR US TO FRY.
CHAPTER SEVEN:
HOME

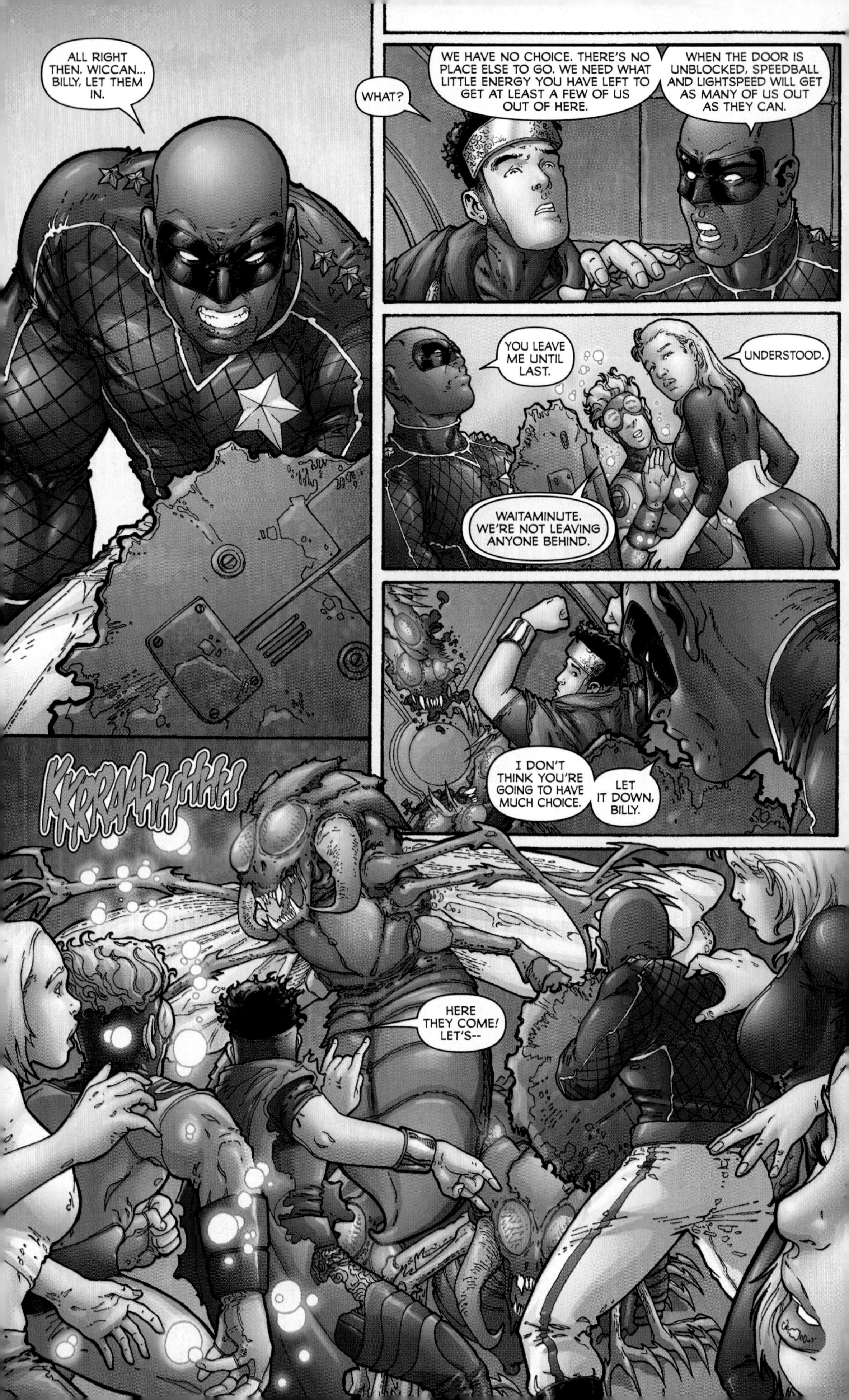
ALL RIGHT THEN. WICCAN... BILLY, LET THEM IN.
WHAT?
WE HAVE NO CHOICE. THERE'S NO PLACE ELSE TO GO. WE NEED WHAT LITTLE ENERGY YOU HAVE LEFT TO GET AT LEAST A FEW OF US OUT OF HERE.
WHEN THE DOOR IS UNBLOCKED, SPEEDBALL AND LIGHTSPEED WILL GET AS MANY OF US OUT AS THEY CAN.
YOU LEAVE ME UNTIL LAST.
UNDERSTOOD.
WAITAMINUTE. WE'RE NOT LEAVING ANYONE BEHIND.
I DON'T THINK YOU'RE GOING TO HAVE MUCH CHOICE.
LET IT DOWN, BILLY.
KKRRAAHHHHH
HERE THEY COME! LET'S--

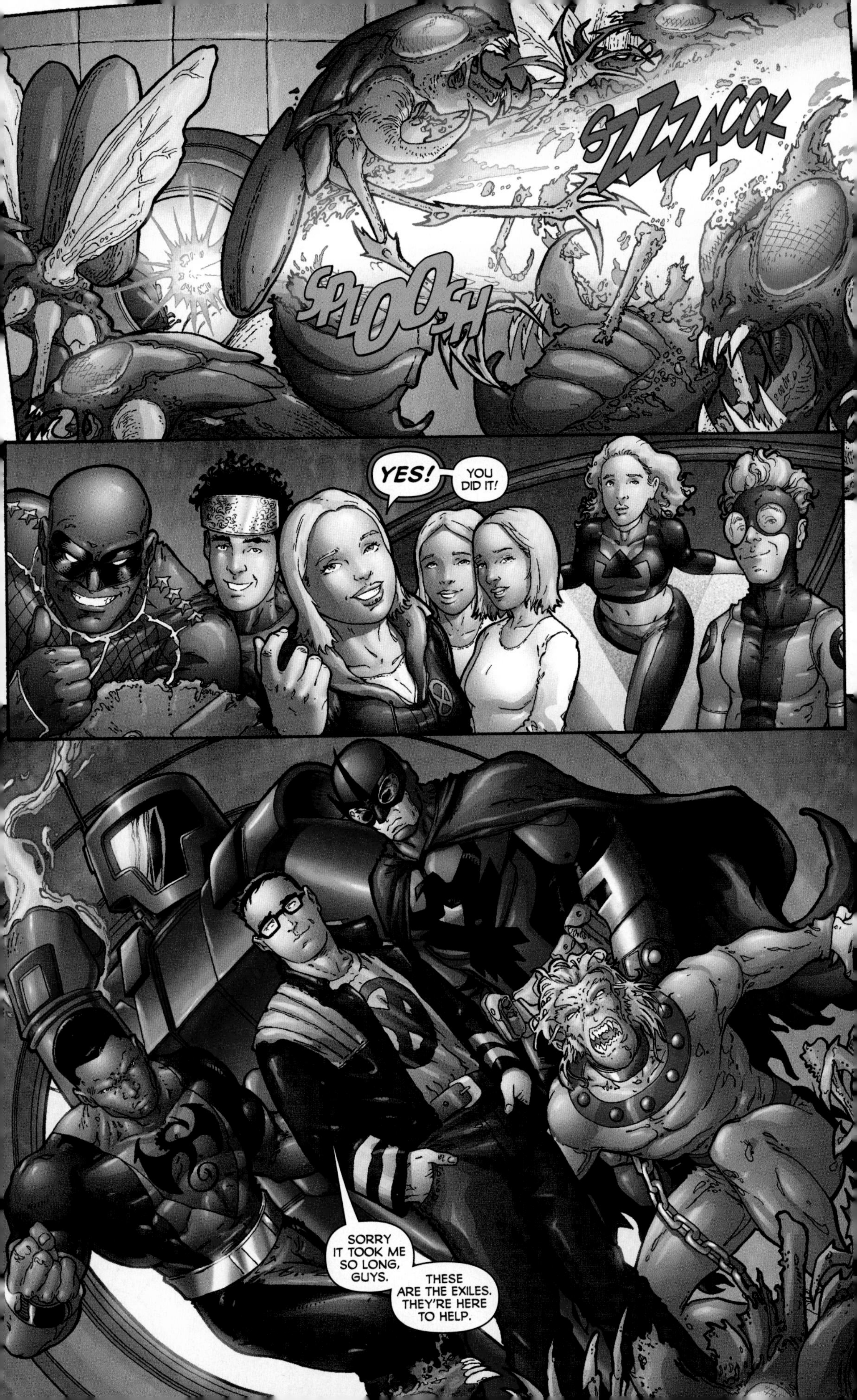
SZZZACCK
SPLOOSH
YES!
YOU DID IT!
SORRY IT TOOK ME SO LONG, GUYS.
THESE ARE THE EXILES. THEY'RE HERE TO HELP.

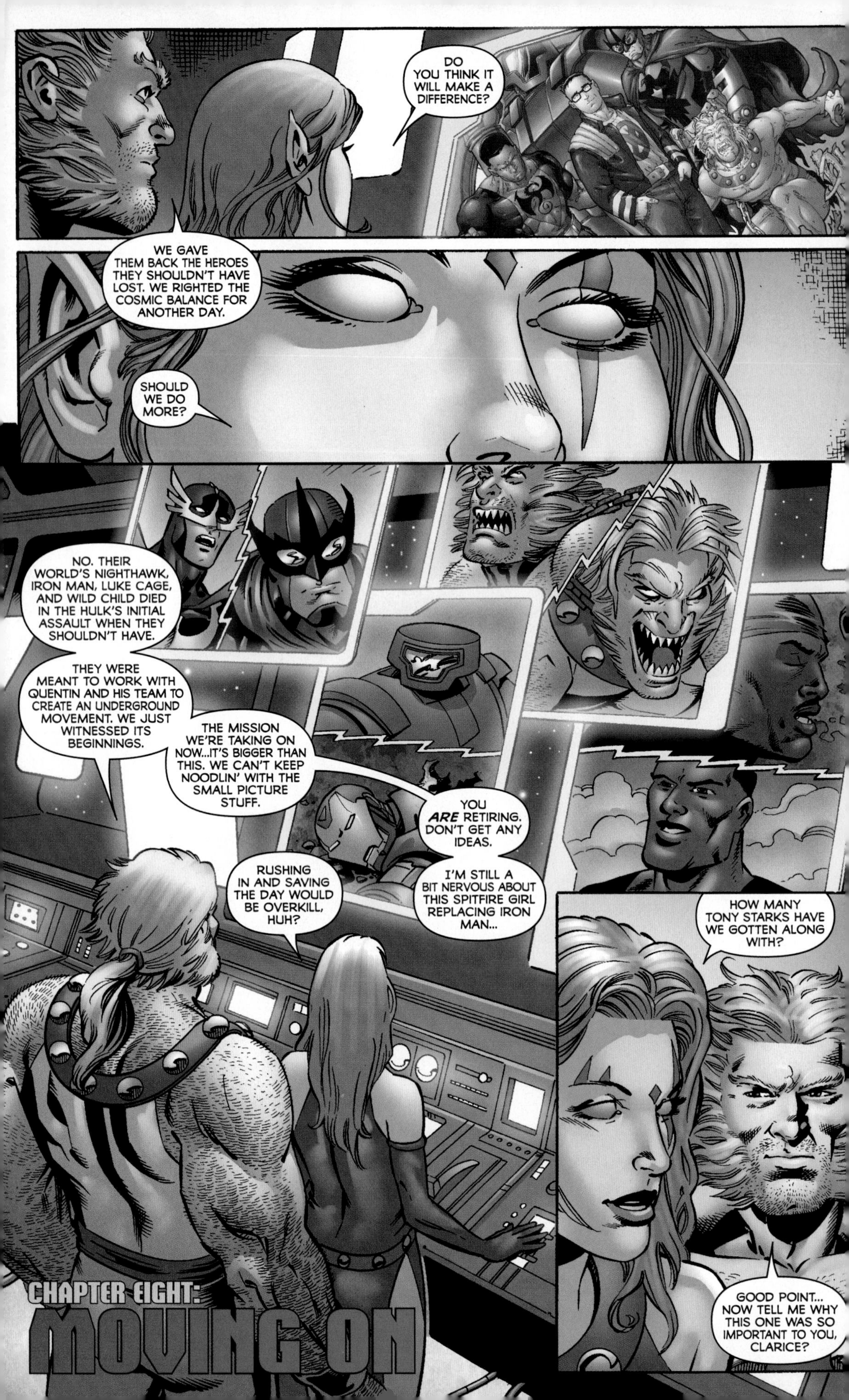
DO YOU THINK IT WILL MAKE A DIFFERENCE?
WE GAVE THEM BACK THE HEROES THEY SHOULDN'T HAVE LOST. WE RIGHTED THE COSMIC BALANCE FOR ANOTHER DAY.
SHOULD WE DO MORE?
NO. THEIR WORLD'S NIGHTHAWK, IRON MAN, LUKE CAGE, AND WILD CHILD DIED IN THE HULK'S INITIAL ASSAULT WHEN THEY SHOULDN'T HAVE.
THEY WERE MEANT TO WORK WITH QUENTIN AND HIS TEAM TO CREATE AN UNDERGROUND MOVEMENT. WE JUST WITNESSED ITS BEGINNINGS.
THE MISSION WE'RE TAKING ON NOW...IT'S BIGGER THAN THIS. WE CAN'T KEEP NOODLIN' WITH THE SMALL PICTURE STUFF.
RUSHING IN AND SAVING THE DAY WOULD BE OVERKILL, HUH?
YOU ARE RETIRING. DON'T GET ANY IDEAS.
I'M STILL A BIT NERVOUS ABOUT THIS SPITFIRE GIRL REPLACING IRON MAN...
HOW MANY TONY STARKS HAVE WE GOTTEN ALONG WITH?
GOOD POINT... NOW TELL ME WHY THIS ONE WAS SO IMPORTANT TO YOU, CLARICE?
CHAPTER EIGHT:
MOVING ON

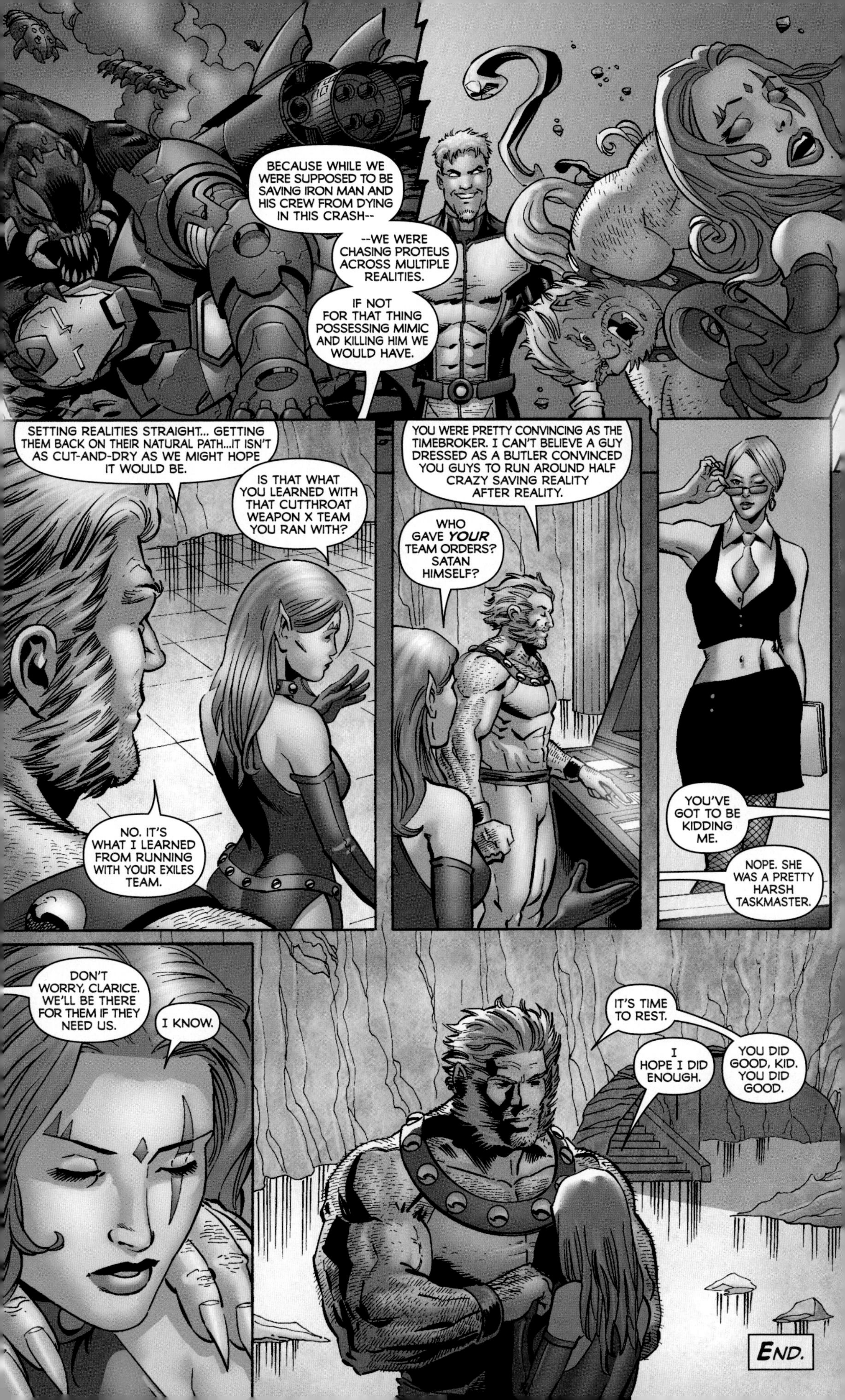
BECAUSE WHILE WE WERE SUPPOSED TO BE SAVING IRON MAN AND HIS CREW FROM DYING IN THIS CRASH--
--WE WERE CHASING PROTEUS ACROSS MULTIPLE REALITIES.
IF NOT FOR THAT THING POSSESSING MIMIC AND KILLING HIM WE WOULD HAVE.
SETTING REALITIES STRAIGHT... GETTING THEM BACK ON THEIR NATURAL PATH...IT ISN'T AS CUT-AND-DRY AS WE MIGHT HOPE IT WOULD BE.
IS THAT WHAT YOU LEARNED WITH THAT CUTTHROAT WEAPON X TEAM YOU RAN WITH?
NO. IT'S WHAT I LEARNED FROM RUNNING WITH YOUR EXILES TEAM.
YOU WERE PRETTY CONVINCING AS THE TIMEBROKER. I CAN'T BELIEVE A GUY DRESSED AS A BUTLER CONVINCED YOU GUYS TO RUN AROUND HALF CRAZY SAVING REALITY AFTER REALITY.
WHO GAVE *YOUR* TEAM ORDERS? SATAN HIMSELF?
YOU'VE GOT TO BE KIDDING ME.
NOPE. SHE WAS A PRETTY HARSH TASKMASTER.
DON'T WORRY, CLARICE. WE'LL BE THERE FOR THEM IF THEY NEED US.
I KNOW.
IT'S TIME TO REST.
I HOPE I DID ENOUGH.
YOU DID GOOD, KID. YOU DID GOOD.
END.

HISTORY: When an unidentified species of insectoid alien explorers discovered an ancient abandoned observatory outside of space-time, they set about studying it. Naming it the Panoptichron, later the Crystal Palace, they quickly learned that its equipment allowed them to observe every other reality in the Omniverse. Apparently accessing the Reality database of Merlyn and Roma's Core Continuum, they launched expeditions into other realities in order to map each one. These expeditions led them to numerous realities including Earth-1610's "Ultimate" reality with its young X-Men mutant group and the government strikeforce Ultimates, Earth-41483 where a female vigilante became the Punisher, and many others. They became more relaxed as their expeditions became more routine, and eventually accidentally caused all of creation to become displaced and damaged. Discovering how to fix their error, they devised a story about the realities becoming naturally "broken" and sought out beings from various realities to help correct their mistakes. Using their communication equipment along with a holographic device, they created a humanoid image and called it "Timebroker." The insectoids removed various beings from their realities and had the Timebroker tell them that they had been unhinged from time, and that they must repair broken realities before they could return to their own realities. The first groups were not very successful and forced the insectoids to find replacements. Their first successful roster was Blink of Earth-295 ("Age of Apocalypse"), Magnus of Earth-27 (son of Magneto and Rogue), Mimic of Earth-12 (where Professor X saved Mimic from his darker side), Morph of Earth-1081 (who was a member of both the Avengers and the X-Men), Nocturne of Earth-2182 (where Wolverine took over from a retired Professor X), and Thunderbird of Earth-1100 (where he had become a Horseman of Apocalypse).

The Timebroker gave Blink the Tallus, a communication device that would explain each mission. Calling themselves the Exiles, since they were essentially "exiled" from their own realities, the team had its first mission on Earth-1815 where all superhumans had been jailed, executed or aborted in an act of zero tolerance by humanity. Mimic completed their mission by killing an evil Charles Xavier, but Magnus sacrificed his life to save the reality. Joined by Magnus' replacement, Sunfire of Earth-2109, the team subsequently teleported to another reality. Unbeknownst to the group, the deceased Magnus was teleported back to the Crystal Palace and placed in a stasis wall by the insectoids instead of being returned to his own reality. Arriving in the Blue Area of the Moon orbiting Earth-8649 during the trial of the Phoenix, their mission was to ensure Jean Grey was killed. Disguising themselves as Imperial Guard members, they reluctantly joined the X-Men in killing Phoenix. Seeing that this team was reluctant to kill when required, the insectoids gathered a second team. Calling themselves Weapon X, alternate reality versions of Deadpool, Kane and Sabretooth were used for missions deemed too brutal for the Exiles. Eventually, the Exiles crossed paths with Weapon X — now consisting of Sabretooth, Deadpool, Hulk, Spider, Storm and Vision — on Earth-2600, a world where Sentinels eliminated all mutants and advanced humans. Instructed to kill a young David Richards, the Exiles and Sabretooth refused, resulting in a battle with Weapon X. Sabretooth seemingly slew Deadpool while the Exiles defeated the rest of Weapon X. Sabretooth decided to remain behind to raise David and save the world from destruction, ensuring he wouldn't turn into the monster the Timebroker claimed he eventually would become.

As the Exiles continued their missions, Blink and Mimic developed a romantic relationship while Nocturne and Thunderbird did the same. When the team was given a week vacation on Earth-9212 after stopping a bank robbery, Morph and Sunfire developed a strong friendship with each other. Undertaking increasingly dangerous missions, the Exiles frequently lost members only to gain new ones. Thunderbird was rendered comatose during a battle with the Galactus in Reality-5692 and was replaced by Sasquatch (Heather Hudson) of Earth-3470 (where she married and was eventually forced to kill Wolverine). After battling the Vi-locks on Earth-8545, Blink was sent home and replaced with Magik of Earth-4210. The Exiles battled Havok, who was subspatially joined with every other Havok in existence, and the lupine mutants the Dominant Species on Earth-616 alongside that reality's X-Men. During a battle with vampiric Avengers on Earth-3931, Union Jack cast a spell to separate the team as they teleported, sending them to different realities. Sasquatch and Morph fought a feral Wolverine on Earth-9927 while Sunfire and Nocturne returned to Earth-8545, where Sunfire developed a relationship with that reality's Spider-Girl. Mimic, meanwhile, arrived on Earth-2942, where he spent four years battling the Brood. When the Exiles were reunited on Earth-312, Mimic was overcome by an implanted Brood egg while battling a rampaging Thing and killed Sunfire, resulting in Blink rejoining the team.

After Hyperion joined Weapon X and defied the insectoids' orders in order to rule a planet instead of fixing its reality, the insectoids decided to cut their losses and ordered the two teams to battle each other until only six remained. The Exiles' Magik and Weapon X's Firestar, Hulk, Gambit, Ms. Marvel, Spider and Hyperion were

CURRENT MEMBERS: Morph/Proteus (Kevin MacTaggert), Psylocke (Elizabeth Braddock), Mystiq (Raphael-Raven Darkholm), Rogue (Anna Raven), Sabretooth (Victor Creed), Sage (Tessa), Shadowcat (Catherine Pryde)
FORMER MEMBERS: Beak (Barnell Bohusk), Blink (Clarice Ferguson), Heather Hudson/Sasquatch, Holocaust, Magnus Lehnsherr, Longshot, Magik (Illyana Rasputin), Mimic (Calvin Rankin), Morph (Kevin Sidney), Namora, Nocturne (Talia Wagner), Power Princess (Zarda Sheldon), Spider-Man (Miguel O'Hara), Sunfire (Mariko Yashida), Tanaraq, Thunderbird (John Proudstar)
WEAPON X: Angel (Warren Worthington III), Colossus (Piotr Rasputin), Daredevil (Matthew Murdock), Deadpool (Wade Wilson), Firestar (Angelica Jones), Gambit (Remy LeBeau), Hulk (Bruce Banner), Hulk (Jennifer Walters), Hyperion, Iron Man (Arno Stark), Kane (Garrison Kane), Maverick (David North), Mesmero, Ms. Marvel (Carol Danvers), Spider (Peter Parker), Storm (Ororo Munroe), Vision
WOLVERINE SQUAD: Albert, Elsie-Dee, James Howlett, Major Logan, Patch, Weapon X, Wolverine (zombie), numerous other Wolverine variants
BASE OF OPERATIONS: Panoptichron (Crystal Palace), located outside space-time
FIRST APPEARANCE: Exiles #1 (2001)

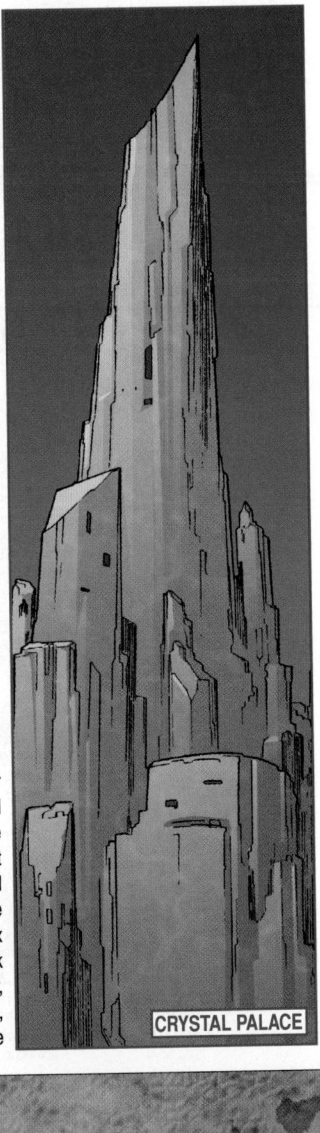
CRYSTAL PALACE

all seemingly slain and teleported into stasis within the Crystal Palace. Joined by Earth-2189's Namora, the Exiles returned to Earth-616, where Beak joined the team while Nocturne remained behind. New missions took the Exiles to Earth-14845 to battle the Impossible Man, Earth-5423 to help that reality's Mimic (aka Big M) redeem himself, and Earth-26292 where eating a danish stopped a Shi'ar invasion via the "Seahorse Effect." The Timebroker then seemed to develop a vicious side, sending them on vague, irrational and sometimes nonexistent missions. Eventually he sent them to Earth-37072 to stop Kulan Gath. There, Tanaraq, the Great Beast linked to Sasquatch, overpowered his host Heather Hudson; however, she was saved at the cost of her powers after the Exiles consigned Tanaraq to another dimension. When the team returned to Earth-2600 for their next mission, Heather was not among them. They eventually found Sabretooth and discovered he had failed to save David Richards. The Tallus then instructed the Exiles to kill Mimic. When they refused, the Timebroker teleported them along with Sabretooth to Earth-295, home to both Blink and Sabretooth, where they found Holocaust had replaced Beak as their newest member. When the team refused to kill that reality's heroic Magneto, they used the reality-bending M'kraan Crystal to travel to the Crystal Palace where they discovered that a revived Hyperion had usurped control. The Exiles battled Hyperion, losing both Holocaust and Namora to his power before he was defeated with the aid of two other alternate reality Hyperions (Earth-712 and Earth-5764) enlisted by Beak. The battle's aftermath left Mimic injured, but he recovered after mimicking Deadpool's healing factor. The Exiles found their former teammates in stasis at the Palace and buried Sunfire on Earth-8545, where she was most at peace in life.

While attempting to return Beak to his own reality, the Exiles found themselves in the wake of the Scarlet Witch altering Earth-616 into Reality-58163 ("House of M"). The Exiles encountered the body-snatching, reality-altering Proteus who took possession of Mimic's body and, upon doing so, absorbed all of Mimic's memories and discovered other realities to visit in order to find the perfect host. Leaving Beak in his own reality, the Exiles followed Proteus from reality to reality in an effort to stop him and save Mimic. When Proteus burned out Mimic's body, he moved to another body and continued his search for a perfect host. While following Proteus, the Exiles were joined by Longshot of the Mojoverse, Spider-Man of Earth-6375, and Power Princess of Earth-712. When Proteus took possession of Morph's body on Counter-Earth, he had found the perfect host due to Morph's transmutable physiology, which did not burn out like other hosts. The Exiles stopped Proteus by placing a behavior modification device on him, reprogramming his mind to make him believe that he was actually Morph.

No longer controlled by the insectoids (now dubbed Timebreakers), the Exiles returned those in stasis to their home realities and continued to fix broken realities under their own terms; however, when the entire group left the Crystal Palace, the Timebreakers "fired" the Exiles and organized a series of new teams consisting of alternate versions of Wolverine, chosen because he was "the best there is at what he does," to repair Earth-127. Unfortunately, each team dispatched there fell under the mental control of Brother Mutant until the Timebreakers contacted the former Exiles for help. Alongside another Wolverine Squad, the Exiles stopped Brother Mutant, after which the various Wolverines were

EXILES

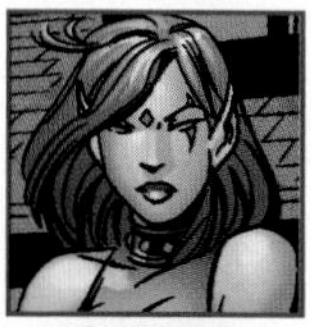
BLINK-295
(Clarice Ferguson)
Joined in Exiles #1 (2001)

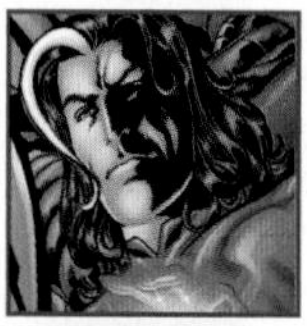
MAGNUS-27
(Magnus Lehnsherr)
Joined in Exiles #1 (2001); deceased

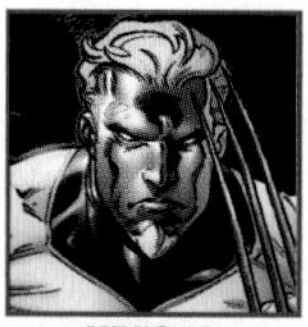
MIMIC-12
(Calvin Rankin)
Joined in Exiles #1 (2001); deceased

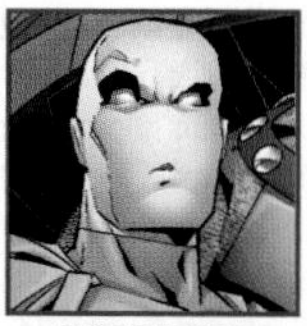
MORPH-1081
(Kevin Sidney)
Joined in Exiles #1 (2001); presumed deceased

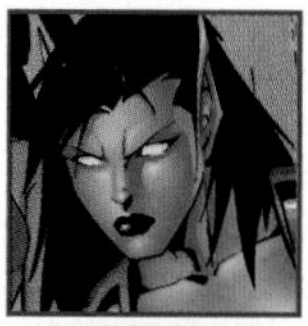
NOCTURNE-2182
(Talia J. Wagner)
Joined in Exiles #1 (2001)

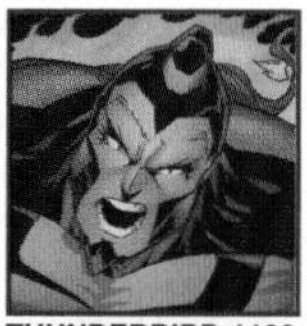
THUNDERBIRD-1100
(John Proudstar)
Joined in Exiles #1 (2001)

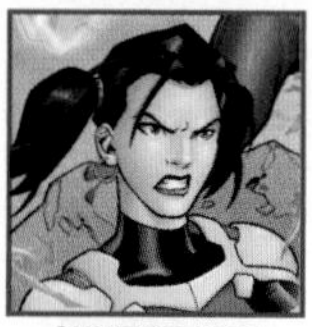
SUNFIRE-2109
(Mariko Yashida)
Joined in Exiles #2 (2001); deceased

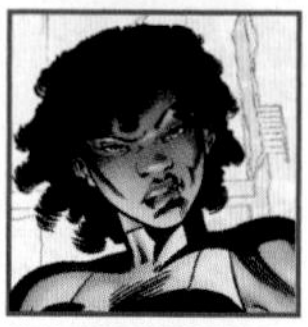
HEATHER HUDSON-3470
(Sasquatch)
Joined in Exiles #10 (2002)

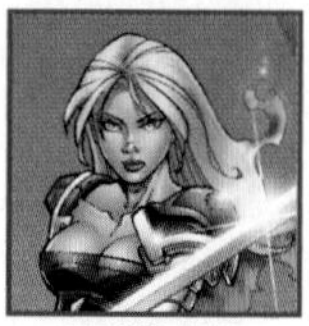
MAGIK-4210
(Illyana Rasputin)
Joined in Exiles #22 (2003); deceased

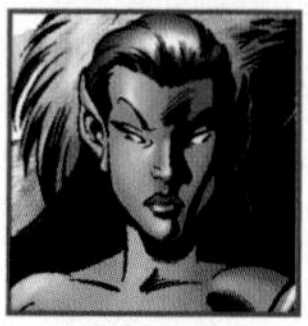
NAMORA-2189
Joined in Exiles #46 (2004); deceased

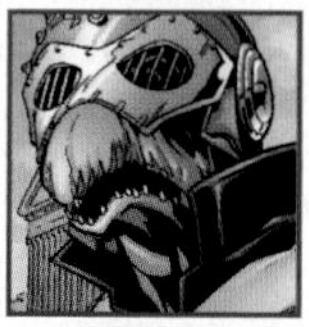
BEAK-616
(Barnell Bohusk)
Joined in Exiles #48 (2004)

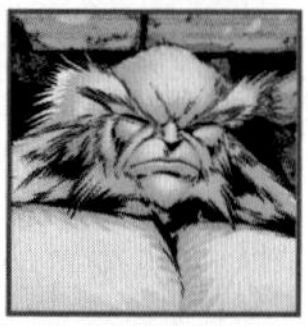
TANARAQ-3470
Active in Exiles #57 (2005)

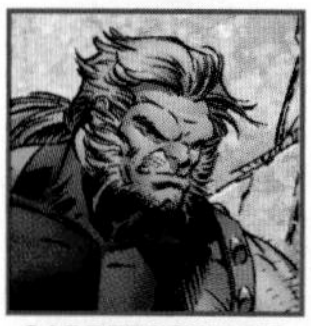
SABRETOOTH-295
(Victor Creed)
Joined in Exiles #59 (2005)

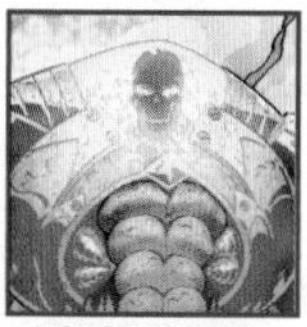
HOLOCAUST-295
Joined in Exiles #60 (2005); deceased

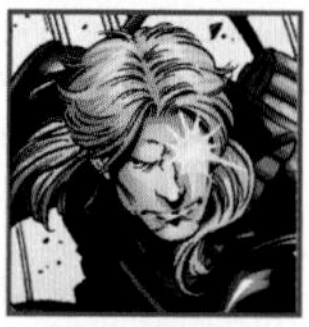
LONGSHOT (MOJOVERSE)
Joined in Exiles #74 (2006)

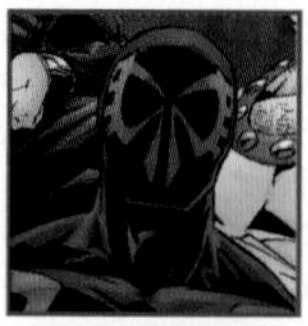
SPIDER-MAN-6375
(Miguel O'Hara)
Joined in Exiles #76 (2006)

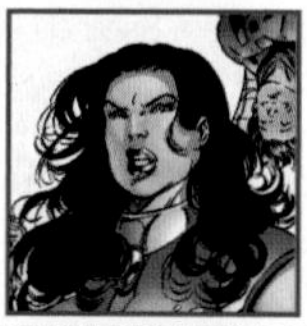
POWER PRINCESS-712
(Zarda Sheldon)
Joined in Exiles #78 (2006)

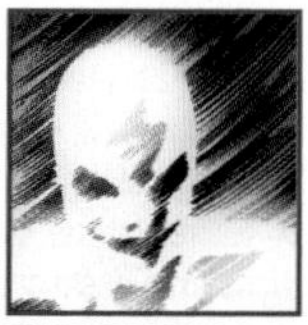
MORPH/PROTEUS-58163
(Kevin MacTaggert)
Active in Exiles #82 (2006)

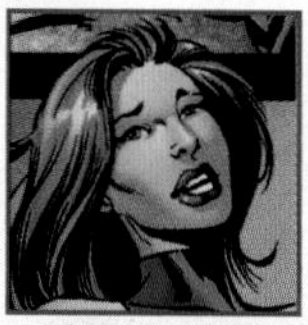
PSYLOCKE-616
(Elizabeth Braddock)
Joined in Exiles #91 (2007)

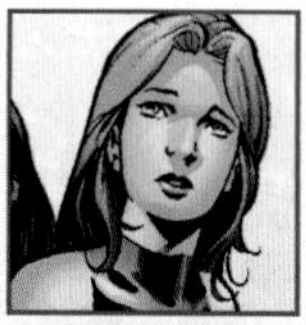
SHADOWCAT (UNREVEALED)
(Catherine "Cat" Pryde)
Joined in Exiles #97 (2007)

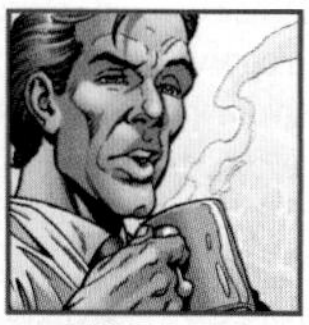
MYSTIQ-797
(Raphael-Raven Darkholm)
Joined in Exiles #99 (2007)

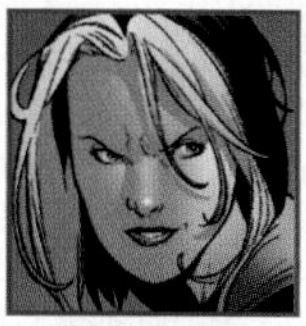
ROGUE-1009
(Anna Raven)
Joined in Exiles #99 (2007)

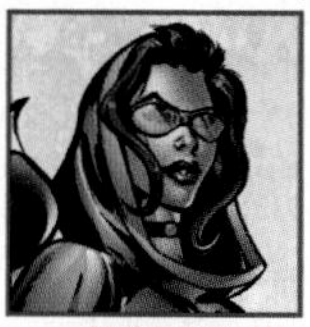
SAGE-616
(Tessa)
Joined in X-Men: Die By The Sword #5 (2007)

returned to their home realities. Power Princess then returned home while a mysterious, god-like figure visited the Crystal Palace to ensure Earth-616's Psylocke would become their newest member. During a mission on Earth-1720, the planet was seemingly destroyed, causing Heather to believe her teammates had perished. She returned to her own reality to live a normal life, leaving the Crystal Palace empty until the Exiles eventually returned. Their next mission took them to Earth-187319, where everything seemed too perfect. Violence, famine and war had been eliminated, but only at the cost of free will with everyone controlled by their ruler Dr. Doom. The Reed Richards of this reality sacrificed the entire planet and all its population to prevent Doom's control from spreading to other realities. This catastrophic event again displaced the Exiles across space and time. Meanwhile, back in the Crystal Palace, Psylocke encountered the young mutant Shadowcat from an as-yet-unidentified Earth shortly before Thunderbird awoke from his coma. Together, the three heroes repelled an assault by Doom-187319's troops before searching for the Exiles. They located Sabretooth on Earth-797 after he had saved Mystiq from assassins and Morph on Earth-1009 after helping Rogue escape from the Royal Avengers. Finally, Spider-Man was located on Earth-22506 living a peaceful life and so the team opted to leave him there. Blink was teleported through time to the Crystal Palace and met with its previous caretakers, who transported her back to the rest of the team.

During a trip to Earth-616 so Psylocke could visit her brother Captain Britain and Thunderbird could be reunited with Nocturne, the Exiles teamed with British group Excalibur to stop James Jaspers and the Fury from destroying the Omniverse. Longshot's memory returned and he joined Excalibur to be with his lover Dazzler while Nocturne rejoined the Exiles to be reunited with Thunderbird. After becoming the unwitting recipient of the sum of the apparently deceased Roma's knowledge, Sage joined the Exiles. With Nocturne recovering from a stroke, Thunderbird having only recently awakened from his coma, and Blink emotionally exhausted from everything, the three decided to take a sabbatical and relocate to Heather's dimension, leaving Sabretooth as leader with Morph, Psylocke and new members Mystiq, Sage and Shadowcat as sole protectors of the Omniverse.

WOLVERINE SQUAD

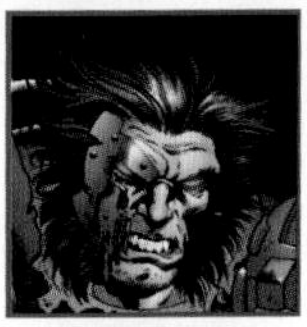

ALBERT-50211
Active in Exiles #85
(2006); deactivated

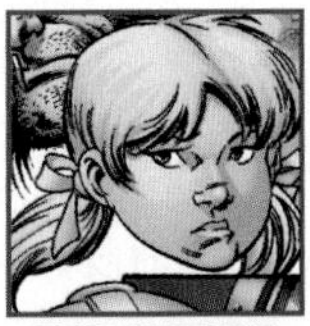

ELSIE-DEE-50211
Active in Exiles #85
(2006); deactivated

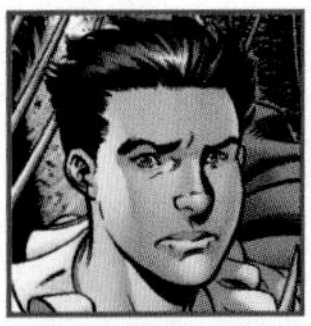

JAMES HOWLETT-1880
Active in Exiles #85 (2006)

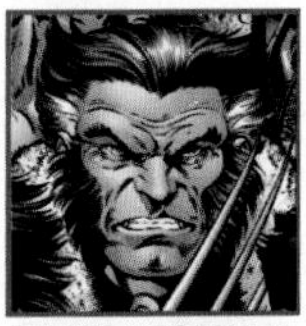

MAJOR LOGAN-811
Active in Exiles #85
(2006); deceased

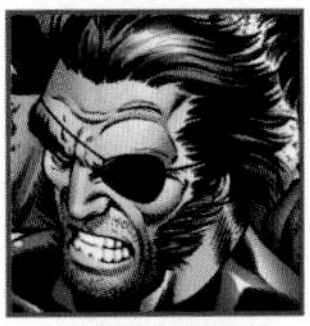

PATCH-181
Active in Exiles #85
(2006); deceased

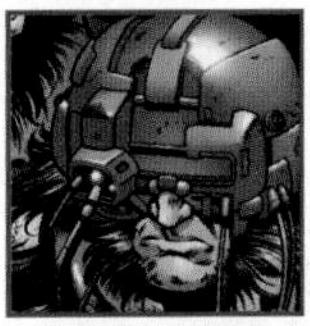

WEAPON X-520
Active in Exiles #85
(2006); deceased

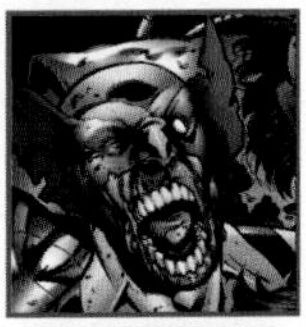

WOLVERINE-6195
Active in Exiles #85
(2006); deceased

WEAPON X

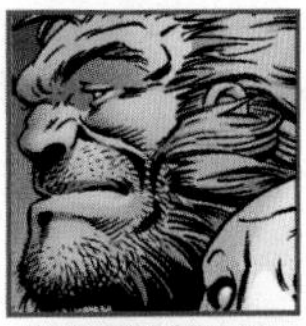

SABRETOOTH-295
(Victor Creed)
Active in Exiles #5;
member of Exiles

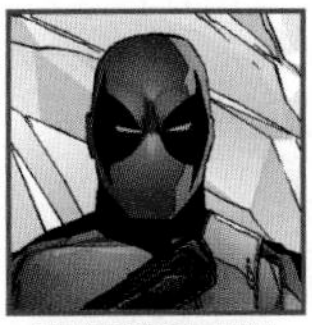

DEADPOOL-5021
(Wade Wilson)
Active in Exiles #5
(2001); deceased

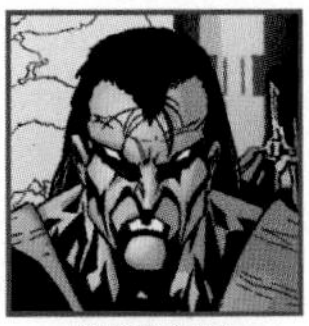

KANE-3031
(Garrison Kane)
Active in Exiles #5
(2001)

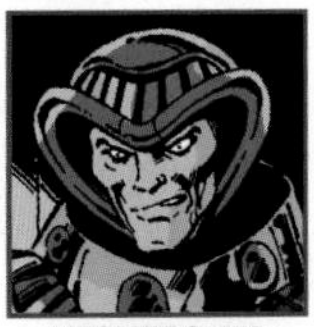

MESMERO-653
Active before Exiles #5
(2001); deceased

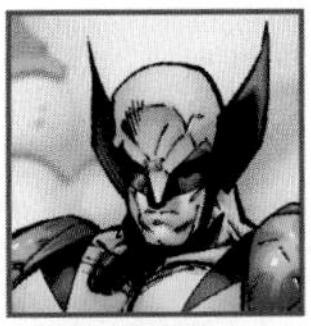

WOLVERINE-172
(Logan)
Active before Exiles #5
(2001); deceased

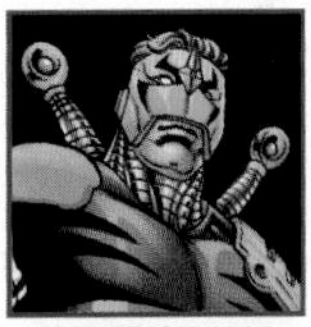

MAVERICK-1287
(David North)
Active before Exiles #5
(2001); deceased

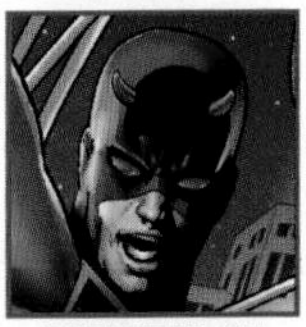

DAREDEVIL-181
(Matthew Murdock)
Active after Exiles #6
(2002)

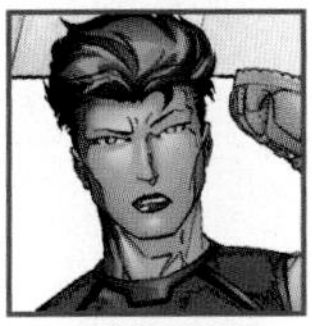

HULK-1029
(Jennifer Walters)
Active in Exiles #12
(2002)

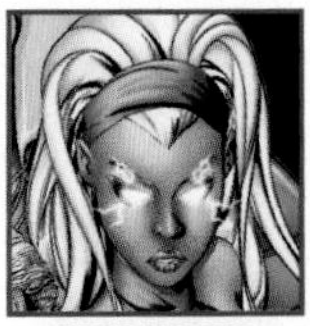

STORM-23895
(Ororo Munroe)
Active in Exiles #12
(2002); deceased

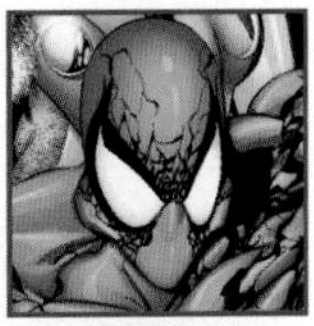

SPIDER-15
(Peter Parker)
Active in Exiles #12
(2002); deceased

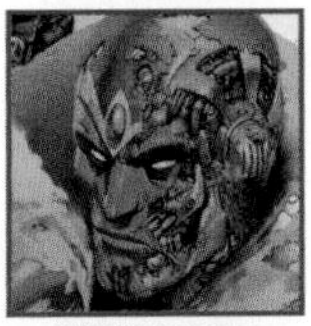

VISION-10101
Active in Exiles #12
(2002); deactivated

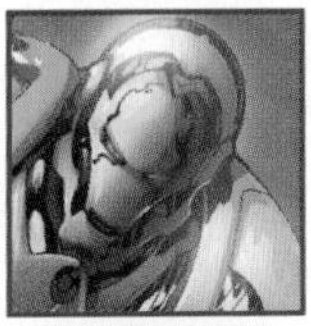

IRON MAN-2020
(Tony Stark)
Joined in Exiles #13
(2002)

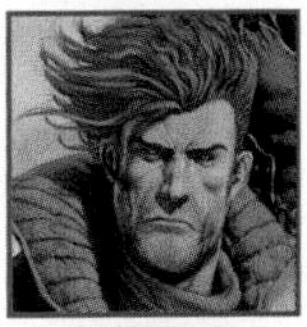

GAMBIT-731
(Remy LeBeau)
Joined in Exiles #23
(2003); deceased

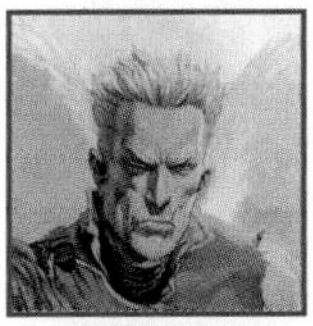

ANGEL-714
(Warren Worthington III)
Joined in Exiles #23
(2003)

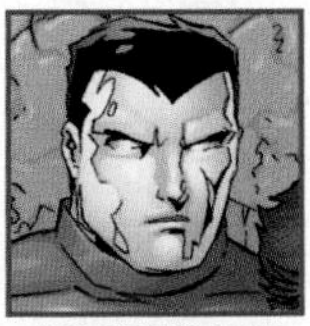

COLOSSUS-1917
(Peter Rasputin)
Joined in Exiles #24
(2003); deceased

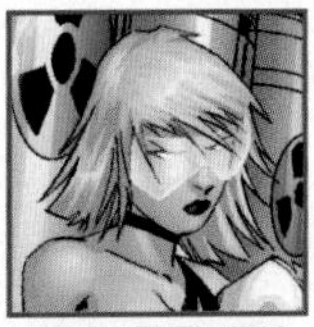

MS. MARVEL-4732
(Carol Danvers)
Joined in Exiles #38
(2004); deceased

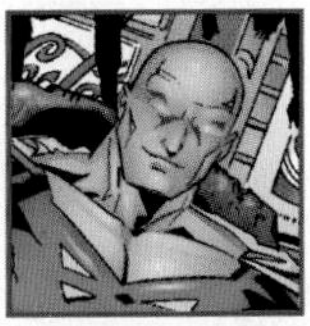

HYPERION-4023
(Zhib Ran)
Joined in Exiles #38
(2004)

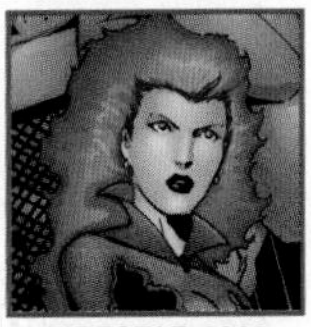

FIRESTAR-3062
(Angelica Jones)
Joined in Exiles #40
(2004); deceased

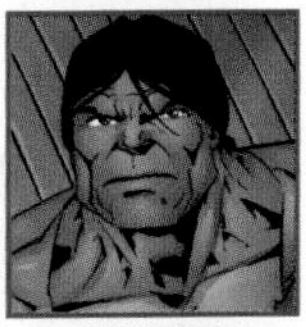

HULK-873
(Bruce Banner)
Joined in Exiles #40
(2004); deceased